This book is the first attempt to study the early history of the Protestant revival movements of the eighteenth century not simply in an Anglo-American context, but from a European perspective. Professor Ward examines the crisis in the Protestant world beyond that established and protected by the Westphalia treaties, and its impact upon the morale of Protestant communities which enjoyed diplomatic guarantees or other forms of public protection. He traces the widespread outbreak of striking forms of revival to the emergence of a common Protestant mind, shaped by the appreciation of common problems, and especially the development of the modern 'police' state or phenomena perceived to be like it. The religious effects of widespread emigration produced by persecution, war and distress are traced, and the chronology of the familiar revivals of the West is related to the crises of Eastern and Central Europe. The connexion of the English revival with these continental movements is also explored.

*The Protestant Evangelical Awakening* is based on a wide variety of archival resources and published scholarly work extending from Eastern Europe to the American colonies, and marks a major contribution to our understanding of the religious history of both continents.

# THE PROTESTANT EVANGELICAL
# AWAKENING

# THE PROTESTANT
# EVANGELICAL
# AWAKENING

## W. R. WARD

*Emeritus Professor of Modern History, University of Durham*

CAMBRIDGE
UNIVERSITY PRESS

Published by the Press Syndicate of the University of Cambridge
The Pitt Building, Trumpington Street, Cambridge CB2 1RP
40 West 20th Street, New York, NY10011 – 4211, USA
10 Stamford Road, Oakleigh, Victoria 3166, Australia

First published 1992

Printed in Great Britain at the University Press, Cambridge

*A catalogue record for this book is available from the British Library*

*Library of Congress cataloguing in publication data*
Ward, W. Reginald (William Reginald)
The Protestant Evangelical Awakening
W. R. Ward
p.   cm.
Includes bibliographical references and index.
ISBN 0 521 41491 1
1. Revivals – Europe – History – 18th century. 2. Protestant
churches – Europe – History – 18th century. 3. Europe – Church
history – 18th century. I. Title.
BV3777.E9W37   1992
280′.4′09409033 – dc20   91-23665 CIP

ISBN 0521 41491 1 hardback

The history of the eighteenth century is in my eyes the most important I know in the almost boundless field of history – at least it is the richest in great events unexpected by our forebears, or even our contemporaries…Alterations in states and in the realm of knowledge have always had their mighty influence upon the church. But never were those influences so quick and instantaneous as in the present century.

J. R. Schlegel, *Kirchengeschichte des achtzehnten Jahrhunderts*
(3 vols. Heilbronn, 1784–96) 1: 1–2

In his *Dissert. de Studio Theolog.* the blessed Abbot Breithaupt has well noted that in church history we ought to observe closely not only the *dominantis cleri magnificentiam, sed piorum quoque pauperculorum suspiria & desideria.*

*Fortgesetzte Sammlung auserlesener Materien zum Bau des Reiches
Gottes* pt 25 (1735) Foreword

# Contents

# Maps

# *Preface*

I am very grateful to the Syndics of the Cambridge University Press for undertaking to publish a very substantial book on a very unfashionable subject. To meet their requirements the original draught has had to be cut very considerably, and, in particular, the critical apparatus, which amounted to some 35,000 words, has been drastically simplified. I hope that the basic support for scholarly readers will nevertheless remain adequate, and that some of what is lost may be made good by a bibliographical study of German Pietism which I have in hand.

Extended study abroad has been made possible by the financial generosity of the University of Durham, the British Academy, the British Council, the government of the former German Democratic Republic, the Deutscher Akademischer Austauschdienst, and the American Antiquarian Society, to all of whom I am deeply obliged. To many librarians and archivists at home and abroad I am indebted for assistance; perhaps I may mention especially the willingness of the Moravian archivists in Herrnhut and London to accommodate the inconvenient visits of a student with many other preoccupations.

My former colleagues in Durham extended their usual tolerance to my hobby-horses and Dr Anne Orde and Dr Jeremy Black gave special help. My wife has nobly endured a study of revival which has hardly granted the refreshing showers of grace envisaged by its promoters. To them all I am grateful.

# Abbreviations

| | |
|---|---|
| AFSt | Archiv der Franckeschen Stiftungen, Halle |
| *AHE* | *Acta Historico-Ecclesiastica* |
| *AÖG* | *Archiv für Österreichische Geschichte* |
| *BJRL* | *Bulletin of the John Rylands Library of the University of Manchester* |
| *BWKg* | *Blätter für Württembergische Kirchengeschichte* |
| *CH* | *Church History* |
| *CHSB* | *Connecticut Historical Society Bulletin* |
| DG | Diozesanarchiv, Graz |
| *GHQ* | *Georgia Historical Quarterly* |
| Herrnhut MSS | Archiv der Brüderunität, Herrnhut, Oberlausitz |
| *HJLg* | *Hessisches Jahrbuch für Landesgeschichte* |
| *JAH* | *Journal of American History* |
| *JBKg* | *Jahrbuch für Brandenburgische (later Berlin-Brandenburgische) Kirchengeschichte* |
| *JEH* | *Journal of Ecclesiastical History* |
| *JGGPÖ* | *Jahrbuch der Gesellschaft für die Geschichte des Protestantismus in Österreich* |
| *JGNSKg* | *Jahrbuch der Gesellschaft der Niedersächsischen Kirchengeschichte* |
| *JHKgV* | *Jahrbuch der Hessischen Kirchengeschichtlichen Vereinigung* |
| *JPHS* | *Journal of the Presbyterian Historical Society* |
| JRL | John Rylands Library, University of Manchester |

| | |
|---|---|
| *JSKKg* | *Jahrbuch für Schlesische Kirche und Kirchengeschichte* |
| *JTS* | *Journal of Theological Studies* |
| *JVSKg* | *Jahrbuch des Vereins für Schlesische Kirchengeschichte* |
| *JVWKg* | *Jahrbuch des Vereins für Westfälische Kirchengeschichte* |
| MCA | Methodist Church Archives, John Rylands Library |
| MCH | Archive of The Moravian Church in Great Britain and Ireland, Moravian Church House, 5 Muswell Hill, London N10 |
| *MNEKR* | *Mitteilungen und Nachrichte für die Evangelische Kirche in Russland* |
| *MRKg* | *Monatshefte für Rheinische Kirchengeschichte* |
| ÖSA | Österreichisches Staatsarchiv, Vienna |
| ÖNB | Österreichische Nationalbibliothek, Vienna |
| *PMHB* | *Pennsylvania Magazine for History and Biography* |
| PRO | Public Record Office, London |
| *PuN* | *Pietismus und Neuzeit* |
| *PWHS* | *Proceedings of the Wesley Historical Society* |
| *SCH* | *Studies in Church History* |
| *SJH* | *Scandinavian Journal of History* |
| SLG | Steiermärkisches Landesarchiv, Graz |
| *SMBRG* | *Sammlung auserlesener Materien zum Bau des Reiches Gottes* |
| SPK | Staatsbibliothek Preussischer Kulturbesitz, Berlin |
| *STZ* | *Schweizerische Theologische Zeitschrift* |
| *THSC* | *Transactions of the Honourable Society of Cymmrodorion* |
| *TLCAS* | *Transactions of the Lancashire and Cheshire Antiquarian Society* |

| | |
|---|---|
| *UF* | *Unitas Fratrum* |
| *UN* | *Unschuldige Nachrichten* |
| Walch, *Religionsstreitigkeiten* | J. G. Walch, *Historische und theologische Einleitung in die Religionsstreitigkeiten ausser der evangelische-lutherischen Kirche* (5 vols. Jena, 1733–6) |
| Wesley, *Journal* | *Journal of John Wesley* ed. N. Curnock (8 vols. London, 1909–16; repr. 1938) |
| Wesley, *Works* | *The Works of John Wesley* (Bicentennial edn) (34 vols. Oxford & Nashville, Tenn., 1975– (in progress)) |
| *WMQ* | *William and Mary Quarterly* |
| *WVLg* | *Württembergisches Vierteljahresheft für Landesgeschichte* |
| *ZBKg* | *Zeitschrift für Bayerische Kirchengeschichte* |
| *ZGNSKg* | *Zeitschrift der Gesellschaft für Niedersächsische Kirchengeschichte* |
| *ZHT* | *Zeitschrift für Historische Theologie* |
| *ZKg* | *Zeitschrift für Kirchengeschichte* |
| *ZSP* | *Zeitschrift für Slavische Philologie* |
| *ZW* | *Zinzendorf Werke* ed. E. Beyreuther & others (Hildesheim, 1962– (in progress)) |

# CHAPTER I

# The Protestant frame of mind in the eighteenth century

### THE CIRCULATION OF INFORMATION: (I) LETTERS

This study of international religious revival in the Protestant world in the eighteenth century may without paradox commence with a postscript, perhaps the most breathless postscript of the century:

P.S. As to the churches in Germany, you'll inquire how their discipline is exercised, and particularly the discipline of the Lutheran churches, their worship and government; how the affair of the union between them and the Calvinists stands. All you please to send anent the present state of the Barnavelt and Arminian party and Cocceians in Holland, with the conditions of religion there, will be most acceptable. You will likewise be fond to know the present numbers of the confessors and new converts in France; and, if you have as much time, I would fain know the state and issue of that affair between the Cardinal Noailles and the Bishops who join him anent Father Quesnel's tenets, and the rest of the clergy in France who adhere to the Pope's Bull; and if there be any numbers in France that are in any way breathing after a reformation, as we hear there are. Anything anent the success of the Gospel in the Dutch and English plantations, in the East Indies and the Danish missionaries in Malabar; of the state of the Greek churches ... May I expect anything anent the much forgotten Jews in Africa, Asia, or Europe? You'll inquire likewise into the design of sending over a suffragan Bishop to America, and the bearing down of our brethren of New England; and you will not forget to inquire into the efforts for spreading the Liturgy, and Ceremonies and Hierarchy, in the Protestant churches abroad.

The writer, Robert Wodrow, minister of the country parish of Eastwood near Glasgow, was not going to spare his correspondent, a brother minister of the Kirk, on the occasion of a visit to London. Should a friend venture to Leiden he became even more importunate, calling for a full report of the state of the Reformed churches in the Netherlands, Switzerland and the Empire; the state and organisation of the Lutheran churches; the condition of Protestantism in the

Palatinate, Savoy and the alpine valleys; in Silesia and Poland (including the state of Socinianism); in Hungary, Bohemia, Transylvania and Scandinavia. What did the Dutch think of the French prophets, and did they, as he understood, hold no witchcraft trials? Were their professors given to apocalyptic studies? What was the latest estimate of Francke's reputation and of the institutions at Halle? Wodrow, indeed, thought nothing odd about writing to Boston, Mass. for news of the health of an aged minister no further away than Glasgow.[1] Wodrow was unusual among contemporaries in having professional interests in recent ecclesiastical history, but he was in no way singular in believing that even for the standpoint of a narrow confessional interest the whole Protestant world mattered. For a generation organised international prayer had been pitted against persecution.

Wodrow's method of learning by letter was so widely followed, especially by the opponents of 'dead' Orthodoxy and 'formalism', as deeply to mark the history not only of the letter, but of religion itself. The movements of renewal and revival of the eighteenth century sought their legitimation in the hand of God in history; their characteristic achievement was not, like the Reformers of the sixteenth century, to offer a confession of faith for public discussion, but to accumulate archives which would support their understanding of history. Molinos, whose *Spiritual Guide* was read by all the evangelicals, was discovered by the Inquisition after his death in 1696 to have accumulated 20,000 letters. Bengel in Württemberg wrote about 1,200 a year. Francke had about 5,000 correspondents, and was in constant touch with three to four hundred. International archives, large to huge, were accumulated by all the leading religious figures of the age, by Spener and Turrentini, by Wake and Wesley, by Cotton Mather and Isaac Backus, by numerous Scots, and by the ecclesiastical machinery they created or used – the SPCK, for example, or the Classis of Amsterdam and Synod of North Holland. Where correspondence plumbed the wiles of the heart it strengthened the women who gathered round all the leading men of God; where it conveyed information and opinion it was used devotionally to raise the spirits of the faithful and lift their vision beyond the present trial;[2] and it gave the cue to diplomats who bought themselves confidential

[1] *Correspondence of the Rev. Robert Wodrow* ed. Thomas M'Crie (3 vols. Edinburgh, 1842–8) 1:614–15, 388–92; II:10–11.
[2] Samuel Urlsperger, *Detailed Reports on the Salzburger Emigrants who Settled in America* ed. G. F. Jones (6 vols. Athens, Ga., 1968–) 1:31; III:71; IV:101, 104.

correspondence for professional purposes. International letter-writing paid a toll to war and espionage. Heinrich Melchior Mühlenberg, who kept in regular touch from America with his sponsors in Halle, normally sent two copies of his letters and kept a third in his journal; but in the Holy Roman Empire, at least, the efforts of the Baron von Taxis to beat down the resistance of Emperor and cities to his postal service made it easier to communicate by letter across frontiers. The sheer bulk of surviving correspondence shows how much was achieved and by what devious routes; Gotthilf August Francke, son of the great August Hermann, received news of the revival in New England from English sources via the German community in Pennsylvania, and friends of his late father in the Rhineland.[3]

### THE CIRCULATION OF INFORMATION: (2) PERSONAL CONTACTS AND THE PRESS

One of John Wesley's jobs as a chaplain and missionary in Georgia was to help with the postal difficulties of the Salzburgers. On their distant frontier of European civilisation he also grew wise to Central Europe. Wesley arrived in Georgia in February 1736 with favourable impressions of the Moravians. Among the first to greet him was August Gottlieb Spangenberg, then the head of the Moravian enterprise in Georgia, who instructed him further in their faith and practice. What Wesley may not have known was that the current phase of the revival in Europe was being given shape by an intense feud between the Franckean institutions at Halle, and Zinzendorf's Moravians. In this battle there were issues of principle, but also acute personal animosities centring at this stage on Spangenberg. Suspected of disloyal coquetting with separatists,[4] Spangenberg had been abruptly dismissed from an academic half-appointment in Halle, and had thrown in his lot with Zinzendorf. Halle had dispatched two pastors to take spiritual charge of the Salzburgers, and from one of them Wesley received chapter and verse of that ill character of Spangenberg which (in the Halle view) was at the root of an international religious conflict in Central and Northern Europe.[5]

In its turn Wesley's early career contributed to the enlightenment

---

[3] Theodor Wotschke, 'August Hermann Franckes rheinische Freunde in ihren Briefen', *MKRg* 23 (1929) 24, 26.
[4] G. C. Knapp, *Beiträge zur Lebensgeschichte A. G. Spangenbergs* (1792) ed. O. Frick (Halle, 1884) 114–19.     [5] Urlsperger, *Detailed Reports* IV: 143, 170, 117–19.

of Halle. At a very early stage, certainly by the summer of 1733,[6] the younger Francke had received reports of what was afoot in Oxford, and the German community in London had sent translations of the first defence of that circle in print – *The Oxford Methodists* (London, 1733) – which was to have a longer run in Germany than in England. By 1740 Wesley was personally commending himself to Halle through German third parties.[7] Long before this date, however, the interest in the Oxford Methodists aroused in private communications had spilled into print. Benjamin Ingham, who accompanied Wesley to Georgia, returned home in September 1737; already the first part of his Georgia diary had been published in translation in the journal now edited by the Protestant apostle to Silesia, Johann Adam Steinmetz.[8] In 1739 the Württemberger Pietist and public lawyer Johann Jakob Moser published in his journal a favourable account of the Methodists received from Kensington (Ziegenhagen's address) and Steinmetz followed suit with a translation of the original edition of the *Oxford Methodists*. The editors of the fathomless Orthodox repositories of ecclesiastical knowledge maintained at Weimar and Leipzig must now compete. The *Acta Historico-Ecclesiastica*, which had a special concern for the Salzburgers in Georgia, had reported the arrival of the Oxford circle by 1737, the dealings of the brothers Wesley with the Salzburgers the following year, and in 1740 a large-scale account of the movement from its earliest days in Oxford, including all the material which had appeared in the Pietist publications. The even more strait-laced *Unschuldige Nachrichten* in two successive years reviewed the literary polemic stirred up by the new movement.[9] By now the diplomats of Europe, aware that religious changes often had political results, had spoken to their masters. The French Foreign Ministry received two very full and well-informed accounts of the religious ferment in England, and, a little late in the day, the Senate and clergy of Hamburg received a formal report in the technical language of Orthodox theology, Latin, which gave pride of place to Whitefield, and in America, to the Tennents.

In the Habsburg lands the need to travel abroad for education enlarged clerical horizons and made the clergy exotic contacts.

---

[6] SPK Francke Nachlasse K30 fos. 537–49; 30.2 fos. 770–1.     [7] *Ibid.* 31.1 fo. 244.

[8] *SMBRG* 6 (1737) 498–539. Steinmetz wrote personally to Wesley in 1741. Wesley, *Works* XXVI: *Letters* II:49–51.

[9] J. J. Moser, *Altes und Neues aus dem Reich Gottes…* (Frankfurt/Leipzig, 1733–9) 22:293–5; *SMBRG* 2 (1733) 700–18; *AHE* 2:405–24; 3:1087; 4:287–303, 727–824; *UN* 1740 'Früchte' 45–7; 1741 'Früchte' 74–5.

Slavonic peoples, and especially Slovaks, found Jena cheaper than Leipzig, and in the century and a half before the revolution of 1848, interrupted only by wartime, Jena contributed importantly to their development. If war restricted the movements of the Habsburgs' subjects, the Thirty Years War drove many Germans abroad, not least to the Netherlands and England. To Oxford in particular they continued to come right into the Hanoverian period; H. L. Benthem's 1,300-page guide to English educational institutions for discriminating German students was reprinted as late as 1732.[10] At Halle there were not only an English table (1709) financed by Queen Anne and an English house (1711), but Czechs and Slovaks, Silesians and Poles, Wends and Sorbs, Hungarians of most varieties, Russians and South Slavs, Esths, Letts and Swedes; and they were student members of an institution dedicated to international regeneration, acclaimed as such by Jonathan Edwards in his *History of the Work of Redemption* (1739). Swiss theological students would go to Saumur as long as the authorities permitted, and pursued their studies in Heidelberg and Herborn, in Leiden, Franeker, Groningen and Utrecht; and those who went to the Netherlands normally took in England as well. Hungarian Lutherans depended very heavily on Wittenberg, where their countryman Cassai (1640–1725) had left an endowment, a house and a library for them; Hungarian Reformed repaired to the Netherlands, Switzerland and Oxford in that order of importance. The connexions formed during an international education might have a practical value; for all the time the pull of preferment and the push of persecution kept clergy on the move. Persecution in Hungary might lead them to Siebenbürgen (the modern Transylvania), Hamburg[11] or the galleys (and thence to Switzerland). Many Lutheran clergy in Poland in the early eighteenth century had taken refuge from Silesia and some were imported from Saxony. The first German Lutheran pastor in New York had been expelled from his parish in Upper Hungary by the Turks, and the first German Reformed minister in Pennsylvania had been turned out of his parish in Bern as a Pietist.[12] Virtually all the clergy

[10] Paul Schaffhausen, *Commentatio historico-litteraria*... (Hamburg, 1743); H. L. Benthem, *Neueröffneter Engelandischer Kirch- und Schulen-staat*... (Leipzig, 1732). Cf. Georg Wilhelm Alberti, *Zustand der Religion und der Wissenschaften in Gross Britannien* (4 vols. Hanover, 1752–4).

[11] Friedrich Teutsch, *Geschichte der evangelischen Kirche in Siebenbürgen* (2 vols. Hermannstadt, 1921–2) I:491; Johannes Borbis, *Die evangelisch-lutherische Kirche Ungarns in ihrer geschichtlichen Entwicklung* (Nördlingen, 1861) 92–3.

[12] Eduard Kneifel, *Die Pastoren der Evangelisch-Augsburgischen Kirche in Polen* (Eging, 1967); H. J. Kreider, *The Beginnings of Lutheranism in New York* (New York, 1949) 50, 63–4; *JPHS* 14 (1930) 28–31.

serving in America (outside New England) in the early eighteenth
century were brought in from abroad, whether from England,
Scotland, Ireland, Sweden, Germany, the Netherlands or Switzerland.

The demand for expatriate clergy was created by broader
population movements, movements sometimes occasioned by religious persecution but also reflecting economic pressures and
inducements, and defying the efforts of every state to hang on to its
labour force. Losses of population in the Thirty Years War had
attracted considerable net immigration to the northern Reich in the
seventeenth century, some of it like the German and Czech migration
from Bohemia into Saxony, the Defereggers who got into Swabia,
Nuremberg and Frankfurt, or the Protestant Lorrainers who made
off for Prussia in the late 1730s,[13] the direct result of religious
intolerance of the Habsburgs, the archbishop of Salzburg and
Stanislas Leszczynski respectively; and the Prussian government,
which took handsome advantage of the Revocation of the Edict of
Nantes in 1685, continued to recruit systematically down the
eighteenth century, picking up over 70,000 immigrants. Once the
Turkish tide was rolled back there was an insatiable demand for
German colonists, irrespective of confession, in Hungary, which took
three times the number of immigrants to America, there was a steady
leakage into Poland, and after the Seven Years War there were major
settlements in Russia and Galicia.

Many settlers from the West also went east, but the recruiters for
America operated so successfully that German settlers in the
American colonies all tended to be called Palatines. Religion was
prominent among the early motives for migration. Penn came on
missions partly evangelistic and partly promotional for his new
colony in Pennsylvania, concentrating his efforts in towns where
there were Mennonite meetings and successfully recruiting among
Mennonites for both Quakerism and Pennsylvania. But the first huge
surge between 1709 and 1712 was clearly motivated mainly by
famine, and immense numbers escaped famine to meet other
disasters. Many never reached England; of those who did, many died
in the camp at Blackheath, thousands of Catholics were sent back to
Germany, and thousands of Protestants fetched up in Ireland. This
emigration owed much to the overpopulation of Switzerland and the
south-western territories of the Reich, but it owed something also to

---

[13] J. G. Schelhorn, *Historische Nachricht vom Ursprunge…der evangelischen Religion in den Salzburgischen Landen* (Leipzig, 1732) 348; *AHE* 5:160.

the misery produced by repeated brutal French aggression and by the religious policies of the new Catholic dynasty in the Palatinate towards their Reformed population. Men spiritually depressed were specially exposed to the blandishments of the recruiting agents who took their harvests after 1709 mostly in the intervals of the great transatlantic wars. Franz Daniel Pastorius, the collaborator of Spener, who took out the first party for Penn, founded Germantown, just outside Philadelphia, in 1683, and the migrants of 1709 who managed to reach that goal made it into a magnet for all the Germans who followed. Those who manipulated these population movements were knitting the world together; Oglethorpe, for example, who in the 1730s was anxious to acquire Salzburgers, Germans and Swiss for the new colony of Georgia, had served under Prince Eugene in the brilliant Balkan campaign which led up to the Peace of Passarowitz (1718) and was familiar with the problems and techniques of Habsburg frontier settlement.

Thomasius, the fountain-head of the German Enlightenment, observing that persecution led to emigration, pronounced in 1688 that one of the causes of the decline of kingdoms was the power of the clergy; those seeking to make religious sense of the business turned to Exodus themes. Valentin Ernst Löscher, the latter-day spokesman of Saxon Orthodoxy, perplexed and moved by the great emigration of Protestant Salzburgers in 1732, explained that[14] 'the exodus of Israel from Egypt was a type of the emergence of the Christian church from heathenism and Judaism and the holy reformer Luther; there was also an anti-type or counter-picture; and the hunting out of the Salzburgers is an after-picture (*Nachbild*)'. The spiritual verse of Protestant Silesia was full of 'Songs of comfort by pious exiles' and pilgrim hymns on the theme

> Ein Wandersmann bin ich allhier
> In dieser Welt auf Erden.

Wesley, who learned German by studying German hymns with the Moravians on the Atlantic passage, began to translate them on his arrival; Rothe's words 'Wird alles andre weggerissen, was seel und leib erquicken kan' were transformed into a clear Exodus reference: 'Though waves and storms go o'er my head', while Paul Gerhardt's metaphor of release from incarceration: 'Gott wird dich aus der höhle...mit groszen gnaden rücken' is similarly transposed:

---

[14] Christian Thomasius, *Monatsgespräche* (4 vols. repr. Frankfurt, 1972) II:474; Valentin Ernst Löscher, *Drey Predigten von der Erkänntnis und Ehre des Sohnes Gottes...* (Dresden, 1733) 32.

'Through waves and clouds and storms he gently clears thy way.'[15]
The Exodus metaphor was in vogue; it sharpened the perpetual
dichotomy between religious experience and religious organisation,
and fuelled American nationalism with a picture of England's
'rulers...madly rushing like Pharoah and his host, through a sea of
blood, on their utter destruction'.

The migrations of European peoples enlarged minds by producing
strange bed-fellows; both the migration and the enlargement were
much facilitated by the striking growth of the European press,
convincing readers that they were now more fully and rapidly
informed about world events than any of their predecessors. The
Strasbourg journal which commenced in 1609 with the title of
*Furnemmen und gedenckwürdigen Historien so sich hin und wider in Hoch und
Nieder Deutschland auch in Franckreich Italien Scott und Engelland Hisspanien
Hungern Polen Siebenbürgen Wallachey Moldau Turckey etc.* set the pattern
for innumerable successors, and by the end of the century the
ordinary weekly press was supplemented by journals with titles like
*Theatrum Europaeum, Diarium Europaeum, Europaische Fama, Europaischer
Staatssekretarius*. The ordinary newspaper press was a cosmopolitan
agency because so much of its material was cannibalised from other
papers. The great information-gatherers were the French-language
Dutch papers which exploited the relative freedom of information in
the Netherlands, and the political network built up by the great
Huguenot diaspora. British papers drew on them heavily, but adeptly
used commercial sources in Hamburg and elsewhere to provide a
reasonably comprehensive guide to the rise of Russia. The confessional issue in European diplomacy ensured that to English readers
(what is now) Czechoslovakia was not a distant country of which
they knew little; and in the later seventeenth century the European
press made the labyrinthine struggles for religion and liberty in the
much more distant kingdom of Hungary a matter of domestic
relevance to English observers, calling upon them to abandon
domestic brawls and come to its defence.[16] Except in 1739 and 1740
when Whitefield hogged the limelight and most of the column-
inches, the American papers were almost entirely composed of
material taken from British and European sources. Thus in 1731–2,
for example, the Philadelphia *American Weekly Mercury* did well on the

---

[15] 'Here on earth I am a pilgrim'. J. Mutzell, *Geistliche Lieder...aus Schlesien...* (Braunschweig,
1858) 68–71, 7, 165; J. Nuelsen, *John Wesley and the German Hymn* (Eng. tr. Calverley, 1972)
24, 60–1, 129–130.

[16] Béla Köpeczi, *Staatsräson und christlicher Solidarität. Die ungarischen Aufstände und Europa...*
(Vienna, 1983) 274 n. 61.

negotiations over the Pragmatic Sanction, and on the Protestant flight from Salzburg. And in every country the regular press was supplemented by broadsheets without number whenever events took an exciting turn.

Men of faith read the ordinary press and wrote for it on newsworthy subjects. When Christoph Martin Wieland was studying with Steinmetz, the Protestant apostle to Silesia, he learned classical languages and philosophy, but also read the English weeklies, the *Spectator*, the *Tatler* and *The Guardian*, which were as popular in Germany as in England.[17] Wesley was Georgia correspondent to the *Gentleman's Magazine*, while Jonathan Edwards in 1745 sent a full military report on the Cape Breton expedition to the Glasgow *Christian Monthly History*. Before the end of the seventeenth century the great international repositories of scholarship, literature and discussion were in circulation, the Paris *Journal des savants* (from 1665), the Leipzig *Acta Eruditorum* (from 1682), the English *History of the Works of the Learned* (1699 to 1712) and the Amsterdam *Nouvelles de la république des lettres* (from 1684). Lutheran Orthodoxy could do no less and gave rise to the Leipzig *Unschuldige Nachrichten* (Wittenberg, 1701; transferred to Leipzig the following year) and the still more valuable *Acta Historico-Ecclesiastica* (Weimar from 1735).

There was a Christian demand for news for less familiar purposes. Much chiliastic steam remained in parts of the Protestant system, and all who believed that they lived in the end-time required accurate news of events which might portend the ultimate denouement. Whatever their scheme of interpretation, all understood that the final consummation would not take place in a corner. Spener and many of those close to religious revival did not expect an instant eschaton, but still wished to interpret the signs of the times. Jerichow and Steinmetz used their journal to report the current progress of the kingdom of God, a service which the Scots evangelical minister John Gillies developed into a modern Acts of the Apostles. To Johann Jakob Moser this kind of journalism even offered an antepast of heaven, since 'no small part of the eternal bliss among the elect will be the discussion and praise of the leadings of God'. Conversion too needed to be documented, it being 'not a question only of a *raptus* or *paroxysmus*, since splenetic or melancholic people may imagine something of that sort for a time'. Men of this turn of mind were bound to report their news on an international and interconfessional

---

[17] J. G. Gruber, *Wielands Leben* (Leipzig, 1827) in *C. M. Wielands Sämtliche Werke* L:26.

basis; convinced 'that from the times of Luther... no single witness of the truth arose who did not witness against this... abomination of Protestant Orthodoxy, and... suffered all manner of hardship from carnal teachers', they needed every evidence for the prosecution.[18]

## TRANSLATION; THE PRESTIGE OF BRITISH RELIGIOUS LITERATURE

The meeting of minds took place on many levels, not least those of commercial and technological interchange. Science also created its own community independent of nation or confession. And the religious world profited from more general cultural changes. The ability to translate had been steadily moving north since the Renaissance. The Italians were the first to provide Latin versions of Greek texts; the French to render Latin into the vernacular. They were followed by the Germans, English and Dutch. As vernacular practice improved, translation began among the various vernacular tongues on a more or less equal basis.

These developments left their mark in the world of religion. No one was more hostile to the scholastic Latin of Protestant Orthodoxy than the Pietists, yet Spener at once put his programmatic writing, the *Heartfelt Desires* (1685), into Latin for international discussion, and Francke, who encountered Molinos just before his conversion, contributed to the spread of Spanish mysticism in central Europe by translating two of his tracts from Italian into Latin. It was the eighteenth century before the English of German theologians was equal to any great amount of translation from the English direct, but they took on board a great deal of English work at second hand, from Latin, French and Dutch.[19] By the early eighteenth century the Dutch occupied the central position in the world of vernacular translation they had assumed in the dissemination of news. In the Netherlands it was confidently maintained 'that the English nation surpasses other nations in the speculative knowledge of theology (oh, that they were so happy in the practice thereof)'.[20] Great quantities of Puritan literature (followed later by belles-lettres) found their way into Dutch, often *en route* for other languages such as German,

---

[18] *SMBRG*; J. Gillies, *Historical Collections Relating to Remarkable Periods of the Success of the Gospel...* (4 vols. Glasgow, 1754–86); *Altes und Neues* 1:12–13; J. S. Carl, *Geistliche Fama* (n.pl, 1733–43) 22:37.

[19] Udo Sträter, *Sonthom, Bayly, Dyle und Hall. Studien zur Rezeption der englischen Erbauungsliteratur in Deutschland* (Tübingen, 1987) 25–35.

[20] C. W. Schoneveld, *Intertraffic of the Mind* (Leiden, 1983) 70.

Swedish and Hungarian.[21] The popularity of English theology in the Netherlands considerably exceeded what some English spokesmen considered decent, Bishop Thomas Sprat complaining that 'our famous divines have been innumerable, as the Dutch men may witness, who, in some of their theological treatises, have been as bold with the English sermons as with our fishing; and their robberies have been so manifest that our Church ought to have reprizals against them, as well as our merchants'.[22] The plagiarism continues to provide employment for modern literary detectives, and the translation went on right into the age of latitudinarianism.

In Protestant Europe generally English theology and devotional works enjoyed a prestige which has not come their way in the last two centuries for two quite different reasons. The period c. 1650–c. 1750, from, say, Descartes's *Les Passions de l'âme* (1649) to Adam Smith's *Theory of Moral Sentiments* (1759), was a golden age in the history of moral philosophy, and one in which concern for the study of the passions and their influence on behaviour ran very close to the interests of those, Catholic and Protestant, who were concerned to jack up the general level of religious devotion. And from the time when Hobbes had insisted on direct observation without preconceptions British moralists had been of the first importance.[23] British literature, religious and secular, also benefited from British political and social prestige. When Sigmund Jacob Baumgarten came, in the mid eighteenth century, to apply historical criteria to theological studies, he created a whole translation factory to put works of British history into German dress, all because British liberty had produced a nation of characters larger than life, who 'yield more notable examples of the most glorious virtues or most shameful vices, of the exceptional use and misuse of unusual capabilities and advantageous opportunities and of the most rapid and unexpected changes of good and ill fortune than other nations'.[24]

Baumgarten's list of heroic Englishmen, from Cromwell to Baxter and Marlborough, had been anticipated half a century earlier in Reitz's Pietist history of the regenerate which featured England

---

[21] J. van der Haar, *From Abbadie to Young…* (Veenendaal, 1980); *The Role of Periodicals in the Eighteenth Century* ed. J. A. van Doorsten (Leiden, 1984); Bengt Hellekant, *Engelsk Uppbyggelsellitteratur I Svensk Översättming Intill 1700 Talets Mitt* (Stockholm, 1944) 287–8.

[22] Thomas Sprat, *Observations on Monsieur Sorbière's Voyage into England* (Oxford, 1665) 270–1.

[23] N. Fiering, *Jonathan Edward's Moral Thought in its British Context* (Chapel Hill, N.C., 1981) 5; and, more generally, his *Moral Philosophy at Seventeenth-Century Harvard* (Chapel Hill, 1981).

[24] S. J. Baumgarten, *Samlung von merkwürdigen Lebensbeschreibungen grössten Teils aus der britannischen Biographien übersetzet…* (4 vols. Halle, 1754–7) 1: Preface.

strongly in the succession of saints from Edward VI and Lady Jane Grey to Baxter and Bunyan.[25] Bunyan was already a hero in Protestant Germany within a decade of his death in 1688. *Pilgrim's Progress* was translated in 1685 and followed by a series of other works done into German from either English or Dutch versions. He was among the authors prescribed for reading in the Halle Orphan House on Sundays when there were no public prayers, and he received the radical accolade of a life and bibliographical notice in Gottfried Arnold's *Leben der Gläubigen* (1701). But Bunyan was only the last of a line of Puritan writers who had flooded into Germany on their merits long before British constitutional prestige or moral philosophy could affect the issue. Edgar Mackenzie has calculated that between 1600 and 1750 nearly 700 English religious works, most of them devotional in character, were translated into German and ran to about 1,700 editions and impressions. Some were very large business indeed. Lewis Bayley's *Practice of Piety*, which flew the Puritan flag everywhere, went through at least 68 editions, Joseph Hall's *Arte of Divine Meditation* at least 61 in that period, 30 of Baxter's works were translated.[26] The first port of entry into the Protestant Empire was Switzerland, Bayley being translated into French in Geneva, thence into German in Basel, speedily followed by other editions in the Reformed towns of Zurich and Bremen. In 1631 a Lüneburg edition was produced by one of the two great Lutheran devotional presses, and after that they never let it get out of print. It was a similar success story with the *Gulden Kleinodt der Kinder Gottes* of Emanuel Sonthomb, the anagram for E. Thompson, a member of the Merchant Adventurers of England living in Stade in the early sixteenth century. Another English author very fully received in Lutheran Orthodoxy was Joseph Hall. Nowhere was the penetration deeper than in Strasbourg, where the reception of Johann Arndt and of the English Puritans formed the immediate background to the rise of Spener. English sermons were equally in demand, most of all Stillingfleet, Tillotson and Watts. The Lutheran Orthodox differed as to the number of preaching methods, there being advocates for two, four and a hundred; of course the vogue of the English pulpit necessitated a recommended text-book on the *Engellische Prediger-Methode*.[27]

The extraordinary enthusiasm for English devotional literature

[25] J. H. Reitz, *Historie der Wiedergebohrnen*... (5th edn Berleburg, 1724).

[26] Edgar C. Mackenzie, 'British Devotional Literature and the Rise of German Pietism' (unpubl. Ph.D. thesis, University of St Andrews, 1984).

[27] Martin Schian, *Orthodoxie und Pietismus im Kampf um die Predigt* (Giessen, 1912) 14, 132–4.

which won for the Puritan tracts a more enduring importance abroad than they ever enjoyed at home, did not proceed unchecked. Everywhere there were those for whom the English represented an evil principle. They shared the ill repute of the Dutch for piracy and dealing in slaves; their hot blood could be readily fanned to produce the trembling phenomena of early Quakerism; a slightly stronger wind would blow their delusions back to Germany in the shape of Fifth-Monarchy men, Quakers, the English disciples of Jakob Böhme, or even the sad illusions of Eva Buttlar.[28] Even Thomasius, one of the most faithful disciples of Locke in Germany, filtered English thought through his own understanding of Christianity, and drew the line at the more sceptical portions of Hobbes and the deists.[29] Despite the personal union of Hanover and the United Kingdom, the theological faculty of the Hanoverian University of Göttingen resolved in 1747 to confer no doctorates upon English or Reformed theologians lest they undermine respect for the Augsburg Confession at home. It was indeed pretty generally true that the Orthodox parties in the Lutheran and Reformed worlds (like their high-church counterparts in England) favoured intellectual and political isolationism, while those who wished, for latitudinarian, rationalistic, or pietistic reasons, to dent the Orthodox monopolies, adopted broader perspectives, knowing that they could not 'go it' alone. Indifferentism, the great Orthodox bugbear, had been a daily reality in the Thirty Years War when each side in a conflict ostensibly for confessional survival had employed troops without respect to religious allegiance, and men and officers had changed sides according to employers' ability to pay; to the Orthodox it now seemed rampant everywhere, and especially in the new science which delivered its goods irrespective of denomination.

## BIBLICAL CRITICISM; ATHEISM

The Orthodox were very narrow – they left even hymn-books, the great popular source of doctrine, to be produced by private commercial enterprise – but they acknowledged at least two obligations, one beyond the *Landeskirche*, the other beyond that of the confession. One of the glories of the confessional age had been the willingness of churches to provide for persecuted brethren in the faith. The outstanding case of this was the Swiss support for throngs

[28] J. Reiskius, *Commentatio de Monarchia Quinta...* (Wolfenbüttel, 1692).
[29] Walther Bienert, *Der Anbruch der christlichen deutschen Neuzeit...* (Halle, 1934) 242–7. With a similar penchant for Dutch thought, Thomasius also rejected Spinoza. *Ibid.* 249–51.

of often unpalatable Huguenot refugees (not to mention Alsatians, Palatines and Waldensians) and for the decaying Reformed diaspora in the Rhineland after the Thirty Years War. The Orthodox were, moreover, prepared to take seriously the exegesis of separated brethren. When a classified catalogue was provided for the great theological library at the Tübingen Stift in 1766, Orthodox principles still reigned in the main theological classification. This read: Dogmatici, Polemici, Morales et Casuales Lutheranorum, Reformatorum, Remonstrantium, Pontificorum, Fanaticorum, Turcarum, and apparently made no provision at all for the library's considerable holdings of Anglican work. For Exegetici super universam scripturam, however, the theological classification was entirely dropped, and the works of the Bible scholars stood side by side in a common enterprise.[30] More importantly the great Orthodox journals, the *Unschuldige Nachrichten* and the *Acta Historico-Ecclesiastica*, for generations abundantly reviewed the English (rather than British) output without specially hostile intent. The result was that by the time the *Aufklärung* had established an orthodoxy of its own in parts of Germany, an admirable work like Schlegel's *Kirchengeschichte* could distil a vast theme into the proposition that English scholars, churchmen and dissenters, 'through their energy in research illuminated many dark spots in theological scholarship; and through the outspokenness with which they made their discoveries known inspired the spirit of research abroad', especially in Bible studies and the philosophy of religion.[31]

This last discipline mattered because the Orthodox of every confession were engaged in constructing water-tight positions not only against each other, but against a threat they perceived in common, that of atheism. The debate was the more urgent and confused because it could be not be confined to scholarly circles. It was noted in 1701 that 'the name "atheist", despite its Greek origin, is now so well known that many simple and unlearned men are familiar with it and know what it means'.[32] Not that they were given much scholarly assistance in understanding, for writers far outside the Orthodox pale were so convinced of the merits of their own key to meaning as to assume rather readily that all else was meaninglessness and therefore atheism. Spener was convinced that atheism

---

[30]  Martin Brecht, 'Die Entwicklung der alten Bibliothek des Tübinger Stift in ihrem theologie- und geistesgeschichtlichen Zusammenhang', *BWKg* 63 (1963) 31.

[31]  J. R. Schlegel, *Kirchengeschichte des achtzehnten Jahrhunderts* (3 vols. Heilbronn, 1784–96) II:814; I:248–471.

[32]  H. Leube, *Orthodoxie und Pietismus* (Bielefeld, 1975) 75 n. 2.

was much more widespread in the Catholic than in the Lutheran world, and in his extreme Christocentrism Zinzendorf did not shrink from declaring that all who were not in Christ were atheists. No Christian apologist could evade the scripture warnings against supposing that there was no retribution for sin, nor fail to treat both speculative and practical atheism.[33] That the latter abounded in post-Thirty Years War Europe was made perfectly clear in the church courts. In England the Toleration Act of 1689 seemed to herald a free market in religious opinions (and hence 'atheism'); with statute law now at loggerheads with canon law it was impossible to proceed against practical atheism in the church courts in the traditional way. As Humphrey Prideaux put it, toleration 'hath almost undone us, not in increasing the number of dissenters but of wicked and profane persons...all pleading the license, although they make use of it only for the ale house'.[34] Even the lapsing of the Licensing Act in 1695 did not introduce a free market in the publishing of opinions, but it opened the way to endless public controversy on matters which seemed scandalous to the Orthodox, and created the impression in Germany, that, for good or ill, the English were a nation of singular intellectual boldness.

Speculative and practical atheism seemed closely linked at the top of the social pile. The great exemplars of speculative atheism were the ancient Greeks; they had been mediated to the modern world by the Italian humanists, and nothing now sapped the spiritual fibre of the upper classes quicker than the Grand Tour. The Orthodox were clearly up against Protean changes in public mores, habits of mind, and knowledge of the world at large. And when natural reason was turned against the scoffers in, for example, the physico-theology, annoying new difficulties appeared. Too late it was noticed that for Leibniz, at least, the evidence for the existence of God was the basis for theodicy and not vice versa.

### POOR PROTESTANT MORALE

An interlocking network of personal connexions and channels of communication would not of itself have generated a Protestant frame of mind. What was needed was a recognition that beyond the differences of nation and denomination, there were common problems affecting the whole Protestant enterprise, a recognition which

---

[33] Walch, *Religionsstreitigkeiten* 1:674; S. J. Baumgarten, *Geschichte der Religionsparteien* (Halle, 1766; repr. Hildesheim, 1966) 25.
[34] *Letters of Humphrey Prideaux...to John Ellis* (London, 1875) 154.

need not involve the bugbear of 'indifferentism'. The striking characteristic of Protestant mentality in the late seventeenth century was low morale; this notwithstanding that one great church, the Church of England, had recovered its position after twenty years of revolution, and engaged in major reconstruction. But everyone knew that the Protestants had lost perhaps half their numerical strength; and almost every change seemed to be for the worse.

The Protestant demonology was headed by the institution which ought to have given least worry, the Papacy. According the Papacy the cosmic dignity of being Antichrist obscured the fact that the Popes of the late seventeenth and early eighteenth centuries had much the same difficulties with the leading Catholic powers as had the Protestants. Clement XI (1700–21) could not prevent the War of the Spanish Succession being wound up largely on the terms of the Protestant powers, nor the cantons of Zurich and Bern increasing their hold on the Swiss federation in the Toggenburg war. The map of Italy was shaped and reshaped by the Catholic powers with scant regard to the Holy See. Quite early in his reign the Emperor Charles VI, narrowly Catholic as he was, showed that he would use the church to strengthen the royal supremacy rather than to serve the purposes of the Counter-Reformation and the authority of the Holy See; and his policies were pursued with much consistency by Maria Theresa and Joseph II. The popes of the twenties, Innocent XIII (1721–4) and Benedict XIII (1724–30), were preoccupied with domestic affairs, and when Clement XII (1730–40) was elected, he was already seventy-nine and became totally blind two years later. Corsini, his secretary of state, fearful of his early demise, avoided taking measures of importance so as not to jeopardise his own future career.

The Protestant demonology was similarly adrift in its understanding of the special tools of the Pope, the Jesuits and Jacobites. The German press combed every last corner of Bohemia to locate every Jesuit, and should have concluded that so meagre a number, however influential their situations, hardly constituted the menace they alleged. Moreover they ought to have perceived, as the eighteenth century proceeded, that vast as was their torrent of anti-Jesuit polemic, it was now surpassed by Catholic anti-Jesuit polemic.[35] The Habsburgs, recognising that the Jesuits had failed to

---

[35] *AHE* 3:715–28; B. Duhr, *Geschichte der Jesuiten in den Ländern deutscher Zunge* (4 vols. Freiburg &c., 1907–28) IV/ii:556.

convert their Protestant subjects, were turning elsewhere. Moreover, the Catholic party in the Empire smarted under Clement XII's attempts to restrict the accumulation of benefices in the hands of individuals, and were on the look-out for anti-papal arguments of their own.

The Jacobites were a real menace, and, coming after the constant threat to the Protestant Succession in the reigns of Charles II and James II, were mightily feared especially in Scotland. How deep these fears went was shown in 1695 at the sacrament Sunday in Edinburgh 'Colledge', when 'there came such a downpowring of the spirit of God on the whole Congregation (supposed to be 3 or 4000), that they all cryed out, not being able to contain themselves: so that the Minister could not be heard…For the Lord came down with the Shout of a King among them, so that they could have been content to have built Tabernacles there; which has dash'd the Jacobite party more than all the King's forces could doe'.[36] A generation later these would have been recognised as the marks of revival. The Hanoverian succession ushered in the Jacobite rebellions, rebellions which menaced not only the English political settlement but the Westphalia treaties abroad. What the Protestant interest could not see (and the house of Hanover dare not admit) was that the Hanoverian succession was a double insurance against a Jacobite triumph; the Jacobites would not succeed without foreign backing, and it was less risky for Britain's enemies abroad to put the squeeze upon Hanover than to gamble on a Stuart *Putsch* across the Channel.

However ineffective, the popes still gave ground for Protestant suspicions. The Papacy had solemnly protested against the Westphalia settlement, the great bulwark of the Protestant interest, and had Johann Jakob Moser arguing that the religious peace was a perpetual bargain established between the Catholic and the Protestant states of the Empire for the management of religious and ecclesiastical affairs, founded on the principles of the Catholic faith or upon religion as such, and thus not vulnerable to the authority of the Pope or the Council of Trent.[37] The Westphalia settlements unhappily proved as leaky as a sieve. In the 1690s the French ran amok in the Palatinate, and remained till the peace settlement of

---

[36] *Diary of Samuel Sewall* (2 vols. New York, 1973) 1:352.
[37] J. J. Moser, *Teutsches Staatsrecht* (21 vols. Nuremberg &c., 1737–54) 1:123–4, 171. New England also protested: *The Diary of Cotton Mather* ed W. C. Ford (2 vols. Boston, 1911–12) 1:256, 397.

Ryswick in 1697. Behind the French troops the building of Catholic churches in this Protestant state recommenced; in places Catholics were permitted to use Protestant church buildings. To the Protestants this was a clear breach of the Westphalia agreement, accomplished under duress and not binding in conscience; the Catholics replied menacingly that Westphalia itself was an act of force in which they had been pillaged by the Protestants with foreign assistance from France and Sweden. This bitter confrontation poisoned the atmosphere of the Empire for half a century; Clause IV of the peace settlement provided that in the places the French now gave up, Catholicism should retain its present status. To this encroachment on the fundamental law of the Empire the Papacy gave total support. During the negotiations which ended in the Utrecht settlement (1713) Clement XI determined to uphold Clause IV at any cost; his agent, Passionei, was prepared to buy off English backing for the German Protestants by dropping demands for the relief of Irish Catholics, but the Pope, still protesting against Westphalia, would have no compromise at all.

In 1715 the Pope put to his cardinals his view of the balance of advantage and disadvantage for the church in the great peace settlements,[38] finding especial pleasure in the maintenance of Clause IV, and especial pain in the failures of the Stuarts and the confirmation of the Westphalia settlements. The evidence of the terms on which that archetypal cavalier, Augustus the Strong of Saxony, had been received into the Roman Catholic church in 1697, terms which left the Lutheran church of Saxony in full possession of its status and property, was that the Papacy would push an advantage gingerly; but the Pope now appeared to confirm the view that he held the peace of Europe and the agreements which secured it as of small account beside the advantage of the church.

### THE WESTPHALIA SETTLEMENTS

This reading of the matter gained strength from events in the Empire since the Westphalia settlements. In general, things had gone the Protestants' way in the century between the Reformation and the outbreak of the Thirty Years War; but for the next century the process went into reverse, a reverse which was checked but not halted

---

[38] Ludwig von Pastor, *History of the Popes from the Close of the Middle Ages* (40 vols. London, 1891–1953) XXXIII: 108–9.

by the Westphalia settlements. The factors which had once encouraged princes on the make to take up Protestantism now encouraged conversion to Rome. English churchmen whined rather unreasonably about the seduction of 'poor protestant flies' to Catholicism; but in the Empire converts were of the very best blood, and almost every Protestant princely house had one or more to show by the beginning of the eighteenth century. By that time the Reformed house of the Palatinate whose claims to the Bohemian crown had let loose the Thirty Years War had died out, and been succeeded by a Catholic branch of the family; while the conversion of the head of the Saxon house had left the Corpus Evangelicorum in the Diet under Catholic leadership. In 1712 one Swiss statesman 'would not dare to trust to paper all [his] fears for Protestantism in Germany: humanly speaking, only the King of Sweden can prevent its ruin';[39] and there was nothing the king of Sweden could do to safeguard the local application of the Westphalia settlements.

Those settlements had established 1624 as the normative year for determining confessional boundary disputes. Legislation by reference was bound to create difficulties; and the bitter Protestant experience was that, as in politics at a grander level, the tide went consistently against them. Without application to the law-books, to publications like Professor Struve's history of religious grievances, or the endless proceedings of the Corpus Evangelicorum at Regensburg,[40] it is impossible to grasp the immense proportion of the time and energy of the public authorities in Germany taken up in trying to implement what was supposed to be the fundamental law of the Empire.

One case may stand for the rest by virtue of its intrinsic triviality, that of Cronenberg, a small property not far from Frankfurt, though by that proximity held to be peculiarly damaging to the reputation of the Reich. For a time in the sixteenth century Cronenberg had been owned by the princely house of Hesse, and had been reformed by them. When in 1541 they returned the town to the *Ritterschaft* family which had previously owned it, they did so on the condition

[39] *Lettres inédites addressées à J.-A. Turretini* ed. E. de Budé (3 vols. Paris/Geneva, 1887) 1:349. The relief in the Pietist county of Sorau in Lower Lusatia when Charles XII actually turned up was almost inexpressible. Hans Petri, 'Der Pietismus in Sorau, N-L', *JBKg* 9/10 (1913) 160.

[40] Burcard Gotthelf Struve, *Ausführliche Historie des Religions-Beschwerden…im Teutschen Reich* (Leipzig, 1722). Cf. Struve's *Neueröffnetes historisch- und politisches Archiv…* (5 parts Jena, 1719–22); E. C. W. von Schauroth, *Vollständige Sammlung aller…Verhandlungen des…Corparis Evangelicorum…* (3 vols. Regensburg, 1751–2).

that Protestantism be maintained, a condition observed till 1626, when Catholic practices began to be reintroduced. This, however, was after the normative date of 1624; so in 1649 the *status quo ante* was restored by a *Reichsdeputation*, merely excepting that the private practice of the Catholic religion be permitted in the castle. As there were very few Catholics in Cronenberg apart from the ruling house, their needs could be met by this device. In 1704, however, the Cronenberg family died out, and the property went to the great Catholic archbishop-elector of Mainz. He began to push the Catholic cause in every way he could, including knocking down the town hall to build a huge Catholic church next to the Protestant one, and making the Protestants contribute to the cost. The Cronenberg case went in and out of the courts and political institutions of the Empire, the backing obtained by the Protestants being checkmated by the archbishop's insistence on his *jus reformandi ac diocesanum*, and it was still going strong in the 1750s. The papers show how many issues of local status, power and convenience were dragged into the sour affray. It was a matter of power that the Protestants choose their own pastors, schoolmaster, organist and other local officers, and present them to the archbishop for appointment. It was a matter of status that only Protestants be allowed to ring the bells for church services, and that the shrines be removed from the town gates. It was a matter of convenience that the archbishop return the town bleaching-ground he had made into a garden, that Protestant services be not disrupted by Catholic processions, that for funerals the Catholics take no more of the Protestant biers, they having already had one and destroyed it in what was described as an accident. How much of ordinary German life could be dragged into the confessional divisions of the Empire, how frail the constitutional supports on which the Protestants had put their trust, how dark remained the shadow of the Thirty Years War a century after it was supposed to be finished, needs no further emphasis.[41]

In 1719, indeed, that war appeared about to recommence over an issue like that of Cronenberg writ large, once again on the initiative of the (now Catholic) electoral house in the Palatinate. The church of the Holy Spirit, regarded as the cathedral of Heidelberg, reflected only too accurately conditions in that unhappy territory. The choir, owned by the electors who were buried there, had been used by the

---

[41] J. J. Moser, *Vermischte Berichte von Religionssachen* (2 vols. Stuttgart, 1752–4) 1:124–223, 432–54, 597–8; *AHE* 3:491–553, 989–1024; 4:1–28; 14:797–812; 15:48–70; 16:153–246; *UN* 1739 'Früchte' 12–14.

Catholics for forty years, and separated from the rest of the building by a wall from top to bottom. The wall was now pulled down and the Reformed turned out, with, indeed, specious promises designed to induce them to forgo their internationally guaranteed status, and prospectively that large part of the ecclesiastical revenues of the Palatinate attached to the church. Moreover, concluding that the glosses to the eightieth question of the Heidelberg catechism to the effect that the Mass was 'abominable idolatry' were not part of the original catechism he was bound to tolerate, the elector set about the seizure of all the copies he could find. The politicians, especially in England and Hanover, were deeply convinced that the affair had been worked up by the Curia to get the Emperor out of Italy and embroil him with England in Germany. A tremendous diplomatic crisis built up, maintained to the brink of war. The Palatine Protestants regained their rights, and, much more importantly, as statesmen quickly recognised but the ordinary faithful could not, a serious check was given to the advance of the Counter-Reformation in the Empire over seventy years.[42]

### CONTINUING FEAR OF CONFESSIONAL WARFARE

Outside the Empire the outbreak of confessional war on a yet more savage scale seemed presaged by the atrocities at Thorn in Poland. Thorn, the first town to be founded by the Teutonic knights, had been ceded to Poland in the fifteenth century, had gone over to the Reformation in the sixteenth and had kept its German character into the eighteenth even while suffering horribly as a Polish town in the Great Northern War at the hands of Swedes, Russians, Tartars, Kalmuks, Cossacks and Saxons. The acquisition of the Polish crown by a Saxon house which had to work its passage into Catholicism helped to bring what were clearly very bad communal relations in Thorn to a head; it encouraged Catholic aggression in a place where the Protestant academy, though now rivalled by a Jesuit gymnasium, did yeoman service in educating Protestants from the hard-pressed evangelical communities in Poland, Hungary, Siebenbürgen and Silesia, as well as Prussia, Pomerania and the Alt-Mark. To the

[42] K. Borgmann, *Der deutsche Religionsstreit der Jahre 1719–20* (Berlin, 1937); Andreas Biederbeck, 'Der deutsche Reichstag zu Regensburg im Jahrzehnt nach dem Spanischen Erbfolgekrieg, 1714–1724' (unpubl. Ph.D. thesis, University of Bonn, 1937); Turretini, *Lettres inédites* III: 375–82. A concise view very hostile to the Jesuit proceedings, from within the Vienna government, is given in ÖSA W 514. Protestants 1712–1777 et Poppenheim fos. 289–90.

Jesuits the moment seemed particularly apposite, as the Orthodox Lutheran establishment in the town was just being challenged by a Pietist movement from below. How the troubles began is disputed in the testimony, though the date, 16 July 1724, the feast of the Virgin of Mount Carmel when her image was carried through the town, was a tense one. In the Catholic version of the story, a Lutheran apprentice kept his hat on and made abusive gestures with a view to creating an uproar; he had his hat removed by a Jesuit student. In the Protestant version, the Jesuit student used main force to get reverent bare-headed onlookers to their knees. Communal violence followed, with each side taking prisoners and with some damage to church furnishings. No account could be offered of how some pictures of the saints and the Virgin got to a bonfire. The President (or mayor) restored order, and offered satisfaction to the Jesuits. They, however, complained to the supreme court in Warsaw, demanding a commission of inquiry in Thorn, which should consist entirely of Catholics; it sat in the town for four months at the town's expense. The Jesuit campaign mixed xenophobia and class consciousness to attain ends which had nothing to do with law and order in Thorn, and did so with an extravagance which led even the papal nuncio to counsel caution.

The Holy Mother of God…protected Poland against the Tartars but has now fallen to a Tartarish heathenism in Thorn…The wickedness of the Jews against the crucified Lord has ceased to rage at Golgotha, only the blind frenzy of the inhabitants of Thorn…God gave the image at Czestochova 1000 wounds because it was twice cut by a heathen hand. Should not the town of Thorn now requite her honour to the Mother of God by the cession of her churches which they misuse to the blasphemy of God…Is not Thorn a real London, subject to English and not Polish laws?

This gauntlet was not declined by Protestant Europe. George I of England became a Protestant crusader; Prussia, Denmark and Sweden also intervened, and the international pamphlet controversy recalled that occasioned by the Revocation of the Edict of Nantes. The final judgment was in keeping. The academy was closed and the one remaining Protestant church handed over to the Catholics. Catholics were to have parity on the town council. Worst of all, twelve Protestant burghers, led by the President, were beheaded in a public carnage which gave Protestant Grub Street its best copy for years: 'the hand of the executioner through weariness mangling the bodies of the condemned…one boy was cut open, and his noble parts torn from his entrails and flapp'd in his face, and the youth afterwards beheaded and quarter'd'. John Wesley soberly assessed the diplomatic consequences for his mother. Here was the rub. Thorn confirmed every dark Protestant fear,[43] and those fears at once took centre stage in the European diplomacy to which the Jesuits had appealed.

In the mid-twenties when these events had brought the English press to a high pitch of anti-Catholic excitement, there were reports of renewed persecution of the Huguenots in France. Thom, the London envoy of the duke of Brunswick-Wolfenbüttel, approached Walpole with a proposal from the Corpus Evangelicorum at Ratisbon that Britain head a general collection among the Protestant powers 'for the preservation and propagation of the faith [which] would be much more dreaded by the Roman Catholicks than a powerful army'.[44] To Walpole this doubtless smacked of enthusiasm, but in 1725 Austria and Spain formed the Alliance of Vienna 'against the Turks and the Protestant princes', which was believed to contain secret articles for the annihilation of Protestantism.[45] England's counterblast was to form the Alliance of Hanover, in which Prussia and France were principal partners. This was not quite a Protestant bloc, and was not a Protestant bloc at all after the defection of Prussia in 1726; but it spoke of the threat of war through the violation of the Peace of Westphalia, and, in a separate article, of the proceedings at Thorn and the violation of the Peace of Oliva which the three powers had guaranteed.

As long as the dominant Catholic powers on the continent were divided among themselves, the London government could not pursue a foreign policy based on Protestant solidarity; moreover, the rising power in the East, Russia, could not be accommodated within the framework of Western confessional hostility. Hanover too had interests which could make relations difficult with Protestant Sweden and Prussia. But the confessional issue obstinately refused to go away

43 T. Wotschke, 'Der Pietismus im alten Polen', *Deutsche Blätter in Polen* 4 (1927) 435; 6 (1929) 478–9. Modern accounts of the episode are given in F. Jacobi, *Das Thorner Blutgericht, 1724* (Halle, 1896) and Arthur Rhode, *Geschichte der evangelischen Kirche im Posener Land* (Würzburg, 1956) 107–9.
44 Cambridge University Library. Cholmondeley Houghton Collection. Correspondence no. 1232. I am grateful to my former colleague Dr Jeremy Black for drawing my attention to this document. Cf. Schauroth, *Vollständige Sammlung* 1:343.
45 W. Michael, *Englische Geschichte im 18. Jahrhundert* (5 vols. Hamburg &c., 1896–1955) III:410ff.

in favour of the balance of power or any other grand simplicity, and continually refuelled the inherited suspicions of the Protestant mind. The thirties began with the expulsion of some 30,000 Protestant Salzburgers, and in the middle of the decade the Prussian government received, apparently from an agent in Vienna, a German translation of what purported to be a memorial of the Congregation of Cardinals (1735). This maintained that since sects of all kinds were an abomination unto God, they should be rooted out by a combination of Bourbon and Habsburg. The contest between these houses which had done so much to perpetuate the Reformation, and had recently been so damaging to the church in the War of the Polish Succession, should be terminated by frontier agreements, and a territorial share-out in which Gibraltar and Port Mahon should go to Spain. A large joint naval expedition (disguised as a campaign against pirates) should make an attack on Scotland with a view to restoring the Stuarts and preparing for the destruction of the Dutch. Fattened on these spoils, the Catholic powers should turn against all the heretics separated from the church of Christ, finally destroying Sweden by hunger, fire and sword.[46]

Droysen, who (like Ranke before him) held that this document was genuine, published it in the certain knowledge that it would be used as ammunition for what became the *Kulturkampf*; and it then attracted the whole fire-power of Catholic defence. True or false, it differs little in its implications from Clement XI's address to the cardinals in 1715 (published by Pastor himself), and it vividly illuminates why sober English statesmen again began to call for a Protestant league, why official British diplomatic correspondence was weighed down with concern for Protestants in the Habsburg lands or the Empire,[47] and when a sceptical Frederick the Great marched into Silesia in 1740 a much less sober English public dedicated a host of licensed premises to his Protestant chivalry and revelled in pornography on the theme of 'The Queen of Hungary Stript'.

One recent analysis of the War of the Austrian Succession has presented that struggle as a confessional conflict reaching its head in

---

[46] J. G. Droysen, *Geschichte der preussischen Politik* (14 vols. Berlin, 1855–86) IV/iv:416–33.
[47] PRO SP 80/117 Robinson to Harrington 5, 12, 13 August 1735; 80/118 Robinson to Tilson 27 August 1735; 80/120 Harrington to Robinson, 12, 23 March 1736; 80/122–3 *passim* and 84/359–60 correspondence of Robinson and Horace Walpole. Cf. SP 90/44 Dickens to Harrington, 21 June 1738, and Walpole's letter of 27 May 1738.

Silesia.[48] Certainly Frederick II went out of his way to make it so appear and he convinced both sides. Catholics believed, quite erroneously as it proved, that the Catholic interest in Silesia or even the whole of Germany was at stake. In 1742 the Associate Presbytery meeting at Dunfermline proclaimed a solemn day of humiliation,[49] 'considering that... the Protestant interest and liberties of Europe seem in hazard of being swallowed up by the subtile intrigues and bloody sword of Popish powers'. Two years later Robinson groaned to Carteret: 'What for my poor part... I pray to God for in particular is, that the present war may not degenerate into the worst of all wars, that of religion.'

By this time confessional conflict had cast its shadow into the New World. In 1742 Jonathan Edwards had been able to declare the revival 'a more important war' than that with Spain; but in May 1744 controversy over Whitefield's third visit to the American colonies was cut short by news of renewed war with France. This was the end of a generation of more or less peaceful isolation. If France was to triumph in North America she would have to conquer New England; if she was to be defeated and the New England Way preserved, New England shipping and manpower would be indispensable. Whitefield and Gilbert Tennent among the revivalists encouraged recruiting,[50] and so did their opponents. A splendid victory at Louisburg was followed by terrible casualties inflicted by disease and by the Indians. The judgments of the Lord were indeed inscrutable; New England was no longer safe.

The reversal of alliances of 1756 by which Austria and France at last came together, though made possible by the emergence of Russia as a great power, would alone have suggested to Protestants that the long-feared confessional war was about to begin. In fact the whole period between the War of the Austrian Succession and the Seven Years War was filled with steadily mounting religious tension exploited by the political leadership on both sides. As we shall see, once free of the war, Maria Theresa set about a final solution of her domestic Protestant problem, and in Styria, Carinthia and Hungary the confessional issue became acute again. In the Empire there were

[48] G. Jaeckel, 'Die Bedeutung der konfessionellen Frage für die Besitzergreifung Schlesiens durch Friedrich den Grossen', *JSKKg* NS 34 (1955) 79–121.
[49] *Newcastle Journal* 6 March 1742; PRO SP Austria 80/64 5 August 1744.
[50] G. Tennent, *The Late Association for Defence Encourag'd...* (Philadelphia, 1748); G. Whitefield, *Works* (6 vols. London, 1771–2) V: 79–93.

the usual cases of local Catholic aggression, and when in 1751–2 von Schauroth published his three great volumes of the proceedings of the Corpus Evangelicorum he prefaced them with the heart-felt prayer 'that the God of peace will fill all Christian hearts in such a way that Germany may know *for the first time* what conduces to its peace'.[51]

Moreover, the Habsburgs took a leaf out of Frederick's book, and the Imperial chancellery began to compile a complete list of Catholic complaints against Protestants since 1747; the archbishop of Cologne looked to the extirpation of Protestantism. Kaunitz began to blame the cooling of Britain towards the Austrian alliance on Protestant zeal and to make veiled threats of using the Jacobites to overthrow the Hanoverian throne. The House of Denmark began to fear the outbreak of religious war, and to call for the formation of a Protestant bloc. This atmosphere was ideal for both the diplomacy and propaganda of Frederick the Great, who was in the most exposed position. He put constant pressure on the Protestant governments, especially the British government, sought to get up resistance to the Habsburgs in Protestant Hungary, and took academic advice in the field of public propaganda; but the war all but undid him. One of Frederick's abiding impressions of the previous war was that the gentry, clergy and bureaucracy of the Habsburg lands were all venal, that the enduring force was that of religious fanaticism; and he could not have prepared more thoroughly to be the aggressor a second time by presenting himself as the champion of the persecuted.

His campaign had the desired resonance. With the Dutch the Protestant theme could be used to reinforce renewed fears of French expansion. Protestant Swiss needed little persuasion. Lacking an international champion since the days of Cromwell, they had pinned their hopes of safety to the rivalry of Habsburg and Bourbon. Those hopes were now in dust. Swiss Catholic clergy began to talk of the final annihilation of Protestantism; the great abbot of St Gallen and the Catholic Toggenburgers who had been worsted in the last confessional conflict were restive; blows were exchanged on the frontiers of Zurich, where the cantons of Zug and Schwyz began to hold military exercises. When the Seven Years War broke out the Swiss crisis also came to a head, and, receiving reports that Richterswil and Wadenswil were in flames, the town council of Zurich closed the gates and brought out the cannon and munition

[51] Schauroth, *Vollständige Sammlung* I: Preface.

trains.[52] At the other end of the Protestant front in England, there was the same alarm. Whitefield preached patriotic sermons and Howel Harris, the Welsh revivalist, acted out the role of a minuscule Gustavus Adolphus:[53]

Mr Harris was in much concern least [*sic*] our privileges and liberties should be taken away from us; especially the liberty of the gospel, which should the Papists succeed we should be robbed of... [In 1759, becoming alarmed at the risk of French invasion he accepted a commission in the Breconshire militia and went to Yarmouth, writing] 'I am resolutely, and cooly determined to go freely, and conscientiously, and die in the field of battle in defence of the precious word of God, the Bible, against Popery.'

Samuel Davies, the Presbyterian revivalist in Virginia, sought to out-recruit the Anglican gentry with his volunteer companies from Louisa and Hanover counties.

### WHY CONFESSIONAL ARMAGEDDON NEVER CAME

Yet the head-on confessional conflict so long awaited had failed to arrive, and could no longer be employed proleptically to interpret the relations of states, the general atmosphere changing rapidly after the Seven Years War. But in the early history of religious revival the facts that reasonable men could believe that Armageddon was just around the corner, and that it never arrived, were almost equally important. What then were the motives, not of the Papacy, but of the great Catholic powers which took the lead in the great European game?

France's age-old struggle with the Habsburgs had led her into alliances in the Empire, irrespective of confession, with a view to protecting her eastern frontier, alliances with that restive daughter of the Pope, the Republic of Venice, and, outside the Christian world, with the Turks. Louis XIV had brought French power to its apogee, brutally handling Protestants at home and abroad, and combining genuine professions of Catholic piety with a willingness to deal roughly with the Pope (complaining indeed that Innocent XI was not anti-Protestant enough)[54] and sections of his Catholic subjects.

[52] Paul Meyer, *Zeitgenössische Beurteilung und Auswirkung des Siebenjährigen Kriegs...* (Basel/ Stuttgart, 1955) 25, 135, 138 147–54. Cf. R. Feller, *Geschichte Berns* (4 vols. Bern, 1974) III:376–7.
[53] [B. La Trobe], *A Brief Account of the Life of Howell Harris Esq.* (Trevecca, 1791) 84, 87–9; Tom Beynon, *Howell Harris, Reformer and Soldier (1714–1773)* (Caernarvon, 1958) 58–146.
[54] *Recueil des Instructions données aux... Ministres de France...* (29 vols. 1884–1969) XVII: *Rome* ed. G. Hanotaux 2.55.

The Revocation of the Edict of Nantes set endless problems to Louis's successors. It destroyed the French lobby in the government of Bern, and broke the old French connexions with the Protestant states of the Empire, turning Brandenburg into a bitter enemy. Huguenot emigration created an international network of anti-French conspiracy and propaganda. Again, the ravages of French arms in the Empire and in Salzburg created a bitter revulsion which was crucial in the history of popular religion. French mores, progressive absolutism, standing armies, Popery, formed a single syndrome to be repudiated by a revived Puritanism. Particularly in Württemberg this fitted precisely with a country politics directed against a dynasty which turned Catholic. But there was the same spirit abroad in New England.

In the war of the Spanish Succession the French were not merely defeated, but had to accept an enormous increase in the power of the Habsburgs, not least in the Balkans and Italy. For a generation, therefore, French policy was devoted largely to mending old fences; in particular at the time of the Austro-Spanish Treaty of Vienna in 1725, Chavigny was sent into Germany to make a drive for allies. In 1685 the instructions to the French ambassador in Vienna had been to encourage the Emperor to make all his subjects Catholics; by 1723 the message was that the Westphalia settlement had aimed to put a brake on the power of the Emperor, and that was why the Habsburgs had always been trying to undermine it.[55] Clause IV of the Peace of Ryswick, it was admitted immediately after Louis' death, had been the king's dearest desire, but had not produced the intended result. Chavigny's realistic instructions for the Imperial Diet in 1726 were that 'His Majesty intends on all occasions to support the Catholic religion when he can do so with success',[56] but that he would not incur unnecessary Protestant hatred by consistently supporting it in principle. A policy of this kind might be painful but not perilous to Protestants.

The Habsburgs had inhibitions of their own. Like the Bourbons, they had been late to adopt the Counter-Reformation as a platform, but had profited enormously by doing so, and were now covering their territories with baroque churches, great monasteries and other

---

[55] *Recueil des Instructions données aux...Ministres de France...* I: *Autriche* ed. A. Sorel 108, 208–10.

[56] *Recueil des Instructions données aux...Ministres de France...* XVIII: *Diète Germanique* ed. B. Auerbach 95–6, 161, 165; *Recueil des Instructions données aux...Ministres de France...* XVI: *Prusse* ed. A. Waddington 243–4.

religious monuments beloved of public authorities. A memorial of 1705 assured the house of Austria that 'the promise of prophecy [to you] is to extirpate heresy and undo Islam; and in your eyes heretics have always been as abominable as Mohammedans'.[57] Throughout the Habsburg family lands this process of extirpation went forward, becoming the more brutal the further east it went. It was at its worst in Hungary, where about a third of the population was Protestant, and there was aristocratic leadership prepared to gamble on rebellion. The Thirty Years War had left Bohemia and Moravia in Habsburg hands; and having got the Protestant aristocracy, clergy and professional classes out of the country, they attempted to carry through an irreversible social revolution, the confiscated property being used to endow religious houses and a Catholic aristocracy which tied up their estates in entails. The Habsburgs had no sharper critics than the Protestant aristocracy thus forced into exile, but could offset this liability by the immense new patronage they gained by the expansion into the Balkans and Italy; this proved a magnet to the Catholic aristocracy throughout Germany, and sweetened invitations to conversion for selected Protestants, such as J. J. Moser.[58] Add to this that the Emperor was by virtue of office the lay head of the Catholic world, that his Reichsvizekanzler in the early eighteenth century was Friedrich Karl Graf von Schönborn, himself bishop of Bamberg and Würzburg and a member of an outstandingly successful family of ecclesiastical magnates, with relatives in the sees of Speyer, Konstanz and Trier, that he was interested in retuning the machinery of the Reich and pursuing a Catholic forward policy, and all the materials were at hand for a great conflagration.

In fact nothing was quite as it seemed. The Habsburg monarchy was and remained to the end a narrowly Catholic monarchy, but from about 1700 it began to pursue new policies of church reform with great consistency, if need be without or against the Popes. The same memorandum which urged the extirpation of Protestantism urged the Emperor to 'wrest from the Popes of Rome what they have usurped over the Empire. Do not confound the usurper with the vicar of Christ.' Moreover, the great captain of Habsburg victory in the field, Prince Eugene, had a reputation for Jansenism, and, in the great library in which he gathered his especial intimates, collected

[57] Droysen, *Preussische Politik* IV:iv:251.
[58] J. J. Moser, *Lebensgeschichte vom ihme selbst beschrieben* (n.pl, 1768) 20–31.

books in every area of knowledge without respect to the Index, including a section on the relations of church and state in which anti-papal works were strongly represented. Among his intimates were Protestants, and, in the thirties, still more remarkably, the nuncio in Vienna, Passionei, an advocate of church reform in head and members. These political interests had access to a system of government, the Hofkanzlei, separate from the Reichskanzlei through which Schönborn operated. This institutional duplication was now important. The reputation of the Empire as a device for conflict resolution and damage limitation stands higher at the present day than at any time since its dissolution; but at the beginning of the eighteenth century it seemed constricting to the larger players. Saxony, Brandenburg, Hanover, Hesse-Kassel, all sought crowns outside the Empire; the Habsburgs too developed a dynastic, as distinct from Imperial, interest in the South and South-East. Among the forces pushing them in these directions was the Catholic nobility of Bohemia. They helped to build up the institutions in Vienna which balanced those of the Empire. Many of them had profited enormously by Catholic advance in terms of capital gains, but they had paid heavily in terms of income. They wanted no new Spanish adventures, and hoped to round off the Habsburgs' Central European holdings by advances in the South and South-East and the incorporation of Bavaria. Prepared to fight to keep out the French, they wanted their northern flank protected by agreements which allowed Saxony and Brandenburg to acquire crowns outside the Empire, and Hanover to acquire a ninth electoral title within it. Though no Protestant could be expected to see it, a Catholic victory in the Empire was postponed to the Greek Calends by the very parties appointed to seal the triumph of the Counter-Reformation in Bohemia.

To this pressure Charles VI was doubly vulnerable. He was much tempted by economic projects, some of which, like the Ostend Company, provoked more trouble abroad than he bargained on. More importantly, after the early death of his only son, Charles VI had only daughters born to him. He provided against this possibility in 1713 by a family statute called the Pragmatic Sanction; his possessions were to pass whole and undivided to his male heirs; failing them to his daughters, and failing them to the archduchesses, the daughters of his deceased brother. It was by virtue of this ar-rangement that in 1740 Maria Theresa succeeded him, not in the

Empire, but in the various crowns and titles by which the Habsburg family lands were held. To secure international recognition of this arrangement, Charles must pay the necessary price. In particular, at the time of the Protestant *cause célèbre* in Salzburg in the early thirties, Charles sacrificed his freedom of action in the Catholic interest to the need to secure recognition of the Pragmatic Sanction. And already by that time, in fact between the Catholic withdrawal in the Palatine crisis of 1719, and the Austro-Spanish Treaty of 1725, Schönborn's hopes of a forward policy in the Empire had covertly fallen victim to superior forces within the family lands.

POLITICAL ASSIMILATION AND THE ROLE OF THE CHURCHES

In between wars and major crises Habsburg policy towards their own Protestant subjects remained brutal, a monument to the fact that, to every ruler, the usefulness of the church at home was a different matter from the confessional interest abroad. In both Catholic and Protestant countries the Reformation had led to a great extension of state regulation; Protestant church systems had to be organised, Catholic systems defended and revitalised. The disasters of the Thirty Years War permitted no turning back. In the Empire the state's desire to get a grip on its subjects might take the form of establishing a single lordship in a territory, succeeding to persons or institutions which possessed the dignity of *Reichsunmittelbarkeit* and to their votes in the Diet.[59] There was much straightforward assimilation. Imperial Sweden sought to master Bremen and Verden, its territories on the south side of the Baltic, in Lapland and Finland, the United Kingdom to secure Scotland, Ireland and the American colonies. Everywhere this process created responsibilities, gladly accepted, for the established churches in teaching, civilising and redeeming. Most of the comprehensive *Landesordnungen* of the sixteenth and seventeenth centuries began with rules relating to church attendance, the observation of the Lord's Day and the preservation of orthodoxy; everyone accepted that the way to improve peasants was to care for their salvation, and in 1661 an ordinance in electoral Saxony for the regulation of police, marriage, dress, day-labourers and artisans, began with the proposition that 'the total destruction and ruin of the

---

[59] J. J. Moser, *Von der Teutschen Reichstände, Landen…* (Frankfurt/Leipzig, 1769) 106.

fatherland by the just wrath and judgment of God [was] to be feared'
from the abuses it proposed to remedy.[60]

In the seventeenth and eighteenth centuries, as in the twentieth,
assimilation proved to be a good deal more difficult than anyone
supposed at the outset. In Germany it created a set of social castes
which long disguised the fact that amongst the most valuable
innovative groups were ethnic and religious outsiders. The laudable
attempts of Lutheran Orthodoxy to lift religious discourse above the
locally circumscribed Low German dialects hindered peasant religious observance right through northern Germany, and led to
downright racialism in the South and East. Mühlenberg found the
Slavonic population in the parish of Grosshennersdorf in Upper
Lusatia, belonging to Zinzendorf's aunt, 'uncommonly rotten and
lazy... If we want to get anything done, we must go peddling with the
word of God like grocery dealers... The old learn mostly to jabber a
little German, the young are taught German in our schools'. A
modern commentator on Silesia as Frederick the Great seized it
reports: 'The Polish population was coarse, lazy and drunken. The
spreading of the German language seemed the only way to raise
them.'[61] The well-meant efforts of the English religious societies to
assimilate Wales, and the Scots Kirk to conquer the Highlands for the
English language were not dissimilar.

Assimilation, however, could cut two ways. The Scots Kirk had a
mortal and well-founded fear of popery and Jacobite conspiracy in
the Highlands. It fought its way into the Highlands on the basis of
Lowland culture and the English tongue. Yet all the time it feared it
was itself succumbing to English mores. 'I sometimes fear we be sifted
with Erastianism, from the head of the English church' lamented
Robert Wodrow in 1709. In Ulster 'the wild Irishes [were] coming
down and taking the leases our countrymen had, and swarming out
in such numbers as very much threatens the British interest in that
kingdom';[62] while Moderatism implied assimilation to English ways,
to the politics of patronage and manipulation perfected by Walpole.
Reasonable men might prefer any fate to that. Enumerating the signs
of the times in one of his unpublished revival sermons, Jonathan

---

[60] H. O. Lichtenburg, *Unterhaltsame Bauernaufklärung* (Tübingen, 1970) 15; Leube, *Orthodoxie und Pietismus* 90.
[61] *Die Korrespondenz Heinrich Melchior Mühlenbergs...* ed. Kurt Aland (2 vols. Berlin/New York 1986–) 1:4–5; Alois M. Kosler, *Die Preussische Volkschulpolitik in Oberschlesien, 1742–1848* (Breslau, 1929) 9–10.     [62] *Wodrow Correspondence* 1:49, 426.

Edwards spoke for many in Old England as well as Scotland and New England:[63]

> We are a country dependent on them [the English], we are such to their government, we have our books, and our learning from thence, and are upon many accounts exceedingly liable to be corrupted by them. This country is but a member of the body of which they are the head, and when the head is so sick, the members it is to be feared, will not long be in health.

The revivalists' belief that the personal and public danger might be averted by fanning the dying embers of faith and conscience presumed to survive in the depths of the hardest heart was one of the several possible responses. New Englanders shifted between compromise, withdrawal and revival, responses which will concern us later.

In the cockpit of central Europe Upper Lusatia also exemplified the surprises sprung by assimilation. Even before the Thirty Years War it was clear that this territory would lose its independence to one or other of the competing orthodoxies, Reformed (should the Winter King maintain his hold on the Bohemian throne), Catholic (should the Counter-Reformation triumph) or Lutheran (should Saxony get its way, which in 1635, after more than a decade of holding the province in pawn, it did). At just this time, almost as in protest, Jakob Böhme, the shoemaker of Görlitz, produced the alternative religion and science which for the next hundred years did yeoman service over much of Europe to those who were sick of pretentious Orthodoxies. The Saxons of course extended their system of church government to the province. The process of absorption was resisted by the Lusatian aristocracy, led by the Friesen family, one of whom, Henriette von Gersdorf, was a very capable blue-stocking to whom fell the bringing-up of her grandson, the famous Count Nikolaus Ludwig von Zinzendorf. Their resistance was inflamed by the defeats of Saxony in the Great Northern War, and the incursions of Swedes, Poles, Saxons, Danes and Russians into Lusatia. The war also intensified an old problem of public order. It multiplied the number of 'loose people' (*losen Leute*) by adding to the immigrants, beggars and vagabonds, numerous wounded troops, deserted and escaped serfs. Loss of labour added to the pressure for intensified serfdom, and this in its turn provoked a crescendo of peasant risings and flights.[64]

---

[63] Perry Miller, 'Jonathan Edwards's Sociology of the Great Awakening', *New England Quarterly* 21 (1948) 54–5.

[64] J. Leszczynski, 'Die Oberlausitz in den ersten Jahren des Nordischen Krieges (1700–1709)', in *Um die Polnische Krone. Sachsen und Polen während des Nordischen Krieges* ed. J. Kalisch & J.

The Lusatian aristocracy had their own methods of dealing with these problems. They were amongst the first to try to raise the religious level of their enserfed Sorbs and Wends by providing vernacular religious literature in languages for which there had hitherto been little in print; and, when it became available from Halle (which of all religious institutions the Saxon Orthodox most detested), they imported it. Their answers to loss of labour (especially as some of it was disappearing over the Bohemian border to the von Dietrichstein estates) was to recruit Protestant refugees in Bohemia and Moravia. The difficulties here were that the Czechs were very unwilling to accept serfdom in Lusatia; that all the refugees were loath to grant more than nominal allegiance to Saxon Orthodoxy; and that the Emperor put pressure on the Saxon government to stop the haemorrhage (thereby adding to the friction between Saxony and the Lusatian aristocracy). Finally the Slavs in exile proved extremely footloose, willing to gather in force wherever preachers to their taste appeared, and convincing the Orthodox clergy of the province that the ground was quaking beneath their feet.[65] Rival schemes of assimilation produced an *impasse* from which three methods of escape were found, expulsion, flight, and a religious revival, issuing, totally unforeseeably, in a mission to the universal church.

Policies of assimilation were designed by states to bind their subjects together, and separate them from the lieges of others, but experience of the process created bonds of sympathy among many European Protestants, and these bonds were strengthened by the reactions of heads of church and state to common pastoral problems. Both in England and in Europe the wars of the middle of the seventeenth century and the long subsequent period of economic recession created problems which the churches could not solve without the sympathetic assistance of the state. This assistance was generally forthcoming, though on terms which the straiter sort of Orthodox found increasingly irksome. There was a daunting contrast between official professions of faith and the private conduct of too many of those who made them. The crass contrast in Restoration England led to the formation of a pastoral ideal of 'primitive

---

Gierowski ([East] Berlin, 1962) 70–94; A. Mietzschke, 'Lusatica aus dem Anfang des 18. Jahrhunderts' *ZSP* 17/ii (1941) 123–42.

[65] [C. F. Demelius], *Vollständige...Nachricht von der Herrrnhutischen Brüderschaft...* (Frankfurt/Leipzig, 1735) 10–12, 41–2; Arend Bucholtz, *Die Geschichte der Familie Lessing* (2 vols. Berlin, 1909) I. 111–12.

Christianity'; yet a distant son of that ideal, John Wesley, could still find 'the grand stumbling-block' to the spread of the gospel to be 'the lives of Christians'.[66] In Switzerland it was alleged that 'Catholics, Jews, Turks and heathen "if only they become new creatures" are, through their good works, better than Christians who know the will of God but do not fulfil it'. In Germany in 1690 'some [went] so far as to say that the present condition of the church [was] to be compared with an *ecclesia plantanda*, a church which still has to be planted, not *quoad doctrina* (as to doctrine) but *quoad vitam* (as to life)'.[67] The radicals scoffed at the idea of defining the church by the pure Word and the sacraments: 'he alone stands in the Christian faith who is united to Christ through faith, enters into the spirit and mind of Christ, denies the world and its desires, and in love shares everything in common with his fellow members'.[68]

It was not the case that the ecclesiastical machine did not care about this state of affairs; the great complaints came from within the machine itself. The Scots lament that 'the Lord seems in a great measure to have withdrawn from his servants, people and ordinances' (in this instance apparently through lack of gentry support) was almost universal; in New England Increase Mather saw 'sinfull security [as]... the great disease of the last times', and the Württemberger church complained of every evil, spiritual, social and moral. Perhaps if the clergy visited more strenuously things might improve. Where feudal obligations were multiplying, the gentry were the villains of the piece. In Prussia their demands forced peasants to desecrate the Sabbath; in Mecklenburg a fair degree of Sabbath conformity was achieved, but services on apostolic festivals were threatened with collapse because masters would not release their men.[69] And the public entertainments which might now be described metaphorically as distancing the participants from the official religion of the parish, might then distance them literally; in Protestant Württemberg, Sunday dancing was prohibited, and those who wanted it slipped off to Catholic places. The chorus of complaint indeed baffled credulity in the age of Enlightenment. Johann Rudolph Schlegel, that model of what Wesley called 'a man of reason

[66] Wesley, *Works* II: *Sermons* II:495.
[67] *Wahrhaffter Bericht... von einem Collegio Biblico zu Giessen* (n.pl, 1690).
[68] Christianus Democritus [J. K. Dippel], *Auffrichtiges Glauhens-Bekänntnüss und kurze Nachricht...* (n.pl, 1732) 53.
[69] E. Peschke, *Bekehrung und Reform* (Bielefeld, 1977) 46–7; Karl Schmalz, *Kirchengeschichte Mecklenburgs* (3 vols. Schwerin &c., 1935–52) III:109.

and religion', thought (erroneously) that the lamentations were the work of Pietist enthusiasts;[70] David Hume thought they proved that churchmen were always trying to have their bun and eat it. When trying to extract concessions from the state they described mankind as

sunk into the deepest lethargy and unconcern about their religious interests. Yet these same divines when they refute their speculative antagonists, suppose the motives of religion to be so powerful, that, without them, it were impossible for civil society to subsist; nor are they ashamed of so palpable a contradiction.[71]

### SUPERSTITION AND NON-CHRISTIAN BELIEF

What the churchmen of the late seventeenth and early eighteenth centuries missed was what John Livingston, the Scots revivalist who had been at the Kirk o' Shotts in 1630, had called 'the hunger of my hearers [which] helped me more than my own preparation'. They could titillate the religious appetite by liturgical reform, improve church-music, building or art; they could deal with those deviant forms of religious practice, officially classed as superstition, which people favoured; they could give more attention to those more vulnerable and less corrupted, the children. The attack on superstition was itself ambiguous. The sterling examples of popular Christian commitment were afforded by people, the Harz miners, for instance, with a strongly supernatural view of the world, which included a great many things besides Christianity; and those in authority were making new distinctions between religion and superstition. It was still too soon in 1700 to say that belief in witchcraft had become superstitious; many at all levels of society still held that a belief in evil spirits was an integral part of belief in God. But witch-trials ceased in Bern after 1680, and by that date had passed their peak even in Bavaria and the Austrian alpine country. For the witch-craze had grown up with the rise of modern absolutism and was intertwined with the great conflict between Catholic and Protestant. When the Counter-Reformation had made Catholic territories safe against Protestantism, it went on to secure them

---

[70] M. Scharfe, 'Subversive Frömmigkeit', in *Kultur zwischen Bürgertum und Volk* ed. J. Held (Berlin, 1983) 117; Schlegel, *Kirchengeschichte* II: 360.

[71] David Hume, *Dialogues Concerning Natural Religion* pt. 12. Norman Kemp Smith's edn (London, 1947) 220–1.

against witches. Protestants replied in kind, and over most of the Empire the trials reached their peak during the Thirty Years War when life of any kind was cheap. After the war, the powers were more keen on attracting population than on hunting out deviationists. By the turn of the century Bekker in Amsterdam and Thomasius at Halle could write openly against belief in witchcraft, and critics of the witch-hunts began to offer theological reasons for their views. In the West general religious apologetic began to turn to arguments based on natural religion, universal agreement, and the need for a first cause. Again, no one believed more firmly than the Pietists in the existence of the devil; but they envisaged a cosmic struggle of the kingdom of God against that of the devil which dispensed with both witch-trials and exorcism at baptism. The historians of the Salem witch-trials of 1697 note that in 1735 Jonathan Edwards directed a similar situation at Northampton to an entirely different end, that of religious revival.[72]

Plain superstition was still entertained in high places (Augustus the Strong tried to foretell the future from geomancy books[73]) but *Volksreligion* was a new elite discovery, equated with popular superstition, against which states were now prepared to act. In 1669 in the county of Mark the elector required his clergy to read an ordinance from the pulpit against a huge catalogue of customary practices[74]

such as putting leaves in the water on St Matthew's eve...putting pigs' hair on the fire, binding trees on New Year's day, of putting St John's wort...on the walls, spirits are driven out, there are Easter bonfires accompanied by all sorts of songs taking the name of the Lord in vain, and a great deal of devilry goes on, soaking meat in water tied up with bread, butter, lard and the like, hanging up St John's wreaths or crowns, making sacrifices.

Doubtless little progress was made under this legislation; certainly in Switzerland ordinances classifying magic among other forms of behavioural deviance were still being adopted in the middle of the eighteenth century without undermining the peasant conviction that it was safer to believe too much than too little. And the standard

[72] P. Boyer & S. Nissenbaum, *Salem Possessed: The Social Origins of Witchcraft* (Cambridge, Mass., 1974) 27–30.

[73] C. Gurlitt, *August der Starke. Ein Fürstenleben aus der Zeit des deutschen Barock* (2 vols. Dresden, 1924) II:83.

[74] H. Heppe, *Geschichte der evangelischen Kirche von Cleve-Mark und der Provinz Westphalen* (Iserlohn, 1867) 188n.

reading of Protestant peasantry from Central Europe to Russia, devotional works apart, continued to consist of almanacs and ghost stories. Nevertheless the mounting hostility of governments to superstitions not practised by themselves probably did unsettle minds on one of the Protestant frontiers, east of the Baltic, where the penetration of Christianity of any kind was remarkably shallow.

The ancient religion of Livonia, the latter-day Estonia and Latvia, had been a nature-religion in which 'trees and flowers, groves and forests, stones and hillocks and waters were endowed with miraculous life-giving forces... All manifestations of the earth's fecundity were lovingly cared for and protected.'[75] The Balts were also great venerators of fire. Fire was sacred and eternal. Tribes had official sanctuaries on high hills and on river banks where fire was kept, guarded by priests, and in each house was the sacred hearth. 'Only once a year, on the eve of the midsummer festival, was it symbolically extinguished, and then kindled again. Fire was a goddess who required offerings'.[76] Subjection by German conquest and incorporation into the Holy Roman Empire in the thirteenth century brought the Balts into the Catholic fold, but their belief in immortality and capacity for syncretism enabled them to take on the new faith with the minimum of alteration to the old. Nor did the Reformation (which did not penetrate to neighbouring Lithuania) make any difference; like the original conquest it was a German imposition, the property of the much-hated German Baltic nobility. Absorption by Sweden (by submission in the case of Estonia (1561) and conquest in Livonia (1621)) heralded eventual change. The official basis of faith was now the Augsburg Confession as it was upheld by the Swedish imperial church; Sweden introduced the basic elements of ecclesiastical as well as secular organisation, schools and a university, and sought, amid the usual difficulties, to offer the resources of Protestant spirituality in the languages of the serf populations. In 1689 a Lettish Bible was produced, largely at the cost of Charles XI of Sweden; but only 1,500 copies were printed owing to the hazards of getting paper from France. The ship carrying the paper fell into the hands of a pirate who, on learning the purpose of the paper, provided an edifying evidence of providence by releasing both the ship and its entire cargo. But copies speedily became so rare

---

[75] Valdis Mezezers, *The Herrnhuterian Pietism in the Baltic...* (North Quincy, Mass., 1975) 34.
[76] Olafs Bruvers, 'The Spiritual Influence of the Moravian Brethren in Latvia in the Eighteenth Century' (unpubl. M.A. thesis, Fuller Theological Seminary, 1982) 23.

as to trade at famine prices.[77] No love was lost between the Swedish government and the German nobility which continued to take its education in Germany. This facilitated the early inflow of Pietism, which of all things the Swedish government most abominated. Added to all this, the Swedish crown brought its relations with the German nobility to crisis point by its policies of *Güterreduktion*, and, after the defeat of Charles XII at Pultava (1709), lost its Baltic provinces to a horde of enemies led by Russia. By the capitulation treaties of 1710 and the Peace of Nystadt (1721) Peter the Great agreed to maintain the Swedish ecclesiastical arrangements. But inevitably the Swedish reorganisation was left uncompleted, the war and its aftermath, disease, wrought havoc among the clergy – twelve of the fourteen in Riga died, all three in Reval, about half those in Kurland; and very long vacancies followed. And in so far as Peter had sympathies in the Lutheran world they were with Halle Pietism not Swedish Orthodoxy. Meanwhile the German nobility poured into the Russian bureaucracy and ran the area very much to suit themselves, filling vacant parishes with their boon companions.[78]

Among the worst affected areas was the island of Oesel, to be important later in the story. Oesel had provided the pension which ex-Queen Christina spent in Rome and was mercilessly rooked by Charles XI. Under his *Reduktion* policy he got many of the local gentry and aristocracy off their property, and left half the island to his favourite, Mannerburg. His administrators oppressed the peasants, and the lessees of the 'reduced' estates were required to pay their rents in kind to metropolitan Sweden, so that there was always a food shortage. Under Charles XII not even the clergy were exempt from war contributions and the billeting of dragoons, and to these exactions were added those of invading Cossacks and Kalmuks. After the war plague exacted a huge toll, including a majority of the clergy. It is said that in the parish of Wolde only one peasant and the pastor's daughter survived, and 'since no pastor and no witnesses were to be drummed up, they celebrated their marriage like the first men in Paradise'.

Livonia was no paradise, and governments right through the Swedish and Russian years continued to hunt down the paganism

[77] *AHE* 3:1058–60.
[78] *Baltische Kirchengeschichte* ed. R. Wittram (Göttingen, 1956) 87–152; Guntram Philipp, *Die Wirksamkeit der Herrnhuter Brüdergemeine unter den Esten und Letten der Bauernbefreiung* (Cologne/Vienna, 1974) 53–109.

which was barely beneath the surface. In 1677 the upper consistory required preachers to report to the provost or superintendent 'household gods, "oracula" in the trees, as also utterers of blessings, magicians, salt-blowers, together with anything else against the first and second tables'; and in 1693 the Swedish governor-general issued an ordinance against superstition and idolatry, ordering peasants to 'tear down the things which...were dedicated to them, crosses, groves, bushes, trees, stones and the like, to hew them down, to burn them with the sacrifices, to purge and root them out in every possible way, so that not the least memorial may be left over which could be used for further superstition'. In 1731 the preachers' conference at Reval took counsel how to deal with the 'heathenism' still present in Estonia.[79] To that problem the Moravians were shortly to find a new answer.

The case of the Eastern Baltic is a telling example of how remorselessly states now harrowed the frontiers of the Protestant world and linked them with central policies. If Prussia was raising Protestant recruits for the Baltic frontier, and both Sweden and Halle in their different ways were trying to christianise the natives, the Habsburgs were populating the Ottoman frontier with Protestants at whatever cost to their own confessional purity, and England was importing others to secure the Georgia frontier against Spain. If the Protestant gentry in Upper Lusatia were strengthening their labour force by smuggling out Protestant refugees from Bohemia and Moravia, Catholic lords were seeking to smuggle others back in, and the Spanish in Florida were trying to promote the mass flight of negro slaves from Georgia. The creation of a genuine confessional conviction, even among suppressed ethnic groups neglected for centuries, was now beginning to matter in a quite new sense. And the recognition that this was so was one of the things helping to constitute a common Protestant mind.

### INDOCTRINATION OF CHILDREN

The same was true in a more complex way of another submerged group, the children. In a classic work Philippe Ariès argued that in the seventeenth and eighteenth centuries the European world generally began to recognise that children were a distinct social

---

[79] T. Harnack, *Die lutherische Kirche Livlands und die herrnhutische Brüdergemeine* (Erlangen, 1860) 20; *SMBRG* 1 (1732) 408–29.

group requiring special treatment; this treatment led to curious contretemps between adult efforts to control and juvenile protests in favour of traditional proto-adult rights.[80] In fact attitudes towards children varied with different social levels and with different convictions, especially between those who believed in the primacy of the intellect over the will, of reason over the passions, and those who saw the will as the great battleground between God and the devil. Indeed children were themselves a battleground; they were bound to be influenced by their parents' fears for the future of the Protestant religious system, and in the Habsburg lands there were intermittent attempts to separate them from their parents altogether.

Here as so often the heritage of the Reformers was ill-tended by their successors. As it was neatly put by Bugenhagen in the Hamburg church ordinance of 1525: 'the father and mother of a household are bishops in their own house and are to instruct the children and servants as simply as they can', the instruction to include the decalogue, the creed, the Lord's prayer, the sacrament and prayers at table. This programme was very imperfectly fulfilled, and became less natural as families were less frequently a productive economic unit. Nor were family failures made good by the church. Under an ordinance of 1574 the church of Hesse was the only Lutheran church to crown its training of children by confirmation. This practice only became widespread in Lutheranism in the later seventeenth century through the agency of Spener, a man who, significantly, had made his name as an expert catechist. Even in Hesse preparation for confirmation needed tightening up after the Thirty Years War. Hesse now reflected a much wider movement of opinion which helps to explain the tremendous resonance of Spener's proposals in the *Pia Desideria*. In Württemberg, Franconia, and Nuremberg[81] schemes for the better instruction of children were on foot incorporating methods and literature adapted to children's understanding, as Bugenhagen's ordinance had not. There had always been plenty of advice on the religious raising of children in the *Hausvaterbücher*, but now there came very successful and long-lived publications designed for the purpose, Anna Hoyers's *Conversation of a Child with Its Mother on the Way to True Godliness* (1st edn 1628) for example, and, most striking

---

[80] P. Ariès, *The Centuries of Childhood* (Eng. tr. London, 1962).
[81] C. Kolb, 'Die Anfänge des Pietismus', *WVLg* 9 (1900) 40–2; F. W. Kantzenbach, 'Der Separatismus in Franken…', *ZBKg* 45 (1976) 33–5; *Nürnberg. Geschichte einer europäischen Stadt* ed. G. Pfeiffer (Munich, 1971) 326–7.

of all, the public recognition that the Bible was a daunting reader for the young. Collections of Bible stories like those of Justus Gesenius (three editions 1656–1719) and Johann Hubner (printed innumerable times, and prescribed in many ordinances 1714–1902) were now provided. Not all the improvements were the work of Pietists; but they pressed the work forward on so broad a front that their enemies were able to publish great lists of child prophets they had led astray,[82] and the first decade of the University of Halle (1694–1703) has with some justice been described as a youth movement.

There were similar developments in the Reformed world. Even in Scotland the drawbacks of using the Bible as a school textbook of the English language were acknowledged by the early eighteenth century, and here too collections of excerpts were made available, better adapted to children's capacity to read and remember. The picture of children grouped around Jesus is prominent in the late-seventeenth-century literature of Reformed Orthodoxy, before the Lockean psychology with its emphasis on children as impressionable began to take effect. An English work of this kind was one of the most successful in the whole Reformed world, *A Token for Children; Being an Exact Account of the Conversion, Holy and Exemplary Lives and Joyful Deaths of Several Young Children* (1670) by the nonconformist divine James Janeway. This was republished in German at Lübeck in 1700; by 1746 it had gone through at least ten editions, and had been greatly amplified by lives of German children, inspiring German works of the same kind. The *Token* was enormously successful in New England too, and, in Old England, was one of the works on which Watts built in his famous *Divine Songs Attempted in Easy Language for the Use of Children* (1715). Like the *Token*, this was dedicated to parents, teachers and all connected with the education of children.

The impact of all this pedagogy was strikingly manifest in New England. The Reformed churches of New England began by requiring a profession of conversion for membership, but, in the last third of the seventeenth century, gradually but generally went over to the Half-Way Covenant. This created a class of church members, admitted when young, who could not profess conversion, but understood the doctrine of the faith and accepted the authority of the church; their children were to be baptised. Here the church proposed to get a grip on people outside (and in terms of age, below) the ordinary membership. In due course it became normal for candidates

<hr />

[82] Casparis Sagittarius, *Untheologische und abgeschmackte Lehr-sätze von Pietismo...* (*n.pl*, 1691).

for membership to reach that goal via the Half-Way Covenant, and the flow of full members increased. Not everyone was satisfied. When Jonathan Edwards came to apply the gathering-in of the guests from the highways (Matt. 22 : 9–10), he proclaimed that 'the saving mercy of God in Christ extends to all sorts of persons', and proceeded to a sociological analysis of what sorts there were in the parish, beginning with children and young persons. Not surprisingly these groups were prominent in the revivals he wrought.

In secular life children did not accept dependence on the superior wisdom of their elders without resistance; and in the field of religion the youth problem was most powerfully illumined by spectacular examples of the young assuming a precociously adult role in a crisis. Where Protestant communities were deprived of a regular ministry, as in the late seventeenth century they were in France and parts of the Habsburg lands, fathers of families must assume a more than normally priestly role, and in desperate circumstances, so must children. In the Camisard rebellion schools of child prophets were produced who were attached to the Protestant commandos and prophesied as to the killing of prisoners and other matters. The young, who might prophesy in their sleep, seemed to have sidestepped the corruption of original sin, and were the most moving testimony to their elders that their own sufferings had not been in vain, that the true church survived despite all past failings.[83] The Camisard children did not perhaps convert their parents, but the public knowledge of what they did assisted innumerable eighteenth-century children to convert theirs. Moreover, the terrible events in the Midi had a demonstration effect for which the adult world was unprepared. Early in 1708, in the wake of Charles XII's victorious army in Silesia, children began to hold camp-meetings like those which the Swedish troops had held, praying all day for the restoration of Protestant schools and churches, a subject as politically sensitive as could have been conceived. The Halle interest saw to it that these events were known all round Europe, including the British Isles; this time parents were converted. To those of millennial propensities one of the signs of the end-time became 'the strange impulses and motions of the children of Silesia'[84] in defiance of all authority. There was a lineal continuity between the events in Silesia in 1708 and the revival there in the early forties; more importantly Silesia had its own

[83] Hillel Schwartz, *The French Prophets* (Berkeley, Ca., 1980) 28–33.
[84] *Praise out of the Mouths of Babes and Sucklings* (London, 1708); [R. Roach], *The Great Crisis...* (London, 1725) 9.

demonstration effect in an almost endless series of children's revivals all over Protestant Europe in the thirties. What had begun in pastoral concern for a specially needy group, ended with the evidence, unmistakable to men like Wesley, that the young constituted an area of specially active operation by the Holy Spirit.

## EUROPEAN CONSCIOUSNESS OF AMERICA

If the religious imagination of the Protestant world was being stretched downwards (so to speak) by the discovery of ethnic differences and of children, it was being stretched outwards by the discovery of America as a psychological fact. The contacts made between Europeans and other cultures since the fifteenth century made their way only slowly into general European consciousness, but at the end of the seventeenth century public demand for information of this kind rocketed in the western states, followed at a modest interval in Germany. Before questions of comparative culture arose, however, Christian thinkers sought strenuously to fit America into a religious perspective which steadily modified the Euro-centric viewpoints from which it was undertaken. Seventeenth-century Orthodoxies had a low opinion of America. To the Lutherans it was the outer darkness of the Gospel where the lost were cast with weeping and gnashing of teeth; and an English view that the colonies consisted of 'colluvies of wild opinionists, swarmed into a remote wilderness to find elbow-roome for [their] phanatick doctrines and practices' was no more flattering.[85] Joseph Mede, in his *Key of the Revelation* (London, 1643), had a difficulty in locating the forces of Gog and Magog which would assail the saints when the seventh vial was poured out, and thought that America, suitably remote from the central drama, might well be the place.[86] The poor reputation of America was, however, an advantage from some standpoints. Johannes Kelpius was not so enamoured of the toleration in Siebenbürgen that he did not date the inbreak of the millennium at the turn of the century 1699/1700, and in 1694 pushed off with forty followers to create an opportune settlement in the wilds of Pennsylvania, complete with telescope on the roof to observe the signs of the times. Kelpius contrived to marry an ascetic viewpoint with the

[85] E. Benz, 'Pietist and Puritan Sources of Early Protestant World Missions' *CH* 20 (1951) 32–3; N. Ward, *The Simple Cobbler of Aggwam in America* ed. R. M. Zall (Lincoln, Nebr., 1969) 6.
[86] J. W. Davidson, *The Logic of Millennial Thought* (New Haven, Conn., 1977) 54.

philosophy of Jakob Böhme and with a reading of Rev. 12: 1–6 which speaks of a woman giving birth to a male child destined to rule the nations, while being threatened by a dragon. 'Her child was snatched up to God and his throne; and the woman herself fled into the wilds where she had a place prepared for her by God.' Kelpius understood this passage to mean that the fall of the Apostolic church was caused by the dragon which wanted to devour the male child Jesus. When the woman, the Virgin Sophia, fled into the wilderness, the dragon turned on her other offspring, the remnant of the true church. Here the American wilderness qualified by virtue of being a real wilderness; it would enforce an ascetic existence and the prophetic journey into it would act as a catalyst for the dramatic events immediately in prospect. Salvation depended on the church's flight into the wilderness as also upon the journey of the soul into its own inner wilderness. Like all the Philadelphian groups Kelpius's brethren found it difficult to reconcile their group ideals with the obligation to bring the saints into their Philadelphia – Kelpius sent Daniel Falckner back to Germany (and, of course, to August Hermann Francke) for recruits – and the company finally disintegrated. Kelpius confessed: 'I went into the wilderness as into a rose-garden and did not know that it was a fiery furnace of tribulation.'[87]

This was a candid admission that the America of the apocalypse was not the 'real' America on the ground; but the views of those who founded Pennsylvania were not very different from those of Kelpius. Penn first came to Germany in 1677 not just to preach a Quaker gospel, but to make contact with continental groups which were alienated from the state churches, Mennonites, Labadists and radical Pietists, and gather them for the unsectarian church of Philadelphia, the comity of free minds and brotherly love. Names and sects and parties were indeed about to fall, and the great harvest of true believers was about to be reaped.[88] Once again the real America was too much for the dream, and Quakerism had to change.

Contact between this America and Germany continued – the Inspired on both sides of the Atlantic corresponded, Oglethorpe advertised for settlers for Georgia in Jerichow's *Sammlung auserlesener Materien* in 1734, and the American Schwenkfelder Abraham Wagner

[87] Elizabeth W. Fisher, '"Prophecies and Revelations": German Cabbalists in Early Pennsylvania', *PMHB* 109 (1985) 299–333 esp. 322–4; K. Deppermann, 'Pennsylvanien als Asyl des frühen deutschen Pietismus' *PuN* 10 (1984) 208–9.
[88] *A Collection of the Works of William Penn* (London, 1726) 51, 58–9, 65–72, 209–15, 236.

wrote to Tersteegen. But as German migration westward turned into a flood, powered by hunger and political misery, German radicals feared it would extinguish 'the little light of nature and virtue among the poor savages' and the Germans would become savages themselves. The surprising turn came with the great Protestant emigration from Salzburg in 1731 which compelled the admiration of Orthodox and Pietist alike. A small number of the Salzburgers fetched up with two pastors from Halle in Georgia, and their history was traced year by year in great detail by Samuel Urlsperger, the Pietist senior of Augsburg. He also got the Orthodox *Acta Historico-Ecclesiastica* of Weimar to take up their cause. In 1736 a new section appeared in that journal entitled 'Of the spreading of the Christian religion among the unbelievers', featuring the Salzburgers at the head. This concession made, the *Acta* had to go on to the Danish missions in Tranquebar, and Callenberg's work for the Turks and Jews. This missionary study became a permanent feature, always with the Salzburgers in first place.[89] At last the Orthodox had broken the narrow bounds of the *Landeskirche* and had an eye to the gospel work which needed to be done in the world.

The Orthodox were as fascinated as the radicals with the news of the revival in New England when it came. In the forties Lutheran Orthodoxy at home was engaged tooth and nail with the Moravians, and America was now a favourable arena in which to put Zinzendorf down. Even Gilbert Tennent could be dragged in as a witness for the Orthodox prosecution. Moreover, it shortly became clear that Mühlenberg, Hallesian though he might be, was organising a real Lutheran church in America, though one owing nothing to any act of state. Emigration to the New World ushered in not Zinzendorf's supra-confessional church of the latter days, but an extension of the church systems of the Old World; it reconciled old church enemies, not in the New World, but in the Old. A real America was changing Europe even as Europe strengthened its hold on the American peoples.

### THE SEPARATION OF RELIGIOUS FROM ECCLESIASTICAL LIFE

The Orthodox parties in the Lutheran and Reformed worlds and their high-church counterparts in England confronted these stresses with some success. The abuse they suffered from Pietists and *Aufklärer*

[89] *AHE* 2:405; 3:66–90, 1084–1125; 6:882–939.

cannot obscure their achievement in reconstruction after the Thirty Years War. The Orthodox policy of underpinning religious establishment with a highly articulated systematic theology fitted well with the 'routinisation' of the secular bureaucracies. If the third generation of the Reformation had fallen into a 'crisis of piety', the age of Orthodoxy had begun with Arndt, often hailed as the fountain-head of Pietism, and ended with Valentin Ernst Löscher, whose motto was *Doctrina et pietas*; and it was a great age of church-building, church-art and church-music. This, however, was where the problems began. Löscher understood his motto strictly in terms of cause and effect; mysticism might promote the inner growth of Christians, always provided they had been renewed on the basis of the doctrine of justification forensically understood, the doctrine which had seemed so alien to Penn when he encountered it in Spener's circle. Löscher could never escape the embarrassment of insisting that justification must be accepted as a fact to which the mystical experience was secondary. Orthodoxy was already in straits with its heavy dependence on the scripture principle. This had once seemed a way to interpret reality at large, but was now fruitless for confronting the proto-Enlightenment. To insist, as Löscher had to do, that scripture was the only way to the true knowledge of nature was to accept exclusion from a major intellectual industry.

Piety alas! involved a much larger public than science. If the scripture principle, the great bulwark against popery and indifferentism, were to be preserved, there was no way of coping with Pietists who understood God's gracious gift as the New Birth, and regarded this as the decisive presupposition not merely for sound theologians, but for sound theology. A thousand Orthodox pamphlets proclaimed this to be the one comprehensive hydra-headed heresy of quakerish enthusiasm (even *quakerische Methodisterei*) descended from the Anabaptists. In 1690 the clergy of Hamburg even took oath to repeat their subscription to the symbolic books,[90] 'and to reject the lately notorious *Pseudophilosophos, Anti-scripturarios, laxiores Theologos* and other *Fanaticos*, especially Jakob Böhme, and *Chiliasmum tam subtiliorem quam crassiorem*'. To such narrow defensiveness had the Orthodox been driven by the war against popery, indifferentism and atheism. From the side of humanism Thomasius would now object

---

[90] A. Ritschl, *Geschichte des Pietismus* (3 vols. Bonn, 1880–6) II : 178; Hermann Rückleben, *Die Niederwerfung der hamburgischen Ratsgewalt...* (Hamburg, 1970) 108–31.

that the scholastics were a thousand times more damaging to the church than the mystics.[91] And from the side of practical piety Löscher's mechanical bracketing of *doctrina* and *pietas* looked uncommonly like magic, especially when it was wedded to religious establishments whose liturgies spoke of every deceased baptised person as a Christian, and appeared to equate legally-exacted conformity with the Christian obedience born of conviction.

This was a serious matter. One of the fruits of studies in seventeenth-century bibliography has been the discovery that the demand for devotional literature, for what might be called the pabulum of *pietas*, was overwhelming, that it had never been possible to meet it from the Bible and Protestant sources alone, and that this state of affairs continued until the age of revivals in the 1730s. To take the most popular of all, *The Imitation of Christ* of Thomas à Kempis went through 188 editions in Latin and the vernacular languages in the sixteenth century, 444 in the seventeenth. Two Catholic authors were very widely read, Molinos, whose *Spiritual Guide* was put on the Index in 1687, and François de Sales, whose books went through 100 editions before 1740. English Puritan devotion was indispensable; Lewis Bayly's *Practice of Piety* going through 59 editions in English and 45 in German, French, Welsh, Hungarian, Romanian, Indian and Italian up to 1740; and, as we have seen, Bunyan and Baxter were in great demand. All were outdone by Johann Arndt whose *Four* (later six) *Books of True Christianity* from their first appearance in 1605 up to 1740 were published 95 times in German, and 28 in Latin, English, Dutch, Danish, Swedish, French, Czech, Russian and Icelandic; almost an edition a year. The German editions amounted to probably 100,000 copies, and were found everywhere; even amongst the persecuted Protestants of Carinthia, it is said that every peasant who possessed three or more books had at least one edition of Arndt.[92] And Arndt made no bones about his dependence on Tauler, Thomas à Kempis and other pre-Reformation writers, a dependence enlarged by modern inquiry to 'a broad spectrum of late medieval mysticism'. Likewise Puritan devotional literature was in a great measure modelled on earlier Roman Catholic literature. Funeral sermons, which were also a form of devotional literature and constituted a succession of the saints emulated in other literary forms, were also published by the hundred; statistically speaking their

[91] Christian Thomasius, *Monatsgespräche* v: 1130.
[92] Oscar Sakrausky, 'Evangelisches Glaubenleben im Gailtal...', *Carinthia I* 171 (1981) 191.

*Blütezeit* fell between 1620 and 1740.[93] As late as 1740 devotional works constituted 20 per cent of the total book production in Germany (compared with the 5 per cent devoted to belles lettres). In short, while the *Zanktheologen* polemised against indifferentism, ordinary Protestants stayed themselves against a century of trial and terrible defeats by appeal to a spiritual tradition common to Catholic and Protestant. The men who ushered in new ways of christianising their world, Spener and Francke, Baxter and Watts, Doddridge and Wesley all appeared as middle men of one kind or another. Someone needed to mediate between the world of ecclesiastical precision, and the world of spiritual nutriment; and the fact that the reading of Luther's Preface to Romans or his commentary on Galatians proved the royal road to conversion showed that the mediators were going to have to go behind the scholastic Orthodoxies of recent generations to do it.

By that time the spiritual life of Europe was escaping confessional control. At all social levels there was practical eclecticism between Christianity and superstition and among spiritual writers of various confessions; there was also an eclecticism amongst 'ancient' truths, the pursuit of a core of mystical experience, the study of more than one alternative to the kind of science which so alarmed the Orthodox. This kind of position had been given a fresh repute and new intellectual content in the early seventeenth century by the famous shoemaker of Görlitz, Jakob Böhme. As we have seen, he provided an alternative science, religion, and philosophy to the Orthodoxies allied with the big battalions of the day, and when those battalions triumphed in Upper Lusatia in 1624 Böhme died.

No man more completely mistook his situation. In 1690 the Lutheran Orthodox Ehregott Daniel Colberg dedicated two fat volumes to refuting the 'fanatical spirits' in *Platonisch-Hermetisches Christentum*, and his successive chapters on Paracelsianism, Weigelianism, and Rosicrucianism, on Quakers, Behmenists and Anabaptists, on the followers of Bourignon, Labadie and Molinos testified to an important fact. Böhme had given respectability to a way of regarding things which spread right across Europe into the Netherlands and Britain with as much organisation as an anti-institutional movement was ever likely to have, took off to Pennsylvania, drew into itself the very widespread interest in those Catholic mystics who

---

[93] Rudolf Lenz, ed., *Leichenpredigten als Quelle historischer Wissenschaften* (Cologne, 1975–9).

fell foul of the church in the late seventeenth century, was taken up by a scholar like Thomasius as an antidote to Cartesianism, and, when interest in the logic of Wolff waned in the third quarter of the eighteenth century, had the vitality to return as the immediate background to Goethe[94] and indeed to Kant. Wesley struggling with this as part of the heritage of William Law is a characteristic, not a lonely, figure.

Behmenism also fitted comfortably with two final features of the Protestant frame of mind, millennialism and great weariness with confessional strife. It was normal in the seventeenth century for Orthodox preachers to call on their congregations to recognise that, like Israel, they were subject to God's chastisement, and to repent before his judgments. Too many of the Orthodox went further, and applied a leverage to conscience by asserting that the final judgment was near, and that the time for repentance strictly limited. Some millennialists believed that the Last Judgment would come at the imminent end of the Fourth World-monarchy, some, in the chiliastic tradition, believed that the end of the old order of this world would be followed by Christ's return and the inauguration of his thousand-year kingdom. Either way the chronology of salvation-history yielded certainties very relevant to the day. One of the signs of the end was to be 'the slaying of the witnesses' (Rev. 11: 3), and Protestant witnesses were being slain in such profusion as to lend plausibility to almost any computation of the end-time. The Popish dragon raged with a fury attributable to the wound he had suffered in the Reformation, and, until late in the seventeenth century, the Turk penetrated ever deeper into Christendom. Were anyone not sufficiently alarmed, a plethora of comets was outdone only by the number of broadsheets interpreting their significance. Why some theologians succumbed to apocalyptic obsessions while others escaped, is not clear; English theologians were especially vulnerable, though there were among them those who shared the view represented by Luther and Calvin that the millennium was already past. The Reformed tradition was more susceptible than the Lutheran, perhaps because the Reformed were more often subject to extreme political pressure, and more often unable to see any way, short of the final intervention of God, in which righteousness could triumph. The Orthodox parties made much of apocalyptic speculation, for the seventeenth-century world seemed hopelessly in the toils; and one of

---

[94] R. C. Zimmerman, *Das Weltbild des jungen Goethe* (Munich 1969–) 1: 22–6.

its growth industries, scientific astronomy, looked likely to put the study of at least one group of signs of the times on a much firmer basis. But a religious body cannot for ever proclaim the imminence of the end; and long before the disappearance of famine, the long-term economic upswing, and other circumstances made people in eighteenth-century Europe more optimistic about their future, the pioneers of new ways in religion proclaimed a 'hope of better times'. Spener, who introduced chiliasm into the Lutheran world, held that the end would not come until all God's promises to the church had been fulfilled; more precisely, Bengel calculated for the faithful of Württemberg that the Second Coming would not occur till 1836. Oppressed saints would not have to wait for ever to be vindicated, and need not now secede from a distressed establishment. Moreover, by viewing justification as the real improvement of the regenerate, and preaching the prospective real improvement of the church, Spener provided a new leverage upon the consciences of those numbed by the continual deferment of the end-time.[95]

Behmenism and chiliasm also answered to another feature of the religious mood, the longing to go behind the present confessional division of Europe into a larger religious unity. This movement took many forms. The continuing popularity of the devotional works of Arndt was a testimony to the existence not of a 'school' of Arndt – his readers came from every corner of the theological spectrum – but of a desire to escape from polemic to a better life. There were those who had had enough of the institutional burden of seventeenth-century Christianity. For them it was time to achieve life at the expense of the law, the spirit rather than the letter. Quakers, mystics, Philadelphians were of this style. Kelpius, who had fled Europe for the wilderness of Pennsylvania, in 1699 perceived a 'revolution in Europe...which in the Roman Church goes under the name of Quietism, in the Protestant church goes under the name of pietism, chiliasm and philadelphianism', and evidenced 'by ecstasies, revelations, apparitions, changings of minds, transfigurations, translations of their bodys' and 'paradysical representations by voices, melodies and sensations'. The Philadelphians were a group which had originated in England in the 1650s and by the end of the seventeenth century were led by a widow, Jane Leade. Basing themselves upon

[95] H. Lehmann, *Das Zeitalter des Absolutismus* (Stuttgart &c., 1980) 124–34; *PuN* 14 (1988): *Chiliasmus in Deutschland und England im 17 Jahrhundert*; J. Wallmann, 'Reformation, Orthodoxie, Pietismus', *JGNSKg* 70 (1972) 196; J. Wallmann, *Philipp Jakob Spener und die Anfänge des Pietismus* (Tübingen, 1970) 307–35.

the prophecy of Rev. 3: 7–13 which held that only the church at Philadelphia would survive the trial coming upon the world before Christ's return, they began to hold public meetings in London in 1697, announcing that 'the society is not a church, but preparatory to the church at Philadelphia; consisting of those who have associated to wait in the unity of the Spirit for its glorious appearance and manifestation'. Jane Leade's writings were speedily translated into Dutch and German, and made more stir on the continent than at home. They were taken up by the Petersens, husband and wife, who had been married by Spener. And like Kelpius they had an international vision:

the Philadelphian Society…must be considered as a part of the great movement for awakening spiritual life which [has] broken out like a new reformation in Germany under the name of Pietism, and which had also appeared in other countries, such as France, Italy, and the kingdom of Naples.[96]

The hopes of the Philadelphians were not borne out by the millennium, but they recall the international vision of the Puritan movement in the middle of the sixteenth century, and they survived as a common element in the self-assessment of all the evangelical movements in the eighteenth century, right through to the time when they were re-evaluated in Germany after Wesley's death.[97]

If the Philadelphians nourished hopes of unity by escape from the church, at another social level, church unity itself appeared to be an ideal within practical grasp. Leibniz served under both Catholic and Protestant masters who were interested in securing confessional unity to foster common action against the Turks. The Hanoverians who employed him for thirty years had of course an interest in sustaining an irenical reputation until they succeeded to the British throne, Toland even claiming that no clergy were more moderate, and no princes more wise than those of Hanover.[98] The desire of rulers for the domestic convenience of a single church, or for a bloc against Rome, the instinct of latitudinarians that ecclesiastical isolation was ruinous, and the convictions of men like Wake, based on relatively unbiased scholarship and evidenced in negotiations with the Gallican church

[96] *Diarium of Magister Johannes Kelpius* ed. J. F. Sachse (Lancaster, Pa., 1917) 47; Nils Thune, *Behmenists and Philadelphians* (Uppsala, 1948) 92, 94. Cf. C. W. H. Hochhuth, *Heinrich Horche und die philadelphischen Gemeinden in Hesse* (Gütersloh, 1876) 104.
[97] J. G. Burkhard, *Vollständige Geschichte der Methodisten…* (2 parts Nuremberg, 1795) i: 2–3.
[98] J. Toland, *An account of the courts of Prussia and Hanover* (London, 1706) 57.

immediately following a war in which Louis XIV had moved heaven and earth against Protestantism and the United Kingdom, all pointed to the church-union negotiations which still ruffled Orthodox feathers in the 1720s.[99] The turning of Habsburg ambitions away from the Empire deprived these schemes of the political relevance they needed, and the running was then made by a Prussia geared to state-managed schemes of toleration rather than church union.

Church union, however, staged a come-back in the age of Enlightenment, and by then Prussia was playing its part. In his political testament of 1752 Frederick the Great had declared that 'I am neutral between Rome and Geneva. I try to unite them by showing them they are fellow-citizens', while adding, as a Protestant *Aufklärer*, 'I advise posterity not to trust the Catholic clergy without authentic proofs of their fidelity.' By the time of his second political testament in 1768 those proofs seemed largely to have been obtained, and 'the odd priest, abbot, or canon who fancies martyrdom and the Austrian connexion' could be watched in time of peace and kept under close surveillance in time of war.[100] By that time the movements both of revival and renewal had had to rethink who were their friends and who were their enemies, and a surprising number had converted their old xenophobia into a new nationalism.

---

[99] *UN* 1721 1048–57; 1723 835–8, 915–24.
[100] O. Hegemann, *Friedrich der Grosse und die katholische Kirche...* (Haida, 1904) 12; *Politische Testamente und andere Quellen zum Fürstenethos der frühen Neuzeit* ed. H. Duchardt (Darmstadt, 1987) 235.

# CHAPTER 2

# *The beginnings of revival: Silesia and its neighbours*

## RELIGIOUS POLICY IN BRANDENBURG–PRUSSIA

Within the Protestant world and operating upon the common Protestant mind were particular driving centres, areas of special activity which, from the middle of the seventeenth century, moved ever further from the old Protestant heartlands in central Europe. Heidelberg and Hamburg kept some kind of contact with Germans overseas, Reformed and Lutheran; Sweden continued to supply pastoral assistance to the Swedes of the former New Sweden on the Delaware; the Pietist monarchy of Denmark gave its patronage to the celebrated Tranquebar mission: Amsterdam was more important than them all, but gradually yielded the palm to London. The Great Elector's dying words were 'London and Amsterdam',[1] a prophecy as precisely fulfilled in the ecclesiastical as in the political sphere. In the non-hierarchical Protestant churches of the continent the link between church and state was normally formed by the court chaplain, and, from 1705 when Queen Anne's consort, Prince George of Denmark, appointed as his chaplain the Pietist Anton Wilhelm Böhme, the Great Elector's successors had a spokesman for their policies at the British court. Their Dutch connexions proved more problematic. In 1613 the Elector Johann Sigismund went over from the Lutheran to the Reformed confession, less, it seems, from the hope of furthering his claims to Reformed territories in the Rhineland, than from genuine admiration for what was then the most dynamic religious confession in Europe. This conversion had far-reaching implications. Dutch influences remained strong in Brandenburg; and the Reformed interest at the court offended not only the confessional and xenophobic instincts of Brandenburger Lutheranism, but also its well-founded judgment that many of the new court were men of no

---

[1] Carl Hinrichs, *Friedrich Wilhelm I. König in Preussen* (Hamburg, 1943) 7.

deep religious conviction. The electors could neither reform their Lutheran churches on Calvinist principles, nor continue to govern them on the old Lutheran basis of being the senior lay member of the congregation. When the Great Elector received Huguenot refugees after the Revocation of the Edict of Nantes, Pufendorf argued that his sovereign rights included the oversight of all confessions and that the religious freedom of individuals must be preserved.[2]

Since toleration rather than union was the best the electors could achieve, they were attracted to religious movements which sought to go behind the entrenched confessional divisions of Europe, to syncretism, rationalism and Pietism in turn; and, within the wider Lutheran world, to any movement which challenged Lutheran Orthodoxy. Orthodoxy formed the official platform of their immediate neighbours, Saxony and Sweden. The Lutheran Orthodox, of course, scented the sale of truth for indifferentist Mammon; but establishing toleration gave the electors three great prospective advantages: in whichever way their domains expanded no new problem of confessional relations could arise: they could help make good their losses of population during the Thirty Years War by canvassing for immigrants among oppressed religious minorities abroad; and when, to acquire the crown of Poland, the electoral house of Saxony turned Catholic, the way was open for the Hohenzollerns, the Reformed heads of an overwhelmingly Lutheran people, to seize the practical leadership of the Protestant interest in the Empire on an undenominational principle.

Moreover, the battle against the Orthodox could not be avoided if a state was to be built in Brandenburg, for it was simply a special aspect of the electors' conflict with their estates. The Orthodox party owed its strength in the church to the ecclesiastical patronage which Lutheranism conceded to the gentry. The Great Elector's great weapon against the estates was a standing army, so far as possible self-financing by means of subsidy treaties with foreign powers. The army in its turn offered an inducement to the impoverished nobility to come to terms by affording a career in military service. The nobility were further cushioned by a tax policy which sacrificed the economic interests of the towns to the Junkers' concerns in corn-growing and -exporting, and a social policy which enabled them to fix their labour force to the soil by steadily intensifying serfdom. Corn exports were indeed the one great resource of the old Brandenburg; and since the

[2] Otto Hintze, *Gesammelte Abhandlungen* (3 vols. Göttingen, 1967) III: 72–3.

natural outlets at the mouths of the Oder and Elbe were in foreign
hands the dynasty sought to provide alternatives in its possessions on
the Weser and the Lower Rhine by road-building and canal-
construction. Of the canals the most important was that between the
Spree and the Oder, opened in 1669, which put Berlin across the
route of the transit trade between the South-East and Hamburg, and
gave it direct access to Breslau, one of the most important German
cities, and the starting point of the Russia trade.

This Friedrich-Wilhelm-Kanal was also significant from two other
points of view. The Great Elector established claims on hereditary
grounds to the principality of Jülich-Berg, to the duchy of Pomerania,
and to Silesia; France and Sweden encouraging him to pursue the
last to accommodate Swedish claims in Pomerania. About 1670 the
Great Elector drafted a plan for the acquisition of the whole of Silesia,
and from the time that Prussia acquired the Oder mouth at Stettin in
1714, a drive to seize the whole Oder valley was to be expected, the
more so as it would sever electoral Saxony from her new crown in
Poland. The importance of the Berlin–Oder connexion was also
enhanced by the acquisition of the duchy of Magdeburg in 1680. At
that time a thoroughly run-down asset, Magdeburg was prospectively important as a junction to the Hohenzollerns' possessions in the
West, as a bridgehead against Saxony, and as an asset capable of
rapid improvement. Under the new management the mines of salt,
copper and hard coal began to boom, the Saale was made navigable,
the population doubled in two generations, and manufactures were
exported by the Silesian route to Hungary and Moravia. The
industrial extremity of the territory, the town of Halle, sat auda-
ciously almost on the doorstep of Leipzig, the seat of an ancient and
famous university, the home of an international trade fair, one of the
two leading German book markets, and the chief place of a Saxony
which was itself the chief mining and manufacturing state in
Germany. But the Berlin government meant business, and as became
their wont, they made it plain by founding a university at Halle. A
Lutheran university to turn out clergy and officials for the state was
indeed required. Duisburg and Frankfurt-on-Oder were both Reformed schools; and when Wittenberg, the stronghold of Saxon
Orthodoxy, resisted the liberalising policies of the Great Elector by
producing a yet more exclusive version of the Formula of Concord, he
prohibited it to his theologians.

All these threads in the development of Brandenburg-Prussia were to be crucial in the history of Pietism, and, at one remove, in the early history of religious revival.

### ORIGINS OF PIETISM

Pietism has constituted one of the most relentlessly contested battlefields of modern historiography, disagreement about when it began being so well balanced by its obscurity as a concept, and the whole so confused by the application of often arbitrary theological preferences or varying degrees of national self-isolation among German scholars, that inevitably a French critic has appeared to ask whether it ever existed at all.[3] Ambiguity there was from the beginning, but sense can be made of the story by keeping it on a concrete and personal basis. Philipp Jakob Spener, who began his professional career in Strasbourg, and attained fame as senior of Frankfurt (1660–86), made his name originally as an expert catechist. A churchman to the core, he set out a programme of church renewal in 1675 in an introduction to the sermons of that most devotionally minded of Lutheran theologians, Johann Arndt, republishing it separately under the title *Pia Desideria, or Heartfelt Desires for an Improvement of the True Evangelical Church Pleasing to God, with Some Christian Proposals to That End*. In this tract Spener castigated all classes for their responsibility for the poor state of the church, making proposals for improved clerical training and preaching. The crux, however, was the inner spring of spiritual vitality, the New Birth, a doctrine which became a Pietist party badge not because it was peculiar to them but because of the prominence they gave it. The essence of the matter was how best to realise the priesthood of all believers. Here too Spener had his proposal, the *collegia pietatis* or class-meetings, in which the faithful should teach, warn, convert and edify each other; in a word, they should practise the general (or spiritual) priesthood, testifying to Spener's conviction, that Christianity was a way of life, learnt by doing. Spener's class-meeting at Frankfurt began as an elite society, much like the groups already gathered by Jean de Labadie, but it was soon joined by artisans and servants of both sexes who surprised him with their knowledge. It was clear to him that the work of the Holy Spirit was not circumscribed

---

[3] Michel Godfroid, 'Le Piétisme allemand a-t-il existé? Histoire d'un concept fait pour la polémique', *Études Germaniques* 101 (1971) 32–45.

by boundaries of class or education,[4] and, like the doctrine of the New Birth, the class-meeting, an apparently ideal way of supplementing the regular devotions of the church, became the badge of Pietism everywhere.

The beginnings of Pietism were, however, no guide to what it speedily became. What Spener offered was not a protest movement of the 'spiritualist' or quakerish kind, but a response from within the church to a felt spiritual need. He thought the church in no danger from those abused by the Orthodox as 'fanatics', and maintained warm personal relations with men like Gottfried Arnold, Johann Wilhelm Petersen and Friedrich Breckling even after they had separated. Closer to home, Spener's right-hand man who had much to do with the founding of the *collegia pietatis*, Johann Jakob Schütz, took up with Labadism and led a separation, part of which confirmed the worst fears of the Orthodox by emigrating to Penn's Quaker colony in America. If one set of misunderstandings was generated by Spener's associations with people who were in important respects unlike him, another set was created by the immense resonance which the *Pia Desideria* obtained amongst Germans, some of whom were not Lutherans and great numbers of whom were never Pietists.

The vivid response to Spener was such that in 1686 he was appointed court chaplain to the elector of Saxony, in effect primate of Lutheran Germany; and both the vivid response and the violent reaction which followed hard upon it owed something to the special position of Frankfurt in the ecclesiastical geography of the Empire.[5] Down the Rhine were churches like that of Jülich-Cleves and Berg which had never received the Formula of Concord, and being subject to a dynasty which had turned Catholic in the middle of effecting a constitutional reform, had lost their old synodical constitution without ever gaining an effective monarchical consistorial constitution. Self-help and ways of business characteristic of their Reformed neighbours were here unavoidable. In the Upper Rhine area princely initiative had been maintained, but the Reformed and Lutheran churches were not only intermingled, they had both undergone a powerful Melanchthonian influence, were beginning to approximate to each other in constitution, and in the nineteenth century were to accept union schemes relatively willingly. The

---

[4] J. Wallmann, 'Geistliche Erneuerung der Kirche nach Philipp Jakob Spener', *PuN* 12 (1986) 29.

[5] M. Goebel, *Geschichte des christlichen Lebens in der rheinisch-westphalischen evangelischen Kirche* (3 vols. Koblenz, 1849 52) II: 438–9, 159–60, 511–25. See more fully in Chapter 6 below.

Lutheran churches of this area had many features which in Saxony were regarded as Reformed. In Strasbourg, for example, the church exercised church discipline through elders, and maintained public catechisings, public confirmation, communion without confession, and baptism without exorcism. To churches of this kind, suffering a decay of discipline traceable to established status, Spener offered a means of revitalising the sanctions of conscience by using semi-Reformed methods which were not unfamiliar.

The explanation of the storm which descended upon Spener soon after his migration to Saxony is thus partly personal and partly institutional. In the race for the court chaplaincy Spener had defeated Johann Benedict Carpzov, a Leipzig Orthodox theologian of formidable polemical violence, yet a man who (like so many elsewhere) had been prepared to give a sort of Spenerism a trial by encouraging two of his students, August Hermann Francke and Paul Anton, who at that time had no personal connexion with Spener, to found a *Collegium Philobiblicum* in which to practise exegesis.[6] The students' movement could not, however, be confined to academic channels, and Carpzov was soon moving heaven and earth not merely to put them down, but to raise as much of Lutheran Germany as he could against a new enemy of the truth. The groundswell of opinion to which he applied with the predictable argument that Spener's friends substituted piety for faith, arose from the fact that the Saxon church and those which followed its lead embodied a Lutheranism very different from that of the Rhine churches, and felt committed to protecting the gospel from what they saw as Reformed contamination. Between 1689 and 1692 a fearful drive was put on against Spener and Francke, and their friends and relatives, who were clearly bound for the underworld of visionary enthusiasm if some new protector did not turn up. That protector was found in the Reformed elector of Brandenburg, and what became the Pietist party was the battered remnant of a ferocious hue-and-cry gathered under his liberal aegis.

This was an odd alliance, for the Elector Frederick III (who after becoming king in Prussia in 1701 took the title of Frederick I) was a less obviously pious man than either his father, the Great Elector, or his son Frederick William I. But there was nothing in the undenominational Protestantism to which he, like so many later Hohenzollerns, clung (despite Roman Catholic attempts to purchase his conversion)

---

[6] A. Ritschl, *Geschichte des Pietismus* (3 vols. Bonn, 1880–6) II: 168; G. Kramer, *Beiträge zur Geschichte A. H. Franckes…* (Halle, 1861) 39n.

to take offence at the Pietists, and they could hardly question his determination to be independent of the churches in political matters. An influx of eminent and interesting religious refugees was beginning to alleviate the tedium of Berlin as a garrison town. Moreover the Pietists had something to offer in return for protection. Should the policies of Protestant union which the elector pursued with his chaplain Jablonski (the grandson of Comenius) and the great Leibniz fail, as fail they did, the Pietists would enable him to regain a foothold in a live movement in the Lutheran churches (and a now blessedly anti-Saxon one to boot). It would be politically advantageous in the Empire to have Lutherans near the throne as well as Reformed. And the Pietists might be useful in social policy. For Spener justification was not just a forensic transaction based on faith; it was a real transformation of the regenerate. The world too might be improved through this real improvement worked by faith. And in so far as Spener had a theological position peculiar to himself – his optimistic eschatology – he afforded another motive to strive for the kingdom of God on earth. For in his 'hope of better times', he offered another stimulus to the active conscience.

In the years 1691–2 the bargain was struck. A senior church appointment in Berlin was found for Spener, protection was offered to his friends, and, most important of all, the *Ritterakademie* at Halle was upgraded to a university. The moving spirit here was Christian Thomasius, who had defended Francke in Leipzig; but the theology faculty was staffed by Francke and other Pietists, mostly young. These appointments were guaranteed to evoke a venomous riposte from the local clergy and from the estates of Magdeburg, but this was the kind of battle the dynasty was now used to fighting and winning. Significant differences between the theologians of Halle and the king did develop in the last years of the reign, 1709–14, but these were offset by Francke's success in winning the crown prince, the future Frederick William I, to his cause.[7] After this relations continued close until Francke's death in 1727, and, though somewhat less intimate, till the accession of Frederick the Great in 1740.

[7] Hinrichs, *Friedrich Wilhelm I* 583–99; C. Hinrichs, *Preussentum und Pietismus* (Göttingen 1971): 93–101; K. Depperman, *Der hallesche Pietismus und der preussische Staat...* (Göttingen, 1961) 165–71; *Der Soldatenkönig und die Stille im Lande* ed. J. Klepper (Berlin, 1938) 10–30.

## THE HALLE FOUNDATIONS

The crown prince was won by an inspection of the astonishing institutions which Francke had raised at Halle. No one could have foreseen when Francke, a young man who stood close to the 'spiritualistic' radicals and echoed their complaints against the world, was taken up by Berlin that he would turn out to be one of the great visionaries and also one of the most remarkable organisers in the whole history of Christianity. In quite the Leibnizian style Francke produced in 1704 a 'Great Project for a Universal Improvement in all Social Orders', known later for short as the *Grosser Aufsatz* or Great Essay. In this essay Francke gave an account of his stewardship and unfolded a scheme for systematic social improvement with a logic worthy of the great system-builders among his contemporaries. The core of the plan was educational.[8] Francke proposed three different types of education for the three orders of the old Prussian society, though the children of the Orphan House were to be fitted into the system according to their gifts rather than their social origin. Above all the cavalier-style objectives of upper-class education were to be displaced by practical training for the bureaucracy and the army. In the same cause (and incidentally to advertise his institutions on the international charity market) Francke obtained permission to publish the country's first newspaper; after a year's struggle with the Halle postmaster, who did not wish to lose his commission for circulating foreign papers, the *Hallesche Zeitung* appeared thrice weekly in 1708.

There was paradox in beating the drum of the New Birth and that of education simultaneously, but Francke camouflaged it skilfully by virtue of being a great systematiser of the Christian life. After the Puritan manner, but heavily influenced by his own dramatic conversion experience, Francke analysed the stages of the Christian life, beginning with a conviction of sin under the law, working through fear of the wrath to come to a total breach with the old Adam, a faith and a real sanctification continuously tested by rigorous self-examination. This was the kind of model which Methodist class-leaders were later supposed to apply in examining the religious experience of their class, and its very existence as an expository device created the presumption that the Halle system was capable of educating its subjects towards conversion.

[8] G. Oestreich, *Strukturprobleme der frühen Neuzeit* (Berlin, 1980) 294–5; W. Oschlies, *Die Arbeits- und Berufspädagogik A. H. Franckes* … (Witten, 1969).

What struck the ordinary observer was not the theory, nor the work of the theological faculty, but the charitable institutions which Francke created outside the walls of the town, the Orphan House, the dispensary, the schools, the teacher-training institutions, the Bible Institute. Here Francke followed Dutch models, but the scale of his enterprise was unheard of, and it gave a shape to charitable activity all over the Protestant world. His Orphan House bore no resemblance to the minuscule reproductions of it set up by Wesley in Newcastle and Whitefield near Savannah in Georgia. One of the biggest buildings in Europe, and still an impressive example of high-density construction, it provided, before Francke's death, accommodation for 3000 people to live and work. The dispensary was the first producer of standardised branded medicaments on a commercial scale, able and anxious to sell a complete public health kit for a city or a province, and marketing its wares by brochures in Latin, French, English, Dutch and Greek. How else was the vast enterprise, an institution of neither church nor state, to be paid for? The Halle institutions received royal privileges which had a cash value; there were charitable collections all over Europe and in America for which Francke's regularly updated *Blessed Footsteps of the Loving and Faithful God…at Glaucha by Halle* provided the appeal; but the machine relied on commercial ventures on an enormous scale, Francke's spiritual agents tapping markets for a wide range of products all the way from Venice to the Far East. On the nearer East and the Russia of Peter the Great Francke indeed staked so heavily as to give historians of the former German Democratic Republic the impression of prefiguring the Eastern bloc. In Hungary he was prepared to exploit national rebellion to start a Pietist movement and back it up by trade in Hungarian oxen and wines.[9]

The great business of Halle, however, was the supply of medicaments and of Bibles and other religious literature. The press speedily became one of the chief in Germany, publishing not only in German and Greek and Russian Cyrillic type, but in a whole range of Slavonic languages where nothing of the kind had been available before. Francke here profited from his labours to keep in touch with *Deutschtum* abroad from America to Russia and from the network of personal connexions bequeathed by Spener. Spener had been a

---

[9] Among the customers for the Hungarian wines were the crown prince of Prussia and the duke of Marlborough. Hinrichs, *Preussentum und Pietismus* 83.

protégé of the Countess Agathe von Rappoltstein, née countess of Solms-Laubach, and had been linked by her with a connexion of Imperial counts stretching away to Lusatia and Silesia. They formed the backbone of the Pietist party and constituted the lay cabinet of the Halle interest. Some of the Slavonic output of the Halle presses was for the benefit of Wends and other enserfed populations on their estates; but still more was for the restless Protestant populations of the Habsburg lands. To these people the Bible was a forbidden and revolutionary book, and to reach them Francke hoped to create a second Halle at Teschen, the point at which Silesia made a junction with Hungary and Bohemia. It was here that a Pietism which offered a programme for a church in decay but was not itself revivalist encountered Protestant religious revival for the first time. And it was here too that the universal aims of Halle most closely coincided with the strictly limited aims of the Prussian royal house. Carl Hinrichs believed that the devotion of the Halle interest to the development of the Prussian army and bureaucracy, and the compromises to which Francke was forced to retain his position, turned the Halle movement into a Prussian state-religion and undermined its wider ends. But the long-term connexion of Halle with the movements of religious revival would not have been possible had not the objects of Pietism always been both narrower and wider than those of the Prussian state. In Brandenburg-Prussia Halle contained but could never rout its rivals; on the other hand in the Tranquebar mission, in the Baltic, in America, its objectives were broader than those of the Hohenzollerns could ever be.[10]

### CONFESSIONAL AND SOCIAL CONFLICT IN SILESIA

The Westphalia peace settlements have hitherto appeared as the somewhat shaky guarantees for what has been called 'the establishment' of Protestantism. Such as they were, however, those guarantees were purchased at the expence of the huge numbers of Protestants who found themselves outside the ring-fence created by the peace settlements. Paragraphs 38–40 of the peace of Osnabrück made special provision for Silesia: the exercise of the Protestant religion was to be permitted in the duchies of Brieg, Liegnitz and Münsterberg-Oels together with the town of Breslau (to adherents of

---

[10] *Ibid.* 88, 175; K. Deppermann, 'Die politischen Voraussetzungen des Pietismus in Brandenburg-Preussen', *PuN* 12 (1986) 51–2.

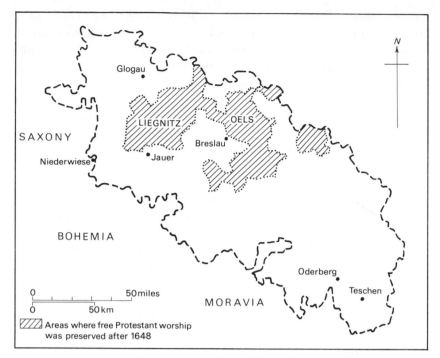

Silesia after the Thirty Years War

the unaltered Augsburg Confession, but not to the Reformed);
counts, barons and nobles (with their subjects) in other Silesian
duchies, and counts, barons and nobles in Lower Austria (but not
their subjects) were not to be required to emigrate on account of their
faith, and were to be permitted to attend services at neighbouring
places outside their territory; Protestants were to be allowed to build
three churches outside Schweidnitz, Jauer and Glogau (of wood and
loam only and without tower or school). For Protestants in Bohemia,
Moravia, Austria and Hungary, there was the worthless reservation
of a right to Sweden and the Protestant estates of the Empire to
petition the Emperor for greater religious freedom; for those in
Salzburg and Poland, nothing at all.

Beggarly as the concessions to Silesia were, they nevertheless
constituted that province a special case, and permitted various
powers some colour of a claim to interfere. Basically a prosperous
province, Silesia nevertheless suffered from war and Turkish advance. The Thirty Years War was extremely damaging. Most of the

towns did not recover their old population till after the turn of the eighteenth century, and some not for a further hundred years; but by the time Prussia acquired the province population was being drawn in from most parts of Europe on a big scale. Silesian agriculture gave powerful support to its linen- and woollen-textile industries, and there was a great range of mines of coal, saltpetre, base and precious metals. But Silesia had other troubles than the legacy of the Thirty Years War. There was continuous ethnic conflict between Pole and German. In the later middle ages and the sixteenth century the German towns of Upper Silesia were steadily polonised, and in that part 'Silesian' came to mean the mixture of old Polish inhabitants and denationalised Germans who distinguished themselves from new Poles whom they regarded as adherents of the Polish state.[11] At the same time there was a steady crescendo of rural conflict. In the half-century after the Thirty Years War this was stimulated partly by events in Bohemia and Moravia and partly by direct reaction to the continual intensification of the burdens of serfdom and to eviction. This conflict between peasant and lord was in so great a measure also a conflict between Pole and German as to enable Polish Marxist historians to arrange the whole history of Silesia in this period around Polish championship of the downtrodden.[12]

The ethnic struggle was complicated by bitter religious conflict between Catholic and Protestant. The Reformation had strengthened the German element in Silesia, particularly in the duchy of Teschen in Upper Silesia where many thousands of the old Polish inhabitants were now Protestant. But in the second half of the seventeenth century the driving force behind German supremacy in Silesia was the ruthless catholicising interest of the Habsburgs. The German Protestant cause in Silesia was thus caught in the crossfire of a conflict between Habsburg determination to wrest confessional supremacy quickly, and the long-term pressure of Polish immigration which ultimately proved the most powerful force of all. How stability was undermined by the interweaving of ethnic and religious conflict may be illustrated by two cases: as long as the Protestant duchies in Silesia lasted they were a refuge for Polish unitarians who had no legal title to practise their religion there at all; and in Upper Silesia, where an organised Protestant church system collapsed quickly, religious ordinances were at first dependent on the secret infiltration

---

[11] H. Patzelt, *Der Pietismus im Teschener Schlesien 1709–1730* (Göttingen, 1969) 18.
[12] *Beiträge zur Geschichte Schlesiens* ed. Eva Maleczynska ([East] Berlin, 1953) 300–35, 356–400.

of Protestant preachers from Hungary where confessional oppression was repeatedly answered by rebellion.

Even during the Thirty Years War large numbers of Protestants had seen the writing on the wall and left. In Upper Silesia the injury to the mining industry caused by the exhaustion of seams was aggravated by the emigration of Protestant miners; most of the Protestant population of the county of Glatz emigrated in 1623, abandoning extensive property. The haemorrhage led to the foundation of a rash of new Silesian villages in Brandenburg, Saxony and Poland, and the enlargement of the numerous frontier places in those states where churches were built to accommodate Silesians exercising their right to go abroad for their ordinances. And the ink was barely dry on the guarantees of the Westphalia settlement when the Habsburgs (aided by the chances of mortality in Protestant ruling families) set about undermining them. Hundreds of Protestant churches were confiscated and the clergy and schoolmasters driven out. What force could not accomplish was to be made good by an impressive array of Jesuit colleges, residences and missions, Capuchin settlements, great baroque monasteries and pilgrimage places. Protestant Silesians must now face a crisis for which Spener and Francke had not prescribed, the total collapse of a church system, and prospective assimilation into either a nationality or a religion they did not want or into both.

Some resources they had, social, religious, cultural and political. There was still the remnant of a Protestant aristocracy in Silesia[13] such as the Promnitzes, heavily propertied but residing in safety at Sorau in Lower Lusatia, or the Counts Henckel of Oderberg, who were able to purchase a family refuge from the Counter-Reformation at Pölzig in Thuringia. Families like the Henckels had a lively sense of Protestant solidarity from having had, for many years, to make religious provision for the Protestant aristocracy of Austria, and both they and the Promnitzes were of the inner circle of lay advisers to Francke's enterprise at Halle; one of the later Henckels, Erdmann Heinrich (1681–1752), who could be seen praying in the open air with the company at Oderberg, produced a great literary monument to the whole group which added to the *Busskampf* (or penitential struggle) required by Francke a second condition of salvation – the struggle for the faith against a confessional enemy who reappeared as

---

[13] Catalogued in *Historische Nachricht von dem Zustand der Religion in Schlesien* (n.p., 1707) 9–10.

often as he was defeated.[14] Early in his time at Halle, Francke built up a considerable circle of correspondents in Silesia, and this connexion was maintained by his son until conditions changed altogether with the Prussian invasion in 1740.

## THE BEGINNINGS OF REVIVAL

The spiritual resource of the Silesian Protestants has been described rather flatly as 'lay religion'; in fact it added another dimension to the word *Erweckung* or revival. The annihilation of organised Protestantism in Bohemia and Moravia after the Battle of the White Mountain implied the same fate for the Protestant churches in Silesia at no great distance. From 1610 onwards the church in the duchy of Teschen and from 1635 in the lordship of Bielitz was without leadership and organisation, and from 1654 without pastors or teachers, churches or schools. The centre of gravity of the Protestant faith moved into families and private houses. At this point the rights granted to the nobility in the Westphalia settlement to maintain private devotions, keep a private tutor and have him educated abroad, became important. By this device connexions could be maintained with the centres of religious life in Lower Silesia, with the universities in Saxony and Württemberg, and with foreign sources of religious literature. But the Emperor whittled away the rights even of the aristocracy, until, as in Austria, they began to flee. Working Protestantism (as in Austria) began to be concentrated in the hills and in the farm kitchens of miners and shepherds. With ever severer measures being taken against the *Wald-* or *Busch-prediger* (the Silesian equivalent of the later Methodist field-preachers) who had brought in encouragement from Hungary, these informal *collegia pietatis* which Spener had advocated as a supplement to the regular devotions of the church came to bear the entire burden of christianising successive generations. New and unsacramental as this situation was, curious echoes of the past remained; the rural congregation of Kurzwald in Bielitz refused to give up its communion vessels to the religious commission of 1654 and kept them hidden under the threshold of a house until 1782, after Joseph II's Edict of Toleration.[15] What began

---

[14] *Die letzten Stunden einiger der evangelischen Lehre zugethan...Personen...* (4 parts, Halle, 1720) i:21; A. F. Büsching, *Beiträge zu der Lebensgeschichte denkwürdigen Personen...* (6 vols. Halle, 1783–9) IV:4–50.
[15] Oskar Wagner, *Mutterkirche vieler Länder* (Vienna, 1978) 51.

in Upper Silesia extended gradually everywhere; only the city of Breslau and the duchy of Oels-Bernstadt escaped forcible catholicisation.

Breslau differed from the hills culturally as well as politically. In 1639 it had had to admit the Jesuits, and by 1702 they had created a university there, clearly to cream off the upper strata of the Protestant population. But Breslau Protestantism possessed innate strength as well as the backing of the town council and the international guarantees of the peace settlement. Confessional co-existence was possible there as it was not possible over most of Silesia and Hungary. The two Protestant gymnasia were excellent institutions which coped with Jesuit competition. And the inspector of churches and schools, theology professor at the two gymnasia and theological adviser to the town council in the later seventeenth century, was a remarkable man of international standing, Caspar Neumann. Though the son of a Breslau merchant and city chamberlain, and early apprenticed there to a chemist's shop, Neumann could easily have been lost to Silesian Lutheranism. Like so many of his fellows with a clerical career in view, he trained at Jena in a faculty not yet under the sway of Buddeus, but already embodying the mediating position which made him an important figure in the background of the revival; Jena was also distinguished for a mathematically constructed natural philosophy. In 1673 Neumann was recommended to Duke Ernst the Pious as travelling chaplain to his fifth son, who later became Duke Christian III. Him he accompanied to Italy and all the southern regions of the Protestant world. When the duke died in 1675, Neumann returned to Silesia, and, despite receiving calls from Hamburg and Lüneburg, he stayed, engaged in preaching, pastoral care, study and diplomacy. At Jena he had read with Weigel, a sort of Central European Locke, who made no great scientific advances but promoted scientific enquiry on the score of its usefulness, and because he believed, as a primitive physico-theologian, that God could be known in nature, and that even the doctrine of the Trinity could be based on reason and experience. There could thus be religious education in a profound sense; and among Weigel's pupils were no less than Leibniz and Pufendorf. At one remove Caspar Neumann's pupil, Christian Wolff, who became the uncrowned king of the early Enlightenment in Germany, illustrates very vividly the eclectic approach to knowledge, and the combination of mathematics and theology for which Weigel had stood.

The breadth of background which enabled Neumann to keep in touch with the Leibnizes of his world, to be a member of the Royal Society of Sciences in Berlin and a correspondent of the English Royal Society, enormously enhanced his value in Breslau. There the Protestant professional men, in no mood to surrender learning to the Jesuits, were making a distinctive contribution to the early German Enlightenment as they sought a substitute for a local university. Already in 1652, before any of the big scientific societies in the West, an Academia Naturae Curiosum had been founded in Schweinfurt and the Breslau doctors soon formed a branch of their own. They launched the world's first scientific medical journal, and developed academy sections to pursue physics and chemistry, mineralogy and meterology, zoology and palaeontology, to the same standard as medicine. The Breslau clergy, concluding, unlike most clergy at most times, that, if they were going to hold forth on the great facts of life and death, they had better know what they were, cooperated with the doctors to produce better tables of vital statistics than those which could be obtained from the Bills of Mortality in England. Caspar Neumann and one of the doctors, Gottfried Schultz, sent the data on to Halley in 1692, who used them as the basis for the first satisfactory calculations of annuity tables. Neumann declared that his object in the work was to make 'fine observations of the providence of God over our life and death... the better to drive superstition... from the understanding... Almost the whole learned world engages in experiment *in regno naturae*, and writes Observations, but no one thinks to do the same *in regno gratiae*, or in theology'.[16] This was not the language to expected from a theologian out of the straitest school of Weimar Reform Orthodoxy, but it was that of the same Caspar Neumann whose devotional writings and hymns were prized all over Germany, who was a preacher in demand, and whose book of prayers, *Kern aller Gebete*, went through twenty-one editions in his lifetime, and was translated into almost all European languages, including English (in 1705).

Neumann's mediating position may be illustrated by comparison with two of his most famous pupils. Christian Wolff became the greatest spokesman of the early Enlightenment in Germany, though he was prepared to strike a blow for metaphysics where he thought it still useful. Adam Bernd (1676–1748), the other, made a successful

---

[16] H. Zimmerman, *Caspar Neumann und die Entstehung der Frühaufklärung* (Witten, 1969).

preaching career in Leipzig. Orthodoxy, in the party sense, was here an indispensable qualification to begin; but Bernd proved not to be Lutheran Orthodox and was ultimately suspended from office and forbidden to preach again. His success as a preacher turned on his conviction that belief or unbelief were not just intellectual or philosophical problems and he set forth doctrine as it bore upon the practical conduct of the Christian life. But Bernd showed that he was not a Pietist in the melancholic autobiography on which his fame mainly rests.[17] The self-observation encouraged in this literary genre by the Pietists is there, but detached from edifying purposes and devoted to practical, medical and literary ends. Wolff and Bernd, in short, developed the legacy of Caspar Neumann in different ways; both were too empiricist to be confined to the limits of Saxon Orthodoxy, though neither wished to break with it altogether. Bernd, in particular, developed a side of Silesian religious experience which he and Neumann shared with many others, an inwardness of faith, a tenderness of piety, which became one of the hallmarks of revival. Neumann had to pick his way carefully in the confessional conflict; many Silesians before him, sickened by this warfare, and now deprived of their church system, had also moved into an interior piety. He had also to keep alert for Pietist excesses which might be politically damaging. He sent his son to read theology under Buddeus at Jena, and to live in Buddeus's house, rightly calculating that Buddeus held a mediating position similar to his own; but, learning that he had acquired a name as a Pietist, took the boy away and sent him to the Orthodox stronghold at Wittenberg. Silesia was one of the few places where the Orthodoxy of Wittenberg could coexist with the Spanish mysticism which elsewhere went into Pietism. It was not for nothing that Jakob Böhme had lived and worked at Görlitz, nor that his 'alternative' religion fostered the absorbing power of a people now substantially deprived of the Orthodox options which were all that were offered by the Westphalia settlement.

### SILESIA AND THE GREAT POWERS

The political context of Silesia underwent transformations as surprising as those of Silesian religion. There would clearly never be a Protestant system in Silesia again without outside intervention. Long before the electoral house of Saxony turned Catholic, Silesian

[17] A. Bernd, *Eigene Lebensbeschreibung* (1738) ed. V. Hoffmann (Munich, 1973).

hopes were pinned on Brandenburg, Hohenzollern claims to Silesian territories were noisily revived and aroused the Emperor's suspicions. The tempo of forcible catholicisation accelerated and the Corpus Evangelicorum was constantly abuzz with fruitless remonstrances; but in 1707 it was not Prussia that intervened, it was the Sweden of Charles XII. Charles's great bid to break the mould of international politics began brilliantly with victories over Poland and its Russian ally. Then, with the Emperor involved in the West with the War of the Spanish Succession, and in the East with another revolt in Hungary, the moment had arrived to salvage the Protestant cause in Silesia. A campaign almost without resistance followed, and finally Charles XII camped out at Altranstädt in Saxony to neutralise the alliance between Poland-Saxony and Russia while he haggled with the Emperor over the rights of Silesian Protestants. By the Convention of Altranstädt 120 churches were to be returned to the Protestants in the indirectly governed principalities in Silesia, 6 new 'Grace' churches were to be built in the Habsburg family lands, and to these and some other churches schools were to be attached. The city of Breslau got back 4 churches in the neighbouring countryside.[18] Charles XII had not been strong enough to destroy the Counter-Reformation in Silesia any more than he had managed to destroy the Russo-Polish alliance; but, while the Silesian Protestants were still second-class citizens, they were freed from the worst pressure.

### THE 'REVOLT OF THE CHILDREN'

The intervention of Charles XII changed the situation in Silesia in two important ways not foreseen in the Convention of Altranstädt. At the time of the Swedish invasion almost all the Protestant churches in Silesia had been confiscated; the Swedish troops therefore held their church parades in the open air, introducing what later became a familiar Methodist word, camp-meetings (*Feldgottesdienste*). When the troops moved on, the children in the principality of Glogau in Lower Silesia, to the general astonishment, accepted their cue, and held their own camp-meetings, gathering round their elected leaders in prayer and singing, often several times a day, and often against parental opposition. Despite the onset of winter, these prayer-meetings, 'the uprising of the children' as they were called, spread

[18] Norbert Conrads, *Die Durchführung der Altranstädter Konvention in Schlesien, 1707–1709* (Cologne, 1971).

across the country, reaching Breslau early in 1708. The ability of the children of Silesia to emulate in their own context the initiatives of the child prophets of the Cévennes caused problems of all kinds, not least because the objects of their intercessions, the return of Protestant churches and schools, were politically sensitive in the highest degree.

The Halle network, moreover, was bent on exploiting the international newsworthiness of the event. The minuscule Thuringian court of the count of Reuss, a prominent supporter of the Halle institutions, published the well-known paper *Europaische Fama*, which carried the story, and at once Josiah Woodward and the English friends of Halle brought it out in English dress as a pamphlet. Somewhat incongruously the pamphlet presented the uprising as the answer to the prayer of the societies for the reformation of manners, side by side with Caspar Neumann's reluctant confession that he had a religious revival on his hands:

> very raw people as country-fellows and soldiers, looking on their devotion, were powerfully affected and moved, even to shed tears... many aged and grown people have been reclaimed; so that they resort no more to places of drinking & of vain diversion: shewing since that time several signs of a sincere reformation... What a strange... thing it is that the children of a whole country should rise, and shew their disobedience therein, that they will pray in spite of all opposition.[19]

Francke had been expecting dramatic events in Silesia as soon as peace had been patched up in Hungary in 1699. He had received his share of Protestant complaints from Silesia, of requests for intercessions, even of the striking results derived from carefully supervised meetings for prayer and singing.[20] But Francke was basically a preacher of reform rather than revival, and he can have had no inkling of the way lay Silesia would break loose in 1708. The *Buschprediger* had been put down by Habsburg authority; but now they reappeared, and the *Busch* services, under less control than the old wilderness meetings in France, became something which the German language, then as now, was ill-equipped to describe; but the mass awakenings qualify them as primitive revival meetings. In the reports reaching the staid if somewhat rational Orthodoxy of Breslau, they were said to be characterised by 'erroneous balderdash leading to fanaticism'. The children's camp-meetings, miraculously orderly

---

[19] *Praise out of the Mouths of Babes and Sucklings* (London, 1708) 21–2, 28–30; *UN* 1709 369–70.
[20] T. Wotschke, 'Urkunden', *JVSKg* 20 (1929) 82, 64, 80–1; SPK Francke Nachlasse 25 fo. 208.

as long as adults were hostile, also showed every sign of getting out of hand once sympathetic wild men began to take advantage of them. Predictably Neumann attempted to get a grip on the only part of the movement within his reach, the children's prayer-meetings; Francke attempted to exploit it well out of range of Breslau. The return of Protestant churches under the Convention enabled Neumann to set some aside for children's use. They now acted under clerical oversight and mingled their prayer with catechising. Their movement was baptised into the church. Neumann, who had done so much to undermine the intellectual and devotional attitudes of the old Orthodoxy, proclaimed: *non vitium pietas, sed pietismus habet.*

## TESCHEN AND THE PIETISTS

In the camp at Altranstädt were not only the diplomats of the nations, but Francke, equal to them all in negotiating skill. No church, not even that of Saxony, had greater distaste for Halle than that of Sweden; no Orthodox critic of Francke was more rancorous than Johann Friedrich Mayer of Greifswald, the little Swedish faculty in Germany. Nevertheless Francke, supported by his knot of Silesian noble advisers, persuaded Charles XII to come to the aid of the Silesians, and to get the most important of the Grace churches for Teschen in Upper Silesia. (For good measure he also carried off a team of Swedish army chaplains to Halle, impressed them with the work, and formed connexions which, by the devious ways of Providence, were to create a future for Pietism in Sweden.)

Teschen had a threefold significance. It had been a Protestant duchy, and although Lutheranism had gone to pieces in and about Teschen itself, the hills at a distance harboured a considerable Protestant population; in fact when the Jesus church was opened it claimed a congregation of 40,000.[21] Then in the immediate vicinity of the town was a zealous nobleman, Baron von Morawitsky; he had married the sister of Count Henckel, one of Francke's inner circle, whose Oderberg estates bordered on the duchy of Teschen. Most important of all, the place was the natural meeting ground of Poles, Czechs and Slovaks, and lay just below the Jablunka pass, the best commercial route into Hungary. Francke was deeply concerned about the fate of Protestantism among the Czechs and Slovaks, who,

---

[21] On them see AFSt A174 no. 23b.

since the Battle of the White Mountain, had suffered much worse at the hand of the Counter-Reformation than the Silesians; still more significant, since 1706 during the Rákóczi rebellion, Francke had had his own man in Hungary, ostensibly dealing in wines but also acting as a Prussian political emissary, Anhard Adelung. He was now commissioned to get the institutions at Teschen going. And what he built first was not the Jesus church but a large house; a large house with cellars for the wine trade, a ground floor for a bookshop and stock-room, a first floor with accommodation for three preachers, and a second floor with a seminary for nobles. What was envisaged was a miniature Halle, uniting propaganda and commerce at a strategic point, where the question of confessional survival was most acute. Were this design not broad enough, the network was extended to the court of Peter the Great, the erstwhile ally of the Hungarian rebels, after the Russians had crushed Charles XII at Pultava in 1709.

Such objectives called for able staff. The first two nominees, Christoph Voigt and Christoph Schneider, were of Francke's inner circle, the former having tutored his children in Halle, the latter the children of his brother who ran a wholesale business in Venice. The disadvantage of them both (which was not lost on the Jesuits) was that they did not fulfil the requirement of the Convention of Altranstädt that the clergy of the Grace church should be Silesians – though some kind of cover was provided by ordination in Silesia – nor did they possess the Slavonic tongues essential in a congregation three-quarters of which was Polish, and destined to exercise a magnetic attraction throughout eastern Bohemia and Moravia. Both were quickly dislodged from Teschen; but Voigt, after a spell in Vienna investigating the possibilities of missioning the Protestants in the Habsburg family lands, was drafted into another of Francke's strategies as rector of the gymnasium at Hermannstadt in Siebenbürgen and then first preacher at Schemnitz in Slovakian Upper Hungary.

The Jesus church itself took shape only slowly because of financial difficulties. But by 1730 the building would seat about 5,000 and, at a pinch, another 2,000–3,000 could be crammed in. The 72-metre-high baroque tower was added only in 1751. Financed in the first instance by the Promnitzes of Sorau in Lower Lusatia and by the Protestant nobility of Silesia, the work was forwarded by collections led by the royal families of Prussia and Denmark and supported all over Lutheran Europe, and by the self-help of the congregation in carting materials. Yet this elaborate edifice was not a symbol but a missionary device. It was, and remained for seventy years, the only Protestant church and school in Upper Silesia, and it served a diaspora, the chief groups of which were in mountain valleys and in the town of Bielitz. Illegal groups of secret Lutherans and Bohemian Brethren from eastern Moravia, and Moravian Wallachia and scattered groups of Protestant Poles looked to it. And despite the early failures, successors of real calibre were found.

The key figure was Johann Adam Steinmetz (1689–1762). The son of a pastor in the principality of Brieg in Lower Silesia, Steinmetz's youth had something of the young Wesley about it; his life was preserved by special providences and he owed much to a devout mother. At the gymnasium in Brieg he was trained on the Latin version of Arndt's *True Christianity*. As a student at Leipzig he suffered much agony of conscience, and, again like the young Wesley, he resolved to devote himself to the academic life. But there was a great shortage of Lutheran pastors in Brieg, he had to make some provision for his widowed mother, and his experimental piety brought instant success in village preaching. A Whitsuntide sermon he preached on the estates of the Baron von Seidlitz encouraged the latter to present him to his next vacant living. This proved to be Töppliwoda in the principality of Münsterberg. Töppliwoda was a small-scale version of Teschen; a populous village whose church served a scattered congregation of 10,000. Here Steinmetz proved a very successful revivalist, reinforcing his preaching with fruitful but politically hazardous class-meetings and prayer-meetings, and developing his pastoral skill by businesslike recording of what he learned in confession and visiting. There was soon scarcely a house in the village where there was not a convert to be found. He aimed to initiate his flock into his own practical experience of justification, and to keep a brake upon the more extravagant phenomena evoked by his preaching. Those who reported ecstasies and visions 'must be in great need, that God must use the extraordinary means in them because he could not attain his end through his Word, and resorted to this means'. The moral results to this revival without virtuosity had a comic consequence. When it became urgent to find a Silesian-born pastor who could get the cause at Teschen on the move again, the two counts Henckel went to Töppliwoda to inspect Steinmetz for themselves. Putting up at the inn, they were treated to the bitter complaints of the innkeeper that he could no longer make a living and that it was all the fault of the pastor![22]

Steinmetz took some persuading to go to Teschen, partly because of inadequate proficiency in Polish; he bargained that an additional Polish preacher should be appointed. There was still no church there, 'only a great barn knocked up from planks, so that it very often snowed in, and, even when it was improved, the Polish peasants often tore off the planks from the top, and sat on the beams to hear the Word of God', such was the hunger for the ordinances among a congregation which had been deprived of them for fifty years. And there were so many Polish boys to be instructed that there was an enormous overflow into the open air, they enjoying 'much good awakening from this devotion'. The Silesian children's camp-meeting had re-established itself by accident.

The team now assembled was an extraordinarily strong one. Johann Muthmann, the first pastor in the place, took charge of the Czech preaching, Steinmetz the German preaching and the general management, and Samuel Ludwig Sassadius, a pupil of Buddeus at Jena and an energetic catechist, took charge of the Polish preaching.[23] Still more fiery were the theological assistants in the school. Georg Sargánek, Andreas Macher, and Johann Liberda were all young, active and trained at Halle in Slavonic languages; Liberda, in particular, in whom the preacher and political agitator were almost indistinguishable, was not only one of the most capable theologians Teschen ever brought forth but one of the most effective revivalists of all time. Moreover, in the Teschen team the future of religious revival can be seen casting its shadow before. When Steinmetz was expelled from Teschen, Zinzendorf helped him to preferment as super-intendent at Neustadt an der Aisch in Ansbach; Liberda was appointed to the Czech exile congregation on the estate of Zinzen-dorf's aunt at Gross Hennersdorf, next to his own at Berthelsdorf; while Traugott Immanuel Jerichow, who was called as rector of the school in 1725, had already served Zinzendorf in the printing and proof correcting of his publications, and after his expulsion was helped by him to an appointment as master of the pages at the Pietist royal court of Copenhagen.

As much through circumstances as by plan, the Teschen Pietists found themselves acting as revivalists. German confessions began at

[22] Most of the secondary authorities on Steinmetz depend heavily on C. F. Jona, *Nachricht von den Lebensumständen ... des ... Herrn Johann Adam Steinmetz* (Magdeburg, 1762).

[23] Patzelt, *Pietismus im Teschener Schlesien* 63.

six on a Sunday morning, and communions, confessions and preaching in various languages went on simultaneously or in succession all day. The great crowds arriving from a distance would spend the time until it was their turn in enthusiastic hymn-singing of the sort that was later to become a revivalistic prescription. What in New England would have been curious echoes of a Puritan past turned up in Central Europe. Revival spread to the inhabitants of Bielitz in 1725; finding themselves with others not far from the church after the Whitsuntide service, they prayed together and ended by concluding a covenant with God. Moreover, there was an enthusiastic character about their new piety: 'they not only avoided all vanity, but spent their time in prayer and with God's word, and with psalms, hymns of praise and spiritual songs'. This was hardly Saxon Lutheranism. And the Teschen staff were less like ordinary parish pastors than circuit riders, dividing up their duties in a rota: one week public prayer meetings and ministerial duties, the second week travelling out to the sick, the third week rest, and the fourth riding out to support the travelling preachers.

All the time Francke was advising, assisting, encouraging, warning the Silesian Protestants,[24] and keeping in touch with the Prussian government; and his concerns went beyond Teschen to Bohemia and Moravia. If the Jesuits succeeded in preventing Teschen from being turned into a miniature Halle, they failed to prevent religious literature produced at Halle from going through Teschen into Bohemia and Moravia to the tune of scores of thousands of volumes, nor could they prevent a jolt being given to an already unstable situation in the old Bohemian kingdom by the Teschen preachers.

### CONFESSIONAL AND SOCIAL CONFLICT IN BOHEMIA AND MORAVIA

The victory of the White Mountain had enabled the Habsburgs to attempt irreversible social engineering in the lands of the Bohemian crown. The Protestant nobility and much of the professional and commercial class were got out of the country before the end of the Thirty Years War, and the peasantry were left to the tender mercies of a new aristocracy and of an alien church which salted away into mortmain huge quantities of former Protestant property. Over most of eastern Europe serfdom was being intensified under a combination

---

[24] SPK Francke Nachlasse 25; AFSt. c680; DIII pt. 2 no. 1495. For what amounted to Protestant encyclicals: Wotschke, 'Urkunden' *JVSKg* 21 (1931) 118–20, 121–2.

of economic and political factors; and in Bohemia religious conflict guaranteed that recatholicisation and aggravated *Leibeigenschaft* would be inseparable. For if the only defence of Protestantism lay in flight, the most obvious way for the new Catholic order to keep its system operating was to shackle its labour force more firmly to the soil by law. Right through the Habsburg lands the Reformation had been a relatively late arrival, and had been a defence of older social customs against innovation as much as it had been a religious or theological programme. And Bohemia had in Hussitism at least the memory of its own form of religious deviance to add an element of nationalism to peasant hostility towards the new order and its expensive baroque monuments. A desperate peasant revolt in 1679–80 encouraged by threats of war from Turkey and France was savagely put down, and the last barriers to recatholicisation seemed to collapse.

The remnants of a church system even in Slovakia were crushed and crusading preachers from Hungary and Saxony kept out. Priests annually submitted registers of suspect persons to the appropriate authorities. The Bohemian Protestants had been so long been under the hammer that their various religious traditions had become blurred at the edges; by the early eighteenth century internal collapse seemed almost complete, isolated groups clinging desperately to fragments of what they had inherited, some calling themselves Israelites,[25] others succumbing to apocalyptic ravings, others again to a kind of deism. Except on the southern edge of the Erzgebirge where for business reasons Protestantism was tolerated among German miners, and in the county of Asch which was only pawned to the kingdom of Bohemia, not incorporated in it, the game seemed up. So great had been the emigration that on the Saxon and Lusatian side of the Bohemian border the population density was now far greater than in Bohemia itself – a fact still instantly perceptible to the visitor – and the Wends had been pushed northwards; but now the outflow was reduced to a miserable and hazardous trickle. The exiled Czechs began the work of sustaining the old cause by publishing abroad, but could not from their own resources salvage anything from the wreck.

The impulse they needed was given by Charles XII's incursion into Silesia. Seven thousand peasants applied to the Swedish authorities for religious freedom in Bohemia and Moravia, and strict

---

[25] Rudolf Říčan, *Das Reich Gottes in den Böhmischen Ländern* tr. B. Popelar (Stuttgart, 1957) 148.

Habsburg measures against them, especially in east Bohemia, began a generation of recurrent and open conflict. If among the Czechs resistance to forced labour combined with secret Protestantism and revolutionary elements in the Hussite tradition, the Bohemian government accompanied a Forced Labour patent in 1717 with an edict against secret Protestant emissaries. In the interior competition for the religious roots of Czech nationalism each side laid claim to symbols from the past. The Habsburgs took up the veneration of a fourteenth-century Bohemian, John of Nepomuk, and pressed it on a great scale. Charles VI and his consort Elizabeth Christine urged Pope Clement XI in 1720–1 to speed his canonisation, and obtained it in 1729. At the crisis of Habsburg survival in 1742, with Silesia lost and French and Bavarian troops in Prague itself, a great veneration of the Bohemian saint began at the court of Maria Theresa. In Vienna itself two churches, six chapels, statues by the score at every bridge and river bank, and religious fraternities with their altars, testified to the new standing of the only Bohemian saint of international significance.[26] Czech Protestants could now hardly avoid a rival attempt to appropriate their country's religious past, and, as we shall see, they generated a religious revival at Herrnhut which not only beat the canonisation of John of Nepomuk by a short head, but considerably outdid him in international impact.

The first tentative revival came, indeed, in 1701, in response to the revival movements in Silesia. The establishment of the preaching station at Teschen and the determined effort from Halle to provide suitable literature greatly raised the temperature of the situation. Protestants found their way out to Teschen and some were converted by Steinmetz's preaching; the preachers and the literature found their way in and restored a sense of direction to the Protestantism which remained.

Not all was gain from a Protestant point of view. As in Germany, Hungary and Silesia, Pietism continued to be a red rag to Orthodox bulls, and was at first rejected in Slovakia. But here as in so many other places the Pietists had in the most literal sense got themselves into a position where they could help an otherwise helpless Protestant population, and the Orthodox had not; they were willing to use the

---

[26] Elizabeth Kovács, 'Die Verehrung des hl. Johannes von Nepomuk...' in *250 Jahre Hl. Johannes von Nepomuk. Katalog der IV Sonderschau des Dommuseums zu Salzburg* (Salzburg, 1979) 69–85. One of the favourite atrocities of the Prussian army in Silesia in 1740 was to bowl over the statues of St John of Nepomuk. A. Theiner, *Zustände der katholischen Kirche in Schlesien von 1740–1758* (2 vols. Regensburg, 1852) 1:4.

lay agency which was all that was available; and their practical preference for scripture over dogma was reminiscent of the Hussites and the Bohemian Brethren. By 1720 their preaching was generating revival among German-speaking remnants of the old Bohemian Brethren round about Fulneck and Zauchtental, but spread to the Czechs and broke out quite independently in other parts as well; even Catholics were drawn in.

In Bohemia, as in Silesia before it, revival offered among other things a great relief from the accumulated sense of guilt at the religious compromises of almost a century, at public conformity and secret practice; but public profession of any kind of Protestant faith implied a clash with authority, whether those who made it proposed to stand their ground or surreptitiously to emigrate. Francke, who produced prodigious quantities of religious tracts and Bibles in Czech and got them into the country, exhorted the king of Prussia in 1725 to find 'encouragement' in the situation. What kind of encouragement was needed by a king who was advertising publicly every year for immigrants to fill the 3,000 vacant peasant plots which he had in Brandenburg alone needs no commentary. Religious refugees would be particularly welcome; they might abscond to Russia, but they could not return home. Besides the trickle of Germans whom Christian David smuggled out to Zinzendorf's estates at Berthelsdorf, Czechs were getting out to Gross Hennersdorf, the adjacent parish owned by his aunt, and to other places. On the basis of their information Orthodox journalists calculated that there were 20,000 secret Lutherans in Bohemia, anxious to escape, and, in 1724, the king of Prussia received a memorandum from two Czechs, craving his protection, and, for further information, sent the Provost of Berlin down to Gross Hennersdorf where Francke's friend and Czech translator, Milde, was organising the Czechs into a congregation.[27]

The far-reaching implications of the revival which the Teschen preachers evoked in Bohemia sufficiently explain the strenuous efforts which the Jesuits began to make to get them out. Now the Orthodox charges that the Pietists were really a new sect enjoying no legal toleration for their class-meetings were used by the Catholics; after a seven-year campaign they succeeded in expelling the Pietists from Teschen in 1730. The early expulsion of Voigt had delayed the take-off of the Teschen enterprise, and the mass exit now was a severe

---

[27] *UN* 1720, 263; E. Winter, *Die tschechische und slovakische Emigration...* ([East] Berlin, 1955) 100.

blow. Steinmetz and his friends raised funds for the cause in Bayreuth, Hamburg and Schleswig-Holstein, but even this did not compensate for the steady decline of the Protestant gentry of Silesia, a group thinned by death, emigration and conversion. The Teschen apostles must increasingly pin their hopes on Prussian protection, and on Prussian schemes in Bohemia. The reversal of roles became apparent in 1736. Hitherto Teschen had been an inflammatory influence in Bohemia; now in response to Bohemian unrest, Teschener peasants and miners descended on the town armed with their staves, forced some concessions to their religious grievances, and Silesian children resumed their prayer-meetings.[28]

Events in Bohemia had indeed acquired a momentum of their own stimulated in a measure by dramatic episodes in Herrnhut and Salzburg. Herrnhut was not the largest or most important settlement of the Bohemian exiles, but it was the most vocal, it impinged upon a huge range of other communities, and had a uniquely divisive influence upon the second generation of the revival movement. The crisis in the archbishopric of Salzburg made public everywhere what was happening to Protestant minorities within the circle of Habsburg influence, and whetted the appetite of the king of Prussia for settlers. In 1732 he had professed willingness to receive 6,000 immigrants from Salzburg, and finally acquired over 20,000. Could Bohemia be milked on the same scale?

The Czechs at Gross Hennersdorf reckoned that 30,000 more could be got out; radical Pietists were prepared to go as high as 100,000. The old apostles of Teschen ensured that neither Halle nor the Prussian monarchy could evade this delicate question. In the summer of 1732 Liberda, with three members of his new congregation at Hennersdorf, went to Neustadt an der Aisch where Steinmetz was now superintendent and Sargánek rector of the school. They agreed to approach Frederick William I and Gotthilf August Francke, who had succeeded his father at the head of the Halle foundations, with a statement of the grievances of the Hennersdorf Czechs against their lord of the manor, Henriette von Gersdorf, Zinzendorf's aunt. These Czechs were now very restive against their conditions of service, their lack of a school and ecclesiastical self-government. Hennersdorf could never become a staging-post for a major Czech outflow without reform. These demands (which Liberda would not discourage)

---

[28] For a fascinating account of Teschen in these years, *AHF* 6:854–82. Cf. Biermann, *Protestantismus in Österreich-Schlesien* 203; *SMBRG* 4 (1735) 109–12, 644–6.

amounted to a request that Prussia deliver Czechs not only from popish darkness but also from Protestant servitude, a quite different matter.

On 31 August 1732 Liberda and a Czech delegation were received by the king of Prussia himself, and came away convinced that they had his support; though it is clear that he warned them not to be precipitate, and wrote hypocritically to Vienna affirming his desire 'not to injure his best friend, the Emperor'. Patience, however, was not in Liberda's character, and he dashed off into Bohemia armed with supplies of his spiritual works, the *Key of David* and the *New Harp*, which had a proved revolutionary effect (the rebels in East Bohemia were called *Harffanisti*). No sooner was Liberda out of the way than the bulk of the Czechs in Hennersdorf, 500 strong, with the old and sick in two waggons, pulled up stakes and made off to Prussia via Silesia, precisely the eventuality Frederick William had been trying to avoid. They reached an outlying Prussian territory at Cottbus, only to be excluded by the king. Not till they had been excluded from Saxony also, and it was midwinter, did Frederick William relent and receive them in Berlin. Once he had them, the king set them to work in a textile concern, and made them one of the basic units of the Berlin proletariat. In due course he provided them with houses, a church and a school. Their preachers were successively the old Teschen colleagues Macher and Liberda; their school lasted into the present century.

The reason for Liberda's haste in returning to Bohemia was that peasant unrest was brewing again, stirred by agitators claiming to bring great promises from the king of Prussia. Liberda drafted them a petition claiming freedom of conscience or an unimpeded passage to Prussia, and they resorted at once to force. This time, however, the Imperial government crushed the rebels without mercy. Of course the reasons for ferment did not change; the emissaries of Halle and Prussia still went to and fro; and in the winter of 1737–8 another peasant uprising began. No vast train of refugees set out for Prussia, but a steady trickle escaped, and it was not healthy for Habsburgs that a similar restlessness became apparent among the Protestant minorities much deeper within their system, in Lower Austria, Styria and Carinthia.

Nor was Liberda to be either the redeemer or the liberator of a nation. Returning to Gross Hennersdorf on October 1732 after the failure of the peasant revolt, he was imprisoned by Henriette von

Gersdorf, who was furious at the loss of her labour force, and was in any case well on the way to having to sell her estate. She sent him off to Dresden in chains, and the Saxon government, under strong pressure from the Emperor, tried him for high treason and put him in the notorious penitentiary of Waldheim. But the Czech congregation in Berlin petitioned the king to get him as their minister, and Frederick William plotted a series of jail-break attempts, finally springing both Liberda and his gaoler in 1737. The liberator had been liberated, but at the price of turning the revivalist into the settled minister of a congregation of exiles, and one too subservient to Halle to be completely congenial to them.

### REVIVAL IN SIBERIA

The chapter in Silesian history which had begun with Charles XII's adventure there in 1707 was closed by that of Frederick the Great in 1740, which remains to be related. The connexions formed in Charles's camp at Altranstadt, however, appended to the history of Silesian revival another revival in which not so much the fringes, as events beyond the fringes, of the Protestant world operated upon the centre.

The Swedish church stood tightly to Lutheran Orthodoxy; as recently as 1686 church law had required all Swedish citizens to confess the evangelical-Lutheran faith as it was embodied in the Augsburg Confession and the Formula of Concord, and even while encamped at Altranstädt Charles XII forbade Swedish subjects to study at Halle 'because all sorts of novelties and harmful opinions are got going' there.[29] There was equal animosity on the Prussian side. It was in at least the short-term interest of Prussia that a brake be put on the Alexander of the North. The crushing defeat of the Swedes by the Russians at Pultava was celebrated in Berlin with illuminations, and Francke subsequently received plain warning from the court that his efforts on behalf of Swedish prisoners of war, the cause which, after the Tranquebar mission, was nearest to his heart, risked incurring the displeasure of Frederick William I. The gap between Francke's ideals of universal regeneration and the necessarily limited horizons of the Prussian state could hardly be more vividly illustrated.

Francke, however, had made his contacts with the Swedish army

---

[29] Hilding Pleijel, *Der schwedische Pietismus in seinen Beziehungen zu Deutschland* (Lund, 1935) 14; E. Winter, *Halle als Ausgangspunkt der deutschen Russlandkunde* ... ([East] Berlin, 1953) 303.

chaplains; he was deeply concerned as a Lutheran for the spiritual fate of the Swedish prisoners; he wanted to make an impression in Russia itself. After Pultava, the number of prisoners was swollen by the 20,000 troops and 10,000 civilian camp-followers taken in the battle, the bulk of whom were pushed off beyond the Urals to Tobolsk, the capital of Central Asian Russia, and the centre for dealings with China. Their plight offered Francke a once-for-all opportunity to enhance the long-distance leverage of Halle. Yet the story which unfolded turned on two twists of fortune which were beyond any calculation of policy.

It was not for nothing that the Swedish imperial church had shouldered the task of assimilating a growing empire; it had an adaptability uncommon among established churches. Though Charles XII himself was regarded in Saxony as an unwashed barbarian, his army preserved an outward respect for religion which was then unusual; and army and church together kept in touch with the Swedish prisoners of war in Russia in a way that must have been the envy of the sorry Protestant diaspora of the Habsburg lands. Wherever there were Swedish prisoners there was a minister; in some places there were church elders and overseers as well. The church, from bases in Moscow, formed the chief administrative link between the thousands of Swedes in Russian exile, and maintained its preaching and piety even in Siberia. Yet the decisive spiritual force was the Pietism which until the second decade of the eighteenth century was forcibly excluded from Sweden itself. And the dragoon captain who did more than anyone to promote the remarkable revival among the Swedish prisoners, Curt Friedrich von Wreech, taken prisoner before Pultava in the spring of 1709, came through none of the channels carefully cultivated by Francke. Francke's diplomacy, like his base in Teschen, simply enabled him to take an opportunity when it came.

Francke had supporters at work among the German community in Moscow, especially two pastors, Thomas Roloff and Justus Samuel Scharsmid. They cared for Swedish prisoners in Moscow, and, when they were sent east, provided them with suitable literature. It was in this circle that Wreech began to read sermons, and underwent a spiritual crisis when the widow of an elderly German of the Sloboda suburb lent him an old German Bible with Luther's prefaces and marginal glosses; in best Hallesian style the crisis was brought to a head by Luther's Preface to the Romans. One of his companions was a German captain from the Swedish army, also in captivity, who had copies of Arndt's *True Christianity* and Francke's Fast sermons, and these deepened their religious experience. When they met up with the main body of Swedish prisoners at Tobolsk their preaching divided the clergy, and caused a great revival among the troops, the converted officers being known as 'Pietists, Quakers and the like'.[30] One of their difficulties was that their converts were always being sent off to other camps, so in June 1713 they decided to write to Francke himself. Francke responded with pastoral care and encouragement, with money and Bibles, with hymn-books, tracts and medicaments, the material assistance coming through Thomas Roloff and the Sloboda.

Revivals began to break out among the Swedish prisoners elsewhere in Russia. Francke characteristically sought to consolidate the results of the revival by education. Wreech and his friends began an excellent school in Tobolsk, based on a school ordinance of the Halle pattern, aspiring to raise the children in a living knowledge of Christianity. This school and others elsewhere attracted the children of the Russian aristocracy; and there were schools for girls and a teacher-training establishment for officers. No protracted meeting of the nineteenth century ever presented its promoters with the opportunities created by the Swedes' fifteen years incarceration in Russia. By the time they came home in 1722–4 the effect had gone deep; they came home in such force as to make a noticeable impact in Sweden; and though the schools they had opened with Francke's cash and books had to close, eminent Russians now sought a similar facility for their children at the Pietist school in Moscow.

THE IMPACT OF REVIVAL IN NORTHERN EUROPE

When the Swedish prisoners got home,[31] they found a world much more receptive to their outlook than that which they had left. Charles XII's attempts to break the mould of international politics upon an

---

[30] Von Wreech's own account of these events, *Wahrhaffte und umständliche Historie von denen schwedischen Gefangenen in Russland und Siberien...* (Sorau, 1725) incorporates a vast correspondence of the prisoners of war. Cf. Christoph Eberhard [Alethophilus], *Der innere und aussere Zustand der schwedischen Kriegsgefangenen in Russland durch ihre eigene Briefe* (Frankfurt/Leipzig, 1718): AFSt A182 no. 65; A170 nos. 4a, 17; DI11 fos. 176, 178; C491; A144 nos. 937, 1002; B8 nos. 56, 63; SPK 25 fos. 37–8; 29 fascicles 4–5; *UN* 1725, 1129–33.

[31] Pietists admitted that the majority of the prisoners came back unconverted. 'In prison they despised the righteous, drank, gambled, made cards and sold them to the heathen in China, so that some [became] rich.' *Briefe an A. H. Francke* ed. T. Geissendoerfer (Urbana, Ill., 1939) 190.

Orthodox platform had collapsed disastrously; absolutism had come to an end, and the desperate politics to which it gave way afforded openings to new ideas. Political calamity had revealed inadequacies in the church; there were now reformers among whom Pietists had the advantage of a well-tried programme. Already many of the new clergy were of the Pietist stripe, and one of them, Herman Schröder, powerful in consistory and parliament, was in constant touch with Halle. A great attempt to democratise the church by law failed, and in 1726 a *Konventikelplakat* was a severe blow to conservative Pietism especially in Stockholm. But, even where a Pietist reform movement failed, it often opened the door to local revival movements. In the North, Nils Grubb brought about a real revival at Amea. There were gatherings in barns and on the hills, under boats and in other secret places, and ecstatic phenomena set in.[32] At Nordalming a smith, Nils Jansson Ulander, set up conventicles with the singing of spiritual songs, gospel reading and extemporary preaching. The *Konventikelplakat*, followed rapidly by the deaths of Francke and the leading Swedish Pietists, marked the defeat of the reform hopes to which the returned prisoners of war had given so powerful an impulse; but the evidence that revival was possible even in Sweden encouraged the new practitioners of the art, and especially Zinzendorf. Meanwhile Curt von Wreech retied the knot with Silesia; he obtained employment at the Promnitz court at Sorau, and there published his history of the revival in Russia.

### THE CONSOLIDATION OF CONFESSIONAL DIVISIONS IN SILESIA

In the long, rather than the short, run Frederick II's triumphal entry into Silesia in 1740 froze the confessional conflict there. Having carefully set up the Silesian invasion to appear as a war for Protestant confessional survival, Frederick sought to keep his gains by promising to maintain Catholics in their present rights. Each side was left to weigh the debits against the credits in the account. A century later the Catholics were still groaning over the fact that he had been welcomed everywhere as a liberator by the Silesian Protestants, that he had brought in his train a dozen Berlin clergy whom he advertised as the twelve apostles of Silesia, and whose business was to urge

[32] For similar events in Finland, N. G. Holm, 'Recent Research into Revivalist Movements in Finland', *SJH* 11 (1986) 317.

people to turn to the crown of Prussia. The Catholic aristocracy and monasteries suffered the first financial brunt of the war, and the former were among its major victims. Their long-standing relations with the Habsburg dynasty were broken, and, still worse, without waiting for a peace settlement, Frederick began the instant administrative assimilation of his new province. Habsburg institutions were replaced by the *Feldkriegskommissariat*, and subsequently by Prussian local institutions. The immediate effect of this was a wholesale ejection of Catholics from offices of any consequence, and, in the longer run, the subjection of Silesia, and especially Silesian towns, to a heavier tax-burden than any other part of the Prussian state. Equally painful, the census which Frederick held in 1755 showed a small but clear majority of Protestant inhabitants in Prussian Silesia, a sorry commentary on what had been achieved by the Counter-Reformation in all its might.

It was not, however, all joy for Protestants. If symbols mattered, they had the mortification of seeing the king occasionally pay to make good the iconoclasm of his troops; Protestants did not, in the main, get back their old churches, even where Catholics did not use them, and they often remained liable to stoll fees to the priests. Regaining the use of bells or cemeteries was often a problem; and the acute financial burden of creating the Grace churches under the Convention of Altranstädt ensured that the Protestant churches which now went up rapidly were no more than barn-like meeting-houses. The Reformed were allowed into four of the main towns for the first time, to serve refugees from Bohemia, Poland and Hungary, their cause being generously supported by the churches of Scotland and the Netherlands, and by English dissenters; but not, to Doddridge's disgust, by the English bishops, Warburton not scrupling to suggest that continentals regarded Britain as a milch-cow.[33]

Above all the Protestants must now live with the divisions which had grown up amongst them since the beginning of the century. For all its initial openness, Breslau Orthodoxy had been forced to the defensive by the emergence of revival, and the Brieg consistory to which even Teschen was nominally subject had not scrupled to support the Jesuit campaign against Pietism as a new sect. They had also made their clergy preach before them weekly on Tuesdays on texts and themes appointed by the Superintendent, to ensure their

---

[33] *Calendar of the Correspondence of Philip Doddridge D. D. (1702–1751)* ed. G. F. Nuttall (London, 1979) nos. 1643, 1649, 1650, 1674, 1679, 1730, 1738.

Orthodoxy.[34] Quite apart from the local conflicts, Silesian Orthodoxy, bruised but not annihilated, was no more likely to favour the 'indifferentism' of the Prussian government than was Prussian Orthodoxy; indeed, having contended for Orthodoxy against both heavy Catholic pressure and revivalist competition, it was less likely to do so. Even at the time of the War of the Austrian Succession it would have been possible to envisage a scenario, actually realised in 1835, when Breslau Orthodoxy, so open in the late seventeenth century, closed its ranks against a Prussian liberalism imposed at the bayonet point, while Old Lutherans seceded to the Middle West of America with the object of creating a 'pure' Lutheranism, and prospectively a pure German state, uncontaminated by the successors of the Protestant saviour of 1741.

In the immediate past it was, of course, mystics and Pietists who had taken to flight – as late as 1725 the last remnant of the Schwenckfelders left for Herrnhut, on their way (as it proved) to America.[35] It was to those who remained that Frederick's incursion seemed most like liberation; the poet Johann Christian Günther recalled in graceful verse how it had felt to participate in the children's awakening of 1707–8, while the Moravians, who came in behind Frederick's army to found a settlement at Gnadenfrei, picked up recruits who could give the most vivid and moving accounts of the same prayer-meetings, and who had stood their ground as converts ever since. The historian of Gnadenfrei goes so far as to say that some villages, especially Schönbrunn, Dirsdorf and Steinmetz's old parish of Töppliwoda, had been so well prepared by past revivals nourished by suitable pastoral care and supported by the aristocratic influence of the Seidlitz family, as to be ready-made for Moravian revival now.[36]

The penetration of Pietism, even of revival, into most parts of Silesia did not, however, set the tone of the province as a whole. In the first place Hallesian Pietism, which in Silesian conditions had so often been transmuted into revival, no longer had the ear of government; indeed Frederick the Great convinced himself that his father had always treated him worst after consorting with the men of Halle. The Halle enterprise, now under the less than charismatic

[34] *UN* 1730, 65–8. Cf. *Ibid.* 1725, 264–5; 1732, 269–70; Gerhard Meyer, *Gnadenfrei. Eine Herrnhuter Siedlung des schlesischen Pietismus im 18. Jahrhundert* (Hamburg, 1950) 39–48.
[35] H. Weigelt, *Spiritualistische Tradition im Protestantismus* (Berlin/New York, 1973) 239–76. The *UN* described them as 'very rich peasants' (1725, 1018–19).
[36] Meyer, *Gnadenfrei* 17–19, 47.

leadership of Francke's son, had to make its way without or against the advantage of official favour. Moreover, Halle had become the conservative defender of an orthodoxy of its own, and was now the venomous antagonist of the new exponents of revival based on Herrnhut. By the 1740s alliances of Pietist and Orthodox to put down the Moravians were the order of the day. Again, nothing had done more to transmute Pietism into revival than intervening in the situation in Bohemia; but with Frederick's armies now operating there directly, he no longer needed to rouse the Protestant minority.

### THE FRONTIER CHURCHES

There was one final way in which Prussian conquest changed the religious situation in Silesia. It put out of date the long chain of frontier churches (*Grenzkirchen*) which had been built around the western and northern frontiers of the province to accommodate Silesians bereft of the ordinances at home. To these churches Silesians, deprived of fellowship, had toiled their way, some having to leave home on Fridays to be in time for the Sunday services. The success or failure of these frontier churches depended chiefly on the incumbent; but clearly they offered the kind of opportunities for revival familiar in the camp-meetings of the American Old South or the great communion days of the Scottish Highlands, or in Teschen. The Saxon church being what it was, its concessions had been chiefly to offer services, especially in summer, in the Bohemian language without derogation from Orthodoxy.[37]

The most remarkable of the frontier clergy, Johann Christian Schwedler (1672–1730), pastor at Niederwiesa in Upper Lusatia from 1698, was of a totally different stamp. Of Silesian peasant stock, Schwedler understood his people as did no one else, and did an immense pastoral, evangelistic and charitable work among them. Having captured an audience of high social level and low, he had them streaming in in such throngs each week as to make it possible to support an Orphan House, Halle style. Schwedler thought nothing of preaching nine hours at a time, and reinforced the word preached with a flood of literature. Though educated at Leipzig, he made contact with Francke as a student, and never lost touch with him thereafter.

[37] J. G. Carpzov, *Religions-untersuchung der Böhmisch- und Märischen Brüder...* (Leipzig, 1742) 406.

Uniting in his ministry a great following in Silesia with a Lusatian parish west of the river Queis of seven towns and eighty-seven villages, Schwedler created an ideal position from which to assist Silesians to escape, and he frequently acted for Zinzendorf's grandmother, Henriette Katherina von Gersdorf, in recruiting Bohemian and Silesian Protestants for the estates at Berthelsdorf and Gross Hennersdorf. It was he who converted Christian David, Zinzendorf's turbulent henchman (who was confirmed in the faith by Steinmetz at Teschen), and passed him on via the mystic, Melchior Scheffer, at Görlitz, to Herrnhut. In due course David smuggled out the earliest Moravian settlers via the revival villages Schönbrunn and Dirsdorf (where Steinmetz's friend and old assistant at Töppliwoda, Sommer, was pastor) to Herrnhut, and this was the region to which Zinzendorf himself turned back after the Prussian conquest. With both the clergy and the aristocracy of this region he had then been acquainted for twenty years, long before there was any question of creating a settlement at Herrnhut.

Thus Schwedler before his death, and long before the Prussian conquest, had created a network which enabled him to move part of the Bohemian and Silesian revival out into Upper Lusatia. Here under the intolerant but mercifully inefficient rule of Saxony it was enabled to take root and expand in every direction, even returning to north-west Silesia in the wake of the sceptical Frederick the Great.

### THE LATER HISTORY OF TESCHEN

It remains to take leave of Teschen. The expulsion of the Pietists in 1730 threatened to cripple the Jesus church and school, both of which were now shunned by many of their former adherents. Moreover Teschen was now the personal property of the Habsburg family, and had to withstand the full pressure of the Counter-Reformation and the cult of St John of Nepomuk. Nor was there any relief at the hands of Frederick the Great; Teschen was strategically too important to the Habsburg system for them to part with it. To be excluded from Prussian Silesia was a bitter disappointment notwithstanding that Steinmetz, now abbot of Kloster Berg and Superintendent of Magdeburg in Prussia, made it his business to bring them encouragement and challenge from the world of Anglo-Saxon revival. Jonathan Edwards's *Faithful Narrative* of the revival at Northampton,

Mass., in German dress[38] afforded the opportunity to talk of the interest the great men of New England had always shown in Halle, to issue the challenge 'that the Lord might finally remove his candlestick from ungrateful Europe and give the glory of Lebanon to the American wilderness', to counsel public teachers to preach for revival, and, when they got it, 'carefully to note all the circumstances' as did the Reformed. The case for Doddridge's *Family Expositor* was simply that (bulk apart) it was the ideal book to sustain the priestly role of fathers of families on which the Silesian revival had been built.[39]

Fragile as these buttresses might be, the results of a decade of revival were very striking. Outside Hungary and the embassy chapels in Vienna, the churches at Teschen and in the county of Asch were the only Protestant churches in the Habsburg lands, and Teschen, though weakened by social tension, persistent emigration and the spiritual torpor which the Fredrician regime bought into the rest of Silesia, came to play the leading role in Austrian Protestantism. Between 1741 and 1800 12 candidates for the ministry were ordained in the Grace church for Silesia, Moravia and Galicia, and, after the Patent of Toleration in 1781, it became the mother church of scores of churches and preaching stations throughout the region. The Jesus school was the precursor of the Protestant theological faculty in Vienna, and one of its distinguished sons was not only the biographer of Liberda[40] but, in 1919, the first dean of the new Protestant theological faculty in Prague.

Perhaps most striking of all, when in the later nineteenth century, one Austrian institution after another fell victim to fears of Slav domination, the Protestantism of Teschen and Bielitz retained its cohesion. The peace settlement in 1920, however, divided not merely the duchy but the town of Teschen between Poland and Czecho-slovakia, the old town with the Grace church and most of the public buildings east of the Olsa going to Poland, the suburbs west of the river with the most important railway station going to Czecho-slovakia. At that point the congregation split up into national groups; peace wrecked what conflict and religious revival had created. At the time of the Sudeten crisis in 1938 the Poles occupied the whole area

---

[38] [Jonathan Edwards], *Glaubwürdige Nachricht von dem herrlichen Werk Gottes welches sich in Bekehrung vieler hundert seelen zu Northampton ... geäussert hat ...* (Magdeburg, 1738).

[39] P. Doddridge, *Paraphrastische Erklärung der sämtlichen Schriften Neues Testaments* (Biel, 1755).

[40] G. A. Skalský, 'Der Exulantenprediger Johann Liberda', *JGGPÖ* 31 (1910).

and dismissed the pastors of the German congregations. Nazi occupation was greeted with enthusiasm, and followed by a most uncomfortable incorporation into the Breslau consistory of the Old Prussian Union, and the same loss of legal status as afflicted the churches in the Warthegau, that model Nazi republic. After the war Polish influence was supreme, and the Tescheners played a preponderant part in the reorganisation of what was left of Polish Protestantism, supplying a series of professors of practical theology to the Kirchliche Hochschule in Warsaw, one of whom had been a wartime exile in England. The historiography of Teschen, however, has remained a German-language achievement. The religious history of modern Teschen has thus retained an international significance out of all relation to its numerical size. Steinmetz built better than he could know.

CHAPTER 3

# *Salzburg and Austria*

## CHURCH AND STATE IN SALZBURG

The most dramatic episode in the story of religious revival, an event which had its repercussions throughout Protestant Europe and America, and taught lessons to the Habsburgs, was the great emigration from Salzburg in the winter of 1731–2. Contemporaries found this an even more 'surprising work of God' than Jonathan Edwards found the revival at Northampton, Mass.; but, like that revival, it had roots in the past.

Salzburg was both an archdiocese and a principality. It was characteristic of the old Europe that the boundaries of the two jurisdictions did not coincide on the ground and were not always harmoniously exercised by the same person. Thus, for example, for purposes of secular government, most of the Defereggertal was subject to the principality of Salzburg, but part belonged to the Tyrol; in spiritual matters the valley was entirely subject to the archdiocese of Salzburg and belonged to the archdeaconry of Gmünd in Carinthia, a territory for secular purposes subject to the Habsburgs. Wolf Dietrich (archbishop 1587–1611), who was suspected of trying to secularise the principality and fetched up in effect a prisoner of the Pope, had begun with an edict getting rid of the Protestant town councillors of his capital city, and requiring all his subjects to become Catholic or leave the country. This achieved the desired result in and about Salzburg. But the archbishop wanted money for grandiose building, so, as a secular ruler, he instructed the administrator of Werfen not to press the edict he had issued as spiritual head, and granted the miners of Gastein and the Dürrnberg the free exercise of their religion according to the principles of the Augsburg Confession. In Gastein indeed a Protestant cemetery was laid out, and the miners put up a clock on their church inscribed 'The

93

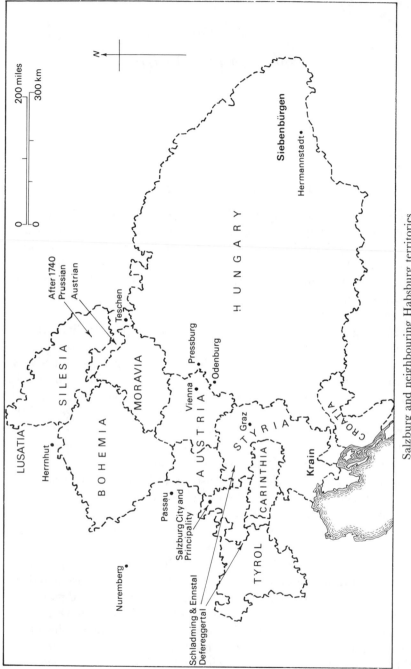

Salzburg and neighbouring Habsburg territories

200 miles
300 km

N

LUSATIA

SILESIA

After 1740
Prussian
Austrian

Teschen

BOHEMIA

MORAVIA

Herrnhut

Nuremberg

Passau

Salzburg City and
Principality

Schladming & Ennstal
Defereggertal

TYROL

AUSTRIA

Vienna

Pressburg

Odenburg

HUNGARY

St Graz

STYRIA

CARINTHIA

Krain

CROATIA

Siebenbürgen

Hermannstadt

word of God endureth for ever'.[1] Only against Anabaptists was he relentless.

In the seventeenth century, archdiocese and principality were nevertheless governed with some consistency on principles common to most of the states in Europe. Salzburg attained a formal independence in the Westphalia settlement, yet remained diplomatically tied to the Habsburg interest; the Habsburgs on their side devoted more pains to influencing elections to the see than to any other, while insisting that the archbishop had no right of interference in their lands nor title to grant the right of asylum to their clergy.[2] The archbishops continued to want money to transform Salzburg into the 'Rome of Germany', and to get a united people to pay it sought to exterminate Protestants, magicians and witches. Campaigns against these three evils, which seem not to have been officially regarded as interrelated,[3] reached a peak in the later seventies and eighties of the seventeenth century, and the last peasant girl was burned as a witch in Salzburg in 1762. The anti-Protestant drive produced simultaneous crises at the Dürrnberg by Hallein and in the remote Defereggertal which both foreshadowed and directly influenced the much greater upheaval which came almost half a century later.

## THE PERSISTENCE OF PROTESTANTISM

No one had any doubt that most of the miners in Salzburg were Protestants, but the scene which was enacted in 1683 seems to have come as a surprise. In the church at the Dürrnberg one of the Austin friars who had pastoral care of the miners for sixty years gave a panegyric upon St Nicholas of Tolentin. In language regretted by Catholics of higher brow, he claimed 'one could through the intercession of this saint easily obtain eternal life'. One of the leading miners, Simon Lindtner, got up and walked out.[4] It is hard not to believe that the timing of this affair owed something to the clearly approaching crisis of the Protestant cause in France; for the excesses of the French troops in the invasion of 1664 had been resented

[1] G. Florey, *Geschichte der Salzburger Protestanten und ihrer Emigration 1731–2* (Vienna, 1977) 52–5.
[2] ÖNB MS s n. 12 109 fo. 77.
[3] Cf. however, G. G. G. Göcking, *Vollkommene Emigrations-Geschichte...* (2 vols. Frankfurt/Leipzig, 1734–7) 1:115.
[4] J. T. Zauner & C. Gärtner, *Neue Chronik von Salzburg* (11 vols. Salzburg, 1803–26) 1:517.

nowhere more deeply than in Hallein, and had provoked a kind of peasant jacquerie. An inquiry set up by the administrator (*Pfleger*) of Hallein predictably revealed that the Dürrnberger miners were slack in church attendance and held secret meetings in the woods. The three ringleaders were Lindtner and two other miners, Mathias Kammel and Josef Schaitberger, who were related not only to each other, but to other miners across the hill in the neighbouring *Probstei* of Berchtesgaden, which was also brought to set judicial inquiries on foot. To cut a long story short, the three ringleaders were imprisoned and subjected to all kinds of pressure to abjure their faith, but to no avail. In April 1686 individual expulsion orders were issued, and over the next five years some fifty to sixty miners and their wives were driven abroad; their property was retained, ostensibly to provide for the Catholic rearing of their children who were kept behind.

### JOSEF SCHAITBERGER

The Protestant powers, especially Brandenburg and Baden, huffed and puffed, and sought to assist the refugees to regain their property and children; but that would probably have been the end of the affair had not Josef Schaitberger separated from the others (who went on to jobs in the mines in Saxony), secured humble manual employment in Nuremberg, developed unsuspected literary gifts, and turned himself into the most notable Protestant propagandist and evangelist over the whole area of Salzburg, Styria and Carinthia. Schaitberger (1658–1733), who always claimed to be Lutheran Orthodox but was lionised just before his death by a Pietist party which had not existed at the time of his expulsion, illustrates both the religious evolution of these years, and the cost, personal and financial, of religious persecution. His father was a peasant and a miner in the archbishop's Dürrnberger mines; his mother, like his first wife (who was a Kammel) and his second wife, was a Berchtesgadener. His parents were both Protestants but he was sent to the Catholic school. The schoolmaster, however, was his brother, who instilled literacy and read Protestant books with him. At thirteen Josef went into the salt mines, and at eighteen on his father's death, inherited property worth about 1,000 thaler. By twenty-five he was married and had accumulated a theological library of some 300 volumes. He had a close circle of friends who 'frequently met, prayed, sang, read the scriptures, the catechism and other good books together'; like so many Silesians he had unwittingly taken the Spenerite *collegium pietatis* and used it, not as a supplement to the devotions of a church now out of reach, but as a substitute for them. And like so many in these years he felt no longer able to sustain the equivocations of the secret practice of the faith.

The cost of the decision, financial and personal, was great. Schaitberger could take little with him in the way of money or books, and was reduced to unskilled employment. The reward of fame at the end of a long life was to be specially admitted to a poorhouse, a former Carthusian monastery, normally reserved for citizens of Nuremberg. But the personal cost was far greater. He forsook his devotional circle on the Dürrnberg. He and his wife had to abandon their daughters; soon after their arrival in Nuremberg she died of consumption and a broken heart, on her death-bed constantly begging him to get their children out. Three times he returned for them, but they had been raised as Catholics and could only regard their father as a stranger. By his third visit one of his daughters was married. Both refused to leave, though it is said that his eldest daughter, at the age of twenty-five, came to visit him with a view to converting him to Catholicism, was herself converted to Protestantism and stayed.

Schaitberger's life and work link together the troubles on the Dürrnberg and those in the Defereggertal, and both with the great emigration of 1731–2 and with the apostles of revival in Silesia and Bohemia. It was while he was considering how he might smuggle his children out that Schaitberger began to write the letters to his Protestant countrymen which made him famous; the very first was a *Sendbrief an seine liebe Landsleute in Salzburg und Tefferecker Thal*, but the letters spread right through Inner Austria and were carried by the exiles of conscience to Pressburg and even to Siebenbürgen at the eastern extremity of Hungary. These letters were designed to comfort, but also to stiffen faith and mark out a Protestant hard line to which oppressed minorities should stick. Yet if Schaitberger was not prepared to spare compromising consciences, he could not address his sorely-tried compatriots simply as a thunderer of Orthodoxy. He had (in the words of one of his own sermon titles) to be a 'preacher of penitence and awakening', and one who sweetened his message by a touching experience of 'the garden of delight of God's word'. He did more than anyone not merely to preserve but to revive the faith of the Protestant communities of Salzburg and Austria; and he had a double reward. Just before his death one of the great trains of Salzburg Protestant exiles came through Nuremberg, and the Pietists who organised them found that 'almost all who could read asked, "Have you any Schaitbergers?" and were delighted when given a copy'.[5] If any further testimony were needed, his works (which exceeded 700 pages of print) remained banned even after Joseph II's Patent of Toleration in 1781; but, camouflaged under the new title of *Devotional Book for Protestant Christians*, they were brought in still by Austrian Protestants.

Moreover at the end of his life Schaitberger was taken up by the Pietist party he had earlier denounced. His most useful biography was published in the journal edited by Johann Adam Steinmetz, now also an exile from his Silesian homeland.[6] And Samuel Urlsperger of Augsburg reprinted his works for the benefit of the exiled Salzburgers, and eased the financial straits of his last days by grants from English subscriptions for the Salzburger exiles. Urlsperger, as we shall see, did more for the Salzburgers who fetched up in Georgia than anyone else, and sang the praises of Schaitberger to the SPCK in England. And to complete the circle, it was Urlsperger's adopted home of Augsburg which provided the chief asylum for the Defereggger exiles, to whom we must now turn.

### THE DEFEREGGERTAL

It is not known how Protestantism first penetrated the remote Defereggertal, but, like the impoverished inhabitants of many other mountain valleys in that region, the Defereggers eked out a living as pedlars and itinerant musicians in Germany, and probably brought back Protestant ideas and books. In 1683 the archdeacon of Gmünd reported that they spoke against the Pope, the Virgin and the saints, and neglected their church duties. There was a civil inquiry launched in the best Ephesian tradition on the complaint of a carver of images who feared for his living, and the archbishop sent in Capuchins to examine the people in their faith and instruct them. The show of force with which they were supported seems to have evoked an informal threat of force in reply. And the Catholic accounts of the event contain two details which distinguish the clash in the Defereggertal from the ordinary confessional confrontations and link it with later events in Silesia and in Salzburg itself: the children were a principal agent in the spreading of Protestantism, and 'the number of

---

[5]  S. Urlsperger, *Der noch lebende Joseph Schaitberger*... (Augsburg, 1732) 21, 8; *Evangelisch in der Steiermark* (Graz, 1981) 85; J. Schaitberger, *Neuvermehrter evangelischer Sendbrief*... (Nuremberg, 1736) 547, 143.          [6] *SMBRG* 5 (1736) 589–621.

Protestants grew daily'.[7] In short some of the common elements of revival were already present; so too were what became the standard responses of the archbishop's government.

The archbishop held that he was not permitted as ruler of the principality to do what he could not do as archbishop, and that the Protestants must either conform or leave the country at very short notice. This they did in a series of trains over the winter of 1684–5 to the tune of about 1,000 persons. One group defied the rule that children under fifteen must be left behind to be raised as Catholics, only to find that at the request of the Salzburg government their children were taken away by the authorities in Innsbruck and returned; while from the meagre stock of property they had managed to salvage, they were required to pay a 10 per cent emigration tax. Most fetched up in Augsburg and Ulm though a few went into Switzerland and conformed to the Reformed faith. A series of desperate adventures followed as parents came back to rescue their children and fortify the remnant with the writings of Schaitberger; some were taken and sold to the galleys in Venice. To try to kill the appeal of Protestant books the school in the valley was closed. When Brandenburg protested that the proceedings were contrary to the Westphalia settlement, the archbishop maintained, as did his successor in 1731, that the Defereggers were a new sect entitled to no toleration under the Westphalia provisions. His attempts to tempt back some of the lost emigrants failed. But the bloodletting did its work; there was no more revival in the Defereggertal and Protestantism there died out. Its chief legacy to the future was the public attention it had earned. One man especially made it his life's work to aid the Protestants who remained elsewhere in the principality: Samuel Urlsperger. Himself the descendent of a Protestant emigrant from Styria, and a pupil of Francke in Halle, Urlsperger had been pastor of the German congregation in the Savoy 1710–12, and, when he left England, became a corresponding member of the SPCK. After a short and disastrous spell as a court chaplain at Stuttgart (1715–18), he went back into the parish ministry, ending in 1728 as senior of Augsburg. He had already established channels for supplying literature to the Protestants of Austria and Salzburg; but Augsburg was to be the great base for his work for the Salzburgers.

[7] Zauner & Gärtner, *Salzburg* 1:502–3.

PERSECUTION RENEWED BY ARCHBISHOP FIRMIAN

In 1727, at the fourth attempt, the Salzburg chapter elected a reforming archbishop, Leopold Anton Eleutherius Freiherr von Firmian. The nephew of a previous archbishop, Firmian had spent much of his time in the diocese; but he had been educated at the Collegium Germanicum in Rome where he had formed firm connexions with the Jesuits. At the age of thirty-nine he became bishop of Lavant. Here he became convinced that the morality of the people was below scratch, and that it would not be raised without a reform of the clergy. In contemporary style he issued minute regulations, anticipating every transgression, and excluding the clergy from public houses and dancing. In the view of his biographer this worked an improvement.[8] In 1724 the Emperor nominated him to the see of Seckau, and here too he showed himself a reformer, bringing in the Jesuits to assist in the work. In Salzburg it was the same again; female dress was meticulously regulated and the Jesuits were turned loose in the hills where there were Protestants, to the number it was supposed of about 5,000. The archbishop also agreed with the Emperor to appoint a joint commission to clear up disputes over spiritual jurisdiction in the duchies of Styria and Carinthia which was a complete success.

The first problem confronting the Jesuits in the hills – it was to recur in Austria – was to distinguish the Catholic sheep from the Protestant goats. Their method was to require the use of the familiar Catholic greeting in South Germany, 'Gelobt sey Jesus Christ' (to which the answer was 'Zu Ewigkeit, Amen!') to which Benedict XIII had attached an indulgence, and also the wearing of a scapular. Notwithstanding that the Salzburger Protestants had conceded a high degree of conformity, these methods, together with the extraction of confidences from children and the hunting-out of forbidden books, evoked a mutinous frame of mind. Moreover all were aware that in the last crisis the Corpus Evangelicorum had been willing to protest on behalf of the Deferegger Protestants. Those protests and the knowledge that expulsion might again be the Protestant fate, coloured the whole course of events. As early as 1729 the first two activists to be expelled from the country, the peasants Lercher from Radstadt and Prambell from Werfen, made straight for Regensburg and had their cause publicly taken up by the Corpus

[8] Karl Amon, ed., *Die Bischöfe von Graz-Seckau* (Graz &c., 1969) 336.

Evangelicorum. The Salzburg ambassador to the Diet, Zillerberg, could only argue that they were not entitled to the Westphalia protection as they had been expelled for disobedience, not religion.

If the archbishop was thus put publicly upon the defensive, the reports he received privately showed how much ground had to be made up at home. In Gastein there was said to be scarcely a family free from heresy, and a long tradition of domestic devotions had bred a race of peasant preachers capable of taking the initiative when the time came. Before the missionaries arrived, peasants were demanding from the priest the right to hold Lutheran services in public; after they came, Protestant gatherings at night were the order of the day in innumerable villages. Under the archbishop's forward policy the situation deteriorated rapidly. To spy out the houses where there were Protestant books, women were used selling chickens from door to door; but over the generations the Protestants had developed such a degree of theological skill in equivocating about what their views were, that the Jesuits found it prudent to begin their inquiries with the weak and the children. All the time the import of forbidden books (and, worst of all, Schaitbergers) went on, and around the books gathered families and friends for worship and preaching. In the eyes of all the Orthodox parties, all this was highly unprofessional; but it was nearer to what the young Luther had wanted in the *Deutsche Messe* than it was to anything in post-Tridentine Catholicism.[9]

## THE INTERVENTION OF THE POWERS; REVIVAL

The two things no one had bargained on were the capacity of the Salzburg Protestants to introduce an international dimension into their conflict, and the solidarity with which they confronted superior force. All the Protestant powers, and especially those represented at Regensburg, were drawn into the fray, while the representative of the archbishop had to move from the argument that their Protestants were an untolerated sect to the claim they were actually rebels. What was undoubtedly alarming was the way peasants and miners who had not previously maintained contact managed to hold a delegate meeting at Schwarzach, to resolve on the public profession of their faith, and get a petition for its free practice signed by 18,000 people and smuggled out to Regensburg. Catholic authorities in Salzburg professed to believe that this conspiracy was got up by Protestant

[9] *Luther's Works* American edn by J. Pelikan & H. T. Lehmann (Philadelphia, 1958) LIII:63–4.

agents from Regensburg; but the last thing the Protestant authorities of the Empire would have encouraged was a demand for toleration. This would have destroyed the whole flimsy basis of the Westphalia settlement. The archbishop also raised the stakes by offering to arm the Catholic population and calling in Habsburg troops to block the passes.

Moreover, though all parties were very short of vocabulary in which to describe what was happening before their eyes, the sharper observers in both Germany and Britain were aware not only that the scale of the Salzburg problem was very much greater than they had supposed, but that it was being magnified by what would now be called revival.[10] It was this which gave the Salzburgers confidence to commence a public trial of strength. The Catholic polemic built up from contemporary sources by Corbinian Gärtner shows clearly enough that styles of piety and religious activity were now put to the service of the Augsburg Confession which did not characterise the churches of that tradition, but were a coarser version of what had happened in Silesia, and were to reappear in America. He speaks of night meetings at Goldegg where they sang hymns and wept so that the whole countryside could hear; there were women preaching – one of the standard signs of the day of the Lord, following Joel ii. 28 and Acts ii. 17–18 – especially at Wagrain. The Mosegger family attracted great repute as preachers, drawing congregations from far and near, one of them preaching so touchingly that his congregation broke out into tears. There were active attempts to proselytise the Catholic population, especially at Abtenau where they ran round like fanatics.[11]

The clearest evidence of all this came in recrudescence of trouble among the Dürrnberger mines, though here there was also industrial conflict, carefully calculated on both sides. The miners had kept clear of the Schwarzach conspiracy and the petition to the Imperial Diet. But at the beginning of 1731 active proselytisation began. This in turn caused the archbishop to begin prosecutions to which the miners replied with the claim that all the miners were now Protestants. The prosecutions were for the moment suspended, but the revival went on with meetings in the woods. Like the opponents of Whitefield and Wesley, the archbishop alleged that the miners were neglecting work

[10] [J. J. Moser] *Acten-Massiger Bericht von der … schweren Verfolgung … in … Salzburg* (Frankfurt/Leipzig, 1732) Vorrede; anon., *The Present State of Germany* (2 vols. London, 1738) 1:344–5.
[11] Zauner & Gärnter, *Salzburg* IV:127–36; Georg Loesche, 'Neues über die Ausrottung des Protestantismus in Salzburg, 1731–2', *JGGPÖ* 50 (1929) 30, 66.

to meet and sing their Lutheran hymns. The archbishop then insured against the worst case by arranging for the authorities in Berchtesgaden to supply him with more miners should he lose his work-force, and informed his men that any who wished could emigrate unharmed provided they paid the usual severance money and gave details and names of all the Protestants. The miners worked even worse, threatened to destroy the salt chambers if force were used against them on account of religion, and secured their own retreat by getting offers of alternative employment in Nuremberg, and later from the Saxon and Dutch ambassadors. Even now it seems that the more prosperous among the miners were for striking a bargain with the archbishop on the basis of the secret practice of their religion; but they were overcome, and the miners finally petitioned the archbishop for permission to leave under the provisions of the Westphalia settlement, not as rebels, they being all adherents of the Augsburg Confession. The archbishop, sensing an opportunity to divide the opposition, sent in missionaries, but this proved the last straw in polarising opinion.

### THE GREAT EMIGRATION

The attitude of the miners was finally stiffened by the trains of Protestants from the hills passing through Hallein; on them the axe had already fallen. In November 1731, in mid-winter, the archbishop issued a patent expelling all Protestants over the age of twelve at eight days' notice, with no other opportunity to clear up their affairs before leaving. The next stage in the story justly formed one of the sensations of the eighteenth century. Protestant Salzburgers, in numbers of which the petition to the Imperial Diet had given no more than an inkling, left the country in spite of the reluctance of neighbouring territories to give them passage. Prussia, popularly cast in the role of an instrument of apocalyptic vengeance on the city and state of Salzburg, made no move, but picked up armies of Salzburgers at different points in Swabia, and marched them in columns, by different routes to ease the billeting problem, to the North-East, retaining some in Berlin, some in Pomerania, some in East Prussia while the bulk settled in Livonia. The whole operation, in which the Salzburgers were paid a daily subsistence allowance on the way, and rapidly settled in peasant lots or domestic service at the other end, was one of the outstanding achievements of eighteenth-century government, the more remarkable as neither the Prussians nor anyone else could forecast the scale on which it had to be carried through. The hapless Salzburgers had to face a second winter in the Baltic lands without proper housing, but they settled and were still recognisable there in 1939; the Prussian government set about providing them with churches, clergy and schools, and made attempts to secure some return for their property abandoned in Salzburg. The business cost the Prussians about half a million thalers, but they got 20,000 settlers, the largest group to be displaced in Germany since the Reformation. All the Protestant powers (not to mention the Hamburg Jews) subscribed largely; the Dutch found 400,000 florins and got 788 Dürrnberger miners, whom they settled partly at Flushing and partly on an island in the Maas estuary where they mostly sickened and died. The English subscribed 228,000 florins and got a first instalment of 200 who were settled by the Georgia Trustees near Savannah with two ministers sent from Halle, and put under the general spiritual oversight of the Wesley brothers. Some are said even to have fetched up near the Turkish frontier of the European system in Siebenbürgen. They seem to have been not Salzburgers, but Austrians from the Salzkammergut; but they celebrated their bicentenary as Salzburgers in 1934. Freudenstadt in the Black Forest was also supposed to have been founded by Salzburgers; the pioneers actually came from Carinthia, but the story is a witness both to the legendary status of the Salzburgers and their continuing contact with their Austrian neighbours.

The Salzburg crisis had both diplomatic and moral consequences. The archbishop, the head of a principality whose finances now became extremely rickety, found his claim to the title of primate of Germany vigorously contested by the Protestant powers, while at the same time he was in hot water with the Pope for not consulting the Holy See and for allowing heresy to become so rife in his diocese. Catholic as well as Protestant powers began to look more than ever to the secularisation of ecclesiastical principalities, including Salzburg, as a way out of diplomatic difficulties, not least of meeting the claims of Bavaria. The Dürrnberger miners failed to shut down their mines; but as they went they tempted out about half the Protestant population of Berchtesgaden, who rewarded the electorate of Hanover for its 90,000 florins subscription by settling there.[12] The Emperor had walked the tightrope with considerable skill. His overwhelming concern at the time of the Salzburg crisis was to secure

---

[12] J. Regula, 'Die Berchtesgadener (Salzburger) Emigranten in Göttingen (1733 bis 1742)', *ZGNSKg* 19 (1914) 209–29. Many of the Berchtesgadeners were serfs; their redemption money was paid by Protestant ambassadors.

recognition of the Pragmatic Sanction and thus enable his daughter Maria Theresa to succeed him in at any rate the family lands. To follow his instinct and secure a Catholic triumph in Salzburg might enable France to get up another religious conflict in Regensburg and destroy his Prussian alliance. To do nothing might drive the archbishop to the side of grasping Bavaria. By doing little more than holding the ring, and blocking the passes, the Emperor prevented a threatened leakage of his own Catholic subjects seeking to take advantage of the flooded land-market in Salzburg, and secured his major objectives. The cost was to allow the Protestant Salzburgers a very much better outcome than the Defereggers had had in 1685 and to encourage all their sympathisers in the Habsburg lands to think that the miracle might be repeated. Nothing was further from the Emperor's intentions.

### INTERNATIONAL REACTION TO THE EMIGRATION

Meanwhile in Germany, and by reprint, quotation and reference, as far away as America, the language of hyperbole, if not of miracle, was standard form. The newspaper press had a field day, and sermons and pamphlets are reckoned to have run to 500 titles.[13] Still more striking were the line drawings and coloured illustrations of the Salzburgers turning their back on their mountain homeland for the sake of the Gospel, a fat baby under one arm and the Luther Bible under the other, or a fat baby under each and Luther's shorter catechism. These remain a splendid source for the history of Salzburger costume because, for the first time, the artists had to pay the lower orders the compliment of naturalistic, not grotesque, representation. There were morals to be drawn by the spokesmen of both the early Enlightenment and religious revival.

Fifty years before Lessing, the newspaper press championed the virtues of toleration on a great scale, and translated a message from the king of England to the Emperor as saying that, with the defeat of the Turkish menace, Christendom needed a healthier basis for its future well-being.[14] For peasants to have accomplished so much showed that, contrary to received opinion, they were educable and therefore fit recipients for the shoal of improving literature provided by *Aufklärer* in the next generation, and presentable candidates for transformation 'from pariah to patriot' thereafter.

[13] A. Marsch, *Die Salzburger Emigration in Bildern* (2nd edn Weissenhorn, 1979) 158ff.
[14] *Reformation – Emigration. Protestanten in Salzburg* ed. F. Zaisberger (Salzburg, 1981) 110–11.

The religious shock administered by the Salzburgers' march across Europe was tremendous. The simple knowledge that they were coming inspired 'moving awakenings' (*bewegliche Erweckungen*); the enthusiasts who stood at the fountainhead of religious revival in the west of the Empire now held that the secret increase of the hidden kingdom of God had reached the point where public outbreaks might be expected anywhere.[15]

The view that the establishment was about to crack under its own weight proved in the event to be an illusion, but at the time it seemed borne out by the Salzburgers' progress across Germany. In every town they were catechised and treated to endless sermons which were sold to raise funds on their behalf. The catechising was intended to show that, despite the allegations of the Salzburg government, the emigrants were Lutherans with rights under the Westphalia settlement. Yet the very existence of Salzburger Protestantism was an affront to Lutheran Orthodoxy. Valentin Ernst Löscher admitted his astonishment that so many thousands should become Protestant against such odds, and without a teaching church. The Salzburgers, even more than the Silesians, had stumbled upon not so much an alternative church as an alternative to the church; the Orthodox had condemned Spener's prescriptions for the informal cultivation of religion as ruinous, but were now intoxicated by the results, not of supplementing but of supplanting the church in this way. 'The Lord is doing a new thing in the land...It makes all things new.'[16]

There is no doubt that the great Salzburger emigration contributed immensely to the promotion of religious revival. The arrival of so large an army of refugees in the Baltic area could hardly fail to weaken the fragile props to religious conformity there, and in this sense pave the way for the preachers of a new religious appeal who followed hot on their heels. In the highly-charged atmosphere of Germany itself, individual men and women (like members of the Oxford Holy Club just afterwards) such as Johann Jakob Moser and his wife[17] were delighted to find that they had independently undergone conversion experiences; and it is hard not to believe that what has been called Zinzendorf's 'turn to Luther', though be-

---

[15] J. S. Carl, *Geistliche Fama* (n.pl. 1733–43) 7:18–34, 42–52; 10:28, 81–2; 23:6–7.

[16] V. E. Löscher, *Drey Predigten von der Erkänntnis...des Sohnes Gottes* (Dresden, 1733) 26; J. G. Hillinger, *Beytrag zur Kirchen Historie des Erzbischoftums Saltzburg* (Saalfeld, 1732); G. Müller, *Zulänglich Erkänntnüss des...Salzburgischen Emigration-Wesens* (Dresden/Leipzig, 1732) Preface 2.

[17] *Lebensgeschichte J. J. Mosers von ihm selbst beschrieben* (n.p., 1768), 55.

ginning in controversy with Dippel, was confirmed by the evidence of Lutheranism among the Salzburgers. And, lastly, events in Austria owed much to their example and direct intervention.

### THE HABSBURG RESPONSE TO THE SALZBURG CRISIS

If the crisis in Salzburg encouraged the hotheads in Bohemia and Moravia, there were fears that it might be immediately reproduced in the neighbouring Habsburg provinces of Carinthia, Styria and the Tyrol, even in Austria itself.[18] The archbishop had long been convinced that that Protestants of these provinces were in league with his own contumacious subjects, while Charles VI had long harried the bishop of Seckau to put on a drive against the Styrian Protestants.[19] Now rumours of all sorts were rife. In Schladming there were tales that the Salzburgers, encouraged by illusory promises from Prussia, were to join with local Protestants in burning places down and do violence against the Catholics. All had conspired together to use force if any of them was arrested. In Carinthia, there were reports of Salzburgers in local dress coming to solicit aid, or distribute Protestant polemic. Some protection against infiltration could be obtained by ordering the military occupation of the passes on the pretext of keeping out cattle plague, but the internal sources of unrest were a matter of anxiety right into 1735. Out of this upheaval were born the main lines of Habsburg policy towards the Protestants down to the Patent of Toleration of 1781. An Imperial resolution of 1733 proposed a combination of evangelisation and force. Missions should be intensified, religious commissions in the provinces should keep the situation under constant review, there should be houses of conversion and better pastoral care (though a reorganisation of the parish system had to await the time of Joseph II). All this was a thin disguise for the mailed fist. The Emperor was to deny the *jus emigrandi* conferred on religious minorities by the Westphalia settlement, and to rebuff the excited interventions of the Corpus Evangelicorum at Regensburg. Determined Protestant communities were to be broken up by forced labour, militia service on the Hungarian frontier, or by transportation to Hungary or Sieben-

[18] The religious press was full of the disturbances in Carinthia and Styria: *AHE* 1:604–40, 758 7, 293–307, 455–64; 2:734–8; 3:1162–6.
[19] Zauner & Gärtner, *Salzburg* IV:112; DG MS xv b 23 , corr. of Charles VI with the bishop of Seckau, 13, 28 September 1714, 3 August 1718, 30 March 1724.

bürgen where attempts to recatholicise the country had ended in bitter failure.[20] On the ecclesiastical side Salzburg could help. There was constant correspondence between the bishops of Seckau and their metropolitan; Salzburg advised on the suspect books to be put down, provided missionaries and money for the church in Styria, and bankrupt as the principality was, it suffered constant criticism in Styria for its miserliness.[21] These measures together with military occupation did not prevent fresh religious unrest in Carinthia in 1738 and 1741 when at the crisis of the Habsburg monarchy a Protestant uprising was feared; but they show clearly enough that the subterranean contact maintained between the Salzburgers and their Protestant neighbours was more than matched by contact between the authorities, and the rival forms of cross-border cooperation continued still more strenuously in the time of Maria Theresa.[22]

Maria Theresa, the zealous Catholic daughter of a Protestant mother, felt deeply the lack of religious unity in her domains, and, confronted by two tremendous struggles with Frederick the Great, could not but be acutely conscious of every weakness of state. Her policies have received a great deal of scholarly attention which has to some extent disguised the fact that her reign was continuous with that of Charles VI not only in the aims, but also in the failures of policy. The fact was that Charles VI could not populate the enormous territories he had gained in the South-East without breaching the Habsburg family contract with the Counter-Reformation. His desperate efforts to stop his Catholic subjects leaking off to replace the Protestants expelled from Salzburg made this as plain as his transports of Protestants to Hungary; the latter were death to a third of their victims, a rate of wastage extravagantly in excess of that achieved by the Prussians in marching the Salzburgers to the Baltic. As a young man the future Joseph II was educated upon documents which insisted that Archbishop Firmian had ruined his principality by depopulating it,[23] and set himself the questions 'how to confront

---

[20] Hans von Zwiedineck-Südenhorst, 'Geschichte der religiösen Bewegung in Inner-Österreich im 18. Jahrhundert, *AÖG* 53/ii (1875) 460–90, 508–26; *AHE* 1:293–307, 455 64, 631–40, 769–80; *UN* 1736 312–14.

[21] DG MS xv b 23, archbishop of Salzburg to bishop of Seckau, 3 March 1730; SLG MS HS XIII.1 nos. 131, 146, 180, 202, 206, 247, 425, 615, 673; HS XIII.2 nos. 22, 104, 118, 137, 466, 505.

[22] Paul Dedic, 'Der Geheimprotestantismus in ... Schladming ... 1753–60', *JGGPÖ* 62 (1941) 70–8.

[23] ÖSA MS w514 fos. 288–9; ÖNB Handschriftsammlung MS s.n 12.109 fo. 110.

the depopulation of the Empire attempted by so many foreign powers, and at the same time to draw advantages from the Empire for strengthening the army and the population of these lands?' The principal answer to both these questions was to be the Patent of Toleration. Thus even in the time of Maria Theresa the Protestants were being persecuted by a government which knew that a 'final solution' to its problem of confessional minorities was not among the options open to it.

Moreover, the government was not able to keep up its own confessional strictness in time of war. Even in the seventeenth century persecution had sometimes been limited in wartime by the non-cooperation of provincial authorities. From a Protestant standpoint the War of the Austrian Succession offered a welcome relief from the exigency of Charles VI, while the Seven Years War formed an interlude between the violent reaction of Maria Theresa in the early 1750s and her vexation with the Moravian Protestants in the last months of her life. Josef Schaitberger had besought his co-religionists to hold firm for the brief interim until they were vindicated in the Last Judgment; in fact relief (though not vindication) came more speedily than he expected, and, in the case of the Austrian Protestants, the wave-like pattern of revival was directly related to the fierce but erratic pressure of hostile governments. Spared, like the Silesians, the worst trials of the Bohemians, like them they better preserved the proportion of faith.

## CATHOLIC RELIGIOUS POLICY

The Habsburg authorities were inhibited not only by physical limitations to what they could achieve, but by intellectual limitations which made it very difficult to understand the efforts of the Salzburgers to reproduce their miracle abroad. The documents of the religious commissions are instinct with the view that the Roman Catholic Church was the one Church, and hence the only missionaries were those it commissioned. Anyone else emulating this line of business was an agitator or an emissary sent by some other authority, and probably a dealer in subversive literature. This view was natural in view of the irritation the Habsburgs had suffered from the agents of Prussia and Halle in Bohemia, but no Prussian agent was ever taken up in Austria, and Halle imprints are notably lacking among the quantities of Protestant literature impounded at the time or surviving in Protestant families into the age of toleration. Yet the administrative documents make it clear that the unrest among Protestant population was fanned partly by homegrown propagandists (*seductores aliorum*),[24] but quite largely by Salzburgers from the West. Relations between the two, even before the crisis, are attested by the fact that some Salzburgers were taken up in Austria, having come to Vienna for communion, and their fellows in the Salz-kammergut appealed to the Austrians for help. From the beginning the new Salzburg preachers were active in Styria and Carinthia, and the Austrian government produced circumstantial evidence to the Reichstag that some were supported by the Corpus Evangelicorum (though the allegation that one varied his disguises with perruques and liveries strains credulity).[25] Special measures were taken to keep them out in 1745, they were there in force during the most vivid outbreak of all generated by the zeal of Maria Theresa in the early 1750s, and they were back again in the 1770s.[26] Small wonder that the government was hostile to the appearance of 'so-called Catholic Salzburgers'. The nature of Protestant survival in Austria was being transformed by Protestant revival in Salzburg.

On the Catholic side, missions suffered from following foreign styles, all of which were losing touch with the tastes of the Catholic population, from being planned by a hierarchy which did not know how it felt to be an Austrian Protestant, and from being executed by a clergy better drilled in giving safe answers than in producing results. The bishop of Passau's instructions to his missionaries required them to brush up their knowledge of agriculture and rural life and to be 'affabiles, urbani, suaves, ab ira alieni…sermone & moribus hilares'. To guide them straight to the market for their wares, an entertaining profile of the secret Lutheran (*signa diagnostica occultorum Lutheranorum*) was included. Beginning with slack attendance at mass and ending with eating meat or pork fat on prohibited days 'sub praetentu oblivionis, voracitatis aut simulatione magnae paupertatis', this would hardly have distinguished a Protestant from the average, carnal, rural Catholic. The missionaries were also instructed to take advantage of the indiscretions of children and to

[24] SLG MS HS XIII.1 nos. 544, 656–7, 687–8, 709, 712, 718, 728.

[25] Zwiedineck-Südenhorst, 'Die religiöse Bewegung', *AÖG* 53/ii (1875) 468–9, 511–15. Cf. DG MS xv b 23, Religionsberichte Protestantismus 1731–5, bishop of Seckau to the Emperor, 3 August, 2 October 1731.

[26] SLG MS HS XIII.1 nos. 534 (there were others from Ortenburg, Bavaria, nos. 459, 561), 1295, 1313. A revival in the Upper Murtal, 1772–4, brought down a religious commission. F. Ilwof, *Der Protestantismus in Steiermark, Kärnten und Krain*…(Graz, 1900) 222.

hoodwink their parents. If, after preaching on the Trinity, in-carnation, Advent, the Holy Spirit, the institution of baptism or the eucharist or any other articles held in common by Catholics and Lutherans, they asked a suspect whether he believed these truths and received the expected confident affirmative answer, they should instantly add 'What about purgatory and the invocation of the saints?' Any hesitation would instantly betray the heretic.[27] Prot-estant ingenuity was not so easily circumvented. The advice from Ortenburg, a Protestant county in Bavaria to which Protestants from Upper Austria resorted for communion, was that the domestic religious instruction of children should cease while they were at school, while the demands of survival had taught the Protestants of the Upper Ennstal to manage the catechism better than their Catholic neighbours. The Catholic missionaries, by contrast, took their cue from their bishop; the best method of conversion, they informed him with depressing unanimity, was 'praescripta mansu-etudo et patientia'. Prescription was the limit of their inspiration.[28]

The second failure of Catholic imagination casts a good deal of light on the inner nature of the Austrian Protestant community. The authorities in church and state were the victims to an extraordinary degree of the myth that Protestantism was the religion of a book. Hence the endless discussions in the documents and the secondary works on how far the troubles in Styria and Carinthia were the work of Prussian agents; hence the fact that, overwhelmingly, the largest item in the indexes to the *Religionsakten* at Graz is the entry *Bücher*; hence also the mountains of repetitive information about the literature accumulated by peasants in holes and corners. Of course, if books had not mattered to the Austrian Protestants, they would not have been part of their ordinary commerce with the outside world, the stock in trade of Ramsauer cattle dealers at Regensburg, of artisans on their travels and the host of itinerant pedlars catering for the housewife's needs and bringing with them Protestant books with the image of the Virgin on the title-page and bogus Catholic approbations and places of origin.[29] The principal sources of supply were Württemberg and Nuremberg, a town once the base of Josef Schaitberger and later that of an interesting merchant who forms a

---

[27] The instructions, dated 1752, are preserved in SLG Box 349, Religions Acta 1752–3, no. 272.

[28] Innumerable missionaries' reports are to be found in SLG Box 350, Religious Acta.

[29] Paul Dedic, 'Die Einschmuggelung lutherischer Bücher nach Kärnten...', *JGGPÖ* 60 (1939) 126, 174; 'Die Massnahmen Maria Theresias', *JGGPÖ* 61 (1940) 110, 113; 'Geheimprotestantismus in Schladming' 60.

link between the first and second phases of the Protestant revival,
Johann Tobias Kiessling (1742–1824). Converted by revival preaching and contact with Salzburger exiles, he devoted himself to getting
books into Upper and Inner Austria in the course of his normal
business in herbs, spices and drugs, and through other channels; he
contributed notably to the founding of the Deutsche Christentums-
gesellschaft and to the reconstruction of Protestant church life in
Austria after the Patent of Toleration.

Austrian Protestants required books of a limited range and used
them in a special way. The bitter resistance of the *Toleranzgemeinden*
to the introduction of the new hymn-books on the grounds that they
were beyond their level of reading-readiness, and their resistance to
the education of their children beyond the point where they could
continue the family tradition of reading the prayers of Habermann
and other devotional works,[30] cast a vivid light upon the role of books
during the years of persecution. Reading, to the old Protestant
peasantry, was a process of deciphering a text heard from childhood
up, a matter of the ear as much as the eye. Those texts, as with
Protestant readers everywhere, had been predominantly devotional
texts. Catechising, which had been a ministerial function, dropped
out. What counted were hymn-books from a variety of sources –
though even here the Austrians' partial independence of the printed
word is attested by the survival of manuscript hymn-books, the
overwhelming bulk of whose contents are to be found in no published
collection – books of prayers and devotions on which family piety
could be sustained (Habermann was the most popular, and there
were also indigenous manuscript collections), Schaitberger, sermons
of Luther and Spangenberg and theological writers like Johann
Arndt who had most given themselves to sustaining practical piety.
Carinthia seems to have been too far south to benefit from the
reception of English Puritanism which was notable in Bohemia. The
Bible came fairly well down the reading list, and, within the Bible the
Book of Revelation was first in importance, followed by the Psalms,
the Gospels and Genesis;[31] strikingly absent are the epistles of Paul,
and especially Romans, on which the founders of Protestant theology
had leaned so heavily. The secret Protestants used those scriptures

---

[30] Franz Reischer, *Die Toleranzgemeinden Kärntens nach einem Visitationsbericht vom Jahre 1786*
(Klagenfurt, 1965) 57.
[31] Oscar Sakrausky, 'Das evangelische geistliche Lied in Kärnten', *Carinthia I* 171 (1981)
271–87; 'Evangelisches Glaubensleben im Gailtal...', *Carinthia I* 171 (1981) 191.

which spoke most directly to their condition and were not too hard to read.

Doblhof, Maria Theresa's commissioner in Carinthia, reported to her in some vexation in 1752: 'Many of these people ... *in Dogmate* are not of the same opinion, each believes what he learned from his parents or read piecemeal in books'. The truth was that the bearer of Austrian Protestantism was not now the church, nor the book, but the family or at any rate the clan (*Sippe*). This is why the pastors often had a difficult time of it when they returned after 1781 and also why the problem which perplexes Austrian Protestant historians, why one valley should stay Protestant and the next not, is not really a problem; it is like those other corporate decisions, buried in the depths of clan rancour which, at the English Reformation, led alternate side valleys in the Pennines to stay Catholic or go Protestant. This is why the manuscript hymn collections show (as Doblhof observed) doctrinal untidiness and evidence even of Protestant–Catholic syncretism at the edges, but show, also, a sustained capacity to translate the original Reformation emphasis on justification into a personal devotion to the Saviour; and it is why a tenderness of piety like that of the Silesians developed here. It was why Austrian Protestantism kept free of the class distinctions of Protestantism in Germany and Hungary,[32] and why what happened when Maria Theresa's government became abnormally oppressive in the early 1750s was not conspiracy, but revival accompanied by a degree of violence and obscenity against the religious statues which were among the obtrusive new features of the Austrian Baroque.[33]

The lessons taught in Silesia, Upper Lusatia, Bohemia and Salzburg, that Protestant communities, fearful for their future, could pull themselves up by their bootstraps and generate an enthusiastic piety not characteristic of the churches of the Augsburg or Helvetic Confessions, lessons which had been taken to heart as far away as Wales, Scotland, England and the northern and middle colonies of America, were now embraced in Styria and Carinthia. There was, for example, a sudden expansion of the movement in Stadel, Upper Styria, where 380 persons suddenly confessed the evangelical faith. The first effect of the Catholic mission in the Ennstal in 1751 was that 200 parishioners declared themselves Lutherans, saying that 'they

[32] J. C. Edelmann, *Selbstbiographie* in *Sämtliche Schriften* (12 vols. Bad Constant, 1969–76) XII:82–5. Cf. *Evangelisch im Burgenland* (Eisenstadt, 1981) 26.
[33] SLG MS HS XIII.1 nos. 125, 127 (and many subsequent papers about Gewiessler), 135; *AHE* 1:605–6.

had formerly had a dead faith, but now a living one, and went home singing and rejoicing'; and they had their peasant preachers too. Revival is also the reason why secret Protestantism issued, not in the Lutheran Orthodoxy of even Schaitberger, and certainly not in the Pietism of Halle or Württemberg, but in 'an awakened Christianity'[34] of a rather unconfessional character, a religion strong enough after all its trials to be capable, with foreign help, of creating a church system, and providing the substance of its life till the end of the nineteenth century.

### HUNGARY

There were four ways in which the Austrian Protestants might confront their harsh predicament – they might accept assimilation; they might attempt flight to a less adverse environment; they might draw comfort and courage from apocalyptic fantasies; or they might fan the embers of religious conviction in revival. Each of these courses was accepted by some Austrian Protestants, many of whom indeed attempted to combine more than one option. It is worth noting that the same intolerant policies were pursued by the Habsburgs in Hungary with a desperate violence deep into the eighteenth century, but with a different result; and that the reaction of the Hungarian Protestants was differently balanced from that in Austria.

The Hungarians retained their church system, under whatever difficulties, and kept a foothold in those social strata with access to power; they had less need for radical departures from the past in order to hold on in a whirlpool in which Catholicism was never as unequivocally equated with Habsburg loyalty as it was outside the Kingdom of St Stephen. Hungary, therefore, had an age of Orthodoxy in a full-blooded sense in which the Austrians did not, and the hirsute and rebarbative bishops of the Siebenbürger Saxons could keep up a war on three fronts against popery, Pietism and Calvinism, long after the Orthodox dinosaurs of Germany had died out. Revival was not a characteristic of Hungarian Protestantism; indeed the only instance in which a religious establishment took up with revival with any enthusiasm was in New England, and even there the association lasted hardly a decade. Hungary represented the rule rather than the exception.

---

[34] A phrase of the Protestant bishop Sakrausky: 'The history of our evangelical church in Austria, though sometimes reduced to small core areas, may be described as the history of a very intensive, decisive and awakened (*erweckten*) Christianity.' *Carinthia I* 171 (1981) 27.

The Hungarian situation was not absolutely different from that in Austria; it was rather that the Hungarians balanced their options differently. It was a great lay age in the Hungarian churches; the growth point among them was also the so-called 'widowed' congregations without a pastor which appeared to the tune of over 1,000 under the Toleration Patent, and which had been kept going by the sort of informal means which were all the Austrians had. The Hungarians also put Philip Doddridge into Magyar dress, and were capable, under the Toleration Patent, of one remarkable missionary effort. Despite all the language difficulties, they got Bohemian and Moravian Protestantism organised again by supplying sixty ministers. But the balance between all this and apocalyptic was quite different. When organised Protestantism collapsed in Bohemia in the Thirty Years War Bohemians took refuge in Hungary and obtained a hearing for their pipedreams of revenge upon the Habsburgs. Of Nikolaus Drabik, who identified the Papacy and the house of Habsburg as Antichrist and Babylon, and forecast their downfall at the hands first of Sweden and then the princes of Siebenbürgen, it was said by a contemporary that 'it is hard to say whether Drabik has falsified his dreams, or whether he is only lied to by them. But it is significant for his personal worth that he was only rational when dreaming.'[35] Hungarian Protestantism was hard-pressed enough without sacrificing reason to these delusions, but the sacrifice was made on a large scale; and when the Reformed got over their eschatological fantasies, they began, like the Reformed elsewhere, a long slide into rationalism.

The Austrians too were addicted to the Book of Revelation, and when, after the Toleration Patent, they built their churches, the highest figure above the altar was commonly the lamb with the flag of victory and the book of the seven seals. That Austrian Protestantism survived to build its altars, however, was due to the fact that in desperation its energies went not into rebellion, but into revival on this side of the apocalypse. Here the Protestants of Salzburg and Austria made a distinctive contribution to the old problem of christianising successive generations which was not lost on their fellows elsewhere.

[35] Béla Obál, *Die Religionspolitik in Ungarn ... während der Regierung Leopold I* (Halle, 1910) 14–17.

# CHAPTER 4

# Zinzendorf and the Moravians

## ZINZENDORF'S RELATIONS WITH SILESIA AND SALZBURG

Zinzendorf's attitude towards the revivals in Silesia and Salzburg was as ambivalent as his attitudes towards most other things. Himself the grandson of an Austrian Protestant émigré, he could not fail to cherish the cause of Protestant survival in the Habsburg lands, even if the peopling of the estate he bought at Berthelsdorf in Upper Lusatia had not depended on it. He was closely connected with the Pietist nobility of Silesia, and also for many years with Steinmetz, the apostle of Teschen. He defended hard-pressed Pietist pastors in Silesia, took up the cause of the Schwenckfelders with the Imperial government, and in 1727 found them a temporary asylum in Herrnhut. But he had a difficult tightrope to walk.[1] He was exposed to plausible charges that he made Silesians (and Upper Lusatians) discontented with their pastors, and, in attacking Steinmetz and his colleagues, the Jesuits made the best of the accusation that he, Scheffer and Schwedler were introducing a new religion into Silesia, not entitled to toleration under the Westphalia settlement.[2] Nor were Zinzendorf's relations with the church and government of Saxony such as to make him desire the hostile attention of that government's patron, the Emperor. The troubles in Moravia which coincided with the great exodus from Salzburg brought on him fresh rebukes from the Emperor, and for years Zinzendorf instructed his sympathisers in Silesia to live quietly and obediently under the authorities. His apologists maintained that he could not possibly make common cause with separatists and fanatics, or with 'Bohemian, Austrian, Carinthian, Salzburger nor any other kind of emigrants, apart from

---

[1] With friend and foe alike Zinzendorf had a reputation for political dissimulation. *ZW* Series 2 IX:61; X:302–3.
[2] *ZW* Series 2 XIV/i:150; XIV/ii: *passim*.

those who have a living experience of the Saviour in their souls and who are of the same spirit with us'.[3] A vein of Silesian spirituality was part of Zinzendorf's make-up, but it did not make political relations easier to manage. In the 1720s Christian David was getting up pro-Prussian sentiment in Silesia, and he also inflamed the uneasy relations between Zinzendorf and the great house of Promnitz of Sorau, which was deeply involved in the Silesian Protestant cause.[4] Embarrassments continued after the Prussian conquest. Annexation was followed by a peasant revolt led by the Poles, and, then, while Zinzendorf was in America, an apparently favourable agreement was negotiated with Frederick the Great by the devout Count Balthasar Friedrich von Promnitz-Halbau, one of the lateral descendants of the Promnitz family, for establishing Moravian settlements in Silesia. What infuriated Zinzendorf on his return was that these communities were subject to no consistory, i.e. were to be regarded as dissenting bodies. Consumed at that time with the idea that his community might retain interconfessional status as a series of 'Tropuses' within the historic confessions, Zinzendorf found this a bitter pill. Prolonged conflict was avoided by Balthasar's unexpected death in 1744; by 1751 Zinzendorf could proudly deduce the 'peculiar right' of children 'to praise our Saviour (for of such is ye Kingdom of Heaven)'[5] and note that the survivors of the children's prayer-meetings forty years before were still in his Silesian congregations.

It was a similar story with the Salzburgers. Zinzendorf must avoid the blaze of publicity which accompanied the Salzburger emigration. But the Salzburgers were too much in the count's line of business to leave alone. As early as April 1728, one of the most gifted of the Herrnhuters, Melchior Nitschmann, together with Georg Schmidt, set out to 'serve the awakened Salzburgers with Protestant encouragement'. They were, however, taken prisoner on the way at Eisenberg in Bohemia. Zinzendorf's protestations to the Imperial authorities that they had no 'intention of persuading men to change from one religion to another' or to get people out of the country, cut very little ice, and Nitschmann died in custody the following year. The next opportunity came when the Salzburger emigration was in full swing. The count's most independent co-adjutor, Christian

---

[3] *ZW* Series 2 xi: 189, 221; *Ergänzungsband* iv: 24–30, 95–6, Vorrede § 12.
[4] E. Teufel, 'Die Beziehungen zwischen Herrnhut und Sorau von 1727 bis 7145', *JBKg* 20 (1925) 172–84.
[5] *ZW* Series 2 xii: 503–12; *AHE* 8: 66–70; MCH MS Gemeinhaus Diary 1751, Week 4.

David, made contact with two large bands of the emigrants on their way to Nuremberg. He found one of their own number, Schmidt by name, admonishing them that the emigration would come to nothing unless they each had a living experience of Jesus in the soul. David supported this with his own testimony and began to distribute among them three hundred copies of the count's controversial edition of the Bible, printed at Ebersdorf. Nothing could have been less welcome to local authorities bent on turning the emigration into a Lutheran demonstration, and they confiscated as many as they could lay hands on. In the following year another deputation was sent to the Salzburgers on the march, Spangenberg artlessly reporting that Zinzendorf 'believed that if some of the Moravian Brethren who had been in similar circumstances to the Salzburgers, could speak with them of the ground of their hope, it would be very useful'.[6] He then negotiated with the king of Prussia about building the exiles an Orphan House in Livonia. The doors to the Salzburgers thus closed in the principality itself, and closed again in Nuremberg, seemed likely to open in the Baltic. Thither the Brethren pursued them, and there they achieved the most spectacular success of all their missions, though not primarily among the exiles.

## ZINZENDORF'S EDUCATION AND VIEWS

Who was the Count Nikolaus Ludwig von Zinzendorf, and why was he casting his net so wide? And what was his relation to the forces of religious revival, resistance and emigration in Central Europe? These questions are important, for what became the Renewed Unity of the Brethren – 'Moravianism' in the usual English shorthand – arose from the conjunction of a small group of German-speaking Protestant emigrants from Bohemia and Moravia with a much larger number of religious refugees of other sorts attracted by the religious toleration which became available at Herrnhut, and with Zinzendorf himself. He had purchased the Berthelsdorf estate on which they settled, and came to pursue his own religious objectives through the motley flock he gathered, as they in turn pursued their objectives through him. By the 1740s writing against the Moravians had become a major intellectual industry, and some at least of the animosity they evoked was due to the difficulty of pinning them

---

[6] *ZW* Series 2 III:753: IV:800–1; H. Beck, 'Herrnhuter und Salzburger vor 250 Jahren: Nürnberger Bibelaktion 1732', *UF 12* (1982) 45–73.

down, there being some solid evidence for all the views of a movement of heterogeneous origin: for the view of some, though not all, of its original adherents that it was a rebirth of the old Unity of the Brethren, a body which had succumbed to the violent pressure of the Counter-Reformation in its old heartlands of Bohemia and Moravia; for the views of its Orthodox opponents that it was either a new sect with no right to toleration in the Empire, or 'indifferentist', i.e. denying the ultimate importance of confessional loyalty on the way to salvation; for the (usual) view of Zinzendorf himself that it was an interconfessional movement, though he had no scruple in accepting an act of the British parliament on behalf of his followers in America in 1749 which claimed that the Unity was 'an antient apostolical and episcopal church'.

In Zinzendorf himself two important features of the Protestant situation in Germany were linked, though perhaps not united. There was the tradition of a family which had grown great in the struggle against the Turks – Zinzendorf himself retained connexions with the Jansenist circle around Prince Eugene[7] – but had finally put confessional solidarity with the Protestants before service with the Habsburgs or the defence of Christendom against the heathen. His grandfather had joined the flight of the Protestant aristocracy from Austria in 1661; his father had become a privy councillor in Saxony, but died in 1700 less than two months after Nikolaus was born. Four years later his mother, Charlotte Justine, née baroness of Gersdorf, married the Prussian Field-Marshal Dubislav Gneomar von Natzmer, like herself a supporter of the Francke foundations at Halle, and left the boy to be brought up by her mother, Henriette Katherina von Gersdorf, née baroness of Friesen. Zinzendorf's upbringing was doubly unusual; he was raised almost exclusively in the company of women the chief of whom was two generations older than himself, and was to boot a remarkable blue-stocking possessed of all manner of languages, a shrewd and strenuous politician in her own right. Her property at Gross Hennersdorf, just north of the Bohemian border, was in Upper Lusatia, Saxony's most recently acquired and restive province. As a Friesen she was in the thick of its politics on two fronts; she shared in the aristocratic resistance to the centralising policies pursued by the Electors of Saxony, now kings of Poland, and held the family view that the enserfed Slavonic populations of the province,

---

[7] *ZW* Series 2 XII: 769.

the Wends and Sorbs, would not be got to acceptable shape without new methods, administrative, educational and religious. For these material was eventually drawn from Halle.[8] Henriette Katherina was not altogether successful in transmitting this heritage to her grandson. She failed to turn him into a politician; but there is no doubt that his markedly aristocratic profile owed much to her milieu. Unlike her daughter, Henriette Katherina was never a slavish adherent of Halle;[9] her grandson was always independent of the Halle interest, and finally hostile to it. He found his own way of dealing with the Wends, who proved to be good material for religious revival. Above all, a man who but for the untimely deaths of his father and grandfather would have been brought up in court society in Dresden became an adopted Lusatian. Spangenberg declared that he loved both the natural and political peculiarities of Upper Lusatia (which meant that he had an ingrained love of independence), and as late as 1753 a German tourist in London was surprised to hear him preaching at the Fetter Lane chapel in 'a quite simple and common Upper Lusatian dialect'.[10]

Zinzendorf's adult testimony to his religious outlook as a young man is all coloured by the great conflict between his own movement and that of Halle which began in the 1730s. Cranz, the official historian of the Brethren, did his best to obliterate the Hallesian background to their story, and thus achieved a smoother transition from what he called the ancient to the modern history of the Brethren than the facts warranted. Zinzendorf's family connexions ensured that he would be sent to Halle for part of his education; he was impressed by the preaching there, and still more by the sense of being at the hub of a worldwide movement of grace. His later claims that Halle could not accommodate a child of his abnormal religious virtuosity (he was nine when he went up), but that he perceived the hollowness of the children's revivals in which Halle claimed such

---

[8] For the von Gersdorf family, W. von Boetticher, *Geschichte des Oberlausitzschen Adels und seiner Güter, 1635–1815* (4 vols. Görlitz, 1912–23) 1:424–608; C. Knauthe, *Derer Oberlausitzer Sorbwenden umständliche Kirchengeschichte* ed. R. Olesch (Cologne &c., 1980); A. Mietzschke, 'Lusatica aus dem Anfang des 18. Jahrhunderts', *ZSP* 17/ii (1941) 123–42.

[9] Henriette Katherina had known Spener as well as the Hallesians; Hochmann von Hochenau, the revivalist, had been a tutor in the family; she gave financial support to the chiliast Petersen. Zinzendorf said of her (as he might have said of that other Lusatian, Jakob Böhme, or of himself) that she adhered to the religion of the heart and 'knew no distinction between the Catholic, Lutheran and Reformed religion'. O. Uttendörfer, *Zinzendorf und die Mystik* ([East] Berlin, 1950) 22–3.

[10] *ZW* Series 2 ii:178; E. Vehse, *Geschichte der deutschen Höfe seit der Reformation* (48 vols. Hamburg, 1851–60) xxxiv:71.

expertise, are, at least *prima facie*, not mutually consistent; and, certainly, out of a revival movement there he gathered a circle of friends who were to form his Order of the Grain of Mustard Seed, his international and interconfessional mission to the whole church.[11] His poems suggest that at this time he combined a sort of Bernardine Christ-mysticism and the contemplation of the sufferings of the Saviour with an impulse to conversion.[12]

From Halle Zinzendorf went on to the Orthodox fortress of Wittenberg where a man of his ilk was something out of the ordinary, and where he was deeply disturbed by venomous attacks on Pietism. With much exaggeration he later claimed to have left 'with Wittenberg theory and Halle practice'. In fact much of his time seems to have been spent on 'things indifferent', on dancing, billiards, balloons, and, worst of all, gambling. But he did some serious study, was impressed by some of the Orthodox theologians, joined a movement to restore union in the church, and formed an Order of the Slaves of Virtue on the model of the English SPG which rejected 'things different' entirely.

The Grand Tour which followed helped to define things which had long been in his mind. In the great contests between the Orthodox and the Pietists over the mystical hymns in the Halle hymn-book he took the part of the latter, and began to go into mysticism, even contending for the possibility of a life without conscious sin. A visit to Holland opened his mind to the virtues of religious toleration, one of the great themes of his life thereafter.[13] A stay in Paris improved his acquaintance with the religious struggles of the Jansenists, Mme Guyon and Fénelon, and brought him the friendship of Cardinal de Noailles, who was later a member of the Order of the Grain of Mustard Seed, and godfather to two of his children. It brought also an exaggerated impression of the amount of money to be made out of Law's Bubble. His journey convinced him that God had his true followers in every confession and that he should never adopt a party standpoint.[14] He had come round to the mystical outlook of the radical Pietist Gottfried Arnold.

Between 1721 and 1727 Zinzendorf obtained an independent position, and, most importantly, in 1722 married Erdmuthe Doro-

---

[11] *ZW Ergänzungsband* III:654; Series 2 XII:174–5, 351.
[12] Uttendörfer, *Zinzendorf und die Mystik* 27.
[13] S. Nielsen, *Intoleranz und Toleranz bei Zinzendorf* (3 vols. Hamburg, 1952–60).
[14] O. Uttendörfer, *Alt-Herrnhut* (Herrnhut, 1925) 144; Herrnhut MSS R20 A1 §7.

thea, Countess Reuss of Ebersdorf. She was very much his second choice as a wife, but she answered his immediate need for emancipation from his grandmother, and proved an admirable helpmate in his work. In the forties Zinzendorf began to behave shabbily towards her, excluded her from the circle in his confidence, and let it be known that after her death he intended to marry one of the Moravians, Anna Nitschmann;[15] but in the early years she brought him invaluable financial assistance, and her head for business, very much better than his own, was sorely missed when he turned elsewhere. The one thing beyond her power was to raise any of her six sons to adult years, though Christian Renatus almost reached his fifteenth birthday. Marriage into the house of Ebersdorf appeared to confirm Zinzendorf's connexion with that network of Imperial counts which sustained the Pietist enterprise. His wife's grandmother had been a highly prized friend of Spener, and the Ebersdorf court was in the inner circle of the policy-makers to the institutions at Halle, maintaining connexions across the Empire from the Wetterau to Silesia. Reputed to be the smallest principality in the Empire, it yet had its Orphan House, which still stands. And Ebersdorf offered a pattern of Christian existence of the sort for which Zinzendorf was now looking. It was not a parish in its own right, and the castle congregation separated easily from the parish church, inviting preachers of their own like the revivalist Hochmann von Hochenau. The important positions at the Ebersdorf court were filled by Christians without respect to sect or party, and it proved possible to hold them together harmoniously in the castle congregation on the basis of a common love of the Saviour. This model deeply impressed Zinzendorf; 'Philadelphian love' was what he hoped for when he built a house for himself and his wife at Herrnhut. As he wrote in 1727: 'Little as I desire that born Lutherans should go over to other sects, I cannot conceive that Catholics, Reformed and separatists who have united with us in love must become Lutheran'. And if Herrnhut never quite became a Philadelphia, the Ebersdorf *ecclesiola* eventually joined the Renewed Unity of the Brethren.

Zinzendorf's Philadelphian ideals were to be realised on an estate at Berthelsdorf which he purchased from his grandmother. His progress towards them was at first inhibited less by the dramatic events which

---

[15] E. Beyreuther, *Der junge Zinzendorf* (2nd edn Marburg, 1957) 212–22; *ZW* Series 3 III:342–84, 428, 268.

took place there than by severe intellectual doubts, the core of which, as for many of his generation, lay in the relation of the Creator to his creation. Like many of the original Halle generation he was at first much attracted to Leibniz (and especially his *Theodicy*); but he had difficulties with philosophy in general and system in particular. Forcing religion into a fine-spun rational harmony was no substitute for faith, indeed it made faith harder by creating the impression that belief was a mathematical problem. The world was not only irrational, it was evil; and philosophy transformed human need into ignorance, and Christian perfection into knowledge.[16] Some relief was provided by that stormy petrel of the early Enlightenment, Pierre Bayle, whom Zinzendorf studied assiduously in 1727 and came to admire. Bayle convinced him of the divorce both in style and substance between philosophy and theology: 'I believe and teach: philosophy has nothing to do with theology... Let people clarify their minds with philosophy as long as they like, but tell them that as soon as they wish to become theologians they must become children and idiots'.[17] The hazards of all this were encountered during the 'time of sifting' (on which see pp. 155–8) in the later forties, but for the moment it protected faith and the Living God against a mechanistic view of the universe and against the Orthodox insistence on the literal inspiration of the Bible.[18] Zinzendorf abandoned his political career to sort out the problems on his estates created by the refugees brought in by Christian David; but he continued to pursue his religious aims, different as they were from those of his new settlers.

## CHRISTIAN DAVID AND THE FOUNDATION OF HERRNHUT

Christian David, who brought the first Moravian settlers to Zinzendorf's Berthelsdorf estate in 1722, was a difficult but very remarkable man. A carpenter from Senftleben in Moravia, he was the son of a Czech father and a German mother, both poor and both strict Catholics. By nature a man of pronounced independence of mind, he took on board many of the animosities created by the Habsburg

---

[16] P. Baumgart, 'Leibniz und der Pietismus: Universale Reformbestrebungen um 1700', *Archiv für Kulturgeschichte* 48 (1966) 364–86; *ZW Hauptschriften* III:xiii, 179–80, 246–7; I (*Teutsche Socrates* Preface, first footnote n.p.); v/i:337–8, v/ii:337.

[17] *ZW Ergänzungsband* I:100.

[18] Zinzendorf noted that the apostles, who habitually quoted the OT scriptures from the Septuagint, could hardly have held the doctrine of verbal inspiration. Cf. E. Beyreuther, *Studien zur Theologie Zinzendorfs* (Neukirchen, 1962) 74–108.

attempt to recatholicise Bohemia, and, by the migratory nature of his trade, obtained the opportunity to sample alternatives to his parents' Catholicism. He first made contact with Protestantism in Berlin;[19] and in Görlitz, one of the six towns of Upper Lusatia, where a fire had created plenty of work for carpenters, he met Scheffer and Schwedler, the evangelists who were getting Protestants out of Silesia. After a prolonged spiritual struggle in which he almost became a Jew, and much Bible study, he was converted to strong Protestant convictions. David's new circle put him in touch with villages in Moravia where revivals were breaking out under local influences and the preaching of Steinmetz at Teschen; with Steinmetz, who discouraged him from bringing out emigrants until he had a prospective refuge where the Christian life could be effectively cultivated; and with Zinzendorf himself, who was considering purchasing the estate at Berthelsdorf from his grandmother with just such a view. One of the immediate fruits of the purchase was that another of David's Görlitz contacts, Richard Rothe, was appointed by the count to the Berthelsdorf living, a nomination which provided the spiritual guarantees for which Steinmetz had been looking. David immediately disappeared to comfort secret believers in his homeland with the news that they need no longer look for liberty to Hungary and Siebenbürgen. The Bohemian crisis was coming to a head. David's contacts were limited to three villages, Sehlen, Zauchtental and Kunwald; they were peculiar in that before the Thirty Years War they had been strong centres of the generally weak German branch of the mainly Czech church of the Brethren.[20] Nevertheless the handful of refugees brought by David, via Schwedler in Niederwiesa and Scheffer in Görlitz, to Berthelsdorf in 1722 were to leave an indelible mark on the history of Protestantism. Zinzendorf was away, but Heitz, his Swiss estate manager, saw the possibility of creating a craft village out of them, and settled them at the far end of the estate around the main road from Zittau to Löbau. On 17 June 1722, Christian David felled the first tree for the first house in what became the village of Herrnhut.

The population of Herrnhut reached 300 by 1727 and 600 by 1734 despite the fact that in 1732, under severe pressure from the Emperor, the Saxon government had forbidden the reception of any more

---

[19] Where he served with the Prussian army sent to wrest Stralsund from Charles XII of Sweden.

[20] *ZW* Series 2 XII: 7–8.

Moravian emigrants. The lot of the new arrivals, faced with the problems of finding themselves housing, work and subsistence, was severe poverty, aggravated by an atmosphere of crisis, external and internal. The threats from the Emperor were bound to evoke the sneaking sympathy of all landlords in an Eastern Europe still very short of labour. In this matter the Saxon government had the willing assistance of the Saxon church. Now that the dynasty had turned Catholic, the Lutheran church in Saxony clung more than ever desperately to its rights as an establishment, and had no love for the toleration prevailing on the Berthelsdorf estate. Moreover the parish clergy throughout Upper Lusatia felt the ground quaking beneath their feet. Apart from their old suppressed Slavonic minorities, the Sorbs and Wends, the area was now full of footloose immigrants from Silesia, Bohemia, Moravia and Hungary, some German, many Slav, and when Schwedler and other revivalist preachers were abroad, they would assemble in their thousands from every quarter.[21] Public order and the parish system were at stake.

The Herrnhuters were also much divided among themselves. Of even the first 300 settlers only half were Moravians. Though well-known figures among them were tradesmen – Christian David and David Nitschmann carpenters, the other David Nitschmann a weaver with six looms, Augustin and Wenzel Neisser cutlers – the bulk were peasants who had had to forsake everything to escape. But the majority of the non-Moravian colonists were artisans, weavers, shoemakers, potters, tailors, turners and the like. And the disparity of origin, social character and religious belief could only be exacerbated by Zinzendorf's recruiting campaigns in Silesia.[22] Religion divided even the Moravians. As the Lutheran Orthodox polemicists insisted, the old Unity of the Brethren had been nearer the Reformed than the Lutheran churches. And the key Moravian with no roots in the old Unity, Christian David, became enamoured of the doctrines of the count's Zurich-Reformed manager, J. G. Heitz. Heitz was not a man for compromise with either the count or Rothe, the incumbent he had appointed. The friction ended with Heitz's returning to Switzerland and rejecting all inducements to come back, and with David's being attracted by the preaching of an enthusiastic separatist,

[21]  E. Beyreuther, *Zinzendorf und die sich allhier beisammen finden* (Marburg, 1959) 155; *ZW* Series 2 XI: 143; Arend Bucholz, *Die Geschichte der Familie Lessing* (2 vols. Berlin, 1909) 1: 91, 98, 109–14. For the further history of the Bohemian congregations in Saxony, *UN* 1741 769–77.
[22]  For the geographical origins of the early settlers at Herrnhut, Herrnhut MSS R6 Aa 17.

Johann Siegmund Krüger. The Moravians divided into a Lutheran party led by the Neisser family and supporting the count and Rothe, and an anti-church group, led by David, wishing to separate itself from the parish.

Given the external threats to Herrnhut, nothing could have embarrassed Zinzendorf more than the emergence of separatism. He came back to reside on the estate, imposed a village constitution, and a religious constitution which should be coordinated into the church structure of the province. This included bands, in which the settlers could share their religious experience. The lay office of elder was revived, and David was chosen one of the twelve. Soon afterwards he was elected by lot one of the four senior elders (*Oberältesten*). The dangers were real for, as the Herrnhut diary records,[23] Christian David moved out of the village, built a new hut, dug his own well, and took to asking what use it had been for him to risk his life bringing souls out of popery, if they were to be entangled in Lutheranism, and, by being kept from conversion, made doubly children of hell.

### THE REVIVAL OF 1727

Herrnhut could not now be saved by seigneurial action alone. But religious revival was in the air, originating in Silesia, spreading in Upper Lusatia amongst Germans, Wends and Czechs, concentrated in the Moravians' own parish by the increasing resonance of the preaching of Richard Rothe. The emotional temperature in Herrnhut was raised by attempts at reconciliation, and by the visits of inflammatory preachers like Liberda and Schwedler; overspill at the parish church at Berthelsdorf reached the point where services had to be duplicated in Herrnhut. Zinzendorf also read the Herrnhuters a German translation of a history of the Bohemian and Moravian Brethren which he had brought from Silesia, from which they concluded that, in the creation of lay offices, they had hit on the principle of the old Unity of the Brethren – 'they were, so to speak, under their fathers' cloud of grace, baptised with their spirit and fire into one body'. News came of great awakenings in Silesia, and signs and wonders began to appear in Herrnhut – 'a great grace was amongst them and in the whole district'. Christian David began to hold men's Bible classes; there were all-night prayer-meetings on the

---

[23] The Herrnhut diary, May–August 1727, is printed in *Zinzendorf und die Herrnhuter Brüder* ed. H.-C. Hahn & H. Reichel (Hamburg, 1977) 95–108.

Hutberg. It needed only one more sign of the recent revivalist past, an intense spirit of prayer among the children, to precipitate one of the most remarkable of all religious revivals.

It began with the personal crisis of an eleven-year-old girl, Susanne Kühnel. Shortly before she had been present at her mother's death-bed, and had been deeply moved by the evident joy with which she had surrendered her life to her Lord. The girl perceived that her mother had something which she lacked, and a powerful conversion struggle was added to her natural distress at personal loss. For three days and nights her distress and prayers lay upon the whole community. Then at one in the morning she awakened her father with the words, 'Father, I am now a child of God, now I know how it was and will still be with my mother.' Three other girls, friends of hers, had been through the same struggle and received the same experience in the same night. The count had them brought to him, fell upon his knees and prayed with them. A dramatic first communion for two of the girls followed, to which the whole community turned out with much weeping and singing. The movement now spread to the adults, and the record in the Herrnhut diary carried self-conscious echoes of the great events in Silesia twenty years before.

On 23 August such an impulse of prayer came upon the boys and girls that it was not possible to hear them without heartfelt emotion, and through Susanne Kühnel an extraordinary movement arose in their assembly which became daily more true and serious. In particular there was to be heard on the night of 29 August from ten at night till one in the morning a heart-rending praying and singing by the girls of Berthelsdorf and Herrnhut upon the Hutberg. At the same time the boys were at prayer in other places. So powerful a spirit prevailed among the children as is beyond words to express.[24]

In this tidal wave of emotion the community at Herrnhut overcame the forces of disintegration in their midst, accepted the elaborate arrangements which Zinzendorf made for pastoral oversight, and discovered a usable past from which the count himself was not allowed to escape. Finding a copy of Comenius's history of the Brethren in Zittau town-library, the Moravians concluded that they had stumbled on the essence of their old church discipline:

So they resolved to stick by it and in the future. Several times afterwards, and especially in 1728 and 1731, the question arose amongst them whether

[24] Beyreuther, *Zinzendorf und die sich allhier...finden* 206–7.

for the sake of peace and to avoid defamation and persecution, they should not abandon their peculiar institutions. But the Moravian Brethren always rejected this and pressed forward the more zealously completely to re-establish the old constitution of the Brethren.[25]

Certainly as the kings of Prussia met their match with the Czech emigrants, Zinzendorf met his match with the Germans. He would have to realise his Philadelphian ideals through their objectives, and it was his particular genius to divert them into a mission to the universal church. This change in scenario was once again assisted by events outside Herrnhut.

### CONFLICT WITH THE EMPIRE AND THE GOVERNMENT OF SAXONY

Despite the confusion in Zinzendorf's mind, confusion between him and the Moravians, confusion between the Moravian and the non-Moravian Herrnhuters, confusion among the Moravians themselves and confusion between them and their parish minister, there had so far been very little interference with Herrnhut from the outside. This was partly because Upper Lusatia possessed no consistory of its own, and partly because the Dresden theologians, who might have regarded its statutes as deviating from Lutheran symbols, lacked the machinery to intervene. But on 15 August 1731 the Imperial ambassador at the Saxon court lodged a written complaint from the Emperor Charles VI against Zinzendorf's practice of tempting away his subjects,[26] claiming that Herrnhut sheltered twice as many as in fact it did. The difference between this complaint and others which had been received earlier was that the Emperor was now justifiably alarmed at the way the Salzburg crisis was coming to a head, knew that the chronic peasant unrest in Bohemia might well issue in the open rebellion which began a year later, and was aware that Gross Hennersdorf, the next parish to Berthelsdorf, was being prepared as a staging-post for a great emigration. For good measure he had provided his ambassador with an exact tally of the emigrants from the manors of Kunwald and Neutitschein, whence many of Zinzendorf's settlers had fled.

In March 1732, when the Salzburgers were on the move in their

---

[25] *ZW* Series 2 XI: 142.
[26] G. Meyer, 'Herrnhuts Stellung innerhalb der sächsischen Landeskirche bis 1737', *UF* 2 (1977) 42–3 n. 50a.

tens of thousands, the Emperor complained again, and this time the Saxon government forbade Zinzendorf to receive any more immigrants, and sent down a commission of inquiry under the *Oberamtshauptmann*, von Gersdorf. He concentrated on the questions whether the Moravians had been enticed to Herrnhut, and whether they adhered to one of the religions tolerated in the Empire, and reported his satisfaction with what he had seen. Without waiting for the commission's report to grind its way through the machinery of government, however, Augustus the Strong, king of Poland and elector of Saxony, issued a rescript on 28 October 1732, banishing Zinzendorf and requiring him, on account of his 'shocking and grave behaviour' to sell his property; he is said to have assured the Imperial ambassador that he intended 'to secure Zinzendorf's person and prevent the further growth of his sect'. Plitt, the historian of the Brethren, connected this violent turn with the Czech peasant rebellion. But Zinzendorf's own family thought he had demeaned himself by his dealings with his refugees, and he had few friends and many enemies at court. Among the former were the Gersdorfs of Bautzen and Görlitz, one of whom, a distant cousin, gave Zinzendorf the good advice, which he accepted, to sell his estates to his wife.

The crisis, however, fizzled out. On 1 February 1733 Augustus the Strong died and, in a display of clemency, his successor temporarily suspended the sentence of exile. Only the Silesian Schwenkfelders who had sought refuge at Herrnhut were expelled. But at once negotiations began for bases abroad, first in Denmark, then in Georgia, in case Herrnhut should become untenable. The Moravians had no option but to become a missionary body. Discussions were set on foot for the separation of Herrnhut from the parish of Berthelsdorf, and for installing Friedrich Christoph Steinhofer, a repetent from Tübingen, as minister. None of these proposals succeeded, but in passing they led Zinzendorf to obtain from the theology faculty at Tübingen an opinion to the effect that, presupposing agreement in evangelical doctrine, the Moravians might keep the institutions and doctrine they had possessed for 300 years and might also 'maintain their connexion with the evangelical church', a sort of institutional pluralism which he believed Luther had provided for in the *Deutsche Messe*. This opinion mattered a good deal more to the count than it did to the Moravians, whose consciousness of distinctness had been sharpened by the crisis. Special toleration had been granted them as a body apparently distinct from the established church of the realm.

And Zinzendorf himself divided the colony at Herrnhut into two parts. The first was to consist of exiles from Moravia only who were to adhere strictly to their peculiar institutions, but hold themselves ready for migration at any time. The others could adhere to the Moravian constitution if they wished, but could expect to stay in Herrnhut. When in 1735 David Nitschmann was consecrated bishop by Jablonsky with the written consent of his colleague Christian Sitkov in Thorn, to lead the second group of Moravian settlers to Georgia, a step had been taken which made no difference at all to Herrnhut, but which was calculated to convince others as well as Moravians that the Brethren were now an independent church. Nor did the Lutheran orders which Zinzendorf acquired[27] do anything to strengthen impressions to the contrary.

## ZINZENDORF IS EXILED

The next crisis had international ramifications but originated mainly within Saxony, and not least within Upper Lusatia. One of the consequences of the great revival of 1727 and of the large number of refugees in the province was that notable diaspora work began, and evoked a good deal of animosity, not least among the clergy.[28] There was a general complaint that the newly awakened were poor attenders at church and at communion, and frequently offensive to the parish clergy. In at least fourteen places there was activity of this sort, and in the Bautzen area where there were heavy concentrations of Wends, whole villages were said to be devoted to Herrnhut. There was peculiar venom in the neighbouring town of Zittau. The catechist Häntzschel assailed the Marche hymn-book used at Herrnhut, and incorporated a memorial from the theological faculty at Wittenberg; Zinzendorf produced a new book. Other clergy attacked Polycarp Müller, an adherent of Zinzendorf and later a Moravian bishop, but at that time rector of the Zittauer gymnasium. Others went for Müller's wife, who attended class-meetings with common people and craftsmen. Zinzendorf, however, believed that the final spur to decisive government action against him was applied by Baron von Huldenberg, as it happened, British envoy extraordinary to the

[27] W. R. Ward, 'Pastoral Office and General Priesthood in the Great Awakening' *SCH* 26 (1989) 325–6.

[28] In 1742 the Orthodox press reported that the Herrnhuters were still swarming about Upper Lusatia complaining that 'Luther was indeed a good man, but the Lutherans of today were damned wretches (*Luderaner*) and stank like beasts (*Luder*)'. *AHE* 8:936.

Imperial court at Vienna, who in 1733 inherited from his father property in Upper Lusatia at Neukirch am Hochwald. Two of the clergy in the village were friends of Herrnhut, and there were supposed to be fifty other adherents there, with whom the elder Huldenberg had dealt pretty roughly. His son now made a scene in the Bautzen parliament, and Zinzendorf replied. The Dresden government reactivated the banishment order against Zinzendorf in 1736 while he was in Amsterdam seeking to negotiate a new Moravian settlement in Surinam; this ensured that he could not give evidence before a second commission now sent down to Herrnhut. And this commission, on which the count had no friends, originated in measures taken by the upper consistory against conventicles, dangerous literature and disorders in the Bischofswerda diocese. The Dutch government was warned against Zinzendorf's dangerous principles.[29]

The second commission arrived at Herrnhut in an atmosphere of considerable excitement armed with an agenda of forty-six points. Clergy turned up from local towns in the hope of sinking the Moravians, but could gain no access. The local landowners appeared, and testified that the Herrnhuters were quiet, industrious people, the victims of clerical malice, but in any case not to be intimidated. The end of a very long inquiry was that little was added to the report of 1732, though Löscher is said to have confessed 'to his brothers and sisters' at Herrnhut that they were in doctrine and practice a God-fearing, Christian congregation, with a discipline lacking in the Lutheran church. The commission itself recommended leaving the constitution of Herrhut in place as the community was a financial advantage to the country. But the mood was clearly moving against Zinzendorf. The clergy and town council of Zittau made bitter complaints about the concourse of people to religious meetings around Herrnhut, and were told to deal summarily with those who despised communion, confession and the pastoral office. The Emperor complained again of his subjects being tempted away; but the Saxon government could now claim that they had taken action, that recent refugees had gone to Prussia, that they had got rid of

---

[29] F. S. Hark, 'Der Konflikt der kursächsischen Regierung mit Herrnhut...', *Neues Archiv für sächsische Geschichte und Altertumskunde* 3 (1882) 12–25; *ZW Ergänzungsband* IV: 135; Ferdinand Körner, *Die kursächsische Staatsregierung dem Grafen Zinzendorf und Herrnhut bis 1760 gegenüber* (Leipzig, 1878) 27–31. The Lutheran Orthodox press added to the weight of Huldenberg's complaints by referring to him as envoy of Great Britain and Lüneburg. *AHE* 3:381.

Zinzendorf himself and rebuffed the efforts of his family to bring him back. The Dresden government, indeed, now had substantially what it wanted. A royal decree of 1737 tolerated the *Brüdergemeine* at Herrnhut, so long as they remained within the doctrine of the Augsburg Confession, avoided conventicles, and did not intrude into strange parishes. But the Privy Council reported that 'great care [was] to be taken that Count Zinzendorf, the originator of such disorders, should not be found again in this land'.

MORAVIAN SETTLEMENTS ABROAD

Zinzendorf was not long separated from his Moravians. By 1738 he had got them off to Marienborn in the Wetterau, and Herrnhut was now peopled by Lutherans proper, so much so that the hitherto successful diaspora work fell into decay for half a century. The refuges in the Wetterau where Zinzendorf hoped to find a guarantee of toleration were all in the territories of petty Reformed princes who both believed in toleration as a principle and for a generation had been selling it for profit to well-behaved subjects.[30] Here the Moravian settlements were never anything but independent of the locally established (Reformed) churches, and the same was true of the communities established in the Netherlands. In England too he obtained an act in 1748–9 for the grant of special privileges in Georgia, which assumed that 'the church known as the Unitas Fratrum is an antient, apostolical and episcopal church'. In England it was easier to secure public recognition of privileges to a dissenting church than to a religious movement (such as Methodism) within the establishment; Germany was a different matter. The Lutheran Orthodox were prepared to argue that the old Brethren were 'complete Calvinists' and that the new ones 'were inwardly filled with many fanatical, enthusiastic, Weigelian, Behmenish and Quakerish opinions'. These charges might be contested, but in the Empire to assert a claim to independent church status, to be a fourth tolerated religion, was to invite the death sentence. Zinzendorf had been angered by the grant of dissenting privileges in Prussian Silesia, and could only reiterate '*my* basic principles, according to which the societies of the Brethren must in perpetuity never become a separate religious body or, at least, if they do, forsake all connexion between me and mine'.[31]

---

[30] On this see Chapter 5 below.          [31] *ZW Ergänzungsband* IV: 127.

The problem was that the Moravians were not prepared to forgo what they believed to be their traditions, while Zinzendorf would not surrender his original Philadelphian ideal. Both needed toleration, and toleration was easier to appeal for in German conditions on the basis of the count's principle. Even so he had the vexation to find that neither the Orthodox nor the Hallesian interpreters of Lutheran traditions would accept the view which he shared with Spener, that Luther himself had provided for community institutions of the sort he had created at Herrnhut within the Lutheran church. His one way out of the dilemma was to establish what he called 'Tropuses' or institutionalised movements within the Lutheran, Reformed or English churches. His language about them was memorably con-torted. He could say: 'we have the lovely Tropus-business as a poison from which the Saviour has prepared a medicine', or again: 'we are only one of ye societies in ye church…ye Moravian church nevertheless abides by itself having her own form & without any other's direction. The Ord[inary] declared that this was none of our own inventing, but within these 26 years he only follows ye thread [of the Saviour's guidance]'.[32] The result of constant pressure from the count's enemies was that, with every year, the Moravian church seemed to become a more distinct body and, in the first instance, to put down roots, not within the bosom of the historic Reformation confessions, but in those lands where the state was prepared to tolerate dissenters, namely in the Wetterau, in the Netherlands, in Britain, in Prussia and Sweden. The Renewed Unity of the Brethren was neither the 'antient apostolical and episcopal church' of the application to the British parliament, nor the new eclectic sect envisaged by Bengel, nor the rump either Lutheran or Calvinist, of the Orthodox propagandists, nor Zinzendorf's Philadelphian ideal; but it contained something of each. Moreover the preaching and propaganda of Halle had contributed crucially to its revival, though neither side now wished to recognise the fact. In the history of religious revival the animosity between the practitioners of renewal at Halle and the practitioners of revival looking to Herrnhut, was much more important than the conflicts which were turning the Moravians into a denomination. This rivalry, which extended from Scandinavia and the Baltic to Georgia and Pennsylvania and, in the

---

[32] *ZW* Series 2 XII: 107; MCH MS Gemeinhaus Diary, 11 November 1748. The rather awkward translations of this document were made for the English Moravian community.

Pietist heartlands, ended the intimacy of Zinzendorf's family connexions with the pious counts, imparted a shape to the history of the
second generation of the revival, as the rivalry of Hohenzollern and
Habsburg had imparted a shape to that of the first. This conflict
involved principles as well as personalities.

### THE CONFLICT WITH HALLE

In January 1734 Zinzendorf concluded that a party had been got up
against him by Halle, that they were determined to destroy his
movement, and had the backing of the pious counts. Certainly when
Count Christian Ernst von Stolberg-Wernigerode took up his pen in
1733 he was clearly briefed by the entire Halle caucus. The hostility
of Halle was reproduced at the court of Zinzendorf's in-laws at
Ebersdorf, where the chaplain, J. P. S. Winckler, a former intimate
of the count, began to denounce him bitterly. Denmark was a total
disappointment.[33]

Zinzendorf had maintained a brisk correspondence with Danish
court circles throughout the twenties,[34] hoping that an appointment
there might relieve him of official drudgery in Dresden. When he
travelled to Copenhagen as the guest of the royal pair for the
coronation of Christian VI in 1731, his hour seemed to have struck.
The head of the most important Pietist court in Europe, the new king
had long been familiar with the count; while the queen had formerly
been on confidential terms with one of Zinzendorf's elder sisters, the
countess of Ortenburg. Denmark was doubly important to him for
the prospect it afforded for colonial missions and for safe European
bases for the Brethren. He was fulsomely received, offered a
ministerial portfolio, the headship of a proposed new university at
Flensburg, and decorated with the Danebrog order. By 1734 he was
banished from the kingdom, his decoration was withdrawn, and
efforts to separate the Moravian settlement at Pilgerruh from him led
eventually to its dissolution. Sharp ordinances in the mid-forties
disqualified Danish subjects who studied in Moravian seminaries
from spiritual office in the kingdom, and prohibited those who went
abroad to Moravian congregations from taking their property with

---

[33] Winckler, who contributed notably to the torrent of propaganda against Zinzendorf in the
forties, claimed to have been turned against the count at Jena by his willingness to press a
personal advantage unscrupulously, and his propensity to frivolous unorthodoxy, in this
case that the children of the faithful suffered no original sin.

[34] Herrnhut MSS R20 C3 nos. 35–223.

them. Nor could later visits by Zinzendorf and his wife undo the damage.[35] This reversal of attitudes was brought about by the Halle interest through Christian Ernst, Count of Stolberg-Wernigerode (whose mother was the sister of the mother of Christian VI). They were helped by Zinzendorf's incautiously lecturing the new king on 'vos tristes sujets à Copenhague, je parle de ceux qui sont les frères de Jésus Christ et les témoins dans cette capitale',[36] and the fact that a revival rallied to him which became embarrassingly successful. Class-meetings spread with his encouragement among both the upper and the lower orders of society, and seemed to the government to be filling up with aspiring politicians. The court banned the expounding of the scriptures by lay people, but repression turned the revival to separatism and to enthusiasts from Sweden and Finland. The Orthodox tried to tighten up the conditions of absolution, and were threatened with dismissal for polemic against Pietists; and the king's confessor was actually dismissed. In this confusion Moravianism took many from the Danish church, though, in the longer run, it returned still more. But the Danish fiasco, the biggest public snub the count had hitherto received, and that at the behest of the Halle party, deeply marked the mind of both.

The conflict is the more surprising since before the thirties relations between Zinzendorf and Halle had been good, almost intimate; he seemed an archetypal 'pious count' of the Halle party. He had thrived on life in Francke's household, and enjoyed a revival in his circle at the end of his time there. He spoke of his 'filial respect to Professor Francke, our dear father in the Lord Jesus',[37] he offered himself to the service of the Halle institutions in 1721, and imitated them in Herrnhut. His personal piety was influenced by the Halle hymn-book. It may be significant that Henry XXIII of Reuss reported of the count's offer in 1721 that Halle 'treated him with every respect, but made nothing special of him',[38] and Francke himself was believed to fear that the work of God in Upper Lusatia might compete with his own institutions in the international charity market. These rubs seemed important only in retrospect. More important was the death of the great August Hermann Francke in 1727. He was succeeded at the head of the Halle foundations by his son, Gotthilf August, a man of much lesser stature, whose very

[35] *AHE* 9:956–60; *ZW* Series 3 III:228–37; Series 2 XII:642.
[36] Herrnhut MSS R20 C3 no. 8.     [37] *ZW* Series 3 II:85. Cf. Series 2 IX:137.
[38] *ZW* Series 2 XII:461.

anxiety to preserve his father's work created a legalism in the Halle mentality from which it once had been free. This was particularly hurtful to Zinzendorf, whose affection for Halle (like his grand-mother's) was real but in no way slavish. In particular he went his own way in the matter of conversion.

CONVERSION

Protestant pastoral theology was perennially exercised by anxious souls who found no difficulty in believing in justification by faith alone, but were tortured by the existential question whether they actually had the saving faith. Both the Reformed and the Lutherans had given their mind to the morphology of the Christian life; and in the early eighteenth century a vogue of collected biographical studies of the regenerate aimed to assist the earnest believer to determine where he stood in the Christian pilgrimage.[39] August Hermann Francke's analysis of conversion, clearly based upon his own ex-perience, but held to be generally normative, was especially influential.[40] Zinzendorf, nothing if not a cheerful Christian, and provocatively willing to admit that, on the Franckean scheme, he was an unconverted person, was temperamentally averse to the *Buss-kampf*, and had acquired other priorities through his experience of revivalism. Revivalism as it had developed among the Protestant minorities of the Habsburg lands was a response of those who must achieve results quickly or go under, who not only had no time for programmes of church renewal to succeed, but for the most part had no institutional church to renew. Zinzendorf early concluded that the highly structured Hallesian pattern of conversion actually delayed the conversion of many; it fixed men's gaze on psychological thresholds which they were unable to recognise in themselves. He must offer something quicker, and this aligned him with the revivalists.[41]

Zinzendorf's own conversion did not conform to the Hallesian pattern, on which he came to pour increasing scorn. 'A Pietist cannot

---

[39] Wesley, *Works* XVIII: *Journals* I:12–21.

[40] A. H. Francke. *Werke in Auswahl* ed. E. Peschke ([East] Berlin, 1969) 4–29; *Studien zur Theologie A. H. Franckes* ([East] Berlin, 1964–6) 1:63–5.

[41] Uttendörfer, *Zinzendorf und die Mystik* 109–10; *ZW* Series 2 XVI:37–8. According to the Ephrata chronicle the Moravians arrived in America boasting 'they could make a Christian in three days'. F. Nieper, *Die ersten deutschen Auswanderer von Krefeld...* (Neukirchen, 1940) 197.

be converted in so cavalier a way (*kavalierment*) as we can; he requires more ceremonious treatment, must have his affairs in better order, an apparent credit balance in his books.' 'Pietism is not a mistake, only another method; we ride and the Pietists go on foot.' 'I hold all general principles as to the way one must conceive the process of conversion in the soul as pedantic, scholastic, fanatical or even nonsensical'. 'The pentitential struggle (*Busskampf*) is mostly a chimera, an imaginary illness, a self-induced sickness.'[42] Christ himself had suffered the *Busskampf* for all mankind; all that men needed to do was to cast themselves upon him. Or in the full extravagance of the language of the 'time of sifting':

practical pietists... those who have their misery and corruption ever before their eyes, & only sometimes cast a look to ye holy side for some consolation... would better bear with & take share in ye labour with those Cross-Airbirds who sit always in ye side hole [i.e. the hole made by the spear in the side of the crucified Christ] & are only sometimes obliged to cast a look into their misery.[43]

Zinzendorf in fact stood on the Enlightenment side of a line distinguishing preachers according to their attitude towards preaching the law, Francke on the other side. Preachers of revival could be classified in the same way. Theodorus Jacobus Frelinghuysen, whom we shall encounter in New Jersey, was on Francke's side; Daniel Rowland in Wales began on Francke's side and ended on the other.

Zinzendorf sniped constantly at the 'methodisms' of Halle; but a method he had to have,[44] and it was that of imaginative identification with the Saviour.

The dear lamb, who died for us, and, though God's son, gave himself for our sins, becoming for every human heart God and Mediator between God and men, preacher of the Law, father confessor, comforter, exorcist, Saviour, throne of grace, example, brother, man, in short to become all this for all through the preaching of his blood and his love to us to death, even the death of the cross. To stray from the dear lamb not a quarter of an hour, neither in suggestion nor in fact.

---

[42] *ZW* Series 2 XII:489–90: *Ergänzungsband* v (*Gegenwärtige Gestalt des Kreuz-Reiches* 27); *Hauptschriften* v/1:205; *Ergänzungsband* III:248, 'One cannot say that [the *Busskampf*] is necessary, for it would of course be better to give oneself to the Saviour without all this resistance, refractoriness and reluctance'.

[43] MCH MS Gemeinhaus Diary 1747, 15 May.

[44] Including an elaborate 'method for converting savages' in twenty-five stages. *ZW Ergänzungsband* IX:90–1.

A man was to be regarded as a child of God as soon as he had received the forgiveness of sins, and showed evidence of the fact in heart and life. Schrautenbach, the count's philosophical biographer, reckoned that his views on conversion were one of the three things which most brought the wrath of critics upon him, and Hallesian Pietists hastened to condemn the 'quick' method as simply frivolous. Zinzendorf once had the grace to admit that there was something to be said for the 'reservedness' of the old Halle Pietists,[45] but his views on conversion helped Pietist and Orthodox to recognise a common unwillingness to cheapen the Christian vocation, which neither had suspected at the outset, and to make a combined onslaught on Moravianism in the forties. Legalism in the Pietist world went deeper than the defence of Francke's heritage.

Disputes over the 'quick' method of conversion were sharpened by a different matter which in the public eye was related to it. The Halle foundations had embodied a new pattern of religious and social enterprise. They were institutions of neither church nor state, and applied the joint-stock principle to the service of the kingdom of God. Zinzendorf, who spent more than all his modest resources in purchasing the estate at Herrnhut, developed it on the Halle joint-stock principle. But he had an aristocratic disdain for money and for the labour required to accumulate it. His financial education took a giant leap forward when he was banished in 1736 and many of his original Saxon creditors called in their 6 per cent loans. Zinzendorf avoided disaster and enlarged his disposable resources by borrowing in the Netherlands at rates of 3 and 4 per cent. The pious merchant circles who bailed him out included Mennonites, Labadists and others alarmed at the progress of rationalism. They continued to find the capital needed to establish settlements in the Wetterau, on the Rhine, in the Netherlands, England and Ireland, in America, and to help establish mission stations from Greenland to the East. Eventually Zinzendorf bought his way back into Saxony by making loans to the Saxon government at rates better than they could obtain for themselves. All this had nothing to do with his 'quick' method of conversion, but the remarkably quick results of other kinds it enabled the count to achieve gave his religious position a peculiar resonance. The contrast between the rapid development of Moravianism and

---

[45]  *ZW Ergänzungsband* IV/i: 38, IV/ii: 73; Series 2 IX: 9; MCH MS Gemeinhaus Diary 1747, 9 June.

the low morale of the Protestant establishments, not to mention Halle foundations now going into the doldrums, was very striking, and embittered their protests against superficial conversion.

### SPANGENBERG

Much of the enduring hostility between Halle and Herrnhut, however, revolved round August Gottlieb Spangenberg, summarily ejected from Halle in 1733, who became Zinzendorf's right-hand man, and, after his death, his successor in the management of the community. Spangenberg's appointment at Halle was negotiated by Zinzendorf in 1731 at the height of his favour in Denmark as a public pledge of the unity of 'all the children of God'. Spangenberg seems to have been nervous about accepting the appointment, but was delighted by his reception.[46] From that point everything went wrong. Spangenberg and Sigmund Jacob Baumgarten were jointly quartered upon the vacancy created by the death of Joachim Justus Breithaupt, the last survivor of the 'great' Halle generation, and each had a very rough ride. Baumgarten, indeed, succeeded to a full chair, but, feeling that theological statements needed to be tested by the strictest criteria available, he made use, first, of the logic of Christian Wolff, who had himself been ejected from Halle in 1723, and then, of history. This was sufficient to bring on him the wrath of Joachim Lange, one of the theological professors, whose doctrinal animus was sharpened by the fact that he lost pupils to the younger members of the faculty. The upshot was that in 1736 Baumgarten would have gone the same way as Wolff and Spangenberg but for the special protection of the queen of Prussia; and thereafter he took good care to maintain a low profile in matters of doctrine.

The weakness of the younger Francke's position at the head of the Halle foundations was that he was all the time trying to restore the intimacy of contact with government which his father had enjoyed, while Lange, for reasons of his own, was trying to alarm Berlin with stories of how wrong things were going. Neither Zinzendorf nor Spangenberg had any inkling of the hornet's nest into which the latter's head was being put, and the fact that Francke, who had appointed Spangenberg in 1732, decided to sacrifice him in the following year filled both with a sense of betrayal.[47]

[46] *ZW* Series 2 XIII: 78–9, 86; XII: 660–2.
[47] Herrnhut MSS R20C 30a 10, 12; R20 AI U41.

In the tense atmosphere of the Halle faculty, however, Spangenberg was always a risk. Like August Hermann Francke in his youth,
he stood near to separatists and used separatist language, complaining of being required to tolerate the mixture of good and evil in
the Francke foundations, and of friends who restrained him from his
duty for fear of a breach. What Zinzendorf viewed as an enviable
capacity to bring separatists back to church appeared to Lange to be
irregularity and disorder of the worst kind. A year after his expulsion
Spangenberg himself admitted that 'I criticised too much in the
Orphan House, even before I was able to offer a cure for the evil.'[48]
The Halle party was too ready to regard itself as the sole vanguard of
religious progress, but it could not fail to act on its view, mistaken
though it was, that Zinzendorf intended to use Spangenberg to
introduce among them his peculiar institutions such as love-feasts
and foot-washing, while Spangenberg himself propagated separatist
ideas on communion and confession.[49] Faculty, state and Orphan
House stood notably together to banish him at short notice. The
breach between Halle and Herrnhut was now public, and it entailed
a breach between Zinzendorf and the network of pious counts.
Everywhere the Spangenberg affair was the gossip of the day.
Messengers went to spread the case against Zinzendorf all round
Europe. There was a general feeling that the count had demeaned his
order by familiar dealings with the lower classes.

    The division of spirits was woefully illuminated by the efforts of
third parties to mediate. Jena Pietism had always been independent
of Halle, and it kept independent of Herrnhut also. But Herrnhuters
played an important role in the student awakenings there; Spangenberg was himself an alumnus of Jena and had first been drawn to
Zinzendorf by the count's preaching there. But Jena could accomplish nothing now. Nor could that other irenic figure, now abbot
of Kloster Berg, Johann Adam Steinmetz. Steinmetz's heroic work
at Teschen early caught Zinzendorf's imagination, and he had
interceded for Steinmetz with the Emperor's Jesuit confessor, Fr
Tönnemann.[50] When Steinmetz's enemies finally forced him out of
Teschen, the count helped him to preferment at an old Franconian
centre of Pietism, Neustadt an der Aisch, and then in 1732 to senior
employment in Prussia as abbot of Kloster Berg. There was a brisk

[48]  *ZW* Series 2 XII:88.
[49]  *ZW* Series 2 XII:671–2. For the Halle material: G. C. Knapp, *Beyträge zur Lebensgeschichte A.
      G. Spangenbergs* (Halle, 1884) 3–66, 93–119.        [50]  *ZW Ergänzungsband* IX:478–9.

correspondence between the two from 1725 to 1737,[51] and Zinzendorf was particularly grateful to Steinmetz for encouraging the Moravians to remain Brethren, and to retain their heritage within the Lutheran church. This intimacy ought to have assisted Zinzendorf's relations with Halle, for Steinmetz was the ablest of all the exponents of Francke's policies in Silesia. But the Spangenberg affair produced a wider rift between the two than could be bridged by mutual goodwill. In his *Life* of Zinzendorf, Spangenberg had to make the embarrassing admission 'that the count lashed out violently about the proceedings in my case and wrote hard letters about it to various people, and especially to Abbot Steinmetz'.[52] The abbot tried to hold a balance, but thought that much of the trouble lay in Spangenberg himself; and he was finally convinced by the Halle charges that Spangenberg was really schismatic, that Zinzendorf's manoeuvres in Pennsylvania were also schismatic,[53] and that the basic trouble with him was his cavalier attitude to the Bible. The Brethren, he believed, taught sanctification along the lines of Wesley, and were guilty of sheep-stealing. Zinzendorf was sorry to lose Steinmetz, and it was paradoxical that Spangenberg, so long convicted of separatism, did more than anyone from the fifties onward to push the Brethren back towards Lutheran Orthodoxy. But if Steinmetz felt compelled to choose between Halle and Herrnhut there was clearly no way in which those parties could be kept together; and harmony was not helped by the propensity of both to wash their dirty linen in the press.[54]

### ZINZENDORF IN AMERICA

To follow the in-fighting between Halle and Herrnhut is not to digress from the history of religious revival. The battle itself aroused widespread interest; as we have seen, Wesley was indoctrinated with both sides of the question as far afield as Georgia. The struggle also illuminates the central biographical problem of Zinzendorf himself,

---

[51] Herrnhut MSS R20C 30a, b, esp. no. 68.

[52] *ZW* Series 2 IV:797. Correspondence of Spangenberg with Steinmetz (with whom he had been intimate) not creditable to the former is given in J. P. Fresenius, *Bewährte Nachrichten von Herrnhutischen Sachen* (4 vols. Frankfurt, 1746–51) II:167; *AHE* 10:944–56. Zinzendorf–Steinmetz correspondence is given in I.C.T., *Sammlung einiger Briefe...* (Hamburg, 1748) 7–16.

[53] Herrnhut MSS R20C 30b no. 83 and packet 'Doubletten zur Correspondenz u^d Controvers. mit Abt Steinmetz gehörig'.

[54] J. A. Steinmetz, *Schreiben an den Herrn Past. Hackert zu Stargard...* (Zelle, 1749) 5–7; Herrnhut MSS R20C 30a no. 66; *ZW* Series 3 II:30–49,; III:179–80; *AHE* 4:784–812; 10:944–56.

his universal ability to make a splendid first impression, and his universal inability to cooperate for long with men of independent mind. (Even Spangenberg, the nearest exception to the general rule, admitted in the count's lifetime that 'his addresses often appeared paradoxical and his methods of business extraordinary'.[55]) The conflict also intensified competition in the evangelistic outreach of the revival, extended its range, and formed the context of Zinzendorf's greatest failure (in America) and his greatest success (in the Baltic). Of each of these enterprises something must be said.

The status and importance of America in the German Lutheran view was changed, as we have seen, dramatically in the 1730s by the Salzburgers. They made Georgia an early theatre of the rivalry between Herrnhut and Halle, the latter sending the first pastors with the Salzburgers, the former sending a party under Spangenberg soon afterwards, and further settlers in the same ships as the Wesley brothers. By the early 1740s Orthodox and Pietist alike were aware that there were 120,000 Germans in Pennsylvania alone. America not only came to host the first national Lutheran church not to be created by a state, and created a dream among hundreds of thousands of Germans, long before the American Revolution, it got the mentality of Central European Orthodoxy out of the rut of *Landeskirchentum*, and by that very fact created common ground between the Orthodox and Hallesian Pietists still living on the back of Francke's *Grosser Aufsatz*. From this remarkable broadening of vision Zinzendorf could hardly have remained isolated, even had there not been pressure to intervene from within his own movement. For America, which in 1740 already possessed in concentrated form the entire gamut of European Christian denominations, was ripe for Zinzendorf's Philadelphian ideal; and the absence of steady institutional christianisation, which had made the term 'Pennsylvania religion' a by-word for godlessness, suggested that the German Americans might offer an abundant harvest to the revivalist. All this became apparent to Spangenberg as he got to know America. He joined a body of men of varied denominational background called 'the Associated Brethren of Skippack' which might prove the nucleus of a wider Philadelphian organisation, what Zinzendorf called 'the congregation of God in the Spirit'. He also wished to evangelise the army of non-practising Germans and attempt primary missionary work among the Indians. These objects were in the count's mind

---

[55] *ZW Ergänzungsband* v (Spangenberg, *Declaration* 18).

when he arrived in Philadelphia in December 1741, bringing with him not only the ambiguities of his relations with the Lutheran churches at home, but also a great sense of urgency; the success of Whitefield's preaching among the Germans suggested that the assimilation they had escaped at home might be their fate across the Atlantic.[56]

For Zinzendorf had heard even in 1737 from Ziegenhagen, the court chaplain in London, that the Pennsylvania Lutherans longed for a pastor. He prepared his mission by temporarily resigning his Moravian bishopric, and emphasising the fact of his Lutheran ordination. He also publicly laid aside his title of count, appearing as Herr von Thurnstein. In this guise he was appointed pastor of the Lutheran church in Philadelphia with Christoph Pyrlaeus as his assistant, and drafted them a church order based on Luther's preface to the *Deutsche Messe*.[57] The Reformed also desired Zinzendorf's ministrations, and a long series of conferences was held with a view to promoting the 'congregation of God in the Spirit'. The count could not endear himself to the separatists by appearing in the character of a Lutheran pastor, and the more meetings he held the worse relations got.

In a country like Pennsylvania was then [reports Schrautenbach] the count was bound to encounter a wondrous variety of critics. To some he was the beast of the Apocalypse, to others the false prophet. His daughter [who accompanied him] was said by some not to be his own daughter but that of a ship's lieutenant whom he had abducted. He was said to have been unfrocked in Germany for drunkenness.[58]

There were unconfirmed reports in the European press that he was taking Christoph Saur, the separatist printer, to court, and in Frankfurt Johann Philipp Fresenius managed to fill some 800 pages of the third volume of his *Bewährte Nachrichten* with circumstantial stories of the count's authoritarianism and the arbitrary distinctions he drew between children he would baptise and those he would not. Still worse, a year after Zinzendorf, Heinrich Melchior Mühlenberg arrived, with the backing of the Halle party, to destroy the count's initial base, and to organise the Lutherans into a Lutheran church. Mühlenberg's mission was a particularly unpleasant cut, for it publicly revealed the count's differences with his own family;

[56] Fresenius, *Bewährte Nachrichten* III : 130.
[57] *ZW Hauptschriften* II : xxi; *Ergänzungsband* VIII : 828–30; IX : 702–8.
[58] *ZW* Series 2 IX : 317–18.

Mühlenberg came straight from running the Orphan House created at Gross Hennersdorf by Zinzendorf's estranged aunt, Henriette von Gersdorf.

Zinzendorf's Indian missions were as unproductive as his attempts to establish the 'congregation of God in the Spirit', and he was fortunate to escape with his life. The end-product of his visit was a considerable strengthening of the Moravians' denominational machinery in America, the very part of the world where such a thing had been thought least necessary. Before he left America in January 1743 (NS) he delivered two heartfelt convictions in maddeningly oracular style:

The first is that America must be washed in the blood of Jesus like Europe, but (and this is the second truth) it must be treated in another way than Europe...In Europe is the house inherited by the Lord Jesus and his people...namely the Moravian Church. The reason why the Moravian Church must be this house is the pressure on conscience which remains in many parts of Europe...In America [by contrast] there is freedom of conscience, especially in Pennsylvania, and where there is freedom the Saviour needs no visible house...a witness of Jesus who has none of your religions is much better fitted to spread the kingdom of Jesus here, than one who has a religion.[59]

This was an odd doctrine from one who had just made the American Brethren more of a separate denomination than they were in Europe. Zinzendorf came home protesting to Edmund Gibson, bishop of London, that he had left behind '*doctores ambulatorii, Methodistorum nomine clari*, Tennent, Findley, Whitefield,'[60] but the overseers of the Lutheran Church in Philadelphia to whom he had gone as pastor repudiated him, and a few years later when he prepared a third, abbreviated, edition of his *Pennsylvanische Reden* for the church in Pennsylvania, he admitted that 'my special connexion and care for the evangelical-Lutheran religion in Pennsylvania [has] ceased'.[61]

### PIETISM IN THE BALTIC REGION

In the Baltic the fortunes of the Moravians prospered, and prospered, whatever the intentions of the participants, in proportion as their efforts proved complementary to those of Halle.

---

[59] *ZW Ergänzungsband* IX: 204–9. By a 'religion' Zinzendorf means a confessionally structured church of the traditional European pattern.      [60] Herrnhut MSS R13A 12 no. 1.
[61] *ZW Hauptschriften* II: xx, xxiii.

East Prussia shared in the history of natural calamity which befell Livonia and other Baltic riparian areas in this period, but differed from them politically. In 1701 Frederick I had taken the title of king of Prussia because only in that duchy was he sovereign, and not subject to the Emperor and the Imperial constitution. To drive the point home all participation in the coronation by the Catholic Bishop of Ermland was excluded, and the anointing performed by a couple of court chaplains (one of them a Silesian Reformed named bishop for the occasion), a public mark of the absolutism under which the church in East Prussia was already being reorganised. A forward policy carried through by Frederick I and Frederick William I guaranteed that Hallesian Pietism would be first protected, then encouraged. In 1699 the elector forbade pulpit attacks on the Pietists, on his coronation day he founded a Königsberg Orphan House on the Halle pattern, and a few weeks later took under his protection a Pietist school which became the Collegium Fridericianum, the most eminent place of university preparation in the state, and later the *alma mater* of Kant.[62] From these bases Pietism made real progress in the province, aided by the changes brought about by royal reorganisation and by population losses caused by the calamitous plagues which swept down the Baltic during the Great Northern War in 1709 and 1711. These cost 200,000 souls, including numerous clergy. The new standing of Pietism was made clear in 1724 when a boy theologian from Halle, Georg Friedrich Rogall (1701–33), came back to Königsberg at the behest of the king and with Francke's warmest recommendations; in the following year he became *Ordinarius* for philosophy and *Extraordinarius* for theology at the university. The Orthodox frustrated his hopes of going on a mission to Livonia, but he trained a whole new generation of Pietist clergy, raised the status of theology at the university, and got some 30,000 devotional tracts, many of them from Halle, into circulation in the province.[63] For some of the new pastoral problems the Halle men were well equipped by the previous experience of those who taught them. The linguistic Babel of the area was aggravated by the energetic recruiting of the kings of Prussia to fill their vacant lots – settlers came in by their thousands, not only from neighbouring Lithuania and Poland, but from middle Germany (Magdeburg and Halberstadt) and the

[62] W. Hubatsch, *Geschichte der evangelischen Kirche Ostpreussens* (2 vols. Göttingen, 1968) 1: 172–96.
[63] T. Wotschke, *Georg Friedrich Rogalls Lebensarbeit nach seinen Briefen* (Königsberg, 1928) 132.

Baltic territories after the Great Northern War

West (Nassau and French-speaking Switzerland). This was the kind of problem with which Halle training had coped in Silesia, Upper Lusatia and (as we shall see) in places nearer at hand like Zezenow. The result of their efforts, abetted by old hands like Steinmetz and at times by Moravians, was that a series of revivals set in of limited scope and duration, subject to setbacks like the abolition of class-meetings by Frederick the Great, but, like those of English Methodism, of considerable cumulative force. By 1759 there was a major revival in Königsberg which spread into other Baltic territories.[64]

The biggest single blow to stability, after plague, was given by the arrival of the Salzburgers, three-quarters of the Prussian contingent

[64] T. Wotschke, *Der Pietismus in Königsberg nach Rogalls Tode in Briefen* (2 vols. Königsberg, 1929/30) 71, 81, 111–12.

to the number of about 14,000, in 1732 before arrangements had been made to settle them. Naturally very high death-rates set in. Those who came via Halle brought with them five preachers, and gradually they were provided with ecclesiastical as well as temporal amenities. A sensation was created by the revivalistic ways they brought with them, reminiscent of the palmy days of Teschen. At Budwethen they were exemplary attenders at church even in weather which kept others at home and forced the grown-ups to wade, and bring the young and the elderly in carts. Arriving at church they still had to wait for the pastor to finish his Lithuanian service, so they gathered outside and 'sang, read or prayed together'. In church they were attentive to the preaching, did their best with the catechism, and (what was not characteristic of revivalists or ordinary Lutherans either) followed the pastor home, 'thanked him and kissed his hand for preaching the Word of God'. On Christmas Eve over forty Salzburgers came to the manse and

right through the night sang prayed and read devotional songs and books. I stayed up with them [related the pastor] and awakened them to praise God for all the goodness he had shown them. Then they began to narrate to each other what they had received of God on their journey and how well accepted they had been. I listened to them all and then fell on my knees and prayed with them. They prayed too in their own words. The simplicity with which it all happened is beyond my power to express. My heart was tenderly moved by it all... I shall never forget that night as long as I live.

Nor was this all. Their children behaved like model Silesians, and, on Ascension Day 1734, held a camp-meeting,

sang songs, read from Arndt's *True Christianity* and the devotional tracts of their countryman Joseph Schaitberger. Germans and Lithuanians joined them, grew stronger in their faith, and they celebrated a common mission-feast, at which the Salzburgers were the hosts. To the clergy it was a matter of astonishment that the Lithuanians frequently attended the Salzburger services, although they did not understand their language. But to see the devotion of these men and to hear their songs moved them.[65]

Many of the churches with which they were provided were barns like those the Prussians built in Silesia, but the Salzburgers introduced their own icons; most emotive of all, to the left of the altar at Gumbinnen, the staff of the leader of the emigrant host.

Zinzendorf, who had dabbled in Salzburger affairs for so long, could not resist the temptation to try again, the more so as one of the

[65] Hubatsch, *Evangelische Kirche Ostpreussens* 1:189–91.

preachers who had accompanied them to Königsberg became a Moravian, and Hofer, a Salzburger who had joined the Moravians, learned Lithuanian in order to hold meetings for that people in their own tongue. Already in 1733 he sent Friedrich Böhnisch and Christoph Demuth[66] from the revival in Pomerania to them, and they arranged for Moravians to visit regularly as they went to and from Livonia.

During the time of Charles XI and XII of Sweden the Baltic German nobility in that province had engaged in a great and damaging struggle against Swedish absolutism. Apart from the physical destruction of war, the nobility in collaboration with the warring parties in Sweden and Russia had managed to swing much of the cost of the conflict upon the indigenous population. The triumph of a very pro-German Peter the Great over Charles XII had left them in a secure position which they used to reverse Swedish efforts to mitigate serfdom. *Leibeigenschaft* was intensified and reached its peak after 1765. The native populations of the area found their pagan culture still under constant attack,[67] and their social circumstances changed sharply for the worse; their hatred of German lordship came out in a nostalgia for the Swedish age which still marks their national propaganda, but did not work to the profit of Swedish Orthodoxy. The German nobility did not repair the ravages of war and plague with the resolution of the Hohenzollerns in East Prussia, but they were subject to some of the same fashions. The *Oberpastor* at the Dom in Reval from 1724–8 was indeed a son of Königsberg, Christian Friedrich Mickwitz, and a stout Hallesian to boot. The Halle interest had been working on Livonia and Estonia before Russian occupation was thought of, and turned them into one of the most powerful bastions of Pietism in the Russian Empire. By the 1740s the bulk of the clergy were of the Halle stamp.[68] And it was on the back of the Halle interest, before the great breach took place, that the Herrnhuters first came into Livonia.

[66] Demuth's testimony was recorded in Wesley, *Works* XVIII: *Journals* 1:289–90, 286 n. 43.
[67] *SMBRG* 1 (1732) 408–29.
[68] E. Winter, *Halle als Ausgangspunkt der deutschen Russlandkunde* 255–89; *SMBRG* 3 (1734) 187–95; 5 (1736) 767–70; T. Harnack, *Die lutherische Kirche Livlands und die herrnhutische Brüdergemeinde* (Erlangen, 1860) 59.

## MORAVIANS INVITED TO THE BALTIC

A Pietist pastor, J. J. Gruner, invited Moravian assistance in 1729, and in the autumn of that year Christian David and Timotheus Fiedler arrived, staying in the Reval area for a year. Earning their living by manual labour, they organised prayer and Bible-study groups, until the Lutheran superintendent of Vidzeme got the city authorities of Riga to bring them in for questioning, and the warning that 'because the time in which we lived was not anything like the time of the apostles when God chose ignorant, uneducated people to teach and preach, we had to stop our activities'.[69] It was clearly urgent for the Moravians to secure the kind of influential lay backing which Zinzendorf had provided in Upper Lusatia, and the pious counts in Silesia. This he found at Wolmarshof (Valmiera), north-east of Riga, the estate of the widow of General von Hallert. He had been a German general in Russian imperial service; she was a Saxon, a von Bülow, a friend of August Hermann Francke, and is said to have been acquainted as a young woman with the future countess of Zinzendorf. She was full of the zeal shown by the Hallesian nobility of Upper Lusatia for dealing with the serf races in a new way; she enabled David to state his case before a meeting of pastors in Reval; she agreed to a correspondence with Zinzendorf, received a visit from David Nitschmann, and eventually allowed her estate to become one of the three main Moravian bases in the area (the Campenhausen estate at Brinkenhof in Estonia being another).

When, therefore, Zinzendorf appeared in Livonia in 1736, making straight for the Generalin von Hallert, there were already a number of Moravian meetings in existence. The main purpose of his visit was to create a good impression on the gentry and clergy, especially Pietists like Mickwitz and his assistant Vierorth, an enthusiast originally appointed as a chaplain by General von Hallert. It was, however, Zinzendorf's genius constantly to be forming connexions with earlier revivals. He met up with friends from the Jena student revivals, former pupils of Buddeus. He became acquainted with old Swedish officers who had participated in the revival in Siberia, and had helped to create the school there. On his return journey he visited the Salzburgers in Prussia and wrote to the king about them. By his preaching and diplomacy he created the impression that the

---

[69] Valdis Mezezers, *The Herrnhuterian Pietism in the Baltic*... (North Quincy, Mass., 1975) 64–5.

Moravians might be good for the pagan natives and would do no harm to the Germans. Even the few representatives of Enlightenment in the area favoured the seminary for Lettish teachers which he organised upon the Wolmarshof estate.

So successful was the count's public-relations exercise that in the next few years some fifty Moravians, a force numerically equal to the entire clergy of the area, came, by invitation, to assist them. They earned a living as tutors, artisans, one even as doctor to Frau von Hallert, and they speedily acquired a popular influence which no one, least of all the clergy, ever expected. The attraction which the long-suffering Salzburgers had held for the Lithuanians was exercised in Livonia and Estonia by the long-suffering Moravians.

The evidence suggests that two generations of public battering, together with the other upheavals which had left the German aristocracy so firmly in the saddle, had weakened the old heathen culture to the point where its adherents were susceptible to a new religious appeal. Even before the Moravians arrived, the occasional Hallesian pastor encountered a revival in his parish. For example, the pastor in the Estonian parish of Urbs, Johann Christian Quandt, converted his schoolmaster, and with his assistance and that of a tract translated into the local language, set to work in 1736 on the children. Adults were affected and were formed into a class in the pastor's house. Numbers grew, and so many adults came to consult the pastor about the state of their souls, that he had to classify them, putting the converted into a class with an experienced leader, and creating a general meeting for the others. The dissatisfaction which this created among the also-rans generated a general revival, so that within a year the whole parish was full of preachers, no building would hold all the people, meetings had to take place in the open air, and the movement spread into neighbouring parishes. From the beginning the revival in Urbs was in the front line of the struggle against paganism. Previous pastors had made assaults on holy places and groves, but these remained no less sacred to the people who used to pray and sacrifice there in cases of sickness and other need. Quandt reports:[70]

Sixty to eighty such places remained in the parish of Urbs, entirely without the knowledge of the pastor. With his schoolmaster the pastor destroyed such places, twenty-four with his own hand within two weeks, the sexton and other young people supported them, and the holy places were ploughed

[70] Hermann Plitt, *Die Brüdergemeine und die lutherische Kirche in Livland* (Gotha, 1861) 101–5.

up and sown, and thus even their memory was expunged. Also the other superstitious customs of the people at work, sowing, ploughing, haymaking, baptisms, marriages and burials, the playing of bagpipes and jumping, fell away without compulsion, etc.

This revival was on the ebb-tide before the Herrnhuters arrived in 1738 and introduced their own organisation and methods of pastoral care, but it shared one characteristic with the revivals which they promoted. The voluntary repudiation of old ways was so vehement that when, over a century later, the folk-lore specialists came hunting for folk-songs, the area south of Dorpat yielded nothing. Even among the Letts the folk-songs were described as 'good for nothing'.

The 'year of revival' among the Letts began in 1739 when that old campaigner Christian David and a Jena theologian called Magnus Friedrich Buntebart, who had come to Wolmarshof in 1737 to learn the language and assist in the new seminary, held their first meeting in Latvian. That summer the movement seized the whole of northern Livonia, winning such a response that the converts had to be divided into classes and choirs, Moravian style, to be coped with at all. In Kurland the Brethren made no progress, the Lutheran Superintendent fighting a successful rearguard action against their missionaries. The movement in Estonia began earlier than in Livonia and went much further, no doubt because the ground had been much more intensively prepared by the Halle interest. Here the movement began in Reval in 1738 and spread from there into the country, the moving spirit being a young German Herrnhuter, Biefer. He was inclined to excess, and for a time successfully ran Mickwitz and Vierorth, who had brought him into the town in the first place.[71] At all events, by 1742 the Moravians had gathered into their own fold some 14,000 members in this part of the Baltic, of whom 3,000 were in Latvian Livonia, 2,000 in Estonian Livonia, and the rest in Estonia and Oesel.

Oesel, the Baltic island which suffered worst of all from the rise and overthrow of Swedish absolutism, had a peculiar place in the history of the Baltic revival. Oesel had enjoyed a revival of its own in 1726; Moravians are said to have had a hand in this, doubtless erroneously, since their own revival had not then taken place. It is clear, however, that one factor in the case was the sympathy of pietistic pastors, and that amongst its abiding fruits were conversions in a number of noble

---

[71] These events were lavishly reported: Fresenius, *Bewährte Nachrichten* IV; *AHE* 8:288–322, 923–31; 14:949–1092; 15:311–476.

families. The great outbreak of 1740 was prefaced in a similar way. In 1738 Gutsleff, one of the Pietist clergy of Reval, who had made Zinzendorf's acquaintance in 1736, became superintendent in Oesel, peasant schools began to be set up, and, on Zinzendorf's initiative, the Bible and hymn-books began to be translated into the local tongues. When revival broke out among the Estonians in Uppa bei Arensburg in 1740 the effects were out of all proportion to those of the previous generation because there was now high-pressure revival among the mainland Estonians and also a Moravian preaching force able to take advantage of an opportunity when it came. Fifty years later one of the noble converts described what happened:

First in the village of Uppa bei Arensburg, Uppa Jurri and his wife were awakened, and praised and glorified God for the unspeakable grace which encountered them in the reconciliation of Jesus, so loudly, that on Sundays people streamed in from everywhere in order to hear the praises and thanks of these children of grace. Soon there was no more room for the crowd of hearers in the village, so the couple and the converts from the village went into the open air to preach to eager hearers while others gave praise and thanks with a loud voice... The gentry and citizens of the towns came out in coaches and... the blessed Superintendent Gutsleff also went out and preached... in the open air to a public hungry for the word... This fire of grace broke into full flame in the neighbouring villages of Kartokulla and finally spread so generally that no village and almost no family in the whole land remained unvisited... Everywhere in the villages they held meetings with prayer and singing, and... upon some estates where there were awakened gentry... They put aside all wordly delights: bagpipes, harps, bugles they burned and totally destroyed. The women put away their headbeads and their pinafores, which were gracefully embroidered with all kinds of ribbons and silver and gold braid, and all their pearls, corals and necklaces, and went into modest and honourable clothing. They no longer went to the pot-houses... At their feasts there was no more stuffing and soaking. On the contrary they spent their time in singing and prayer. They were industrious and obedient towards their masters, went regularly to church and to communion, and prayed quietly and peacefully. In the years 1740–5 not a single criminal case came into the courts. Among the Germans too there was a gracious visitation and almost general awakening. They were most blessedly touched by some Brethren called from the congregation in 1741 and 1742... The nobility and other inhabitants of the province came frequently, and without respect to their outward circumstances, state or prosperity, and took children industriously to town to hear the Word of God and edify each other... To children of the right kind it was a heavenly benediction, a pure festival, and they could not thank the Lord enough for this grace. Every four weeks they assembled in Arensburg church for communion. But alas! this vineyard of the Lord was utterly destroyed in full flower by the wrath of the enemy.[72]


## THE DIVISIVE EFFECTS OF THE REVIVAL

The priesthood of all believers could hardly be exercised at such high pressure without exposing some weak links in the chain. There were admittedly 'excesses of various kinds, which took the form of spiritual *Schwärmerei* and enthusiasm, or even deception and lying', though these are said to have been confined to parishes where the clergy attempted not to guide, but to root out, the revival.[73] Some of the Moravian Brethren themselves were said to have been corrupted by the unwonted experience of gentry favour. Moreover a revival movement which had thrived on popular anti-German and anti-clerical sentiment, but had proved able to sublimate these animosities where those who suffered them had been brought in, was liable to produce strange side-effects. Take the case of Tallima Paap, 'the chap from Reval'. He was a peasant with hereditary rights to the land on the Hahnhof estate near Dorpat. He was early influenced by the Moravians and itinerated in the Reval area. Eventually he parted company with the Moravians, withdrew to Hahnhof and gave himself out as the great prophet who had arisen after the line of the apostles, who worked at the command of Christ and the Holy Spirit, and the one to whom 'the words of Christ, "You will do greater wonders than I"', applied. It is impossible to know how near the mark the defamatory reporting of the Orthodox journals is; but it does not obscure features characteristic of the revival as a whole, or Paap's clear attempts to respond to both the religious and social needs of the peasantry by offering forgiveness of sins, rest for the soul, and apocalyptic with a social reference.

1. On being awakened from the sleep of sin a man must have visions and revelations of hell and those who are in it. Hence, some, young and old, fall down, and for a time seem like dead, and after a time get up and relate how they have seen this one and that one in hell.

[72] Baron P. Sass, "Zur Geschichte der Herrnhutischen Gemeinde auf Oesel', *MNEKR* 40 [NS 17] 155–7.

[73] E.g. Marie Nylander, who had one of a common series of female visions, 'admitted that she had once, on the edge of a melancholic spasm, seen a hand hanging down, dripping blood. She was thankful that Pastor Holmquist had put her right' (Sass, 'Geschichte der Herrnhutischen Gemeinde' 160). Where the clergy were hostile, the visions were likely to become more gruesome, and no pastoral guidance was available to deal with them.

2...Paap has pressed especially for renunciation and the following of Christ...as for example: because Christ and his apostles smoked and sniffed no tobacco, the disciples of Christ must use none. And so on Paap's advice they have burnt many things of this kind, including tobacco pipes, pouches, horns and even tobacco itself. Because Christ and his apostles went about in humble and simple clothes, they have rejected perruques and other German clothes of colour, and want to put them away or even burn them. For this reason they have cut out all red and blue colours from their caps and clothes, and choose instead only what comes out of the earth and is worn by sheep...The reason they allege for this is that the root *Marjama* with which they dye their woollen yarn is gathered on a Sunday...They kiss one another without distinction of sex, and, in their view, from pure love. Indeed for this reason Paap in the last few weeks has begun to run naked, and some others have begun to uncover themselves, and some women have had half to uncover themselves.

3. Whoever reproaches them with such things...persecutes them for Christ's sake, and will pay for it to the devil who was in him...

[4.] The day of judgment will soon come, hence in the last weeks he has forbidden them any more to plough or work, and also not to go to work on the estate...When some said, 'What shall we do in the end when all is consumed?' He answered 'There would be nuts enough.' And then others asked, 'Where will the Germans be?' Answer: 'Over the fence (*Zaun*)'.

[5.] He has an iron rod with which he will pasture all the heathen, and be king over Livonia. One of his followers says that...his view ran ultimately to handsome redemption from their labour services...[74]

Paap and his followers were exposed to a good deal of forcible pastoral instruction. Paap was reported as beyond redemption, but eventually he showed signs of repentance, went back to his farm, and in 1745 gave up his separatism and was accepted again.

Worse than Paap, whose movement seems to have been more noisy than extensive, was the fact that the sweeping gains made by the Moravians had raised the question of where the control of the church in Livonia and Estonia lay. The pastoral assistants seemed to have taken over a great movement of lay Christianity, some of them (as in the case of Biefer and Mickwitz) with scant respect for their hosts. Mickwitz complained that the Moravians had 'led souls from the Words of God to their new fantastic turns of speech, from prayer to social-, band-, and conversation-meetings, from Christ to their community...from the rule of the Holy Spirit to their blind casting of lots.'.[75] A mob was got up against Biefer, who was saved from worse

---

[74] This report was compiled by Quandt, who had presided over the revival of 1736. *AHE* 8:297–304. Cf. 14:1016–20.     [75] Harnack, *Die lutherische Kirche Livlands* 154.

trouble by house arrest, and with clergy and nobility declaring that enough was enough, it was possible to get action in the courts and consistories and even legislation against the Moravians; two commissions of inquiry were appointed, one for the Latvian part of Livonia and another for the Estonian part. Before they could finish their work a worse blow fell; the Czarina Elizabeth issued a ukase in 1743 forbidding the Brethren's meetings, and looking to the confiscation of their meeting-houses and literature. In a particularly brutal act Superintendent Gutsleff, Pastor Holterhof and Dr Krügelstein, who had acted as doctor to the Generalin von Hallert, were hauled off in chains to St Petersburg. Gutsleff died in prison in 1749, Krügelstein died in exile at Kazan in 1760, Holterhof did not receive his liberty till 1762. Back in the Baltic those old friends of revival, the Generalin von Hallert and Pastor Quandt, both died in 1750. In Oesel two-thirds of the gentry retained some kind of connexion with Herrnhut, but the social state of the island continued to justify the suspicions of Tallima Paap. It remained the saddest, poorest and most depraved portion of the whole area.

The vineyard of the Lord seemed indeed to have been destroyed in full flower, yet appearances were deceptive. Elizabeth's ukase was not strictly enforced. Like the revival of 1726, that of 1738–43 left a working capital which continued to yield dividends. The leaven of the Brethren continued to ferment, they bred men able to work under prohibition, and their hymns, translations of devotional classics and music continued to provide a culture to replace the one they had destroyed. There were new revivals in the seventies and eighties, and when the Unity of the Brethren was again legalised by Alexander I in 1817 they had 144 congregations in Estonia and Livonia with some 30,000 members, and they were poised to reach the peak of their influence in the next generation, taking advantage of the strains and stresses occasioned by the abolition of serfdom. The history of the Brethren in the Baltic is a singular one, but it was not singular in taking its rise in the 1730s, and in achieving its full greatness only in the nineteenth century.

### THE 'TIME OF SIFTING'

Zinzendorf's first concerns on his return from America were to visit Silesia and the Baltic, a public acknowledgment that relations with states continued to be of prime importance for his movement, and to pose problems he could not solve. The count bought his way into the Wetterau principality of Ysenburg-Büdingen, but cut the ground under his position by the financial arrangements which he made with the Saxon government to put an end to his banishment; he was then banished from Ysenburg-Büdingen. He secured statutory recognition for the Brethren and constitutional privileges in the American colonies from the parliament of the United Kingdom, but lost the sympathy of bishops and friendly evangelicals by inextricable financial entanglements. The agreement made with the Prussian government in his absence in America, by which the new Moravian settlements were to be subject to no consistory, i.e. treated as dissenting bodies, offended against his view of the nature of his movement. There was no escaping a wide-ranging religious reconsideration which culminated in the 'time of sifting', the most problematic portion of the count's career. The period from 1745 to 1750 was the most productive of his literary life, but it was also one in which he encouraged an enthusiastic piety to run riot. The adoration of the wounds, in an in-language of sentimental diminutives, baffled observers, and the fireworks and feasting contributed to a gathering financial crisis.

In so far as the community later felt constrained to repudiate the extravagances, spiritual and fiscal, of these years it was able to treat them as a 'time of sifting' in which its true nature emerged unscathed.

Zinzendorf had gone to America hoping to realise his Philadelphian ideals on a continental scale; he returned with a romantic vision of the noble savage and the life of nature, with a new distaste for some of what he had left behind in Europe and for changes which had taken place in his absence. The Moravian movement, especially the settlement at Herrnhut, was now more aristocratic than it had ever been, and evinced a sophistication now unwelcome to the blue-blooded prophet of the virtues of nature. Certainly sound management in the community was rashly undermined by the count himself. His financial adventures reached their peak in the forties, and although disaster was held off for a decade, the interest charge exceeded his resources from 1747. Both Zinzendorf and his whole community were incalculably indebted to the countess, Erdmuthe Dorothea, and when she was levered out of the management of the community's affairs the count had to find a fresh impulse and to underpin his own equivocal position.

At any rate in riotous devotion to the wounds, childlike addiction to simplicity and diminutives, and the 'Order of Fools', which filled the later forties, Zinzendorf sought a solution to his difficulties. 'As soon as ye Prince with his open side stept in between, all of the difficulties were removed in one hour.'[76] It is usual to say that he was making a great protest against the pressure of the Enlightenment.[77] This is not at all clear. Doubting Thomas was commended, not scolded, for making 'such an experiment, as one in these days is us'd to do with the electrification'. Zinzendorf, however, was prepared to take up the cause of his Dutch financial backers, a number of whom were alarmed at the progress of Socinianism, and could sound menacingly anti-modernist.

Faith there is no want of [he proclaimed]. Ye people know enough, if they did but practice it, & hereupon have preached up morality with all earnestness & ye philosophers, deists, Socinians & Arians, have directly joined them & strengthened those stupid persons in their idle conceit.[78]

This campaign was consistent with one of the bedrock convictions of Zinzendorf's mind that 'abstract' cosmologies of the Leibnizian or Newtonian kind needed (at the least) to be balanced by the concrete, historically-rooted imagery of the crucifixion.

The distinguishing point between a Christian & a philosopher [is that] a Christian is as abstracted and philosophical & perhaps often means more so in all other matters, but, in the point of wounds, there they us'd their imagination, & the more happy our heart is ravish'd & taken up therewith.

And in less cautious moments Zinzendorf could advocate the doctrine of the wounds as antithetical to reason and even independent of scripture.[79]

Nor in these years can he be acquitted of triumphalism. Moravianism was attractive to Mennonites, he believed, because it countered the intellectual wet rot of Socinianism in a peculiarly effective way. The superior spiritual attitude of the Moravians had not only effected the final and permanent establishment of the Moravian church in the world, it had conferred political advantages in the shape of agreements with the governments of Poland and Saxony, Ysenburg and England. The Moravian church was the first

---

[76] MCH MS Gemeinhaus Diary 1747, 22 February, 12 May, 15 May.

[77] For a different view see my papers, 'Enlightenment in Early Moravianism' in *Kerkhistorische opstellen aangeboden aan Prof. dr. J. van den Berg* ed. C. Augustijn and others (Kampen, 1987) 114–27; 'Zinzendorf and Money', *SCH* 24 (1987) 300–1.

[78] MCH MS Gemeinhaus Diary 1747, 21 May; 1748, 19 February.

[79] *Ibid.* 1747, 5, 19 March; 1748, 5 September. Cf. Uttendörfer, *Zinzendorf und die Mystik* 194–216.

fruit of 'introducing ye blood & cross doctrine amongst mankind', and had profited by not resorting to force like the Protestants of Bohemia, Poland, Hungary and Transylvania.

This self-congratulation, passable when the 'time of sifting' was in full flush, was a great mistake. Zinzendorf's exaggerated Christo-centrism – 'Christomonism' as it has been called – got him into difficulties with the doctrine of the Trinity as conventionally understood, and exposed him to a fearful hammering from the critics, not least Bengel.[80] Spangenberg admitted that the excesses of the time of sifting, the jollifications, fireworks and feasting which went with it, aggravated the financial problems of the community, but could offer no better explanation of the fact than that the Brethren had not kept the crucified Saviour in their eyes and hearts, the very thing Zinzendorf had set out to achieve. He loyally defended the great obsession of those years, the little side-hole, as 'based on a Word of David, "O God, my cleft rock" and merely a child-like translation of that text'.[81] In 1749 Zinzendorf himself had to order 'that no one in future should use a diminutive which has no diminutive in the German Bible', and in 1750 devoted himself at the Synod of Barby to 'getting rid, root and branch, of the sifting which had come upon so many members of the unity, especially the workers'. And there seems no doubt that the 'time of sifting' divided the Moravian movement in Sweden, held up its progress in Franconia, invited the charge that it was like the revival in New England,[82] and undermined its repute in Ysenburg and England. Nor were these setbacks accidental. Moravian missionary strategy was to preach Christ from the outset, to realise a Christian profession within the cultures they encountered, and above all to avoid language unknown or incomprehensible to their hearers. In the 'time of sifting' Zinzendorf himself led his followers into a spirituality and an esoteric in-language which evoked contempt and misunderstanding all round.

---

[80] Beyreuther, *Studien zur Theologie Zinzendorfs* 9–34; *ZW* Series 2 x:73–80.
[81] Ps. 78: 20. Cf. Ps. 94:22, memorably presented in English dress in Toplady's hymn, 'Rock of ages, cleft for me'; *ZW Ergänzungsband* III:151.
[82] Hilding Pleijel, *Das Kirchenproblem der Brüdergemeine in Schweden* (Lund &c., 1937) 23–7; F. W. Kantzenbach, 'Der Separatismus in Franken und bayerischem Schwaben...', *ZBKg* 45 (1976) 49; *ZW* Series 2 xv:431.

### FINANCIAL COLLAPSE

What was to be done? Spiritual shipwreck was avoided by a hair's breadth; the long-threatened financial collapse arrived in 1753. Spangenberg had a remedy and it involved among other things the suspension of Zinzendorf from his offices. A firm system of control was to be applied to every department of the Brethren's life. Spangenberg, pilloried by Halle in his salad days as a separatist, pushed the Brethren back steadily towards Lutheran Orthodoxy in language and systematic theology. Zinzendorf's eccentric language was purged from their devotions, and with it went the light-hearted cheerfulness which had been his redeeming feature. On the economic side the Brethren were to be subjected to the discipline of the market. In Herrnhut Abraham Dürninger, a successful linen-merchant, opened a factory to make profits for the community; the firm still trades. By these devices a modest future was secured for the Brethren, and the count's debts were paid off in fifty years. But the days when the Brethren could excite the world of revival by a new and quick method of conversion, and astonish the world of religious establishment by the speed with which things could be done on Dutch credit were over. The religion of the Unity acquired the burdensome features which had most irked Zinzendorf in Pietism and Orthodoxy. The headlines in the reporting of religious revival passed to others.

# CHAPTER 5

# Revival in the South-West of the Empire and in Switzerland

Zinzendorf and the Dutch money which sustained him for so long were among the forces moving the axis of revival westwards, to the Rhineland, the Netherlands and England. In all of these places, however, he was to find revival already in being or in preparation; and in the South-West a shape was given to his activities by conflict, not with Halle, but with another revival, that of the Inspired. And, different as they were, the Moravians and the Inspired were alike helping to bridge the great gulf in the Protestant world between Lutheran and Reformed, and to plant some of Luther's norms of personal piety in new territory.

## CHURCH AND STATE IN THE WETTERAU

The political and confessional organisation of the Lower Rhine and the North-West of the Empire will be treated in the next chapter. At the very gates of that area, however, many of our present themes, persecution and toleration, state-building and the displacement of old religious shibboleths, emigration and religious revival, were sharply focussed in some tiny Reformed principalities north-east of Frankfurt. Here were a group of counts, constitutionally connected in the Empire by membership of the Wetterau bench, the senior bench of counts. They looked on Frankfurt as their capital, and included key names in the history of German Pietism, the counts of Hanau, the various branches of the Ysenburg family, the counts of Nassau and of Sayn and Wittgenstein, the counts of Solms, with whom Wesley stayed on his way to Herrnhut in July 1738, and who were distantly related to Zinzendorf by marriage, and the Stolberg family, whose main property was in the Harz, who had marriage connexions with the dukes of Mecklenburg and the Danish royal house, and became Zinzendorf's declared enemies. These noble families formed the aristocratic substance of the Halle party.

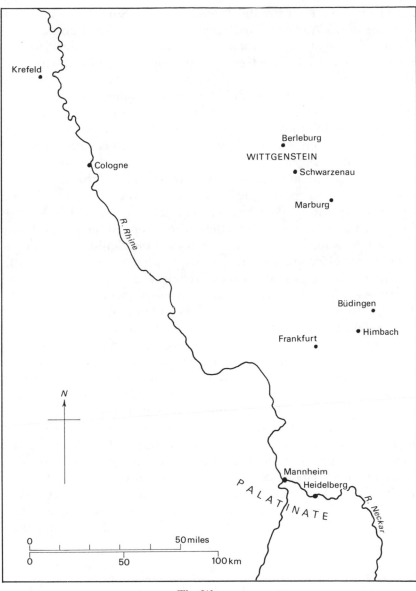

The Wetterau

Many of them were impoverished, both by war and partible inheritance; the baroque exhibitionism of the upstart house of Württemberg was as far out of their reach as the military ambitions of Prussia. Their collective voice in the Reichstag had become

ineffective; service with the Emperor was inhibited by their ad-
herence to the Augsburg and Heidelberg confessions; and administering their domains was not a full-time job. Too refined for the
barbarous pastimes of the German squirearchy, and too ill-educated
to be scholars, they found in religion a serious national and personal
issue to occupy them,[1] as did their innumerable and unenviable
daughters who were too poor to be eligible, and mostly, though not
quite universally, too Protestant to take refuge in nunneries.

Religion also united the counts and their subjects, and afforded a
policy of estate development. In the later eighteenth century, Jung-
Stilling described unforgettably the artisan life of this backwoods
area, the craftsmen reading theosophy in their workrooms and
attaining a vivid, if confused, enlargement of spirit, the charcoal
burners, wood-cutters and smelters who, every Monday, left home
with a week's food for their labour in the forest, cultivating in their
solitude an inner ecstasy.[2] It was no great step to strengthen this
labour force with those suffering religious persecution elsewhere,
even those who did not adhere to the three religions tolerated in the
Empire. In came the oppressed, not merely from the Palatinate, but
from as far away as Switzerland, even before Count Ernst Casimir of
Ysenburg-Büdingen issued his famous decree of 1712.[3] This admitted
all refugees of conscience who were willing to pay a non-citizens' fee,
support themselves by paid labour, crafts or retail trade, and accept
guidelines requiring honourable, Christian and inoffensive behaviour. Under these profitable rules he provided a refuge for radical
Pietists of every stripe who had outworn their welcome elsewhere,
men like Horche, Gottfried Arnold, and Dippel, J. C. Edelmann who
moved all the way from revivalism to rationalism,[4] and not least
Hochmann von Hochenau,[5] a notable revivalist who could not bear
institutional religion, and who was, so to speak, one of the great non-
events of English history. For after much success at the petty courts of
the Wetterau, Hochmann in 1703 tried his hand at the electoral court

---

[1] *Aus dem Leben Casimirs…Grafen zu Sayn-Wittgenstein-Berleburg* ed. F. W. Winckel (Frankfurt,
1842); R. Mack, 'Forschungsbericht: Pietismus in Hessen', *PuN* 13 (1987) 202–10.
[2] Jung-Stilling flourished 1740–1814. His *Lebensgeschichte* is best edited by G. A. Benrath (2nd
edn Darmstadt, 1984). See also Max Geiger, *Aufklärung und Erweckung, Beiträge zur Erforschung
Jung-Stillungs und der Erweckungstheologie* (Zurich, 1963).
[3] M. Benad, *Toleranz als Gebot christlicher Obrigkeit…* (Hildesheim, 1983).
[4] Edelmann described life in the area engagingly in his *Selbstbiographie* ed. W. Grossmann
(Stuttgart &c., 1976) 232ff.
[5] H. Renkewitz, *Hochmann von Hochenau (1670–1721)* (Breslau, 1935; repr. Witten, 1969).

of Hanover. Here, perhaps mercifully, he failed; what the Sacheve-
rells of Queen Anne's reign would have made of a separatist heir to
the throne hardly bears contemplation.

All these men were separated from the popular mysticism of the
area by their literary labours, though they shared its anti-institutional
prejudices; these latter distinguished them from the Halle Pietists,
and from men like Steinmetz who were glad of institutional assistance
against the armed might of the Counter-Reformation from any
quarter. Many of those who now came to the Wetterau had been
forced by their home churches to choose between their confessional
loyalties and their religious experience. To deny their religious
experience was ruinous to their integrity; to affirm it seemed to
involve accepting a hermit-like existence out of the world in the
Wetterau, or, perhaps, in America.

## THE 'INSPIRED'

The 'Inspired', as they came to be known, exemplified all this and
something new as well. They had their origin in the desperate
Protestant resistance to Louis XIV in the Cévennes. The fearful
sufferings of the Huguenots in the eighties drove some to the delusion
that in 1690 the French church would collapse, and the Reformed
church would be raised upon its ruins; this eschatology was what
eighteenth-century English critics understood by 'enthusiasm', that
is, the pursuit of ends without consideration of means. At the worst
times in these wars, strange physical phenomena set in amongst them
which have lately been interpreted by Hillel Schwartz,[6] perhaps the
only working historian who is also a teacher of modern dance. When
resistance was finally crushed, and the prophets scattered to Geneva,
the Netherlands, and England, these strange phenomena and
prophecies made under Inspiration proved almost indefinitely
reproducible. Good men everywhere were loath to deny the
possibility that the Inspired might indeed by visited by the Holy
Ghost, they made converts and were still disturbing the early
meetings of John Wesley's outdoor ministry. Charles Wesley had the
misfortune to share a room with one at an inn in High Wycombe in

---

[6] Hillel Schwartz, *Knaves, Fools, Madmen and That Subtile Effluvium* (Gainesville, Fa., 1978); *The
French Prophets* (Berkeley, Ca., 1980). Cf. Clarke Garrett, *Spirit Possession and Popular Religion*
(Baltimore &c., 1987).

1738; the prophet began to gobble like a turkey-cock, convincing Charles that exorcism was required.[7] In Germany respectable theologians would not exclude the possibility that revelation might be mediated by such means, a notable fringe of doctors, professionally interested in the understanding of dreams and miracle cures, attached itself to the movement, and odd psychic gifts, like second sight, seem to have persisted among the German Inspired. When Max Goebel was doing his fundamental investigation into the movement in the late 1840s[8] and almost all the Inspired were in America, he was astonished to find the American brethren sending home, twelve months in advance, modestly circumstantial prophecies of what was to happen in Germany in the revolution of 1848, which none of the German brethren believed would take place.

Yet, in the main, rejection was the fate of the Inspired. Welcomed at first by the French Reformed church in the Savoy as fellow-countrymen and co-religionists, and by the Quakers as fellow-believers, they were soon excommunicated by the former and cold-shouldered by the latter. The Inspired were unwillingly driven to create a fellowship of their own, and in 1711 to a burst of missionary activity in the Netherlands and Germany, aiming first at the scattered colonies of French émigrés. With them they succeeded little better than with the French Reformed congregation in the Savoy, but, like the Quakers before them, they got a considerable response among the 'Still in the Land' and other mystical groups, and aroused the interest of Pietist circles. But the interest which mattered was that of the police and the *Lumpenproletariat*, and, under their joint pressure, the Inspired were rapidly forced back with the other separatists into the Wetterau. At this point, as in Scotland a generation later, religious revival and separatism come very close together. The principal settlements of Pietists who had fallen foul of successive waves of anti-Pietist laws were in the Wittgenstein territories of Wittgenstein, Berleburg and Schwarzenau, and on the estates of the Ysenburg family of which Büdingen became the most famous. Wittgenstein attracted chiefly settlers from North and East Germany who lived in total isolation from their neighbours of strong Reformed church-manship; Ysenburg attracted separatists from Swabia, and from the

---

[7] Wesley, *Works* XIX: *Journals* II:32–3, 72; Charles Wesley, *Journal* (2 vols. London, 1849) I:138, 152.

[8] Max Goebel, 'Geschichte der wahren Inspirations-Gemeinden von 1688 bis 1850', *ZHT* NS 18 (1854) 275–322, 377–438; NS 19 (1855) 94–160, 327–419.

neighbouring Franconian town of Heilbronn. Their discontents require brief mention.[9]

CHURCH AND STATE IN WÜRTTEMBERG

In the duchy of Württemberg there was a long tradition of Protestant social reform, but it had become quite largely the anti-court politics of the country party in the estates. The court tried to provide for the defence of the duchy, but faced continual *ständisch* opposition to the standing army, and still could not prevent the repeated ravages of the French army during the War of the Spanish Succession. The court adopted French tastes in building and French *mores*; beside the relations of the duke with the Countess von Grävenitz, the age of Walpole looked purity itself. Building schemes wrecked the budget, and led to the allegation that Protestant church revenues were being plundered. As if this were not enough to inflame the Puritanism and anti-French xenophobia of the Württemberger church, the dynasty turned Catholic. Down to the War of the Spanish Succession, Pietist and mystical groups of a Behmenish stamp had held their ground in the church, but the bad times of the war induced an apocalyptic frame of mind in many. This evil age, it seemed, must be hastening to extinction, and the saints must come out of an established church shackled to an utterly corrupt state. When the war ended, the pressure eased, and Bengel, the great scholar of the Württemberger Pietists, on whose *Gnomon* Wesley based his *Notes on the New Testament*, calculated that the Second Coming would take place in 1836; that is, that the faithful would not have to wait for ever to be vindicated, but they need not do anything desperate yet.

By this time, however, there had been a series of separations which fetched up in Ysenburg under leaders of considerable stature, men like J. R. Hedinger (1664–1704), a professor at Giessen,[10] Eberhard Ludwig Gruber (1665–1728), a former repetent in Tübingen, and a learned and pious theologian, and one of his friends, Johann Friedrich Rock (1678–1749), who came from a respectable clerical family, but as a refugee in Ysenburg got a living as the court saddler at

[9]  See F. Fritz's papers, 'Die evangelische Kirche Württembergs im Zeitalter des Pietismus'. *BWKg* 55–7 (1955–70) *passim*; 'Konventikel in Württemberg' pts. 5–7, *BWKg* 50–4 (1950–54) *passim*; H. Hermelink, *Geschichte der evangelischen Kirche in Württemberg...* (Stuttgart, 1949); H. Lehmann, *Pietismus und weltliche Ordnung in Württemberg...* (Stuttgart, 1969).

[10]  R. Mack, *Pietismus und Frühaufklärung an der Universität Giessen und in Hessen Darmstadt* (Giessen, 1984) 239–72.

Marienborn. Unlike the revivalists of the Habsburg lands, but like the Inspired, all these separatists found themselves under the ban of church and state by choice rather than necessity, by their rejection of Protestant Caesaro-Papism rather than popery pure and simple. Gruber was forced by this choice into a position of extreme anti-institutionalism, insisting on not forming a new sect. His followers in the Wetterau lived in complete isolation from everyone except their old connexions in Swabia, with no formal devotion, no prayer, no hymns, communion or baptism, limited to their house services. Life on these conditions was not easy, and they suffered losses to the New Baptists, who were by origin Reformed from the Palatinate and Switzerland, and had come to assert the exclusive validity of believers' baptism before finally departing for America. The separatists, in other words, were looking for a new impulse when the Inspired, as anti-institutional as themselves, arrived in the Wetterau in 1714.

The first of the separatists to encounter the Inspired, Gottfried Neumann[11] and his unmarried sister-in-law, Joanna Margarethe Melchior, were each suffering from spiritual blues. Neumann, oppressed by the apparent decline of the separatists, had joined the Baptists, only to discover a new pharisaism among them. His sister-in-law had undergone a remarkable conversion at the age of thirteen, and had displayed unusual spiritual gifts; but she was now tempted, we are told, by love of the world and a desire to marry, had been given up as lost by the separatists, and was inclined to agree with them. They were impressed by the conversation, the prophecy and the physical contortions of the Inspired, and were finally given a prophecy: 'Your sighs have not mounted unheard, I have heard and sworn to help you, and your petition shall be granted.' Both Neumann and his sister-in-law then fell into convulsions, and, while the Inspired prayed, Melchior came through her distress, and herself began to prophesy. The Inspired went on to the Wittgenstein where, we read, they were 'as voices of God – there were sounds of trumpets, thunder and explosions... they roared like lions and spoke in foreign tongues, and mostly also explained what it all meant. 1 Cor. 14:5–11' (the passage in which Paul explains the superiority of prophecy to tongues). The upshot was that Gruber, the leader of the separatists, after long resistance, was converted to the new ways, finding, after

---

[11] On him T. Wotschke, 'Gottfried Neumann. Der Pietist, Separatist...', *MRKg* 26 (1932) 43–57; M. Benad, 'Ekstatische Religiosität...', *PuN* 8 (1982) 119–61.

sore upheavals, not merely a deeper sense of the forgiveness of sins, and of health and well-being, but the moral bonus of greater personal generosity and patience.

Similarly with his henchman, J. F. Rock;[12] he felt he must confess the burdens which oppressed him, and then searched the scriptures. He found that the Inspired proposed no false doctrine, that they pressed on to love, peace, harmony, denial of the world and of self. Moreover they had sublimated many of the conflicts in the district, and revived the prayer meetings as no one else had been able to revive them. Rock was won only after mature reflection, but, when the moment came, he was seized with violent convulsions at a prayer-meeting and then with powerful laughter. Several weeks later the contortions were followed by prophecy, and prophecy by peace of heart. Neither Rock nor his brethren could doubt that this was the work of the Lord. The separatists, including some of the Swiss brethren, were won for Inspiration.

Inspiration came mostly with or after zealous prayer, singing, Bible study or some other stimulus, and almost always took place in the presence of others, for example in the prayer-meeting. The subject fell into a half-conscious sleep-walking state. Eyes and ears were mostly closed, but the sense of smell and taste were enormously enhanced, and the subject could perform his movements and even go upstairs in this condition. Utterances were usually preceded by a warm feeling of the heart, of the kind experienced by Wesley in his conversion; but with the Inspired this gradually spread over the whole body and the face glowed. First there were movements, then utterances. The gentler the company, the more gentle the movements; the more hostile the company, the more violent and noisy. There was also a heightened sense of community; the voices and thoughts of distant brethren were made known in Inspiration. Indeed the general effect of the Inspiration revival was to counter the isolation and individualism of the separatists, to bring about the formation of prayer-fellowships with public and proselytising functions, which encouraged hymn-singing and writing, held love-feasts, and undertook strenuous itinerant evangelism with a view to gathering in all the children of the prophets, from among all sects and peoples. In this respect they were the successors of wandering Anabaptists, Quakers and Labadists of the seventeenth century, and

---

[12] On Rock: *Lebensbilder aus Schwaben und Franken* ed. R. Uhland (Stuttgart, 1983) xv:86–114.

the forerunners of Zinzendorf's Moravians. Moreover, they described themselves in a phrase taken from Francke as an *ecclesia ambulatoria* or *Wanderkirche*, latching on to an itinerant tradition in the Rhine valley, and foreshadowing the early nineteenth-century discovery that from the New Testament onwards, the true church and ministry had been itinerant. The preaching tours led to the formation of great numbers of prayer-fellowships among the 'Still in the Land' all the way across Swabia to Zweibrücken, and in Switzerland[13] in the cantons of Bern, Zurich and Schaffhausen, which were kept in personal fellowship with the congregations in the Wetterau. Public organisation evoked a fresh round of persecuting legislation, but even this was by no means all loss, for it provoked fresh emigration to the Wetterau. Religious revival was in being.

Yet all was not well with the Inspired. Inspiration did not sublimate their disagreements for long, nor could they escape the classic agony of the eighteenth century, that of distinguishing between valid and invalid religious experience. Having regulated their affairs in 1716, they divided into 'True' and 'False' Inspired, and the 'True' found that their gifts of prophecy began to dry up, their love-feasts to cease. They reverted increasingly to their old separatist ways, and when Rock took the movement over on the death of Gruber in 1728, he was the only one with the gift of prophecy left. Until he began to age in the 1740s he journeyed abundantly over the whole area, as far as Saxony, Silesia and Bohemia, and was away as much as he was at home. Rock was a man of considerable education and spiritual gifts, and he succeeded in embracing men of Reformed and Lutheran origin within the same revival movement.

The Inspired also created their own literary monuments: not only the Berleburg Bible, but an interesting religious journal, the *Geistliche Fama*, edited by (among others) one of the doctors, Johann Samuel Carl. This journal attempted to interpret the signs of the times, and in the 1730s, as events in New England and Old were building up to religious revival – Jonathan Edwards and the Wesleys were watched with sympathetic interest by the Inspired – they believed that the whole structure of authority in Germany was cracking to the benefit of the gospel.

Even the simple peasant class [declared the journal] and especially the mob

[13] P. Wernle, *Der schweizerische Protestantismus im 18. Jahrhundert* (3 vols. Tübingen, 1923–5) I: 159–68; W. Hadorn, *Geschichte des Pietismus in den schweizerischen Reformierten Kirchen* (Konstanz, 1901) 147–219.

in all sorts of countries, gives independent evidence of more understanding and desire to learn than in previous centuries, and they gradually begin to see with their own eyes into the things concerning the salvation of their souls; many thousands of witnesses arise in our way daily, not only in blind Popery, who tear themselves from darkness in Bohemia, Moravia, Austria and Carinthia; but the light is spreading in all sects, most of all among simple and lowly people, ever further.

And in a gross underestimate of the sheer weight of institutions it held that priestcraft had been so far undermined in Sweden, Denmark, North Germany and Saxony that outbreaks might be expected anywhere.[14]

### RELIGIOUS STIRRINGS IN NORTH GERMANY

The immediate grounds for this optimism were the religious and political upheavals in the Habsburg lands, crowned by the great revival in Salzburg. But the Inspired were also buoyed up by random outbreaks of religious revival in the North of the Empire, and, a mirror image of the Orthodox scaremongers, they viewed them as the culmination of all the movements of religious renewal and protest of the last two centuries,[15] as hopeful signs of the times. Of these outbreaks two examples may suffice which have the added interest that they owe nothing to Pietist soteriology.

In 1736 there was a curious case in the village of Zezenow in Prussian Farther Pomerania, not far from Danzig, the background to which was racial oppression. There were only thirty German speakers in this parish; the rest, for whom the church had hitherto provided nothing, all spoke Cassubian, a very low Polish dialect. The squire now secured from Halle a pastor proficient in this tongue; but what opened the people's affections to the new incumbent was not linguistic skill, nor Hallesian theology, but aptitude in folk-medicine. Diagnosing spiritual illness in a man the parish believed to be dying, he cured him with the word of the Lord. When he himself was about to give up in despair, his work suddenly caught fire and spread to the neighbouring villages. Twenty, thirty or fifty would fling themselves on their knees before the Lord together; 120–30 would come into the church together or cry for grace in the fields. Though the people worked all day, they would pray and weep all night, and, even in

---

[14] J. S. Carl, *Geistliche Fama* (n.pl. 1733–43) 23:6–7; *UN* 1732 289–90; *SMBRG* 2 (1733) 570–1; J. J. Moser, *Altes und Neues aus dem Reich Gottes...* (Frankfurt/Leipzig, 1733–9) 13:4–34.     [15] *Geistliche Fama* 10:7. Cf. *UN* 1735 456–9.

winter, they would stay all night in the church, their one place of assembly. The pastor worked day and night without rest, and, if he flung himself on his bed fully clothed, he would be awakened by poor sinners crying for grace. Many received the full assurance of the forgiveness of their sins, and games, dancing, drinking, cursing and the practice of magic stopped. The pastor's preaching was a sort of theology of joy; he practised open communion, and found that they cast off the brutish stupidity of serfdom, developed ready speech and a quick insight into the Word of God.

> He speaks to them [we read] not even of repentance and conversion, which would make them either hypocritical or sulky, but of their professions, arts, studies, newspapers &c. so that he accommodates himself to their temperaments and inclinations... when he preaches almost the whole congregation moves, so that hearers often weep together in such a way that he has to stop preaching. When a stranger comes into the church, even a blasphemer and a scoffer, he is often converted.

Here revival was at least managed from the top, and the pastor was invited to extend it to the neighbouring estates of the von Puttkammer family, into which, a century later, that other religious oddball, the great Bismarck himself, was to marry.[16]

The second case occurred near Halberstadt, just north of the Harz, in 1739, and also involved an element of folk-medicine. Here in the village of Rohrsheim a spring of clear water appeared in a field. It was at first regarded as an arm of a brook flowing nearby which had simply gone underground and reappeared in a new place. But some of those who tried the water became convinced of its healing properties, and people poured in throngs to take advantage of it. This concourse provided an opportunity for a Prussian schoolmaster and former linen-weaver to hold prayer-meetings and open-air services three times daily in the fields, and, it being midsummer, many of the village congregations round about abandoned their churches to hear the exciting preacher at the well. The local clergy complained to their Inspector, who called and found over 500 people listening devoutly and singing with enthusiasm. The Inspector thought the preacher 'disorderly and... unbearable to cultivated minds', but not actually harmful to his immediate congregation. Such irregular proceedings nevertheless encouraged 'the desire for change, peculiar to the people... from which all the sad divisions in the church of God have

---

[16] Moser, *Altes und Neues* 22:3–40.

taken their origin'. His recommendation was that a good medical opinion be obtained whether the spring had healing properties and was a gift of God, and, if so, the devotions at it should be put in charge of the ministers and schoolmasters of the village. The official guardians of religion in this period came in for severe treatment from the religious radicals, but it is notable that they were less hostile to alternative religion than the doctors were to alternative medicine. At Rohrsheim the doctor pronounced the spring to be of no effect, and it was ploughed in. The consistory cited the preacher, but he flitted before proceedings could be taken. To Dr Carl, nevertheless, marvellous cures remained one of the signs of the times; at the least, as the inspector noted, the events at Rohrsheim testified to a popular desire for a change from what was provided by authority.[17]

### ZINZENDORF AND ROCK

The radicals of the Wetterau stood at the junction of the Philadelphian movements of the seventeenth and the revival movements of the eighteenth centuries. They thought that the church was in a fallen state and derived from the Reformed federal theology the idea that church history could be divided into stages yielding an interpretation of the present. The present moment was the time when the true seed scattered among all nations and confessions was to be gathered and the true word hidden in the letter of scripture mystically revealed. Their principal literary monuments were indeed the Berleburg Bible and journals and historical works devoted to the signs of the times. The paradox was that the minuscule events in the Wetterau obtained their historical resonance not from an erroneous belief that the structure of authority in Germany was about to crack, but from two apparently damaging developments. With all Rock's gifts, he could not stop the continual emigration to Germantown, nor the efforts of the emigrants to bring out other brethren. Nor could he avoid conflict with the Moravians, a body in many ways like his own, but with older church traditions to appeal to, a flamboyant leadership and propaganda machine, and an aspiration not open to the Inspired, to be both inside and outside the established confessions.

Zinzendorf first made contact with the Inspired in 1730 when he sent Christian David, David Nitschmann and Leonhard Dober on a missionary journey to Württemberg and Switzerland. On the way

---

[17] *Geistliche Fama* 28:89; *AHE* 7:701–5.

they encountered a thousand of the Inspired in and about Frankfurt. Seeking, in his usual manner, a foothold in other revival movements, Zinzendorf negotiated with them; eventually the need which he shared with them for secure toleration made him their neighbour, with settlements in the Wetterau at Marienborn and Herrnhaag created in 1736 and 1738. Their relations were now unreservedly hostile.

The negotiations between Zinzendorf and Rock afforded the tense excitement of a popular thriller, for each had an unpredictable weapon, the one the casting of lots, the other prophecy in Inspiration. Through the son of Count Casimir of Wittgenstein-Berleburg Zinzendorf got himself an invitation to those territories, and proposed a connexion with them which began with the promising proposition that 'every fellowship based merely upon opinions and forms without alteration of the heart is a shameful sect', and another, less promising, 'plan for the future improvement of the district of Schwarzenau'.[18] Making his usual excellent first impression, Zinzendorf was invited by Rock to go to Himbach 'to examine their faith'. Zinzendorf's hopes of uniting the separatists of Wittgenstein were no more reasonable than his later hopes of success in Pennsylvania, and he could not cope with the satirical Konrad Dippel,[19] one of the most-read and worst-hated writers of the day. Rock, however, seemed more promising. Zinzendorf praised his personal worth, invited him to Herrnhut in 1732, and was friendly till his own movement entered the Wetterau in 1736.

There was a curious mixture of deception and self-deception on both sides of the relationship. Zinzendorf was terrified when Rock went into Inspiration at Büdingen, though he claimed to have suspended judgment because he had not the material to hand to check his motions against those of the ancient prophets.[20] And it was an unimaginative compliment to a man as unsacramental as Rock to invite him to stand as godfather at the baptism of the count's daughter. On his side Rock was the most embarrassing of guests at Herrnhut, repeatedly going into Inspiration at the Moravian public services, and prophesying bitterly against their parades, their spiritual pride, their mixture of church and state. Moreover, Moravians went out of their way to stress that Rock was of respectable

---

[18] *ZW Ergänzungsband* VII:40–4, 361–4.
[19] W. Bender, *J. K. Dippel*... (Bonn, 1882); K.-L. Voss, *Christianus Democritus. Das Menschenbild bei J. C. Dippel* (Leiden, 1970).          [20] *ZW Ergänzungsband* IV:227.

lineage – father a pastor and grandfather a Württemberger *Prälat* – and he felt patronised.

I have been all along a saddler ... to keep myself and my family, under God's help and blessing, by the labour of my hands, without, if I am to serve the congregation, their having to provide for me, and a saddler I will always remain ... You remain a bishop and very great, I will remain a saddler.[21]

Zinzendorf indulged in sheep-stealing, and sustained a secret correspondence with Rock's right-hand man Neumann (who had played the crucial role at the beginning of the movement), attacking Inspiration itself. While Rock was away from the Wetterau in the winter of 1730–1 Neumann introduced the ordinances, customs and doctrines of Herrnhut wholesale, to Rock's fury. After Zinzendorf took refuge in the Wetterau and began to gather congregations from wherever they could be got, it came to outright war. Neumann was admitted to the Moravian community in 1738. One of the factors in the steady rise of the Moravians was clearly the absorption of Rock's followers. Poor Neumann speedily fell out with the count, who sent his daughter for education at Halle, apparently against her parents' will. Neumann returned to his origins, but after his wife's death, about 1748, he again submitted to Zinzendorf's blandishments, gave his daughter back to the community to which they both remained loyal, he till his death in 1782 at the age of ninety-four.

The final balance in the conflict between Rock and Zinzendorf was curiously even. When Rock died in 1749, the game seemed up for the Inspired. Yet the time of sifting cost the Herrnhuters dear, and, within a year of Rock's death, they were expelled from Herrnhaag, and their buildings were taken over by the separatists and the Inspired. In the next two generations the numbers of the Inspired grew steadily by immigration and the Inspirations themselves continued. In 1839 the government of Hesse put a stop to the immigration and assumed oversight of their schools; the dispute ended in 1843 with the emigration of 1,000 Inspired to America, as stately a train as the Moravians had mustered a century before. Meanwhile the conflict left its mark on religious revival in Switzerland and Württemberg.

[21] J. F. Rock, *Des Herrn Grafen von Zinzendorfs und der Herrnhuter brüderlichen Verbindung ...* (Frankfurt, 1741) 16.

### HIGH REFORMED ORTHODOXY IN SWITZERLAND

Switzerland experienced acutely all the factors at work in the Empire. The persecution of the Huguenots turned the Protestant Swiss into the greatest hosts of religious refugees in Europe (even while over-populated Swiss cantons were losing population wholesale to Swabia, the Palatinate and eventually America), and a bottomless well of generosity in the cause of confessional survival. Not only the French, but Waldensians, Hungarian pastors sent to the galleys, and barely viable congregations left stranded by the decay of the Reformed interest in the Rhineland had reason to bless Swiss assistance. If the Empire feared the resumption of confessional warfare, Switzerland suffered it; tension between the great Catholic abbot of St Gallen and his oppressed Protestant subjects, backed by the cantons of Bern and Zurich, came to open hostility in 1712. Their victory secured Protestant ascendancy in the confederation; but the hand which the Habsburgs and Bourbons took in the affair showed what the risks were. A precarious international situation made the government of Bern touchy about affairs at home. Anabaptism, the ancient enemy, was widely reported to be increasing. Certainly Anabaptists enjoyed a good deal of public respect, not least among those who hankered after 'true inward Christianity', and there was a large circle of those described as 'semi-Anabaptists', 'inclined to Anabaptism', 'Baptist-minded'. If they were to develop scruples against military service, the situation would be fraught indeed.[22] And the very existence of this sentiment made things difficult for those who wanted inward renewal, and looked to literary inspiration abroad, Catholic, English, or Hallesian.

Bern flew the flag for a very high Orthodoxy by adopting the Formula Consensus in 1675 and pressing it on her neighbours; but isolation was the result. The Great Elector tried to get it dropped in 1686 when accepting Huguenot refugees who inclined to Amyraldism and the school of Saumur. Werenfels managed to free the church of Basel from it. The clergy of Neuchâtel generally managed to avoid subscription, and there was no question of holding them to it when the territory passed to Prussia in 1707. The great crisis in Germany in 1719 brought repeated pressure on Reformed Switzerland from the

---

[22] R. Dellsperger, *Die Anfänge des Pietismus in Bern* (Göttingen, 1984) 25–6, 52–6. Cf. *UN* 1723 844–6.

king of Prussia, the king of England and the Corpus Evangelicorum not to divide the Protestant front. And there was always internal opposition, not only in Zurich, and in Geneva, which felt the immediate hostility of the French Reformed and finally dropped subscription in 1725, but also in the French-speaking Vaud, chafing under Bernese domination. Neither the stiffness of Bernese high Orthodoxy nor the growth of a desire for a new turn in religious policy are difficult to understand. To try in a position as exposed as Bern to exclude not merely Pietism but Cartesianism was a hazardous undertaking.

### PIETISM IN BERN

This emerged when in 1695 Samuel Schumacher, *Vikar* of the Emmental parish of Lützelflüh, sent August Hermann Francke a fifty-page report on the origins and development of Pietism in Bern.[23] Schumacher had heard in the Netherlands in detail about Lutheran Pietism five years before from an adherent of Spener's brother-in-law, Horb, and had absorbed its sense of being an international movement of grace, a pressing on to Arndt's 'true Christianity'. The same internationalism characterised those whom Schumacher acknowledged as the precursors of Pietism. There was Georg Thormann (1655–1708), pastor of Lützelflüh, who had married a Huguenot, worked mightily on behalf of the refugees, and by his life and writings 'awakened numbers as it were from profound sleep'. There was Elisäus Malacrida, who in 1685 had been preacher to the Swiss colony near Potsdam. On his return to an academic appointment in 1687, he met in Amsterdam the famous separatist Pierre Poiret,[24] the disciple of Antoniette Bourignon, apologist of Mme Guyon, and interpreter of Jakob Böhme. He returned to Bern a changed man and 'awakened very many souls by his devotional addresses and zealous sermons'. The third of Schumacher's precursors was the dean of Bern, Johann Rudolf Strauss. In 1701, in the Orthodox manner, he published a volume of twenty sermons on the one text, Matt. 19:16 ('Master what must I do to inherit eternal life'); and he produced an ethically relevant message.

One of Schumacher's phrases points in the direction of a Pietist movement as distinct from devotional style; he says that Thormann's

---

[23] Dellsperger, *Anfänge* 178–202.
[24] On whom see G. A. Krieg, *Der mystische Kreis. Wesen und Werden der Theologie Pierre Poirets* (Göttingen, 1979).

house was 'to be described rather as a house-church than a piece of domestic management'. The reference here is to the title of a tract, *Die Reformierte Hauss-Kirch* (1677), by Johannes Erb (1635–1701). Erb was the kind of Orthodox pastor thrust by life-experience almost into revivalism. He became pastor of Grindelwald in 1667 just in time to face the dreadful consequences of the plague year 1669; among the victims were the clergy of Aeschi, Adelboden, Grindelwald and Lauterbrunnen. Erb's valiant services throughout the Oberland led to his promotion to the prebend of Oberburg, where he was a neighbour of Thormann. The two distinctive things about Erb, however, were the popular impact of his preaching, and his literary background. Erb was a great divider of spirits. In 1687 a French-speaking seamstress was sentenced to forty-eight hour's imprisonment for maintaining that he was in league with the devil; others maintained that he was to reappear after his death. Erb had taken much of his training abroad, including a decisive spell in England. He translated Baxter and Jeremy Taylor and the prayers and songs included in his *Hauss-Kirch* were drawn from English sources. There is a 'precision' about him reminiscent of Voetian piety in the Netherlands, but his reading extended to the church fathers and the heathen classics. The family head of Erb's house-church was of course to fit domestic devotions to the pattern of parish worship; but in other respects he was a strenuous model of what was being attempted by Protestant fathers right through the Habsburg lands. Erb, an enthusiast only just beneath the surface, was clearly a man not to be bounded by the Formula Consensus.[25]

Schumacher's 'precursors' showed indeed that by 1689 there existed in Bern a demand for new styles of piety and new forms of religious association. It was from these that a Pietist movement crystallised, and, as in Germany, incurred the counter-action of a public authority convinced that the bounds of Orthodoxy were being breached. Schumacher himself dated the beginning of a Pietist movement in Switzerland from the moment in 1689 when he and three fellow students at Geneva, Samuel Guldin, Christoph Lutz and Samuel Dick, began regularly to meet together for prayer and devotional study. It was a moment of personal crisis for Lutz, and a moment of general crisis for Protestantism. Louis XIV had begun his

---

[25] Erb was part of a new wave of Swiss translators of later English Puritan literature comparable with that of the early seventeenth century which shows that there were clergy anxious to spread English ideas of godliness among their flock. K. Guggisberg, *Bernische Kirchengeschichte* (Bern, 1958) 381–2; Dellsperger, *Anfänge* 37–8; Hadorn, *Pietismus* 38.

attack on the Palatinate, forcing the Netherlands and England to war. The Protestant succession in England was saved by a whisker, but the characteristic figure of the day was the Protestant refugee.

In due course all continued their education abroad; Schumacher, Guldin and Dick visited Spener's right-hand man at Frankfurt, Johann Jakob Schütz, who was behind the original *collegium pietatis*. Guldin and Dick went on to the Netherlands and England, Schumacher to the Netherlands and Bremen where the celebrated Theodor Untereyck was at work. Lutz went independently to visit Horb, Spener's brother-in-law at Hamburg, and Spener himself in Berlin. Schumacher went on to Leipzig, whence Augustus Hermann Francke had not yet been expelled. What had begun as a spontaneous association of men who exemplified a change in the climate of Swiss spirituality, ended with a deliberate association with the key centres of Pietism abroad which makes Schumacher's vast report to Francke entirely natural.

On their return to Switzerland the four distinguished themselves by powerful preaching of the New Birth, and by a relationship of both continuity and discontinuity with the main Swiss Reformed traditions. They could properly call upon the *Berner Synodus* of 1532, the first Bernese church order, with its exhortations to clerical oversight of an intimate and personal kind; they could properly be reproached not only with introducing new styles of preaching, but of presenting the doctrine of justification in a much more mystical way than the Reformers would have approved. 'New awakenings' followed in various places; but a movement emphatically within the church came under the hammer of authority in church and state.

In 1699 the council introduced the Association Oath to be taken by all citizens and clergy to maintain uniformity of faith and liturgy; and the following day the Kleine Rat issued decrees against Pietism, which forbade discourses about the millennial kingdom, preaching 'in coarse and unfitting language', the forming of conventicles and private devotions, corresponding with suspect aliens about religious and church matters, and reading mystical writings. To ensure the orthodoxy of the German-speaking country pastors, all were to preach in turn in the Bern minster. The censorship was tightened to exclude almost everything non-scholastic: Jakob Böhme, Schwenckfeld, Tauler, 'the little Kempis', Mme Guyon, Pierre Poiret, Antoinette Bourignon, Petersen, Tennhardt, Hohburg and Molinos now fell under the same ban as, four years previously, Machiavelli and Hobbes. Bern was embattled indeed. Small wonder that Guldin fetched up in Pennsylvania in 1710, to contend mightily against Zinzendorf a generation later. Anti-Pietist proceedings did not spare Samuel König, one of the strong and learned men in the Bern church. He took refuge among the enthusiasts in the Wetterau, becoming in 1711 French court chaplain at Büdingen.[26] It was a question whether forces of renewal and revival could be contained in the church, whether a system which sought survival by treading so narrow a line, could coexist with religious forces which drew strength from their international perspective, whose declared friends were all abroad and included many Lutherans.

### LUTZ AND THE REVIVAL IN THE BERNESE OBERLAND

Pietism made more progress in Bern than in any other canton, and, perhaps because of the stiffness of the official line, moved increasingly in the direction of revivalism. The first group of Pietist theologians were clearly distinguished from Swiss Anabaptists by being an urban, rather than a rural, movement; and they were resoundingly broken by a reaction led by the city clergy of Bern. The future of Bernese Pietism now lay in the country and especially in the Oberland where the old Anabaptism was stirring.

The great name in the church Pietism of the next generation was that of Samuel Lutz (1674–1750), who, fittingly enough, became a hero with Steinmetz's circle in Germany.[27] As a young student he joined the Pietist movement when the trials of the leaders were taking place. The government carefully delayed his ordination, then compelled him to separate outwardly from his friends by taking the Association Oath, and finally sent him off to a newly created post where it was thought he could do no harm, that of German pastor at Yverdon, at the south-west end of Lake Neuchâtel. This was a mistaken calculation; in twenty-three years Lutz made the place a Pietist centre for the whole of the Vaud, and so far triumphed over the Bernese system of religious compulsion as to secure his release from the Association Oath. In 1726 he transferred to the parish of Amsoldingen bei Thun and thrust himself into the leadership of a great revival taking place in the Oberland. Here he held evening class-meetings and dashed about the whole area preaching as a

---

[26] For whom: R. Dellsperger, 'Samuel Koenigs "Weg des Friedens" (1699–1711)', *PuN* 9 (1983) 152–79.

[27] Reports of his work and writing are almost innumerable in *SMBRG* 4–6 (1735–7).

'general apostle'. The government received a constant stream of complaints about his behaviour, but he always managed to put them off by promising not to hold meetings in the forest and to stay at home more – until the spirit moved him to sally forth again.

What made Lutz remarkable was not his activism but an elemental religious spirit, unquenched and perhaps sharpened by the intellectual discipline to which he was subjected as a child.[28] His conversion at the age of twenty-five set the pattern. He was visited in the night by the Holy Spirit, by God himself, and reproached with words of thunder for his failure to do good.[29] Plunged into the depths of hell, he felt close to suicide. The following day he experienced a great breakthrough of grace, the saving hand of Jesus. At a lower level this kind of experience became native to him. He was frequently at grips with the devil, yet always in the hands of his Saviour; always battling with the world, yet always cheerful; unmarried but not ascetic, and with a special partiality for Greek wine. Not surprisingly he felt a close kinship with Christian writers who had endured spiritual struggles like his own, with Augustine for example. Bunyan introduced him to Luther, and Lutz became one of the principal Pietist agents for the diffusion of a piety of Luther's style in the Swiss Reformed world, publishing an edition of the commentary on Galatians in 1717. His sermons could be vast and shapeless, but he hammered away at a restricted range of themes, especially conversion and the New Birth.

That Lutz was a much bigger man than either his style or his doctrine is shown by the response he evoked and by his capacity to innovate. He was given (and especially in his *Canaan Flowing with Milk and Honey and Exalted Highlands of Switzerland* (1731)) to use analogies for the spiritual life taken from the daily experience of shepherd and peasant, from the butter- and cheese-making, the round of rural business and so forth. The stirring of butter in the churn was like God's visitation of the church and the Christian people. 'A cow eats all day long; if you look steadfastly to Jesus day and night, you will never have too much of God's will.' These analogies, predictably offensive to arbiters of taste, were by no means universally acceptable to a Simmentaler flock who knew more about

---

[28] By the age of ten Lutz spoke Latin fluently, read Hebrew and Greek, and had learned the Heidelberg catechism in Greek by heart. Intellectually, however, he remained a rough diamond.

[29] The language was that of Ps. 50, 'The mighty God, even the Lord, hath spoken'.

agriculture than did Lutz. Yet the timeless element in Lutz's religious immediacy sustained his works as standard pabulum in peasant households of the Bernese Oberland till the middle of the nineteenth century.

Again (and in this resembling the pioneers of Primitive Methodism) Lutz suspected that the Reformed tradition pinned too much faith to preaching; people needed intimate pastoral counsel with their difficulties, for in the Oberland as in the Baltic habitual Christianity consorted uneasily with much older non-Christian beliefs. But how to provide this for the inhabitants of Langenbuhl who lived a couple of hours away from the manse, not to mention the throngs that came pouring in from a score of other parishes for his ministrations? Lutz's answer was to get the people of Langenbuhl to choose a time for him to come across, and (again like the English revivalists) to exercise an eye for natural theatre.[30] In the forest was what he wanted,

a shady, very pleasant, broad spot, close to the village and laid out as an open way...They were moved to choose the place by *rationes physicae, politicae, oeconomicae* and *theologicae*, after we had repeatedly tried in the churches and found they would not answer. It possesses an open fresh air, a delightful shade, not to be despised in a hot summer, yet permitting those, like old people and children, who wish to sit in the sun to do so. It is a place where the voice carries well and everyone can clearly understand.

The elders and kirk session could sit on a bench and see that everything was in good order. It was away from the smell and the smoke of peasant rooms and the poor air of barns, and the only outdoor alternative was an orchard where people would have done damage by climbing the trees and the house roofs.

As to the proceedings:

After the people were seated we began with a resounding hymn of praise and vied in song with the forest birds. When this was over and the devotion seemed to awaken prayer, then I offered up myself and the whole company to the heavenly father through our Lord Jesus Christ, imploring his sweet presence, gracious assistance and heavenly unction, that he would open my mouth and the hearts of all...I cried for grace and forgiveness of sins...When prayer was now poured out under the open sky as the throne of God (Matt. 5; Acts 7:48) and the Lord had answered with fire, kindled the heart with joyful flames of love, I sat down again and spoke for a quarter of an hour on a text of scripture. Hereupon I said I was not here to preach

---

[30] *SMBRG* 4 (1735) 354–404.

to them (for they have enough of this in the churches) but to learn what impediments held them back in their pursuit of the heavenly jewel. What hindrances did they have in repentance, in faith, in prayer, in victory over sin, the flesh and the world?

The responses to these timeless questions had themselves a timeless quality.

Must we not desist from oral prayer, I find a resistance to it, and gain no power from it, but mere distraction and desolateness?
   How may I know that my prayer is heard?...But I get nothing. My prayer bears no fruit, I always stay the same.

With these issues Lutz wrestled according to his measure in sessions clearly as memorable as they were irregular. So skilled a practitioner as Zinzendorf's henchman Christian David was impressed.

   One of the things which sustained Lutz in his constant conflict with authority was a sense that his labours were part of the worldwide movement of grace envisaged in Halle. In 1728 he was invited to celebrate the bicentenary of the Reformation in Bern in a special sermon before the chapter in Thun. What he offered was not a panegyric but a jeremiad. The early church had fallen from the perfection of the primitive church; it had been restored at the Reformation but had declined again into the Orthodox state-church; there were now Catholics who received the gospel more readily than so-called evangelicals. The hope for the day lay in the signs of the inbreaking Philadelphian age, the success of the Halle mission to the Tranquebar coast, of Callenberg's mission to the Jews, the flowering of Jesus-poetry, the contribution of women to religious literature, the rise of the desire for church union, the balancing of the idea of justification by that of sanctification, and so forth. The Orthodox might well wonder what distinguished Lutz from a separatist. But Lutz was a churchman, and when in 1738 he migrated to his last parish, Oberdiessbach bei Thun, he won for the church many whose faith was thin, unexercised or uninstructed, and almost all the separatists.

   He kept his finger firmly on the pulse of the world of experimental religion, separatist or otherwise. In his Yverdon years he had been in touch with the awakened at Geneva through François de Magny, corresponded with the Huber family in Lyons, who kept open house to the prophets of the Cévennes, was intimate with lay Pietist circles in Basel. His preaching invitations extended from St Gallen to

Frankfurt, and he had numerous calls from princes in Germany. He entertained Rock, the leader of the Inspired, in Amsoldingen, but tempted his followers back to church in Diessbach. In both places he had worked revival; how had others used the opportunity?

### THE HASLITAL AND CHRISTEN HUBER

That the opportunities were there is shown by the familiar reports in the thirties and early forties of revivals amongst children. At Gutannen in the Haslital in Bern's remotest bounds there were internationally reported events in 1735–6.

Children there banded together to live a devout and loving life and seek Jesus. To this end they meet every morning and evening for prayer and singing. Some have an astonishing gift of prayer which cannot be observed without tears. They keep excellent order among themselves. The children are sixteen or over... The wildest children are become quiet refined lambs. No-one has tried to persuade them into doing it, and they have such an impulse that they can scarcely wait for evening.[31]

A more general spirit of expectation there had been created by another religious original, Christen Huber. He was a former chamois-hunter, and popular legend had it that his conversion in 1723 was due to his having pursued his quarry so deep into the Gelmerfluh that he could finally extricate himself neither forwards nor back, and seemed to face certain death. In fact after an appalling night in which he used his own blood as an adhesive, he escaped, and escaped radically changed in character, though recognisably unchanged in temperament. Still a solitary, he contemplated the work of grace as a hermit, pouring out a stream of devotional prose and verse. And still he needed his prey; the pastor of Meiringen brought him before ecclesiastical authority on charges of unauthorised preaching, and he boasted of direct revelations from on high. He was forbidden to hold meetings at night; but he was not a separatist and was in fact left in peace to hold his gatherings provided they did not compete with church times. Huber not only saved souls, he put the Haslital on the map. Georg Schmid, a Herrnhuter and subsequently a missionary among the Hottentots, extended a Swiss tour to take it in; and in 1738 that old Inspired warhorse, Rock, paid a special visit to deliver an oracle in person. While the establishment was taking the view that

[31] *SMBRG* 5 (1736) 1044–5.

the best way to deal with religiously awakened children was benign neglect, the Haslital was becoming a hive of activity.

What contribution to all this was made by the separatists? The case of the Anabaptists is perplexing. Orthodox and Pietist alike believed that they were increasing in numbers in the early eighteenth century, and in many popular quarters their private character and rejection of public authority were very acceptable. (It was not unknown for the sick to promise God to become Anabaptists if they were restored to health.) One of their teachers, Peter Habegger, went on journeys of visitation as far afield as Alsace and the Netherlands. A stream of ordinances poured out against them, in 1707, 1718, 1722 and 1729; Bullinger's anti-Anabaptist book of 1560 was republished against them in 1734, and the Pietist Thormann attacked their Froschauer Bible. The result was that the Anabaptist community, constantly drained by emigration to Neuchâtel, Swabia, America and elsewhere, and constantly oppressed at home, looked to survival through an increasing legalism in dress and in other ways. When revival reached its peak (in Switzerland as elsewhere) in the thirties and early forties, the Anabaptist community was too hidebound to take advantage of it; and the state-church system showed unexpected flexibility by choosing this precise moment to begin dismantling the apparatus of persecution. In 1742 the *Tauferkammer* was abolished, and the *Tauferjäger* who had hunted down Anabaptists for profit dismissed. This was not so much Enlightenment casting its shadow before, as the recognition by the central government that its grip upon the Oberland, still uncertain where the forces of revival were concerned, had no more to fear from the Anabaptists.

### THE INSPIRED IN SWITZERLAND

Prophecy was a more lively option. Switzerland had, of course, been exposed direct to the Cévennes Prophets, three of whom had been expelled from Bern in 1711. She was also highly exposed to the hybrid variety, Inspiration. Numbers of Swiss religious refugees had fled to the Wetterau; great numbers had emigrated under economic pressure to Swabia and the Rhine valley across the routes of the Inspired into Württemberg; and many who stayed at home still hankered after an absolutely contemporary word of God and made off to the Wetterau for longer or shorter visits. The Bernese Oberland was again strongly represented with the Meyer family of Thun,

Christine Kratzer of Aeschi, who became a prophetess and 'tool', and others, but they came from every part of Protestant Switzerland, and some of what they sought, the opening of hearts and fraternal pursuit of sanctification, was the kind of thing for which Samuel Lutz had uncovered a lively demand in his sessions in the Langenbuhl forest.

At an early stage Gruber and Gleim had treated Switzerland as a mission-field, and four times between 1721 and 1735 Rock extended his journeys into Württemberg to Schaffhausen where he could recuperate in a sort of colony of the Inspired. He also made five major missionary circuits of the country, accompanied at first by a pastor expelled from Zurich, Johann Jakob Schulthess, as companion and translator. Schulthess soon became an independent operator, and with his wife worked the Bernese Oberland. Johann Samuel Carl, the medical adviser to the radicals of the Wetterau and editor of the *Geistliche Fama*, was brought in, and by the time the competition with the Herrnhuters began in the thirties, a great deal of manpower was at work.

They secured their main response in the Bernese Oberland and Oberaargau, making no progress in the more deferential low country, and created a network of conventicles in which the key figure was often an artisan. Women were also prominent, none more so than the blind Christine Kratzer, who claimed at one stage to have taken no solid food for four years, and no liquid for two. In sometimes bizarre forms of this kind the Inspired both exemplified and satisfied a craving for lay Christianity, sharpened the spirit of separatism, and even took aboard some of the old traditions of Anabaptism, forty-five refusing to take part in military exercises at Aeschi in 1730. In the end warfare on three fronts against the Orthodox, the Pietists and the Moravians broke the expansiveness of the Inspired; but although Rock died in 1749 as the age of revival was ending, and the Inspirations died out with him, the community in the Wetterau continued to exercise some pastoral oversight over the Swiss brethren for the rest of the century.[32]

[32] Wernle, *Schweizerischer Protestantismus* 1:178–210; Guggisberg, *Kirchengeschichte* 416–23; W. Hadorn, 'Die Inspirierten des 18. Jahrhunderts...', *STZ* 17 (1900) 184–224.

## ZINZENDORF AND THE SWISS

Even had Zinzendorf not undertaken a struggle against the Inspired, and even had he not as a matter of policy sought a foothold in awakened circles of all kinds (and in Switzerland he recruited largely among separatists, his revival providing them, as Inspiration had provided the Wetterau separatists, with a larger fellowship than they had lost), his attention would have been drawn to Switzerland. For two Swiss were important in the early history of his movement. Johann Georg Heitz, a Zuricher, he had met as steward of his aunt, the Countess Polheim, and appointed as manager of his new estate at Berthelsdorf. It was Heitz who received the first Moravian refugees, and settled them at what became Herrnhut. But Heitz's predesinarian views made cooperation with the count difficult, and in 1723 he left his service for good. His association with Friedrich von Watteville (or Wattenwyl) lasted, however, lifelong.[33] Watteville's father had sacrificed a seat in the Bern council, and his political rights, to Pietist views; he sent his son at the age of thirteen to the school for nobles at Halle, and it was there that he met his contemporary, Zinzendorf. Watteville was converted by the count, already a religious virtuoso, but in 1716 he returned to Bern to pursue a career with his elder brother Nicolas in the family bank. The Malacrida bank, however, fell victim in 1722 to Friedrich's speculations in the South Sea Bubble, the elder Friedrich, having lost his capital, withdrew to his wife's property at Montmirail in Neuchâtel, and the young Friedrich, described as 'half sceptic, half rationalist, his God a question-mark', was free to join the enthusiast Zinzendorf in the service of the kingdom of Christ.

This time Zinzendorf brought about a 'real', painful, almost Hallesian conversion, which made Friedrich his faithful servant for life. In this work he was assisted by another guest they encountered at Ebersdorf, Johanna Sophia von Zezschwitz. She married Watteville in Berthelsdorf in 1724. From now onwards Watteville was employed in managing the Berthelsdorf estate, on evangelistic journeys in France (1725 and 1727) and in Switzerland (1731–2), on all manner of responsible commissions, and in peace-keeping in the community, a work for which he was not always thanked by the count. Even if Watteville's standing in the Moravian community had

---

[33] J. Grosse, *Studien über Friedrich von Watteville* (Halle, 1914); Wernle, *Schweizerischer Protestantismus* 1:359–362.

not been enough to turn the count's eyes in the direction of Switzerland, the estate at Montmirail would have done so. From the beginning it was a base of Swiss operations, the scene of notable awakenings, and, in Zinzendorf's view, a good prospective refuge for Salzburgers and Waldensians.[34]

Watteville had been deeply influenced as a young man by Samuel Lutz; news of the revival at Herrnhut in 1727 was sent over to Amsoldingen from Montmirail, and produced exactly the right response: 'Oh! [wrote Lutz] that Herrnhut might before God be like the little cloud of Elijah, a prototype of the blessed outpouring of the Holy Spirit upon an arid Christendom.' Close relations between the two were established, though there was never any question of Lutz being won for Herrnhut. He and Zinzendorf might both be revivalists, but he was content to cultivate his parish and district, and to watch for the signs of the inbreaking Philadelphia; the count was out to realise that blessed state quickly. Each exercised a slightly prickly candour to the other, and in 1734 it came to a breach. And when the first Brethren, David Nitschmann and Riedel, were dispatched to Switzerland in 1730, they were provided with introductions to the Inspired and separatists of Zurich and Schaffhausen by Dr Carl, the spokesman for the Wetterau and Wittgenstein separatists, and editor of the *Geistliche Fama*.[35]

The Moravian mission in Switzerland enjoyed mixed fortunes. Zinzendorf hoped to use Swiss intermediaries to populate his Berthelsdorf estate with Huguenots; but neither party was open to this negotiation. On the other hand friends in Zurich and in the Graubünden gave generous support to the Moravian overseas missions which now developed very rapidly. The Brethren in Switzerland always recruited most successfully among separatists; but the separatists they attracted were constantly discomforted by the count's evident intention to make his way inside the great religious establishments, his appeal to the faculty at Tübingen,[36] his Lutheran ordination, his clash with Rock. A long series of important Swiss visitors – Holzhalb from Zurich, Annoni from Basel, Emmanuel Wolleb – were tempted off to Herrnhut, and impressed but not converted by what they saw. In the reverse direction, Zinzendorf repeatedly visited Switzerland, but his most successful spokesman was Christian David. During his stay at Montmirail in 1732 he

---

[34] After Friedrich's elder brother, Nicolas, had joined the Brethren in 1739, Montmirail was sold for the benefit of the community; the family repurchased it in 1753.
[35] Herrnhut MSS R21A, 112A, no. 3a.          [36] On which see pp. 193–5 below.

circulated to the important centres a detailed report on the constitution of Herrnhut which convinced sympathetic Swiss that Herrnhut was a model apostolic congregation. And their preachers were out in the Bernese Oberland where there was evidence of a catch to be taken, Amsoldingen, the Simmental, the upper Haslital.

### MORAVIANS IN SWITZERLAND

Relations with Switzerland became more urgent with the founding of Herrnhaag in 1738. The count was now banished from Saxony; Herrnhut was no longer the mainspring of new activities; exclusion from the Lutheran heartland made it all the more important to establish a foothold in the Reformed world. The count's agent has already appeared in connexion with the Baltic revival, Friedrich Wilhelm Biefer, a perruquemaker by original trade. He was now sent to Basel 'to make contact with the children of God there'; what he actually did was to bring about a great revival with 500–600 converts by offering as a new basis of unity among the case-hardened parties of Basel an inward experience of the crucified Saviour of sinners. Examined before the clergy, including old Samuel Werenfels, the Basel apostle of rational orthodoxy, he insisted so firmly on the doctrine of justification as to approve himself, and be given access to the students. Biefer's success, however, was brought to an end by events outside the town. On a visit to Mulhouse, he secured temporary relief from a depressive illness for the mayor's son; but this intervention provoked a great reaction from the patriciate of the town, backed by the clergy, and his expulsion at twenty-four hours' notice. A similar reaction in Basel followed; he had not contented himself with a revival, but had begun to organise his adherents separately, and even to celebrate communion among them. He was recommended to move on; but his work was solid. When he returned he found thirty-two classes of the awakened meeting, with a central organisation of committees, and the powerful support of one of the clergy and one of the merchants of the town. He repeated the performance in Schaffhausen where other Moravians had preceded him, and in Stein. Again he managed to pick up separatists, even some who had gone all the way with English deism. In Stein, however, Biefer was the victim of mob violence, and this sharply limited the success of his mission. The clergy and council of Zurich put out a warning to all the Protestant cantons against this foreign trouble-maker, and successfully barred his way into east Switzerland.

Even the support of Lutz could win him no favour in the city of Bern; only French-speaking Switzerland was left.

In Geneva Biefer was examined by the Venerable Company of Pastors and the straws in the wind all pointed the same way. The chief topics were Christ, faith and the Holy Spirit. The pastors admitted that they had begun to forget the election of grace and were now tolerant. They thought Biefer not tolerant enough on the question of good works, distinguishing too little between men of virtue and evil-doers. They thought Biefer's language about feelings of grace and of the spirit was that of a fanatic; he produced Pauline texts against them. That they were unsympathetic with his activity in the place, Biefer inferred from their repeated inquiry about when he was to leave. His reward for three months' work in Geneva was half a dozen classes, and much criticism among the Brethren themselves. The impression was created in Switzerland that the work of the Brethren there was a sideshow and one which collided with Swiss interests.[37]

The next visit to Switzerland, early in 1740, was paid by Zinzendorf himself, working in the same style as Biefer, and facing a barrage of hostile propaganda from the Inspired and separatists in the Wetterau. This gave the cue to the Orthodox, who replied with both the pen and the sword. The Zurich council resolved that no more Herrnhuters be allowed in, and this put a stop to the conventicles in Stein. The authorities of Schaffhausen concluded that although the meetings and private religious exercises were good in themselves, the risk of separatism was such that teachers from the outside, and all female teachers, must be prohibited. Sympathetic clergy were warned of the 'many perilous and poisonous things in the principles of Herrnhut'. With Basel and Bern swinging the same way, the count's goal, in 1741, was Geneva. The visit, ostensibly to try the ground for his son's education, was an astonishing state occasion, Zinzendorf arriving with a train of fifty. All the Moravian devotions were celebrated in their circle, the party dividing into Lutheran and Reformed when it came to communion. The little flock left behind by Biefer drew encouragement from all the ceremony and increased in number. But diplomatically the visit was a disastrous failure. The religion of reason and morality now dominant in Geneva was abhorrent to the count; his understanding of grace and spirit was abhorrent to the Genevans. The forms of politeness were preserved, but no one was in any doubt as to the situation.

Scouts from Zinzendorf's army were, however, left behind to reconnoitre the situation, and made off to the old stamping grounds in the Bernese Oberland and north and east Switzerland. These visits revealed what setbacks the cause had received since Biefer's first dramatic visit, but also how large a network of connexions remained. The question was whether the Brethren could develop this asset when their own affairs were plunged into the great crisis of the 'time of sifting'. The short answer was that they could not. For what was at stake was not merely the religious and liturgical extravagances of that period, but the attempts of Neisser and Polycarp Müller to force the authority and style of the Herrnhaag community on all the others. The two together were more than the Swiss, whether separatists or churchmen, would swallow. There was more to their objections than republican pertinacity; the claims of Herrnhaag caused a constant emigration and drain upon the human resources of the Swiss movement. It was normal for religious movements of a Philadelphian kind to suffer a tension between the claims of building up the Philadelphia, and those of gathering the faithful into it; here the faithful began to resist the gathering in.

There were also leadership troubles, many of which centred on Zinzendorf himself. The most influential man among the French-speaking Swiss separatists was Hector de Marsay, a disciple of Mme Guyon,[38] now living with his wife in Schwarzenau. They were charmed with the count at first, but later confessed that they had mistaken Antichrist for Christ, an opinion they duly relayed to Switzerland. In 1741 Zinzendorf sent an agent, a former shoemaker, to establish a permanent post in Diessbach, the parish of the aged Lutz. He was instructed to honour Lutz as a father and avoid all controversy. Lutz was generosity itself, and defended him when in 1742 the *Religionskammer* demanded his expulsion. But the Moravian shoemaker had no doubt that they worked on a different religious footing, and not surprisingly correspondence between Lutz and the Brethren ceased, notwithstanding that two of the pastor's nephews joined the *Brüdergemeine*. There was a limit to the amount of proselytising in his parish he would contemplate. Nowhere was the conflict between Herrnhaag and the Swiss sharper than in Basel, the strongest Moravian centre in Switzerland; the Baslers would not

---

[38] On whom: M. Goebel, *Geschichte des christlichen Lebens in der rheinisch-westphalischen evangelischen Kirche* (3 vols. Koblenz, 1849–52) III:193–234.

admit that Jesus was less closely bound to his people in their town than in Herrnhaag, and were deeply disturbed by children being tempted thither, apparently without possibility of return, in defiance of parental disapproval. The breach was completed in 1743. With Hieronymus Annoni, the famous Pietist pastor of Waldenburg, who had close relatives who went over to Herrnhut, there was also frequent conflict. When he moved to Muttenz near Basel, there was open competition between him and the Moravians there. In the mid-sixties, like Samuel König earlier, Annoni was persuaded by the general change in the intellectual situation to patch up his relations with Herrnhut; but this could not be said of Beat Holzhalb of Zurich. Personal observation and the torrent of propaganda exposing alleged Moravian bad behaviour and bad management made him a bitter enemy; he did not take all the Zurich Pietists with him, but greatly assisted those of Hallesian convictions to hold their ground. The leading old Pietists in Switzerland all did so, and the extravagances of the 'time of sifting' gave them no encouragement to do otherwise. Moreover most of the Protestant cantons found means of excluding 'foreign' teachers and leaders of religious organisations and this made things difficult for the Moravians.

Nevertheless, despite resistance on the one side and folly on the other, congregations of the Brethren were established in Zinzendorf's lifetime in Geneva and Montmirail, in Basel, Bern and Aarau, in Schaffhausen and places in Graubünden. The organisation of the Brethren made it possible to send distinguished missionaries, Friedrich von Watteville, and the English bookseller James Hutton, in 1748 and again (for a spell of seven years) in 1756.[39] The exaggerations of the 'time of sifting' were gradually forgotten, and Montmirail proved a splendid setting for corporate celebrations of the scattered flock. A local leadership began to develop. As the hand of reason settled more heavily on the Swiss schools, a minority of theological students found a new attractiveness in Zinzendorf's enthusiastic love of Jesus. The Basel society underwent a further crisis when the settlement at Herrnhaag had to be closed, and many Baslers returned home to create fresh disputes over authority; but in the *Landschaft* the community began to spread. More generally the patient and kindly work of James Hutton reaped its reward.

---

[39] D. Benham, *Memoirs of James Hutton* (London, 1856) 199–204, 312–70. Community politics had united Hutton in 1740, with a wife from Neuchâtel, Louise Brandt, 'in order that there might be a sister in London who should attend to the work of the Lord among the females'. *Ibid.* 56.

In the Bernese Oberland there was little to hope for as long as Lutz and his successor in Amsoldingen, Samuel Hopf, were alive. After they died the leadership gap was filled not by the Moravians, but by the Heimberger fellowship, a body created by converts of Lutz and the Inspired. But in their hostility to legalism the Heimberger fellowship had points of resemblance to the Herrnhuters, and twenty years after Zinzendorf's death there was a fusion between the two which led to the creation of an extensive Moravian diaspora in the Oberland. A strong society developed in Aarau, south-east of Basel, which proved capable of acting as a focus for a diaspora of its own, and, in 1752, in the way that was often to happen during the revival in England, an entirely independent revival near the Hallwilersee, between Aarau and Luzern, came to attach itself to the Aarau community.

East Switzerland remained barren territory to the Moravians, but in the Graubünden they entered into the inheritance of the older ascetic Pietism, provided an organisation which the mystics and adherents of Böhme never had, and attracted noticeable numbers of clergy and gentry. The general run of Bündner people hated foreigners more than they respected their own gentry, and in the fifties the Moravians encountered serious mob violence, and this enabled the Protestant session of the *Bundestag* to intervene. But a goodly heritage remained. Pietism had failed to renew the church, but revival had reached the ends of the country and taken institutional form. And to use a term introduced only in nineteenth-century America, the Bernese Oberland, after the ministrations of Erb and Lutz, the Inspired, the Heimberger fellowship and the Moravians, not to mention the originals of the Haslital, might be termed the first 'burned-over district'.

## THE INSPIRED IN WÜRTTEMBERG

Most of the original separatists who took refuge in Ysenburg were from Swabia, and, after many of them had been drawn into Inspiration, their relations with Swabia continued close. Rock with twenty-seven visits spent much of his time in Württemberg. That duchy had a long tradition of *Konventikel* or private gatherings for religious purposes and it was not difficult to rally some of these to very sharp prophecies against church and state. In 1725 Rock pinned up a jeremiad on the Town Hall in Stuttgart denouncing 'the crazy and wicked people, the evil generation of Christians, and the mad priests, the so-called shepherds and teachers'; 'God would require blood guilt of the princes, authorities, governors and judges, yea, and all the officials, since so much sweat and blood has been sucked out of the poor'. Rock had two quite specific targets in view. Württemberger Pietism was part of a great movement of country politics against the court. Like the Saxon church, the church in Württemberg was confronted by a dynasty turned Catholic; unlike it, it was enabled by the constitution of the duchy to became a powerful vehicle of opposition politics. The bad years for the Württemberger church came in the War of the Spanish Succession, but that corner was turned, and Bengel's confident location of the Second Coming in the year 1836 acknowledged the fact. As the atmosphere of crisis dispersed, the religious temperature dropped and class-meetings began to die out; even the visit of August Hermann Francke in 1717 gave no new impulse. G. K. Rieger, who wrote the history of both the Salzburgers and the Moravians, declared in 1741 that the early years of the century had been the time of the first love in the Württemberger church, implying that like the church at Ephesus (according to Rev. 2:4) it had subsequently left its first love.[40] Rock did not accept the major premise, but was in full agreement with the minor, doing his best to turn the disillusionment to the advantage of his own movement.

Württemberg was, however, almost uniquely exposed, not merely to French invasion, but also to the claims of every group of suffering Protestants from the Defereggers onwards. Collections had been made for all, and refuges found for not a few. The most active friend of the Salzburgers in the West, Samuel Urlsperger, senior of Augsburg, was himself a Württemberger in political exile. A church harrowed so regularly by the sufferings of others, and mindful of its own, responded in the thirties to the forces of revival all round it. Johann Jakob Moser recalled that there was 'a great awakening in Tübingen and throughout Württemberg' and a heightened interest in events in Herrnhut.[41] At this point Zinzendorf intervened.

### ZINZENDORF IN WÜRTTEMBERG

The duchy figured in Zinzendorf's earliest plans much less than Switzerland or Denmark, but in the early thirties his interest in it warmed rapidly. He must now think of new bases, and especially

[40] Fritz, 'Konventikel', pt. 6, *BWKg* 52 (1952) 31, 53.
[41] J. J. Moser, *Lebensgeschichte von ihme selbst beschrieben* (n.pl., 1768) pt. 3 204.

Lutheran bases, abroad, and the malign influence of Halle in Denmark blighted the most suitable opening. Württemberg seemed an attractive alternative. Bilfinger was seeking to ease the way for Enlightenment, to enlarge religious toleration, and raise the general level of piety, while Pfaff had lately been a leading spokesman for church union.[42] Moser was arguing for increased toleration for conventicles. Zinzendorf may have become familiar with Pfaff, Bilfinger, Weissensee and other great names of Tübingen and Stuttgart, while he was in Halle. Certainly in 1733, when he was still generally regarded as a representative of Halle Pietism, he appealed to them direct.

Already in 1730, Zinzendorf sent Nitschmann and Riedel to Tübingen, with introductions to Pfaff and others, and instructions to found fellowships, on their way to Switzerland, and a considerable group of Württemberger clergy with the leave of their consistories made their way to Herrnhut. Of these the most notable were Oetinger and Steinhofer. Friedrich Christoph Oetinger had been studying in Halle in 1730, came to Herrnhut, became tutor to Zinzendorf's daughter Benigna, and did other pastoral work. Oetinger's position, always an odd one,[43] was already suspect to his consistory, and he was fetched back the following September. Friedrich Christoph Steinhofer was a contact made by Nitschmann and Riedel on their first visit, and proved to be Zinzendorf's choice as adjunct to Rothe, to help bear the additional burden of pastoral oversight created by the growth of Herrnhut. In 1731 the count dispatched Christian David to Württemberg, and he was taken round the country by Oetinger, visiting separatists and making a deep impression.

In 1733 Oetinger provided an itinerary for Zinzendorf himself. On this trip Zinzendorf believed he had impressed the theologians of Tübingen, and so he got Steinhofer to put an inquiry to the theological faculty of his *alma mater*, whether the Moravians, assuming there to be doctrinal agreement, 'could and should abide by the institutions they had had for 300 years...and yet abide by their

---

[42] For whom: H. Liebing, *Zwischen Orthodoxie und Aufklärung. Das...Denken G. B. Bilfingers* (Tübingen, 1961); Arnold F. Stolzenburg, *Die Theologie des J. F. Buddeus und des C. M. Pfaff* (Berlin, 1926; rpr. Aalen, 1979); E. Hirsch, *Geschichte der neuern evangelischen Theologie* (5 vols. 5th edn Gütersloh, 1975) II: 336–54.

[43] He is classed by Hirsch among the 'pious outsiders', and, starting from Böhme and Bengel, developed his opposition to the philosophy of Leibniz and Wolff into a christian map of knowledge incorporating Paracelsus, alchemy and kabbalistic ideas. Hirsch, *Ibid.* IV: 166 174; Sigrid Grossmann, *F. C. Oetingers Gottesvorstellung* (Göttingen, 1979); *F. C. Oetingers Selbstbiographie* ed. Julius Hamberger (Stuttgart, 1845); *PuN* 10 (1984).

connexion with the Evangelical Church'. A favourable answer to this question might assist the Herrnhuters in any part of the Lutheran world, and especially in Württemberg, and, written by Bilfinger with an epilogue by Pfaff, it was almost instantly forthcoming. This positive response was a great tonic for Zinzendorf, coming as it did when his orthodoxy was being challenged from opposing sides by the Saxon Orthodox and the Halle Pietists. There were, however, reservations in the Tübingen faculty. Weissmann, the church historian, was on sick leave at the time. He had personal connexions with J. P. S. Winckler, the court chaplain at Ebersdorf, Zinzendorf's inveterate enemy. He felt distrusted by the count and subsequently protested against the document. And the faculty quickly rued what they had done.

From Frankfurt came the allegation that Pfaff opened the door to syncretism, almost the worst slander in the Lutheran dictionary. Still worse, that formidable ex-Pietist champion of Orthodoxy, Erdmann Neumeister of Hamburg, weighed in with the view the 'the grounds of proof look even thinner and more hateful than the seven thin and hateful cows and the seven hard, thin, and dried-up ears of corn which were shown to Pharoah in a dream'. Of course, Calvinists in Saxony had always claimed to be adherents of the Augsburg Confession, even while their brethren were the most zealous persecutors of Lutheranism in Poland.[44] The pretensions of the Tübingen faculty to be a stronghold of Lutheran orthodoxy were, in their way, as great as those of Wittenberg, and the hammering the faculty now received taught caution. On Pfaff's advice, they abstained from further literary controversy on the matter. Zinzendorf believed that the Tübingen opinion accelerated the decree of banishment against him. But it was made superfluous by the development of his community in Reformed territories, and by 1750 the count was prepared to add his own weight to the critics of the hapless Tübingen faculty, telling Pfaff that because they 'answered more than they were asked, they were the real cause of the public controversy'.[45]

This retort, however, was sharpened by events subsequent to 1733. Having obtained Lutheran ordination at Stralsund, Zinzendorf thought first to secure a prelacy in Württemberg, preferably St Georgi, at present used as an endowment for a court chaplain in

---

[44]  E. Neumeister, *Mene Tekel...* (n.pl., 1736).
[45]  R. Geiges, 'Zinzendorf und Württemberg', *BWKg* 17 (1913) 75, 77.

Stuttgart, with a view to restoring the monastic buildings at his own expense, and setting up a seminary to train the converted for church service as catechists, tutors or missionaries abroad. This institution would have been in full union with the Württemberger church. In September 1734 Spangenberg was dispatched to Württemberg to negotiate the matter with the duke. Nothing went right with this mission. The president of the Privy Council was dying; the duke was away at the War of the Polish Succession as a field-marshal of the Swabian circle. The colleges which dealt with ecclesiastical matters were very divided. Johann David Fritsch and his party opposed the plan on canon-law grounds and thought it would lead to separatism. Weissensee's group were very cautious and had great reservations about Zinzendorf (and also about Steinhofer, who had gone off to Ebersdorf without any word to Stuttgart); and as, after Urlsperger's departure for Augsburg, Weissensee was regarded as the leader of the Halle party in Württemberg, his opposition is not hard to understand. And there were, of course, endless complications in allowing a foreigner into a dignity which carried both political representation and prospects of ecclesiastical promotion. Both the Privy Council and the consistory advised against the proposal, and the duke, who feared that such a favour to a Protestant would enrage his Catholic subjects, and encourage anxieties that he was about to convert back to Protestantism, turned it down.

## ZINZENDORF AND OETINGER

Zinzendorf's relations with Oetinger and Bengel may stand for his relations with Württembergers in general, though each was a singular character. Few had greater admiration for and at the same time greater reservations about the count than Oetinger. He did much to prepare the success of Zinzendorf's visit to Württemberg in 1733, and the grandiose and entirely abortive plans for travel to Constantinople and India (in the hope of extraordinary revelations) and as pastor to Pennsylvania (in the hope of gathering congregations which, in turning their back on the churches of the Old World, might realise the kingdom of God in new ways) which testified to his highly individual pursuit of truth, synchronised with Zinzendorf's more romantic fancies. In May 1733 he came back to Herrnhut with a view to a long stay, and plunged enthusiastically into the Moravian work of Bible translation. His consistory began to doubt both his orthodoxy and his willingness to serve the Württemberger church. Baumgarten tempted him to pursue his studies at Halle, and he fitted in medical studies in Bad Homburg, and Böhme studies in the Netherlands. Up to 1737 Zinzendorf pursued him relentlessly, and, trapped among so many claims, Oetinger's health suffered.

His difficulties with the count were never overcome or even eased by genuine personal admiration. They included Zinzendorf's attitude to scripture, which Oetinger had seen at close quarters, his grandiose plans, and his character. To satisfy Oetinger, a world-view had to have its basis in scripture; Zinzendorf, he felt, regarded his own religious experience as normative even for the exegesis of scripture; cavalier and superficial, he got worse in his use of the Bible the more he fell under the spell of mysticism. Zinzendorf was not a scholar; he 'observed the true, the false and the probable according to a certain logic under a divine preservation from all ecstatic leaps'. He was also terrified at Zinzendorf's far-reaching plans for his community. This was perhaps surprising in an Oetinger who could not make do with anything less than a new Christian map of knowledge; but that map indicated that the count grossly exaggerated the significance of his movement. Yet, painful as it was to admit, 'Herrnhut is a magnet to me, more than a hundred glories of the scholars.' It was the same with Zinzendorf himself. His sugary (*zuckersüsse*) professions of personal love to the count are fully matched by his private comments to Bengel. Yet in the end, Zinzendorf, with all his goodness, was a tyrant who used unwarrantable pressure to bind men to him; and, with all his acumen, a tyrant of frequently mistaken views, and of duplicity in tongue and heart.[46] By 1737 Oetinger had broken free, his escape assisted by two factors of more general importance. After 1737, as his hold on the levers of influence in Württemberg loosened, Zinzendorf sent an increasing number of diaspora workers into the duchy, who raised a great many hackles, especially those of Bengel. And from about the same date Oetinger began to enter more deeply into the thought-world of that great man, a thought-world of which something must now be said.

[46] R. Geiges, 'Die Auseinandersetzung zwischen Oetinger und Zinzendorf' *BWKg* 39 (1935) 148; 40 (1936) 114, 108.

## ZINZENDORF AND BENGEL

It is almost the case that there were no relations between Zinzendorf and Bengel except literary relations. Oetinger indeed arranged for Zinzendorf to visit Bengel when he came to Württemberg in 1733. This meeting was thoroughly equivocal, and, never referred to by the principals, is known only through Oetinger's reporting. Oetinger seems to have thought that Bengel might influence the Herrnhut movement for good, but there could be no question of inviting the count to sit at the feet of a (then) unknown Swabian schoolmaster. Bengel, however, pressed on the count his eschatological calculations, and seems to have hoped that the Brethren might disseminate his perspectives on salvation-history world-wide. Oetinger was delighted by the result, reporting that Zinzendorf was completely overcome by Bengel's system. In truth Zinzendorf was deeply orientated against 'system' of any kind, and he was shortly criticising Bengel's ideas, as politically motivated. The principals to the meeting seem rapidly to have appreciated that they would get nowhere with each other. Bengel, hurt at what he felt to be a rebuff, refused to see the count again, and in his later years stalked him relentlessly through his published work. Impersonal as it all seemed, the personal edge was sharpened by the fact that in 1738 Bengel's eldest daughter, Sophie Elizabeth, married a zealous disciple of Herrnhut, Albrecht Richard Reuss.

There was no way two minds as different as those of Bengel and Zinzendorf could be made to meet. Bengel was an extraordinary mixture of breadth and narrowness. As a schoolmaster he had to be a philologist, and his grammar went on being reprinted in Germany until a generation ago, and in the English-speaking world, until well after the middle of the last century. But basically he was a theologian who contributed massively to every branch of his discipline. Zinzendorf was kin to all those who wished to escape the age of Orthodoxy, while Bengel was recognisably Orthodox. He held that it was necessary to believe the basic truths, that the Bible was a system of basic truths, and that theology was a science logically constructed on indestructible biblical foundations. In particular the scriptures contained the basic features of the divine 'economy', God's chronological plan for the destinies of mankind from beginning to end. A knowledge of this scheme was now more than ever necessary for the Christian, for between 1740 and 1834 the 'harvest' and 'autumn' would take place, the taking away of many good and wicked men, prior to the coming of the Lord in 1836. This introverted system spoke to neither the hopes nor the fears of Zinzendorf, neither the prospect of world-wide mission, nor the menace of deism.

The upshot was that Bengel worked out in his own remorseless way the charges already brought by Oetinger, that Zinzendorf was incompetent in the scriptures, that he had 'neither the calling nor the capacity for his exalted undertaking', that he concealed the fact by 'sophistical simulations, dissimulations, baseless charges (*Insimulationen*), reservations, justifications, eulogies, excuses, admissions etc.',[47] that the Brethren were built on the pattern of the founder, and were therefore a mixture of good and bad certainly not based on the *Confessio Augustana*, and certainly not justifying their claim to eminence in the history of salvation. This head of steam was built up gradually. In the years 1743 and 1744 Bengel was asked for private opinions on the Brethren, and between 1746 and 1749 he gave three further opinions requested by the representatives of the Württemberg church government. Bengel, in his bookish way, got down to the study of the Brethren in the mid forties, and completed some 160 octavo sheets, written on both sides. This was the material on which his *Sketch of the so-called Brethren*, written before he came to Stuttgart in 1749, and published in 1751, was based. The combined influence of Bengel and his writings dealt a crushing blow to the hopes of the Brethren in Württemberg from which they did recover till the nineteenth century, a blow reinforced by the famous Pietist rescript of 1743. This gave scope for private religious gatherings within the fold of the church, but drew the line against separation and against the participation of strangers not known to the parson. Württemberg had turned its back on Herrnhut.[48]

### ZINZENDORF AND MOSER

Among those who had brought Bengel to the point of controversy was the celebrated Württemberger public lawyer Johann Jakob Moser (1701–85), whose evolution is also germane to the theme. Moser was already acquainted with Zinzendorf through Halle and Danish connexions when he experienced an evangelical conversion in 1733.

---

[47] *ZW* Series 2 x:286, 303.
[48] G. Mälzer, *Bengel und Zinzendorf* (Witten, 1968); *Bengel. Leben und Werk* (Stuttgart, 1970); J. C. F. Burk, *A Memoir of... J. A. Bengel* tr. R. P. Walker (London, 1837) 157.

His travels convinced him that what he lacked for spiritual progress was the fellowship and combined spiritual expertise of the Pietist class-meeting, and he found this to perfection in the *Schloss-ecclesiola* and the society of the 'pious counts' at Ebersdorf. Here, from 1739, he spent some of the happiest years of his life. From 1745, however, harmony was disrupted by Zinzendorf's finally successful efforts to absorb Ebersdorf into his empire. Moser could not stand the count's preaching, still less the new pressure for 'stillness'. He found himself increasingly excluded from fellowship, and, in 1747, was excommunicated. It was time for Moser to leave and take up an appointment with the Landgrave of Hesse-Homburg. The over-emphasis on the 'blood and wounds theology', spiritual pressure in the community, Zinzendorf's 'popish' authority, had cost the count a man whose ability to harness evangelicalism and Enlightenment ought to have made him useful, and created him another formidable enemy in Württemberg.[49]

[49] Moser, *Lebensgeschichte* 55, 92; R. Rurup, *J. J. Moser. Pietismus und Reform* (Wiesbaden, 1965) 39–40, 42; *ZW* Series 2 xii·561–81. In his newspapers Moser combined favourable views of the Moravians with unfavourable ones of the count. *Altes und Neues* 2:3–40; 3:3–34; 6:49–64; 7:3–33; *ZW* Reihe 2 xv:415–49.

# CHAPTER 6

# Revival in the North-West of the Empire and the Lower Rhine

## POLITICAL AND CONFESSIONAL COMPLEXITY OF THE NORTH-WEST

The Moravians traversed the North-West of the Empire between their bases in the Wetterau, in Denmark and in the Netherlands, as busily as the South-West. Everywhere they went they created new interconfessional connexions – the way they passed Wesley from hand to hand all the way from Rotterdam to Herrnhut and back is especially instructive[1] – and also new disputes; but in this area, unlike the South-West, their history is not an organising principle for that of revival as a whole. For the crux of the religious geography of the North-West was that both revival and Pietist renewal suffered great setbacks, and that Lutheran Orthodoxy staged a notable, if brittle, comeback in the great Imperial cities and in some other important territories. There were good reasons (as we have seen) why religious revival set in first in the little Reformed principalities in the Wetterau, and more importantly, though much more slowly, in the larger Reformed communities. To these developments Zinzendorf's aspirations to create a Reformed Tropus based on Herrnhaag were entirely marginal.

In the North-West political fragmentation had proceeded further than anywhere else in the Empire; nowhere were the religious faiths tolerated in the Empire more confusingly mixed together, and mingled with other faiths not tolerated (in Frankfurt the Jewish ghetto already made up 25 per cent of the population). Nowhere were ecclesiastical oddities more numerous; the bishopric of Osnabrück alternated between Catholic and Protestant, the latter to be members of the Welf family; there was the Lutheran bishopric of

---

[1] Wesley, *Works* XVIII–XIX: *Journals* I:255–66; II:5–12.

Bremen, whose only foothold in Bremen itself, the most important Reformed stronghold in the Empire, was the cathedral; the town council of Frankfurt fought doggedly to preserve the Lutheran character of the place by keeping the Reformed congregation outside the walls, but had in their midst a Catholic cathedral in which the electors formally chose successive Emperors. Equally dogged was the council of the former free city of Strasbourg, where steady French pressure raised the French and Catholic proportion of the population to about a third, and the Lutherans lost the cathedral to the Catholics. The notion that there was such a place as 'the Rhineland', inhabited by Rhinelanders (not to mention Rhine-maidens), was only put about by romantics in the nineteenth century. Yet when, a few years ago, the press association of the Evangelical Church of the Rhineland published a learned analysis of the religious psychology of their own congregations, it transpired that they had a subject, and that its principal feature was the virtue Christian moralists find most difficulty in handling, viz. independence, exemplified especially in lay emancipation and immediacy of religious experience.[2] These modern features can be seen taking shape in the eighteenth century.

Independence in religious experience was a thing which governments wished to encourage only in the most unusual circumstances.[3] Louis XV issued his own edict against Protestants in 1724, many Protestant villages in Alsace were required to share their church with Catholic immigrants, and, as we have seen, Stanislas Leszczynski caused a thousand of his Protestant subjects there to migrate to the Baltic.[4] The literary controversies against Pietists occurred in three great waves, the late 1680s and early nineties, aimed largely at Spener, the first decade of the eighteenth century when Francke was the chief target, and the 1740s when the onslaught was upon Zinzendorf. To an increasing degree these controversies were fought out in the North-West, and they led to many anti-Pietist edicts. Hesse-Darmstadt had long had its anti-Pietist programme. In 1702 the landgrave of Hesse-Kassel published an edict against those who claimed special sanctity, but were in fact subject to 'enthusiastic

---

[2] O. Kietzig, *Die kirchliche Frömmigkeit in den evangelischen Gemeinden des Niederrheins* (Düsseldorf, 1971) 5, 22, 64.

[3] As, e.g., at Altona, where, to develop the place as a commercial rival to Hamburg, the Danish government connived at almost any religious oddity. J. A. Bolten, *Historische Kirchen-Nachrichten von der Stadt Altona*... (Altona, 1790–1).

[4] *UN* 1727 441–6; *AHE* 5:160–2.

visions and revelations', which led them to devalue scripture and pursue Christian perfection in this life. The electorate of Hanover (as will appear) was solidly anti-Pietist. The years 1705 to 1707 saw a series of edicts against innovations in religion in Bremen, Sweden (backed up the theological faculty at Rostock), Denmark, Württemberg and Nuremberg. Some of these condemned especially physical contortions undergone under pretence of special sanctity, others conventicles.[5]

Many were motivated, or justified, by references to the Buttlar Gang (*Die Buttlar'sche Rotte*). Eva von Buttlar (1670–1717) was born into a family, now impoverished, descended from the Lutheran line of a well-known Hessian family; her mother was fifty-two when she was born, and her father died while she was very young. At seventeen she was sent away to the corrupt Eisenach court of one of the descendants of Duke Ernst the Pious, where she married a shady character, the French-Reformed court dancing-master. This union remained childless, and in 1697 she resolved to live as a holy woman, though she seems to have waited another five years before refusing to cohabit with her husband. This decision corresponded with a second spiritual crisis; she now moved to Hesse to set up a Christian and Philadelphian society, taking with her her spiritual circle, her lover, a theologian called Winter, and the five von Callenberg girls, the upper-crust converts of the famous Swiss Pietist Samuel König. Eva gave it out that Winter and a medical student from Jena were God the Father and God the Son, while she was no less than God the Holy Spirit. The press made a meal of the case, and the truth was further obscured by allegations made in the course of divorce proceedings by Eva's husband, the lascivious attempts of the Orthodox propagandists to saddle the Pietist movement with the scandal, and the equal determination of the Halle spokesmen to have none of it. These spiritual unions, it was alleged, were blessed with unspiritual offspring who were disposed of by murder. The rake's progress ended, to Orthodox satisfaction, in the conversion of many of the Buttlar group to Catholicism. The affair shows both how far an unsatisfied yearning for spiritual perfection and personal love might drive members even of the upper orders from their religious establishments, and how determined the Halle Pietists were to stick to

[5] J. G,. Walch, *Historisch- und theologische Einleitung in die Religionsstreitigkeiten der evangelisch-lutherischen Kirchen* (5 vols. Jena, 1733–9; repr. Bad Cannstatt, 1972–) 1:777–85, 808–14.

those establishments and use them.[6] But legislation against religious deviation simply increased the number of religious refugees.

Other religious delusions and possibilities had also been exposed or exhausted. The Orthodox could never be entirely weaned from apocalyptic speculation, but at least the penultimate scenario had to change with the times. Römeling, the garrison preacher at Harburg who adopted rather eccentric Pietist views and lost his job in 1710, proceeded to prophesy the overthrow of Europe's ecclesiastical Babel by the return of the Swedish king, Charles XII, then in exile in Turkey, in alliance with the Turks. This was a conservative vision, featuring the traditional saviour of the gospel faith, Sweden, the traditional enemy of that faith, the Habsburgs, and the Habsburgs' two bugbears, the Turks and the Swedes. It collapsed comprehensively, for Charles XII died in 1718 and confessional peace in Germany was severely tested in 1719. There were then those in East Friesland who looked to the unlikeliest solution of all, an alliance of Wittenberg and Halle, of Orthodox and Pietist. This alliance was only partially realised when Zinzendorf became the menace of the day, and apocalyptic speculation then took a new twist. As we have seen, some of the radicals were convinced by the upheavals of the early thirties that the seduction and tyranny of the age of Balaam and Jezebel was about to end, and that the new dawn was signalled by reformation in Prussia. At an official level Hauber, the Pietist superintendent of Schaumburg-Lippe, was assured that Frederick the Great's incursion into Silesia in 1740 fulfilled the prophecy of Joel. Even Prussia, however, failed to usher in the new dawn, and the war not only directly injured religious enterprise in the North-West but encouraged the nobility of the whole Rhine area to put down Protestants with military assistance in contravention of the Westphalia settlement.[7] The world only too clearly went on as before.

## EMIGRATION

In the West there were men of broad vision distressed by the poor overseas missionary record of the Protestant churches. The maritime states with access to the world overseas seemed more interested in the

[6] *Ibid.* II:768–75; Friedrich Wilhelm Barthold, *Die Erweckten im protestantischen Deutschland während des Ausgangs des 17. und der ersten Hälfte des 18. Jahrhunderts, besonders die frommen Grafenhöfe* (repr. from *Historisches Taschenbuch* ed. Friedrich von Raumer 1852–3, Darmstadt, 1968) 151–84; J. B. Neveux, *Vie Spirituelle et Vie Sociale entre Rhin et Baltique...* (Paris, 1967) 209–14; M. Goebel, *Geschichte des christlichen Lebens in der rheinisch-westphalischen evangelischen Kirche* (3 vols., Koblenz, 1849–52) II:788–809.

[7] *AHE* 7:797–822, esp. 803–5.

slave trade than in the welfare of souls.[8] The conjunction of missions and the slave trade could only recall a recent unsuccessful effort to promote religious revival. For Penn and the Quakers of his generation had sought just this. In England they had picked up Seeker groups (as later Methodism picked up Quakers); on the continent they looked for their first proselytes among the Mennonites, and reinforced their work through Spener's inner circle. Penn himself visited the European mission field in 1671, 1677 and 1683, coming both as an evangelist and as a real estate promoter to gather colonists for his new property in Pennsylvania. Indeed in Frankfurt, with the backing of Johann Jakob Schütz, Spener's right-hand man, he set up a regular emigration society in 1682, with F. D. Pastorius as its secretary. He it was who took out the first group of emigrants from Krefeld, settled them in a compact group at Germantown outside Philadelphia, and by his *Beschreibung von Pennsylvania* (1684) and his constant correspondence with Pietists and separatists, brought out innumerable further groups. He and his Krefelders at Germantown in 1688 produced a memorable application of Bible, English Quakerism, German logic, and the frontier experience of the Holy Roman Empire, resolving, 'never do to another what you do not wish to have done to you; also sell no man as a slave and treat him not like the Turks. If you contend for the freedom of spirit, then be logical and guarantee the freedom of the body.' This first protest against American slavery was to have a long resonance; but the immediate effect of Pastorius's efforts was to ship to the inhibiting climate of North America what might have been a religious revival in the Netherlands and the North-West of the Empire. This experience, as Zinzendorf appreciated, did not entirely destroy the capacity of the Mennonites to generate religious revival. But like the Anabaptists in Switzerland, the Mennonites in the North-West remained marginal rather than central to its history.

LABADISM

Labadism, which fizzled out, at any rate as a communitarian ideal, only in 1744, also remained in the background rather than the foreground of the story.[9] Whereas the Quakers sought to foster the light that lighteth every man, the Labadists were an archetypal elite,

[8]　T. Wotschke, 'A. H. Franckes rheinische Freunde' *MRKg* 22 (1928) 315, 369.

[9]　The large literature on Labadism is surveyed, together with much new material, in T. J. Saxby, *The Quest for the New Jerusalem, Jean de Labadie and the Labadists* (Dordrecht, 1987).

with Jean de Labadie (1610–74) the most elite of all. Perhaps a bastard of Henry IV of France, Labadie was raised there by an ex-Calvinist family on the make, then groomed for stardom by the Jesuits before breaking with them to join the Reformed church and to be hunted from both France and Orange by Louis XIV. After an uneasy pastorate in Geneva, he answered a call to Middelburg in the Netherlands. Here he never got going, and in 1670 left the Reformed church with a select body of disciples, the most famous of whom was Anna van Schurman, and took refuge for a couple of years at Herford, where the Protestant abbey was presided over by Elizabeth, the eldest daughter of the Winter King of Bohemia, and granddaughter of James I of England. Subsequently the Labadists were coolly assessed by Sophie of Hanover, the mother of George I of England, and hunted up and down the Rhineland until a settlement could be found at Altona. Other settlements followed, but, single-mindedly devoted to the kingdom of God, the well-heeled Labadists were not much good at the business of survival. Even less competent in Surinam than Wesley was in Georgia, they would not accept good peasant advice about agriculture in Friesland; and when their more prosperous backers pulled the plug on them at the end of the seventeenth century, they did not last long. Labadie was in truth a rather unsympathetic character, excessively impressed by his own rather voluptuous visions; he had no solution to the ills of a church and world which he scourged continually, other than an erroneous conviction that, when he and his friends inaugurated the millennial kingdom, all the elect would join them. Yet, in a mysterious way, he attracted the veneration of men and women of real substance, and his movement, even more than the Buttlar Gang, testified to the longing, even in the upper classes, to get away from what the churches offered as Orthodoxy. Their secession from the Reformed Church suggested that the Calvinist ethos was hostile to those with aspirations to Christian perfection, and it subtly raised the religious temperature in quarters which stood much nearer than the Labadists to the history of religious revival.

The Labadist determination to achieve the pure church affected the preaching of the Reformed churches in the Netherlands and the Rhineland. A new emphasis on the difference between the converted and unconverted, between the regenerate and unregenerate, is to be observed, a new certainty as to who was in each class; the moral pressure this exerted led to revivals of some scope. At Herford

Labadie's preaching worked a revival which went by the Jansenist name of *resurrectio*. Their settlements attracted religious seekers of quite different origins, enabling the movement to expand considerably after Labadie's death; the parallel with the Moravian movement is striking, and was not lost upon Zinzendorf.[10] The missions of the group in the Netherlands and the Lower Rhine area had a considerable impact; the class-meetings or conventicles which in the Reformed tradition had begun in conjunction with the Sunday service, and which were to become cells of religious revival, spread greatly and became somewhat anti-church in sentiment. Tersteegen (shortly to be introduced) worked in this milieu; his unsacramental mysticism is reminiscent of the Labadists, and his translations of Labadie's hymns got the Frenchman into the German hymn-books. The final dissolution of the Labadist communities also sent their members out into the conventicles. Labadie was an expert publicist who took his own press to Herford and Altona, and employed his own translator to turn work originally published in Dutch, French and Latin into High German. This was important, for the one thing in the Reformed world Lutherans were happy to read about was schism, and publication made Labadism the talking-point of the day. People like J. H. Horb, Spener's brother-in-law, and Samuel Nethenus, pastor of Baerl bei Moers, made personal visits to Labadie in the Netherlands; and publication created other contacts. The library of Johann Jakob Schütz, Spener's collaborator in Frankfurt, was lately discovered in Schloss Laubach, the residence of Spener's friend the count of Solms-Laubach. It contained numerous Labadist writings, including some which urged separation from a corrupt religious establishment, which were actually used in the Frankfurt collegium, complete with Schütz's marginal notes.[11] Schütz, of course, separated as Spener did not; two generations later the Solms family were Wesley's hosts on his way from Rotterdam to Herrnhut. One of the Dutch financial backers of Zinzendorf, Matthäus Beuning, was also a Labadist. Thus Labadism, too elitist to lead a popular revival, left a mark on a much later age which succeeded where Labadie failed. The difficulties confronting Labadie's successors in the West were, nevertheless, formidable, and to them we must turn.

[10] W. Goeters, *Die Vorbereitung des Pietismus in der Reformierten Kirche der Niederlande* (Leipzig, 1911) 276–8; Goebel, *Christliches Leben* II:241, 271–3.

[11] J. Wallmann, 'Labadismus und Pietismus', in *Pietismus und Reveil* ed. J. van den Berg & J. P. van Dooren (Leiden, 1978). Cf. K. D. Schmidt, 'Labadie und Spener', *ZKg* 46 (1927) 566–83.

## THE RIGIDITY OF THE LUTHERAN ESTABLISHMENTS: (I)
### BREMEN, VERDEN AND OLDENBURG

The Lutheran world in the North-West presented an extraordinary picture of outward influence, insularity, and rigidity. The duchies of Bremen and Verden were in Swedish possession until, in episodes rendered famous in Britain by the ructions they caused in domestic politics, they were occupied by Hanover in 1712, and ceded by the Peace of Stockholm in 1719. Sweden replaced the bishop by a general superintendent and consistory, an arrangement which Hanover virtually built into the state machine. This concentration of authority offered at least the possibility of progress, for the efforts of the Swedish consistory to re-establish order and church discipline had been frustrated by peasant indifference. Yet the Hanoverian regime attempted little more than administrative changes, and a steady supplanting of the *neddersassisch* dialect which had succeeded Latin as the language for church purposes at the Reformation. In the mid eighteenth century High German established itself as the official state language and the church not unnaturally followed suit; the cost was separation from ordinary life, and from the *plattdeutsch* of the peasantry. The church of Bremen and Verden still sustained twenty-two different liturgies in 148 parishes, and, still more remarkably for a church which for fifty years had been governed by Sweden, the clergy were not clearly bound to the Formula of Concord, nor to the Swedish ordinances against Pietism. Nevertheless the Swedish government would have no more truck with Pietism here than at home and the Hanoverian government steadfastly followed in its wake, supported by an alliance of gentry and clergy.[12]

Before Bremen and Verden passed to the Hanoverians, they had been briefly occupied by the Danes; and the Danes retained the next territory, the duchy of Oldenburg, from 1667 to 1773. The Danish monarchy, in the eighteenth century the most Pietist royal house in Europe, proud of sending their own missionaries to the Tranquebar coast and letting the Moravians into Greenland to convert the Eskimos, might have been expected to attempt the conversion of Oldenburg. No such thing happened, and very nearly the only Pietist to turn up in the province was Frederick Count Lynar, one of the Pietist aristocracy of Lower Lusatia, who entered Danish state

---

[12] E. G. Wolters, 'Kirchliche und sittliche Zustände in ... Bremen und Verden, 1650 bis 1725', *ZGNSKg* 19 (1914) 1–79.

service, and spent his last few years (1756–66) there as governor. In the whole eighteenth century only eighteen pastors who served in Oldenburg were trained at Halle; some of them must have been Pietists, but they mostly came from outside the province and did not constitute a movement.[13]

### THE RIGIDITY OF THE LUTHERAN ESTABLISHMENTS: (2) HANOVER

The fate of Lutheranism in the North-West would, however, turn largely on what happened in Hanover, the power most clearly on the make, whose ruling house acquired the electoral dignity in 1692, and the British crown in 1714. The Reformation in Hanover had been bloodlessly carried through from above, and it took about a century to penetrate the lower ranks of society. The Hanoverian church was now often troubled by artisan and peasant enthusiasts who found biblical grounds for calls to repentance from the drab conformity to which they had been subjected, and who eventually attracted intellectual leaders, clerical and lay, who sought an alternative religion in the pantheistic mysticism of Böhme and others. An endless stream of ordinances against religious dissidence issued from the Hanoverian government, which were backed up by others to improve the working of the church. By the early eighteenth century radical enthusiasm seems to have fizzled out, destroyed by an unyielding government and its own failure to catch any larger tide of social movement; there were inconsiderable secessions in two fringe areas only, at Harburg in the North and Clausthal in the Harz. The chiliasm of the Hanoverian enthusiasts was also a wasting asset.[14]

The government of Hanover nevertheless remained alert, watching particularly for class-meetings. The very oldest Pietist correspondence for Hanover is that of Francke with his relatives, but the letters brought him little cheer. As one remarked wryly when the first

---

[13] H. Schieckel, 'Pietisten und Erweckte in der Grafschaft...Oldenburg', in *Pietismus-Herrnhutertum-Erweckungsbewegung. Festschrift für E. Beyreuther* ed. D. Meyer (Cologne, 1982) 325–46.

[14] *SMBRG* 4 (1735) 101–7; 5 (1736) 245–56, 622–6; P. L. Meyer, 'Kirchen- und Schulberichte...im Zeitalter der Aufklärung', *ZGNSKg* 19 (1914) 80–146; Kayser, 'Hanoversche Enthusiasten des 17. Jahrhunderts' *ZGNSKg* 10 (1905) 1–72; F. U. Calixtus, *De Chiliasmo cum antiquo tum pridem renato Tractatus theologicus* (Helmstedt, 1692). Cf. G. Meyer, 'Pietismus und Herrnhutertum in Niedersachsen im 18. Jht.', *Niedersächsishes Jahrbuch* 9 (1952) 97–133. On Hanover generally, R. Ruprecht, *Der Pietismus...in den Hannoverschen Stammländern* (Göttingen, 1919); J. Meyer, *Kirchengeschichte Niedersachsens* (Göttingen, 1939).

Hallesian was preferred in the electorate, 'we are so orthodox here, indeed very nearly as pure as in the pulpit of Luther at Wittenberg'.[15] The problem was partly that Hanover and Prussia crusaded competitively on behalf of oppressed Protestants, and Halle Pietism was part of the politics of Prussia. George II of England, indeed, in a long statement of 1735 maintained that the policy in the church since his father's time was not 'to employ anyone other than natives... because most preachers in Brandenburg studied at Halle, and many of them absorbed the well-known Hallesian or so-called pietistic principles'. In 1740 he published an astonishing eighteen page notice against Pietism, claiming that there was just one anti-church sect which disguised itself under different names at different times and places 'among which [were] the Enthusiasts, Anabaptists, Donatists, Quakers, Schwenkfelders, Rothmannians, Weigelians, Böhmists... and especially in our times the Pietists'.[16]

This implausible attempt to roll Halle into one ball with the enthusiasts of the generations was followed by a sharp edict against the Moravians in 1748, and ordinances in 1749. The effect of these was to galvanise Zinzendorf into a personal application to George II in London, to the archbishop of Canterbury and others, which (much to the annoyance of John Wesley) led the British parliament to legislate in the Moravians' favour. This U-turn had its precedents, for Hanoverian church policy was, to say the least, pragmatic. Ernst August, the first elector, was moved by interests of state, and in this supported by his wife, Sophie, who was an adherent of Spinoza. Ernst August offered to the Pope in 1678 to convert to Rome if the temporal administration of the sees of Osnabrück and Hildesheim were handed over to him. The Pope would not negotiate without having first received an unconditional conversion. Ernst August began to make concessions to Roman Catholics, and to obtain the electoral dignity he promised them toleration; having obtained his dignity, he refused the concession, having now an eye to the English succession. Nevertheless negotiations for church union went on, and the cause formerly championed by Leibniz found a second Hanoverian advocate in Molanus. In the same spirit, the Hanoverian accession in England was followed by divergent policies in the two territories.

---

[15]  T. Wotschke, 'Pietistisches aus Ostfriesland und Niedersachsen', *ZGNSKg* 36 (1931) 138.
[16]  *UN* 1735 52, 235–7 (Cf. the ordinance of 1744 forbidding foreigners to preach in Hanover, *AHE* 9:264–5); 1741 201–8; *AHE* 5:218–27, 691–708; Ruprecht, *Pietismus* 9–110.

Nothing changed in the *Landeskirche*; there were important Pietist influences at the court in London.

Even in Hanover, when George II planted an economic multiplier in the most backward corner of his domains, by founding the university at Göttingen, Halle was not held at arm's length. The organising minister of state, Baron von Münchhausen (whose wife had been converted under Francke's influence, and who linked the Pietist networks of Schaumburg-Lippe and Wernigerode),[17] took as his model the University of Halle with its almost unlimited freedom to teach and exemption from censorship, and looked to an 'enlightened Pietism'. The Hanover consistory raged furiously against Pietism, but they could not stop converted students founding, on the Halle pattern, a poor school and an Orphan House, for these became university institutions independent of the consistory. In short, while the Hanoverian church at parish and consistory level continued to be bound to a rigid Orthodoxy, which suited certain interests of the electoral house, gentry patrons, and a local-born clergy shielded almost entirely from outside competition in the struggle for preferment, the same interests of state which had led the Welf house to play with syncretism now drew it to Enlightenment and Pietism. By the 1740s it had the support of a Halle on the look-out for allies against the Moravians. In Hanover the old landmarks were disappearing, though not fast enough to induce religious revival.

### FAILURES OF PIETISM IN (1) WALDECK

In two other Lutheran territories the case was worse; Pietism made a promising start, only to be displaced by the old forces of conservatism. The county of Waldeck had an importance for our theme out of all proportion to its size, because it acted as a catalyst for the opening of the second phase of the enduring conflict between Orthodoxy and Pietism. In the long reign of Count Christian Ludwig (1645–1706) Waldeck became a model Pietist principality, what the radical Bruno Bauer later called an English Philadelphia.[18] The count had married first into the house of Rappoltstein at Rappoltsweiler, the family which had taken up Spener as a young man, and then into the Pietist house of Nassau-Idstein. He was a devout man, with views of a Spenerish kind; and Spener exercised considerable

---

[17] *Ibid.* 135–7.
[18] Bruno Bauer, *Einfluss des englischen Quäkertums auf die deutsche Kultur...* (Berlin, 1878: repr. Aalen, 1972) 25.

influence and patronage in the county.[19] The course of Pietism in Waldeck, however, never ran quite smooth, in at least one instance much to the benefit of the United Kingdom. Anton Wilhelm Böhme (1673–1722), educated at Halle, was appointed in 1698 as tutor to the two young countesses at the court of Waldeck and to take prayers in court. Not liking what he found there, and holding rashly that 'in the whole county there were not four right-minded clergy', Böhme incurred the wrath of both superintendent and count, and was dismissed in 1700. This disaster proved to be the preface to a highly successful career (described in chapter 8) at the English court.[20]

Meanwhile Pietism was reaching its high point in Waldeck. From 1701 to 1711 the most influential man in the government and consistory, the jurist Otto Heinrich Becker (1667–1723), shaped the temporal and religious life of the county on the Halle pattern with the usual educational and social institutions. He enjoyed the full backing of the Halle party, and especially of Francke's leading lay collaborator, Baron von Canstein, whose estates lay just outside the county of Waldeck. Waldeck's importance in Halle's plans for a general world reformation could not be overlooked by her Orthodox enemies. The tide began to turn against Becker with the death of the count, and the accession of Friedrich Anton Ulrich in 1706. He was hand in glove with the anti-Pietist Kammerjunker von Rauchbar and the superintendent Johannes Kleinschmidt. Their opportunity came when the count's sister, the abbess of Schaaken, eloped with the abbey *Informator*, the Pietist Johannes Junker, and, still worse, married him in defiance of all worldly precedence. At this point a vicious pamphlet warfare broke out which involved the Halle spokesmen too, and ended with the leading Pietists leaving the country, an edict against Pietism, a vote against it by the estates, and the publication of a sort of government Black Book of Pietist crime, the *Historia Pietistica Waldaccensis* (1712), prepared by Rauchbar and Kleinschmidt. This was not quite the end of Pietism in Waldeck; Johann Daniel Herrnschmid (1675–1723), who was expected to be Francke's successor at Halle, but predeceased him, served there

[19] G. Menk, 'P. J. Spener und Waldeck' *HJLg* 33 (1983) 171–92; R. Mack, 'Forschungsbericht: Pietismus in Hessen', *PuN* 13 (1987) 200–2; Barthold, *Die frommen Grafenhöfe* 1: 162, 246–8.
[20] Böhme's *Sämtliche erbauliche Schriften* (Altona, 1731–3) contains an engaging memoir and an extensive bibliography. See also Arno Sames, *Anton Wilhelm Böhme (1673–1722)* (Göttingen, 1990). Letters were printed by Wotschke in 'A. H. Franckes rheinische Freunde (Fortsetzung)' *MRKg* 23 (1929) 329, 353.

briefly, and numerous Waldeckers went to Halle to study. But Waldeck was not going to be the catalyst of the Pietist welfare state.[21]

### FAILURES OF PIETISM IN (2) HESSE-DARMSTADT

There were similar disappointments in the Hessian states, and especially Hesse-Darmstadt. Hesse was the theatre of the final violent conflicts of the Thirty Years War, as Hesse-Kassel and Hesse-Darmstadt fought over the division of their common inheritance. The partition enforced in the Peace of Münster proved an enduring one; and so did the burden of economic reconstruction. The most successful prince in this respect was the Landgrave Karl of Hesse-Kassel (1677–1730), who made war, and especially war in the Protestant cause, pay; but his elder son secured the crown of Sweden and left the country to a younger brother; one of his grandsons turned Catholic, and had to be strictly inhibited from interfering with the confessional status of the country.[22] This status, inevitably complicated, since the Hessian territories, predominantly Lutheran, included Reformed and Catholic areas, was further confused by the landgrave's immigration policies; he made his territories the principal reception area for refugees in the West, and Huguenots, Waldensians and Swiss all poured in. The frontiers between the confessions changed all the time, giving the landgrave no option but to look for compromises where they could be found, and to keep the initiative in his own hands. Theodor Untereyck, a Calvinist of the affective kind, became court chaplain briefly (1668–70), but the risks of this kind of religious appeal were writ large in Hesse with Heinrich Horche's itinerant propagation of an ecstatic chiliasm at the turn of the century, and extravagances such as the Buttlar Gang. The landgrave also profited from the ethos of Marburg (the centre for the Reformed diaspora in Upper Hesse) and Rinteln, where Lutheran clergy were educated. Marburg was based on a church system originally Melanchthonian in nature, was early committed to the federal theology, the belief that theological study was inseparable from the life of piety, and the view that their differences with the

---

[21] The best modern treatments of the Waldeck case are by Hans Schneider, 'Die rechte Gestalt der Wolffe in der Kirche' *UF* 3 (1978) 74–110; and 'Johann Heinrich Marmor (1681–1741)', *Geschichtsblätter für Waldeck* 66 (1977) 138–59.

[22] For Hesse: H. Heppe, *Kirchengeschichte beider Hessen* (Marburg, 1876); H. Steitz, *Geschichte der evangelischen Kirche in Hessen ...* (Marburg, 1962); R. Mack, 'Forschungsbericht: Pietismus in Hessen', *PuN* 13 (1987) 181–226.

Lutherans did not touch the essentials of the Christian faith. Rinteln favoured the sort of syncretism developed by Calixtus at Helmstedt. By the middle of the eighteenth century ordinands were required to study for a period at each of these centres, and, not surprisingly, in the nineteenth century, union churches were formed by the Protestant confessions throughout the area. Equally unsurprising, when Francke visited Marburg in 1717 he could find scarcely a friend in the place. When the Moravian diaspora workers arrived in the thirties they found no Pietist circles from which to commence their mission. One Reformed Pietist of note there had been, Conrad Mel, who became *Inspektor* of the principality of Hersfeld, director of the gymnasium there, and eventually founded an Orphan House in the place. He pleased the landgrave by making technological innovations, pleased the princess by his devotional writings, and attracted students from a distance to his gymnasium. But he did not constitute a movement, and found no counterpart at all in Upper-Hesse Lutheranism.[23]

Hesse-Darmstadt was even more disappointing for the new religious forces, for in the age of Spener Pietism failed to consolidate a triumph, and in that of Gotthilf August Francke missed another brilliant opening.[24] After the Thirty Years War the landgrave in Hesse-Darmstadt endeavoured with exiguous resources to develop his land as a model Lutheran state on the pattern of the Saxe-Gotha of Duke Ernst the Pious. One of his assets was the impoverished University of Giessen, which had been built up as a Lutheran rival to Marburg, and continued to attract the professional classes of Frankfurt. As such it also attracted the attention of Spener while he was senior of Frankfurt. Yet such was the resistance to Pietism of the ruling family and their immediate servants, that Spener made no real impression till 1688, long after his Frankfurt days, when Ernst Ludwig took over the government; it then proved possible to manipulate him in religious matters through his wife, the Landgravine Dorothea Charlotte, a most determined Pietist. She could not shift the Orthodoxy of the ordinary clergy, and the Pietist entree was secured in the last decade of Spener's life, after tremendous struggles, at the point of direct state patronage in the University of Giessen. These

[23] W. Zeller, 'Conrad Mel als Theologe', in his *Frömmigkeit in Hessen* ed. B. Jaspert (Marburg, 1970) 151–91.

[24] For Hesse-Darmstadt: R. Mack, 'Die Obrigkeit und der Pietismus in...Hessen-Darmstadt', *JHKgV* 34 (1983) 29–52; *Pietismus und Frühaufklärung an der Universität Giessen und in Hessen-Darmstadt* (Giessen, 1984); Steitz, *Evangelische Kirche in Hessen*.

struggles cost the resignation of the famous radical Gottfried Arnold, after only a few months in his history chair, but his colleague, the Hebrew scholar and friend of Spener Johann Heinrich May, who would also have been glad to make his exit from Babel, stuck out the struggle; he made an impression on a whole generation of clergy and their connexions in the educated classes. Even when the landgravine died in 1705, and the landgrave began to distance himself from the Pietists, May received sufficient support from the minister von Schröder and his immediate successors. When August Hermann Francke came for three days in 1717 he gained the impression of a firmly established position. This was too optimistic a view. The landgrave was loath to be civil to Francke; the attention of his ministers owed more to the feeling that Halle offered a more up-to-date development-programme than Duke Ernst the Pious. Up to 1719 the Pietists occupied the chief offices in the university and the church; but were restricted in their influence by lack of court favour. In Hesse-Darmstadt there was none of the pious counts who maintained the cause of Halle elsewhere, no parallel to the estates which sustained the twin causes of country politics and Pietist sentiment against the dukes of Württemberg. When court favour failed, the Pietists had modified but not broken the Orthodoxy of the clergy, and when the landgrave carried through four university visitations between 1715 and 1725 their academic power collapsed as quickly as it had been created.

An unexpected second chance came their way with the appointment of Johann Jacob Rambach to a chair in Giessen in 1731. Rambach had been born in Halle in 1693, the son of a joiner, and intended to follow his father's trade. An accident made this impossible; so at the age of fifteen he entered the Orphan House school, and from the age of nineteen devoted himself to the study of theology and philosophy. Rambach's future was thus bound up with August Hermann Francke; after four years at Jena, 1719–23, he came back to Halle as an assistant in the theological faculty, became an extraordinary professor in 1726, and, on Francke's death in 1727, ordinary in theology. Academic intrigue in Giessen was fully the equal of that in contemporary Oxford, the more so as the government was so close at hand; and for a man fairly regarded as the flower of the Halle interest to be appointed after the Pietist cause had sunk so low required intrigue of more than normal intensity. There were two key factors. The Orthodox party in the faculty overplayed their hand, proposing the three great names of the party, Valentin Ernst Löscher, the superintendent in Dresden, Ernst Salomon Cyprian, who taught in Coburg, and Benedict Carpzov, a member of a distinguished Orthodox clan whose forebears had got up the opposition to Spener, and who at that time was a professor in Leipzig. The first two were approaching the end of their career, and all three were in posts from which they could not have been tempted by the meagre resources of Hesse-Darmstadt. While the Senate sought a way out of this impasse, the rector, clearly acting at the behest of the government, slipped in the name of Rambach. The ministers seem to have seen in Rambach a man who could do a better job for Giessen and the church than anyone the Orthodox could produce. It was a question whether he could be obtained; Frederick William I was loath to let him go; but relations between Rambach and Gotthilf August Francke were sour, and by paying a salary over the usual Giessen odds the prize was obtained. Their judgment was confirmed by the fact that in 1734 a determined attempt was made to tempt him to the new university of Göttingen. The landgrave, in a personal letter to George II, refused to release him, and the congregation struck a special medal bearing Rambach's image and, on the reverse, the legend: 'The Chrysostom of this age'.

If this was avowedly to gild the lily, Rambach was undoubtedly many-sided. In the Pietist manner there was a strong practical bent to his teaching. A powerful preacher, he contributed so strongly to the theory of preaching, that for a generation after his death nothing new was added to the subject by his religious party. The great features of his style were an unusually heavy emphasis on the awakening of heart and conscience to conviction, a highly scholastic form of presentation, and a tendency to go into too much detail. As Shakespeare helped to liberate German critics from French insistence on the dramatic unity of time, place and action, English preachers, and not least Watts, helped to liberate German pastors from the yoke of their own baroque models. Rambach wrote an introduction to the German translation of Watts's *Death and Heaven* which was speedily rendered into English. He was indeed a middleman between what might be called the proto-revival in England and his fellow countrymen. As we have seen, the substantial life of A. W. Böhme which he prefixed to the latter's works made clear in Germany how receptive the England of Queen Anne and George I was to the influences of Halle; and long afterwards Whitefield made his communion prayers available from a three-volume English edition of his works. In America Lutheran catechists were required to memorise Rambach's catechetical sermons, pass examinations on them, and preach them by heart on Sundays.[25]

Rambach also believed that congregations should be taught how to use Bible, hymn-book and devotional literature; for this purpose a hymn-book which could be used as a doctrinal textbook was desirable. Children in school must be introduced to the Christian life, and the pastoral work of the schoolmaster supported by suitable literature. Likewise the clergy whose initial training could not suffice them for life required a professional journal to keep abreast of theological studies. In all these areas Rambach laboured with energy and success, still enjoying the esteem of the best scholars of the Enlightenment for his reasonable rules of exegesis, a man of peace who took the heat out of the feud between Wittenberg and Halle.[26] That reputation rapidly increased recruitment to the University of Giessen. The greater pity therefore when in April 1735, at the age of forty-two, barely three and a half years after taking up his chair, Rambach died. His post of *Primarius* remained unfilled for twenty years, the Orthodox party regained its old ascendancy, and the principal use they made of it was to conduct a sterile polemic against Zinzendorf. Another opening through which the forces of change had threatened to flood had been dammed up.

### THE ADVANCE OF ORTHODOXY IN THE IMPERIAL CITIES

A similar story unfolded in the Imperial cities, and this against the general tide. For, once the Saxon dynasty had turned Catholic to obtain the Polish crown, Lutheran Orthodoxy was the ideological platform of not a single major German state, and, the Swedish territories apart, it survived mainly in the smaller Saxon courts of Gotha, Weimar, Eisenach and Weissenfels. In the West, however, Orthodoxy staged a remarkable comeback in the Imperial cities. Spener had been bred to his profession in Strasbourg, and made an

---

[25] *Pious Aspiration for the Use of Devout Communicants* ... (London, 1760). L. Tyerman found them 'often beautiful, and always intensely earnest and devout', *Life of George Whitefield* (2nd edn 2 vols. London, 1890) II:440. Cf. *UN* 1728 302–5; *Die Korrespondenz Heinrich Melchior Mühlenbergs* ... ed. Kurt Aland (2 vols. Berlin/New York, 1986–) I:193; *Journals of H. M. Muhlenberg* tr. T. G. Tappert & J. W. Dobenstein (3 vols. Philadelphia, 1942–58) I: 101.

[26] J. R. Schlegel, *Kirchengeschichte des achtzehnten Jahrhunderts* II: 152–3, 351, 370. Cf. H. W. Frei, *The Eclipse of Biblical Narrative* (New Haven, 1974) 38–9. Rambach also notably provided religious literature for children: H. G. Bloth, 'J. J. Hecker (1707–1768)', *JVWKg* 61 (1968) 76.

international reputation as senior of Frankfurt. He quickly secured active friends, relatives and agents in the great South German cities, Augsburg, Windesheim, Rothenburg, Schweinfurt, Nuremberg, Ulm and Regensburg.[27] In Hamburg the pastor Anton Reiser made a great (if unsuccessful) assault upon the city theatre, and in the last years of his life managed to fill two of the four livings in the town with Johann Winckler, a friend of Spener, and J. H. Horb, Spener's brother-in-law. The Imperial cities, which had given so decisive an impulse to Luther's Reformation, might have done the same for Spener's 'second Reformation', and it is a measure of the social change which had come upon Germany in the interim that no such thing happened.

The Pietist cause in the southern towns depended very heavily on Spener's personal influence. Strasbourg had forfeited its status as a free Imperial city by capitulation to Louis XIV in 1681, and from then onwards the German and Lutheran town council tenaciously held out against deliberate French Catholic infiltration, against the fascination of French culture, against diminishing revenues, and in favour of their German and Lutheran university. In this struggle the Lutheran Orthodoxy of the theological faculty set hard, and at the crucial period they appointed as rector no subtler man than Johann Leonhard Fröreisen (1694–1761), a coarse polemical bruiser who pummelled the Moravians.[28]

The popular saying in Frankfurt was that in that city the Catholics had the churches, the Calvinists the money, and the Lutherans the power. The boom in Frankfurt business which followed the Thirty Years War did not directly benefit the governing patriciate, though it did increase the number of immigrants against whom the council adeptly diverted critics of its own privileges. The spiritual democracy which Spener had encouraged was not welcome in the temporal affairs of the town. Among Spener's successors as senior were J. G. Pritius, a Pietist who edited some of Spener's works,[29] and Johann Philipp Fresenius (1705–1761),[30] who had Pietist connexions; but when the Moravians settled in the neighbourhood, he led a violent assault upon them in four huge volumes of heavily documented

---

[27] D. Blaufuss, *Reichstadt und Pietismus* (Neustadt, 1977).

[28] 'Either you are the greatest visionary or the greatest impostor in the world, or perhaps both'. J. L. Fröreisen (to Zinzendorf), *Rede...vor denen...Rathsgliedern der Stadt Strasburg...* (Frankfurt, 1741) Appendix.

[29] *Drey erbauliche Schrifften* (Frankfurt, 1717). Some of Pritius's letters are preserved in AFSt DIII no. 1089.

[30] G. J. Raisig, *Theologie und Frömmigkeit bei J. P. Fresenius* (Bern &c., 1975).

polemic, his *Bewährte Nachrichten* (1741–51). To Fresenius's chagrin, this blockbuster had the greater effect for being pirated all round Germany. The Frankfurt clergy, in other words, vividly illustrated how Pietist and Orthodox were closing fronts against the Moravians. If the complaint of a Pietist at Frankfurt in 1709 that there was no *sensus pietatis* in the town, that everyone 'took very good care not to read the books of Spener, Francke, Schade, Freylinghausen and others, and the booksellers not to deal in them',[31] was not literally true, Frankfurt showed unequivocally that it preferred Orthodoxy to revival. And, given its importance in the Empire and the European book trade, this was a significant matter.

Nearby Wetzlar, the seat of the Reichskammergericht, followed suit. It did not receive a Pietist pastor until 1711, when Egidius Günther Hellmund arrived with the reputation of being a Quaker and a miracle-worker. He soon angered the town council by attempting to reform the school, and introduce prayer- and class-meetings, and was suspended within eighteen months. In touch with Francke throughout, Hellmund defended his meetings, and, perilously for himself, obtained the support of officials of the Reichskammergericht. He was dismissed in January 1713. The issue in this case was that the town council would not have its episcopal authority abridged by allowing the citizens a voice in the choice of pastors, by the democracy they perceived in the class-meetings, or by the courts of the Empire. The Reichskammergericht called on the council of Wetzlar and the landgrave of Hesse as its protector to restore Hellmund to office. Every device for evading this decision was tried, Hellmund was boycotted by the other clergy in the town, and, in 1720, the University of Strasbourg produced an opinion that, although Hellmund's removal from office was inadvisable, he did not teach pure doctrine, and if he did not forswear his enthusiastic, syncretist, Schwenckfeldian and Weigelian opinions, he could not be left in pastoral charge. The only solution to the impasse was for the landgrave to find him another job, and that was the end of Pietism in Wetzlar.[32]

Hamburg was a more important and an even more extraordinary case. The growth of the town had altogether outstripped the capacity of the city clergy to provide pastoral oversight, and had aggravated

---

[31] Wotschke, 'Pietistisches aus Ostfriesland' 111 n. 1.
[32] R. Mohr, 'E. G. Hellmunds gescheiterter Versuch...', in Meyer, ed. *Beyreuther Festschrift* 146–203. For Hellmund correspondence: T. Wotschke, 'Speners und Franckes rheinische Freunde', *MRKg* 23 (1929) 326–8, 331–5, 340–2.

its constitutional and diplomatic ambiguity. Hamburg asserted that it was a free Imperial city, but was always subject to Danish claims; its trade was menaced by French and Allied depredations in turn, and provided arguments for seeking Danish protection. There was no consistory to regulate the relations of the council with the church, and the constitutional relations between the council and the citizens were in dispute. Add to all this that the town was one of the avenues by which English Enlightenment entered Germany and you have a witches' brew. In 1692 J. H. Horb, Spener's brother-in-law, was expelled, and the authority of the town council suffered considerably. In contrast with the big towns of Switzerland, Hamburg Pietism found its support in the upper crust, while Lutheran Orthodoxy was strong among the craft trades. The outcome was a civic uprising in 1708 led by what Tholuck called 'the last of the Orthodox pulpit demagogues, Krumbholtz', and put down by an Imperial commission led by the troops of Prussia, Hanover and Wolfenbüttel. In Erdmann Neumeister, who died in 1756 aged eighty-five, Hamburg appointed a man who associated with the gallant poets in his youth, came unstuck at the Pietist court of Sorau in Lower Lusatia, and later became the most violent of the Orthodox polemicists.[33]

Yet no town showed more clearly than Hamburg how fragile the Orthodox position had become. The last schools of Orthodox clergy were Rostock and Wittenberg, neither of them academic pacemakers. In 1735 Hamburg called Provost Reinbeck of Berlin, a disciple of Christian Wolff (the uncrowned king of the early German Enlightenment); and although Reinbeck was required by the king of Prussia to refuse, he put up in his place Friedrich Wagner, another Wolffian. Orthodoxy had gone straight over to rationalism; Hamburg was blazing the trail for all those German (and English[34]) towns in the nineteenth century which used their ecclesiastical patronage to support the liberal party, a fitting host to the savage Old Testament criticism of its least favourite lay son of the late eighteenth century, Reimarus. It was a similar story in Frankfurt. In 1749 Goethe was born into a patrician family in that town at the height of Fresenius's

---

[33] Friedrich August Gottreu Tholuck, *Geschichte des Rationalismus* (Berlin, 1865; repr. Aalen, 1970) 3; Rudolf Lehmann, *Geschichte des Markgraftums Niederlausitz* (Dresden, 1937) 330–1; Hermann Rückleben, *Die Niederwerfung der hamburgischen Ratsgewalt...* (Hamburg, 1970); G. Daur, *Von Predigern und Burgern* (Hamburg, 1970) 108–24.

[34] Thus Anthony Trollope: 'The free-thinking clergyman of the present time is to be found more often in London than in the provinces, and more frequently in the towns than in country parishes. They are not many in number as compared with members of all parsondom in these realms; but they are men of whom we hear much.' *Clergymen of the Church of England* (London, 1866; repr. Leicester, 1974) 120.

assault on the Moravians; yet by the time he was of student age, he had intimate relations with the Moravians as though Fresenius had never existed. Similarly in Strasbourg. Even in Fröreisen's lifetime, leading old Strasbourg families were sending out their children to Moravian schools, and, after his death, the Moravian diaspora-workers in Alsace were tolerated in the town and made the contacts on which the nineteenth-century revival movement there was built. It is striking that although the history of no two cities was alike, the end-product was the same, a brittle triumph of Lutheran Orthodoxy; a strikingly similar result was produced in Switzerland, where the high Reformed Orthodoxy of the Formula Consensus was sustained by the great Swiss cities, led by the tough-mided patriciate of Bern.

### THE REFORMED CHURCH IN BREMEN

Some light is cast on this common result by the one great Reformed Imperial city, Bremen. The town council of Bremen had been used, long before the Reformation, to struggling for its rights with the archbishop, and, when in 1541 the Emperor transferred to the council the archbishop's rights of church oversight, he was really recognising the *status quo*. The Venerandum Ministerium depended much on the town council, and when, in the second half of the sixteenth century, Bremen abandoned Lutheranism for the Reformed order, the influence of the laity in church affairs increased. Pietism in Bremen had enough friends in the town council to play an important role in the town, but the council had no use for separatism or enthusiasm, and, if they appeared, Reformed Orthodoxy would behave with the same brutal vigour as in Bern or Zurich, or as Lutheran Orthodoxy in other cities. In this they were generally supported by even Pietist clergy in office, with the result that Reformed Orthodoxy was pressed back only very slowly.[35]

### THE LOWER RHINE PROVINCES

In the five lower Rhine provinces of Jülich, Cleves, Berg, Mark and Ravensberg, Reformed and Lutheran congregations were uniquely mingled together, subject to much common development[36] and yet

[35] G. Mai, *Die niederdeutsche Reformbewegung* (Bremen, 1979) 187–242, 309; J. F. Iken, *Joachim Neander* (Bremen, 1880) 34–76; O. Veeck, *Reformierte Kirche Bremens* (Bremen, 1909) 87–108.
[36] On these churches: H. Heppe, *Geschichte der evangelischen Kirche von Cleve-Mark und... Westphalen* (Iserlohn, 1867) 158–296; W. Göbell, ed., *Die evangelisch-lutherische Kirche in der Grafschaft Mark* (Bethel, 1961); Goebel, *Christliches Leben* II; Rothert, 'Die Minden-

bitterly hostile to each other.[37] The Reformed churches of the area, except in Cleves, were like the English Presbyterians of the seventeenth century, in that they never managed to complete their church structure, but they were heavily subsidised by the established Reformed churches of the Netherlands, in whose official handbook they were included right down to the French Revolution. The Lutheran churches of the area were unique. Early in the seventeenth century when the Catholic line of the dukes of Cleves died out, the inheritance was claimed by two Lutheran houses, Pfalz-Neuburg and Brandenburg; they united for the administration of the territory, and things looked bright for their co-religionists. It was arranged that the Count Palatine should marry the daughter of the elector of Brandenburg. Alas! in 1613 when the two met at a banquet in Düsseldorf, they fell out and the elector boxed the count upon the ear. The consequences of the brawl were momentous. The marriage alliance was called off, the count became a Catholic, carried through the Counter-Reformation in Pfalz-Neuburg, attempted to do so in Berg and Cleves, and, through the troops and Jesuits, gave the Protestant Düsseldorfers a terrible time. Soon afterwards, for other reasons, the elector of Brandenburg adopted the Reformed faith, and pushed the interests of his new co-religionists. Ground between the upper and the nether millstone, the Lutherans suffered the worse because the presupposition of the Lutheran church polity, the support of the state, was lacking. Many Lutheran congregations went under, became Reformed or shared churches (*simultan*), and, although some obtained protection from old evangelical towns like Soest, Dortmund, Essen and Lennep, they underwent a peculiar constitutional development. However much the Lutherans might differ from the

Ravensbergische Kirchengeschichte', *JVWKg* 28/29 (1928) 1–169; 30 (1929) 1–111; L. Koechling, 'Minden-Ravensberg und die Herrnhuter Brüdergemeine *JVWKg* 55/6 (1962–3) 69–103.

[37] Of an endless anthology of picturesque abuse two examples may suffice. The Reformed pastor at Hamm in 1743 was scourging his flock for poor church-attendance: 'If you don't want to come to church to hear God's word and learn the way to salvation, then stay at home; you need not come on my personal account. So far as I am concerned you can go away, be circumcised and become Turks and Jews. So far as I am concerned you can go away and worship idols and become Papists. So far as I am concerned you can go to the bottom of the barrel and become Lutherans.' (The temporal authorities fined him 20 thaler; the fine was paid by the congregation who begged him to say it again, they indemnifying him financially from the consequences.) In Dortmund the Lutherans were the aggressors, and in 1708 the Reformed Synod of Mark complained that their co-religionists there were traduced from the pulpit and refused civic rights and employment; they were supported by the Prussian government in 1713 and 1715, but without the least effect. Heppe, *Evangelische Kirche von Cleve-Mark* 219n., 221.

Reformed congregations in doctrine and ethos, they came to differ little in terms of church order. In the very long run the Lutheran deprivation here was an advantage, and late in the nineteenth century it was recognised that their congregations were capable of managing their own affairs in a way unthinkable in parishes in the East, bred for centuries to deference. In the short run, however, lacking the mainspring of their usual system, these Lutheran congregations did badly, and welcomed the new toleration of the Great Elector with perhaps excessive enthusiasm.[38] In general, therefore, the Lutheranism of the Lower Rhine was no more capable of taking a sharp new turn than its half-brother along the Lower Elbe and Lower Weser, and to this general view there seems only one exception. Congregations driven underground by persecution kept themselves going by the informal devices, the class-meeting and the like, later recommended by Spener as supplementary devotions. They found, as hard-pressed Protestants in so many other areas found, that these devices were capable of sustaining their faith in the absence of the ordinary church routines. Moreover, by these means, cells of new congregations were formed which were especially open to Pietist influence. It was unfortunate for the Lutherans that more of these cells were of the Reformed than the evangelical faith.

Right through the area the Reformed church had created its structures against the bitter hostility of governments and, when Brandenburg came in, the independence of the church with its right of self-government were confirmed, and a Reformed university created at Duisburg in 1655. Yet like the Lutherans the Reformed did worst under hostile government, and best where government smiled. The hardest case was that of the Palatinate, which suffered the ravages of French invasion, and where, almost overnight, the Reformed church was transformed from an establishment to an object of persecution. Here many were miserable, throngs emigrated, and a few tried a new approach to an insoluble religious problem, separating from their dilapidated establishment, some as New Baptists. This last solution involved emigration, in the case of the New Baptists to the Wetterau in the first instance, to America later. The most comfortable case was that of East Friesland, up against the Dutch border, and with habitual exchanges of pulpits and other contacts across it. The last three dukes of East Friesland, Christian Eberhard (1690–1708), Georg Albrecht (1708–34) and Karl Edzard

---

[38] Martin Lackner, *Die Kirchenpolitik des Grossen Kurfürsten* (Witten, 1973) 202–49.

(1734–44), were all Pietists, the first a friend of Spener himself. Apart from its distinctively religious appeal, Pietism had for them the same attraction as for the kings of Prussia; it was a device for managing a Lutheran territory with a very substantial minority of Reformed subjects. The dukes hit hard at separatists, and manned their parishes with hard-working Pietists who would do what could be done to keep the ship afloat by honest effort. They did not manage to turn their flock into sacramentalists, but, equally, did not impede the efforts of the Reformed nor their response to currents of thought elsewhere.[39] This openness distinguished the Reformed in this area from the Lutherans, it was to some extent a virtue won from the harsh circumstances in which so many Reformed communities found themselves, and it carried institutional implications in a period when the presbyteries themselves were going downhill.

### CHANGES IN SENTIMENT AMONG THE REFORMED

It was hardly possible for the Reformed to be spiritually or intellectually parochial. The two greatest European reception areas for religious refugees were the Reformed reserves of Switzerland and the Netherlands, those refugees being the in the first instance their own brethren in the Reformed faith. Moreover, theology in the Netherlands was an unusually cosmopolitan affair. William Ames was English, Maresius was French, Coccejus the son of the town clerk of Bremen. Elizabeth, abbess of Herford, daughter of the Winter King and granddaughter of James I of England, had welcomed to Herford philosophers and enthusiasts, Labadists and Quakers, French and English, stoutly maintaining that 'gospel was originally brought from England to Germany, and it is just the same today'. The Labadist crisis affected the Lower Rhine area directly before ever the Labadists got to Herford. The call for a real improvement in the Christian life which in Lutheran Germany was to come from Spener was in Reformed circles recognised by Labadie. The Dutch church had imported conventicles or class-meetings from sixteenth-century London as an adjunct to the Sunday preaching; now they could be revamped as a means by which the spiritual zealots could pursue the kingdom of Christ unencumbered by the dead weight of the parish. Under Labadist inspiration the number of conventicles in

---

[39] Walter Hollweg, *Die Geschichte des älteren Pietismus in den Reformierten Gemeinden Ostfrieslands (um 1650–1750)* (Aurich, 1978) *84*; A. de Boer, *Der Pietismus in Ostfriesland* (Aurich, 1938); Menno Smid, *Ostfriesische Kirchengeschichte* (Pewsum, 1974) 316–427.

the Lower Rhine area seems to have multiplied, and in the larger towns, Wesel, Cleves, Duisburg, Mülheim, Düsseldorf, followed at no great distance by country parishes, the growth led speedily to separations of the sort which Labadism brought in the Netherlands.

The Reformed churches responded to this challenge more wisely than the Lutheran Orthodox. They could hardly repudiate conventicles which had so long a history in the Netherlands Reformed churches; but they required them not to resist regular pastoral oversight, not to appoint their own special teachers, and not to get in the way of the parish services. They also accepted that Labadism posed a genuine challenge to the church as a whole. The Synod of Mark of 1676, and the Synod of Cleve and the General Synod of the following year, resolved that every member of the synod was bound not merely to *orthodoxia* i.e. the Heidelberg Confession and other official standards, but also to the *studium pietatis*. A series of synodical resolutions in subsequent years made it clear that the Lower Rhine churches were to pursue sanctification and inwardness of spiritual life with a quite new determination. Labadism was, so to speak, to be defeated at its own game. In this they remained true to the anthropological orientation of the Heidelberg catechism.[40] Thus in 1687 the town council of Wesel published a resolution that 'Almighty God is to be served not only publicly in the congregations of the church, but also *privatim*', i.e. in class-meetings or conventicles. Free prayer emerged from the private gatherings to supplement the liturgy in church; congregations were helped to internalise the Coccejan doctrine of the covenant of grace in Christ, and a new race of preachers, men like Theodor Untereyck (1635–93) in Mülheim and Bremen, Joachim Neander, the hymn-writer (1650–80), in Düsseldorf and Bremen, and Friedrich Adolf Lampe (1683–1729) in Duisburg, Bremen and Utrecht, gave powerful expression to what nineteenth-century critics thought was a new Pietism; this combined English affective Puritanism with both the bitterly opposed Dutch traditions of Voetianism and Coccejanism, and kept the new movements firmly in clerical hands.

What was happening in the Netherlands to which the Reformed communities in the Rhineland were responding? This has been one of the longest-running controversies in the history of theology and is

---

[40] Rothert, 'Minden-Ravensbergische Kirchengeschichte' 134. On the piety nourished by the Heidelberg catechism, see Heppe, *Evangelische Kirche von Cleve-Mark* 243; J. Tanis, 'The Heidelberg Catechism in the Hands of the Calvinistic Pietists', *Reformed Review* 24 (1971) 156–7.

hardly susceptible of summary treatment. The pastoral problems of the Dutch church are, however, clear enough. After 1660 it had to cope with the universal problem of the misery and poor morale deriving from the great check to the European economy, and with others of its own. The general problem was made worse for the Dutch by the clear evidence that the impetus given to the Reformed cause by the achievement of Dutch independence was now spent. Then, secondly, in the Dutch, as in other parts of the Reformed tradition, the humanistic balance which had been a feature of Calvin's intellectual make-up was lost, with the result that theologians, all of whom wished to be Calvinist, found themselves saying different, and, sometimes, bitterly opposed things. Thirdly, the combination of receptiveness to religious refugees and of economic enterprise greatly multiplied the problems of assimilation faced by the church; a church which knew that one third of the population remained Catholic, and a substantial part of the rest, commemorated by Jan Steen and others of the Dutch school, continued to live for fairs, dancing and drinking in an entirely pre-Reformation way. These acute problems of pastoral strategy were vexed by unavoidable political decisions, by the openness of the Netherlands to the intellectual currents of the day, and by the absence of a highly articulated Orthodoxy of the sort which existed in Switzerland, and in all those Lutheran territories which had followed the lead of Saxony.

The great division in the period 1660–1720 was between the Coccejans and the Voetians, parties which divided not only the clergy, but were also easily recognisable badges of division among the laity. The Coccejans held that the Sabbath was a ritual obligation now outdated, and Heppe reports how ladies of the Coccejan party would sit in the window knitting on the Sabbath with a view to annoying their Voetian neighbours, and that in village congregations side by side, the Voetian congregation would preserve the silence of the grave on the Lord's Day, while the Coccejan congregation might be a riot.[41] The Voetians affected the 'language of Canaan' and plain dress, the Coccejans were modish and their ministers wore wigs. The Voetians were strong in the lower middle class, and in politics devotees of the Orange family and central government; the Coccejans were more notable in the world of wealth and scholarship, and stood for the Patriot opposition to Orange power. In Coccejus the Old

---

[41] H. Heppe, *Geschichte des Pietismus und der Mystik in der Reformiertern Kirche* (Leiden, 1879) 234–6.

Testament and history of Israel were interpreted as images of Christ and the history of the church, and systematised in a series of covenants. His biblical scholarship was admired by Spener,[42] and he anticipated favourite themes of the Pietists, rejecting calculations of the imminent end of this present age, and talking much of conversion and the New Birth, and the way the Christian knows himself to be included in the covenant.

The Voetians were more pastorally oriented, and went more directly for a result amongst their more modestly circumstanced flock. It was through the Voetians that English Puritanism was most directly mediated, and it is worth quoting an English Puritan assessment of Voetius which illustrates very clearly that affective side of English Puritanism which was apt to be recalled when religious revival began. John Quick quotes a Dutch pastor as saying that 'before the Belgick churches were pester'd with the Dogmes of Cocceius, the ministry of the Word was exceedingly successfull, many hearers would weep at sermons, proud sinners would quake and tremble at the word preached, multitudes were converted & reformed, religious worship was strictly and reverently celebrated in congregations & families'[43] under the influence of pastors of the English Puritan stamp. Events at the end of Voetius's life (1589–1676) already suggested that the contest between him and his opponents would be inconclusive. In 1672 the Orange Stadtholdership was re-established, a great political advantage; on the other hand the Labadist schism suggested powerfully that the cultivation of personal piety was not possible within a national establishment, nor indeed within a general appropriation of what culture and scholarship now had to offer. Voetius himself became narrower and more ascetic in his later years, and so did his tradition.

The great cleft in Dutch life came gradually to count for less in the eighteenth century. There were theologians like Witsius who set out to bridge it. More importantly fresh interests led to a theological regrouping as elements in the various schools combined themselves in new ways. The rationalistic and pietistic elements in Voetianism and

---

[42] On Coccejus: Heiner Faulenbach, *Weg und Ziel der Erkenntnis Christi* (Neukirchen, 1972) and his papers 'Johannes Coccejus' in *Gestalten der Kirchengeschichte* 7 : 163–76, and 'Die christliche Persönlichkeit bei Johannes Coccejus' in *Pietismus und Reveil* ed. van den Berg & van Dooren 130–40.

[43] G. F. Nuttall, 'English Dissenters in the Netherlands, 1640–1689', *Nederlands Archief voor Kerkgeschiednis* 59 : 37–8. On Voetius see papers by Aart de Groot, 'Gisbertius Voetius' in *Gestalten der Kirchengeschichte* 7 : 149–62, and 'Pietas im Vorpietismus' in *Pietismus und Reveil* 118–29.

Coccejanism pulled apart as the rationalisers began to take up with new philosophical fashions. On the other hand, middle-of-the-road irenical biblical scholars like Albert Schultens retained an active sympathy with those things commonly described as pietistic, and with the pastoral necessities theology must face. If in the seventeenth century the Dutch escaped a Reformed Orthodoxy like the Formula Consensus, in the eighteenth they eased their way into a range of theological and religious views, with a minimum of dissent from the ranks of the establishment, and with toleration, never easy, to new groups of dissenters from the outside, notably Moravians.

## UNTEREYCK

The German Reformed, some of whom faced much more acute problems than the Dutch, had never been politically polarised like the Voetians and Coccejans, and had thus avoided some of their theological animus. Bremen, indeed, was a town of strict Voetian ethos, and a great stronghold of Coccejan theology. Of Theodor Untereyck, a Coccejan who laid claim to the Orthodoxy of the Synod of Dort, and in his early days in Bremen ran into great trouble with the other clergy both on doctrinal grounds and because he held class-meetings during service times, it was said in his funeral sermon that 'what Spener is in the Lutheran church, Untereyck is in the Reformed'.[44] Untereyck studied under Voetius at Utrecht; his preaching in his first parish at Mülheim in the Ruhr was Voetian in style and like a good deal of preaching elsewhere as the age of precisionism melted into that of revival. He beat the drum about the gulf between the kingdom of Christ and that of the world, rejected every compromise, and looked to every family becoming a house-church with father exercising strict discipline. The object was not, of course, to encourage a works-righteousness, but to present the congregation, and, in the first instance, the house-church as a worthy bride of Christ. Preaching of this kind appealed to those tempted by Labadism; it produced converts who responded to his stress on personal appropriation of salvation, and it also produced suicides. Untereyck powerfully influenced the publicists of the New Birth like Reitz, maintained active contact by letter with Reformed congregations elsewhere in the Rhineland and with the Quakers, and was father-in-God to Friedrich Adolf Lampe.

---

[44] Mai, *Niederdeutsche Reformbewegung* 110–11; Heiner Faulenbach, 'Die Anfänge des Pietismus bei den Reformierten in Deutschland', *PuN* 4 (1977–8) esp. 205–9.

LAMPE

In Lampe many of these incipient changes were fully realised. He was brought up in Detmold by his grandfather, *Generalsuperintendent* Johann Jacob Zeller, a zealous Voetian who had been taken hostage by the French in 1672. After his grandfather's death in 1691, Lampe went to Bremen, which he came to regard as his home, and was educated at the Pädagogium and the Lycaeum, the Bremen theological faculty. Amongst his teachers was Cornelius de Hase, the collaborator and funeral panegyrist of Untereyck. In 1702 he went on to complete his education at Franeker and Utrecht. The former was at that time the most distinguished Dutch university, and Lampe studied under a series of Coccejan professors, who united the exegetical expertise of Coccejus with currents of living piety which Lampe had known from his youth up. Here he underwent a decisive conversion which he celebrated in a hymn of 'Praise to the Lord Jesus' in thirty-six stanzas.

Lampe was soon in Germany again in pastoral appointments, first near Cleves and then in Duisburg. Here he encountered a pastoral problem common in the region. The Reformed congregation had been badly divided, those who hungered and thirsted after righteousness becoming separatists after the manner of Labadie, leaving behind them a thoroughly secularised rump. By preaching of a style to satisfy the one, and energetic house-to-house visiting to keep an eye on the other, Lampe did much to save the day at Duisburg in the three years before he was called back to Bremen in 1709. In Bremen he pursued the same line, admitting that the church could not consist entirely of the elect; it must contain some of the lost for whom Christ had not died. Here Lampe introduced a custom he had already practised in the Lower Rhine area. The conclusion of the sermon was addressed to the elect, and they were required to stand and receive the word directed to them. This was 'discriminating' preaching indeed. He was an active hymn-writer and his theological and pastoral works included the first Reformed theological journal for Germany; he is credited with originating, at any rate in that part of the world, 'the language of Canaan', that bowdlerised form of biblical address which was taken up for theological reasons by Zinzendorf and had a long run in English Methodism.

Thus Lampe united in his own ministry much of what had been divided between the Voetian and Coccejan parties. In 1720 he was called back to a chair at Utrecht which he held till his final call to

Bremen in 1727 not long before his death. At Utrecht he exemplified his wider concerns for the Reformed cause and exercised a wider influence; the one was embodied in a history (published in 1727) of the sorely tried Reformed church of Hungary and Transylvania, the other was effected through very successful catechisms which made their mark in the Netherlands, East Friesland and right up the Rhine valley into Switzerland. Moreover Lampe's career illustrates a common evolution in the Reformed Rhineland and Reformed New England; the necessities of the churches were driving some of the ministry towards revivalism.[45]

### FRELINGHUYSEN

The work they did was confined in its effect neither to the Lower Rhine area nor to the churches. The first may be illustrated by reference to the curious career of a characteristic product of East Friesland, Theodorus Jacobus Frelinghuysen (1692–1747), who in 1717 became pastor of the village of Loegumer Voorwerk near Emden. Social and professional intercourse with the Netherlands was a regular part of the life of the Reformed pastorate in the duchy, and it was on a visit to Groningen in 1719 that Frelinghuysen was put in touch with a pastoral invitation to serve in the Raritan valley in New Jersey, for which the Amsterdam classis was acting as agent. He accepted the invitation, apparently believing that Raritan was a place in Flanders or Brabant, and became one of the earliest revivalists in America, operating on the fringes of British history by his links with the Tennent family, the celebrated Irish revivalists of the Middle Colonies.[46] The European importance of Frelinghuysen is the psychological index he provides to the religious and theological changes already noted; for it seems clear that the history which was compacted in his American ministry was rehearsed over a longer period in the Reformed churches of East Friesland generally, churches which had proved able to unite trends of thought and piety

---

[45] On Lampe: Heppe, *Pietismus und Mystik* 236–40; A. Ritschl, *Geschichte des Pietismus* (3 vols. Bonn, 1880–6) 1:427–54; Mai, *Niederdeutsche Reformbewegung* 252–301; Gerrit Snijders, *F. A. Lampe* (Bremen, 1961); Hollweg, *Älterer Pietismus* 152–3.

[46] J. Tanis, *Dutch Calvinistic Pietism in the Middle Colonies... T. J. Frelinghuysen* (The Hague, 1967). The attempt by Herman Harmelink III to argue that, despite the contemporary estimates of Gilbert Tennent and Jonathan Edwards, Frelinghuysen was not a revivalist at all, actually shows that he was a revivalist who approximated more nearly to the Voetian stamp than those who came later. 'Another look at Frelinghuysen and his "Awakening"', *CH* 17 (1968) 423–88. Frelinghuysen's sermons contrasting the righteous and the ungodly man were on a well-worn preaching theme since the time of Untereyck. *A Clear Demonstration of a Righteous and Ungodly man* (New York, 1745).

which had often been severed in the Netherlands. But a big move in East Friesland waited on an impulse from the Netherlands, and an impulse from the Netherlands waited on an impulse from the New World which Frelinghuysen received in the twenties by actual immigration.

### JUNG-STILLING

Meanwhile what had been happening to the heritage of Untereyck and Lampe in the Lower Rhine? The class meetings begun by Untereyck had a remarkable history. They spread about the neighbourhood and endured. The Thursday meetings in Mülheim stopped in 1740, but the others seem to have gone on and were the seedbeds of revival in the 1840s. In the 1920s the tradition they stood for drove the pastor of Mülheim, Heinrich Forsthoff, to distraction, and its partisans hauled him before his own presbytery; he actually encountered congregations who described themselves as 'Tersteegen-reformed', and denounced them with a ferocity, succinctly deflated by one of his own critics as '*dogmatische* rabies', a failing which broadly hinted that he was to become a German Christian and a leading spokesman for Hitler's religious policies in that area.[47] At Essen, the Lutheran town next door, Pietism had early penetrated and in the 1670s even the mayor, with the support of leading merchants, held class-meetings. In 1702 these were attracting Wednesday attendances of 60, 80 or 150, and 400–500 on Sundays; and were persuading sizeable numbers to abstain from tippling. As the temperature in the Protestant world began to rise again in the twenties, the meetings in the area gave birth to revival movements, and in 1727 they supported what is described as 'a great awakening' in the duchy of Berg.[48] They also provided a congregation for the most fascinating character in the whole history of religious revival, Gerhard Tersteegen.

From a confessional viewpoint, the risk with class-meetings was that gatherings of religious activists, or seekers whose needs were incompletely met by the round of parish worship, might be tempted to sever themselves from the parish altogether. As we have seen, every new religious movement would try to recruit among them, and in the

---

[47] H. Forsthoff, 'Tersteegens Mystik', *MRKg* 12 (1918) 129–91, 193–201; 'Der religiöse Grundcharakter Tersteegens' *MRKg* 22 (1928) 1; K. Scholder, *The Churches and the Third Reich* (2 vols. London, 1987–8) II:5, 13, 14, 63, 160.

[48] Heppe, *Evangelische Kirche von Cleve-Mark* 269–70; Wotschke, 'Franckes rheinische Freunde' 117; *Life and character of Gerhard Tersteegen* (2nd edn London 1834) 9.

Lower Rhine there had long been a profusion of popular alternative religions based on Jakob Böhme and other sources whose adherents formed a prospective market for the class-meetings. Jung-Stilling, who was born into a milieu of this kind in Nassau-Siegen in 1740, moved into Berg as a young man and 'again…met with immense numbers of minor sects, from whose sources flowed all those numerous, ponderous disquisitions on metaphysical philosophy, and the natural history of man'. He believed that the success of the revivalist Hochmann von Hochenau at Elberfeld and Solingen in 1717–18[49] was due to the fact that the iron industry had recruited a workforce of greater intelligence and vitality than was to be found elsewhere, and recalled the educative role of the *Geistliche Fama* twenty years later.

I knew a number of godly men who often sat in groups together on a Sunday evening to hear [a book] read, and who seemed to be transported to the skies by the interesting nature of its aminathemes. This book, if I mistake not, was called *Spiritual Fame*…Its author was a Dr Carl, surgeon to the court of Baden…He had a multitude of correspondents in America, and in the East Indies, in the Turkish empire, and in various parts of Europe, most of whom were of his mode of thinking…He published all kinds of interesting and singular notices from the different quarters of the world, interspersed with accounts of apparitions, miraculous providences…and…stories, all adapted to excite in the minds of the credulous the most intense and powerful excitement.

Jung-Stilling, like so many writers earlier in the eighteenth century, was at this stage an advocate of a middle way, aiming 'to show my German fatherland that the way to true temporal and eternal happiness lies midway between unbelief and religious delusion'; he clearly approved of his father, who 'read all sorts of mystical books and pursued a middle course between a mystic and a member of the Reformed church'. His problem in advocating the middle way (like that of the analytical historian now) was that contemporary language was not equal to the complexity of the phenomena in question.

The term (Schwaermer) in the German Language is not yet…settled; it is employed alike to denote an enthusiast or fanatic, and yet the one differs almost essentially from the other. I denominate that person an enthusiast who clothes, at least *for the most part*, the legitimate deductions of reason or the authorized principles of truth in the light drapery of the imagination…A fanatic, on the contrary, is one who takes all the glowing images of fancy for

[49]  H. Renkewitz, *Hochmann von Hochenau (1670–1721)* (Breslau, 1935; repr. Witten, 1969) 207–8.

actual truth, and gives them out as evidence of divine illumination. Delusionists of this latter class are in the highest degree dangerous, while the former are often beneficent.[50]

Böhme was probably harmless, though not completely so.

### TERSTEEGEN

If Jung-Stilling had difficulty in placing Böhme, modern historians have been in a worse case with Tersteegen. Forsthoff, starting from a familiar, if narrow definition of Protestantism, did not baulk at the adjective 'heathenish', while recent Roman Catholic commentary has seen in him a Carmelite in the thinnest of disguise.[51] The truth is that Tersteegen aspired to the way of Jung-Stilling's father, 'a middle course between a mystic and a member of the Reformed church', though he did not chart it in quite the same way; that the market to which he first appealed was that of the popular mysticisms Jung-Stilling so well describes; that the institutions he first used were those created by Untereyck, now getting away from church control; that the location where he began was where Hochmann had enjoyed his late success; and though Hochmann and Tersteegen were very different characters, Tersteegen was aware that they were seeking to revive the same milieu, paying a respectful visit to his predecessor's grave. Like Zinzendorf he owed a great deal to Dutch financial support,[52] but thought that the great Moravian, in his quest for a quick result, confounded justification with sanctification and opened the door to antinomianism. As a young man he trembled in every limb in the company of the Inspired, and was always well thought of by them; but he took a more rigorous view than they of the 'ecstatic joy and quickening of the soul' imparted to those who succeeded 'in seeing and hearing things of the angelic world'. 'These experiences are always dangerous, and it is possible to change the angelic quickenings for devilish torments, so that one must avoid pleasing oneself.'[53] He did not attend church or partake of the sacraments, but was not a Quaker; he opposed both the doctrinaire views that the sacraments of the church were essential to salvation and that they

---

[50] Heinrich Stilling, *Theobald, or the Fanatic* tr. S. Schaefer (Philadelphia, 1846) 3, 4, 10–11, 23–4, 76–7.          [51] Giovanna della Croce, *Gerhard Tersteegen* (Bern, 1979).

[52] C. P. van Andel, *Gerhard Tersteegen. Leben und Werk* (Düsseldorf, 1973: enlarged from the Dutch edn, Wageningen, 1961) 92–3.

[53] H. E. Govan, *Life of Gerhard Tersteegen* … (London, 1898) 132–3; Max Goebel, 'Geschichte der wahren Inspirations-Gemeinden von 1688 bis 1850' *ZHT* ns 19 (1855) 370–3.

were of no effect. He was indeed half-way between the mystics and the Reformed church. In his *Select Lives of Holy Souls* (1733–53) Tersteegen wished to give biographical shape to the 'truths of interior Christianity', but insisted nevertheless that these were 'truths of faith, grounded in God's Word and in experience'; and at the very end of his life he confessed his faith in the triune God 'according to Holy Scripture and the so-called Apostles' Creed and all the other truths included in Holy Scripture'.[54] At such times he was more than half-way between the mystics and the Reformed church.

Tersteegen was born in 1697 in Moers, still at that time an Orange county in possession of William III of Great Britain. His father was a merchant of modest means, and young Gerhard first arrived in Mülheim in 1713 to begin a commercial apprenticeship to his father's brother-in-law. Mülheim was full of separatist tendencies from Labadism to Hochmannism, and Tersteegen was to come under the influence of one of Hochmann's converts, Wilhelm Hoffmann; he was a candidate in theology but had no hope of preferment because, when cited before the classis in Duisburg, he had refused to express his agreement with the Heidelberg Confession or subscribe to the church order. Tersteegen did not get on well with his master, or with business when he entered it on his own account in the years 1717–19. His real home was the quietistic circle gathered round Hoffmann, meeting in their conventicles. This was the background to his first 'conversion' in 1717, which amounted to the opening of his heart to a mystical piety; his second or definitive conversion took place in 1724 when the divine grace in Christ took the first place in his life.[55] This was marked by a personal covenant with Christ of a quietistic style. In the same year he produced his first book, the *Unparteiischer Abriss Christlicher Grundwahrheiten*, the title of which reveals an abiding Arnoldian streak in the author, the contents exemplifying his dependence on a quietistic milieu, especially Poiret. In the next few years his labours were immense. He maintained himself by bandage-weaving, poured an endless stream of books from the press, many of which, in the baroque manner, were translations (the first being Labadie's *Manual of Piety*). When Hoffmann acquired more work than he could manage in the great Berg revival of the mid-twenties, he delegated much to Tersteegen. The latter was now preacher, pastor and correspondent with care of souls.

[54] W. Zeller, *Theologie und Frömmigkeit* (2 vols. Marburg, 1971–8) II:173, 184.
[55] F. Winter, 'Zur Frömmigkeit Tersteegens', *MRKg* 22 (1928) 142.

Tersteegen, too, must now shed part of his load, and it was characteristic of the man that what he gave up in 1728 was his trade. He now lived in poverty on his royalties and what was contributed by friends. Practising the narrowest possible lifestyle now became part of his spiritual teaching; he pursued his own teaching in this respect so successfully that there was always something in hand for the assistance of the other poor. Moreover, from sources unknown, he acquired a range of medical expertise which was also available at the call of need. In this he resembled not only the scattered North German revivalists we have seen already, not only the Francke institutions at Halle, but also the mystics with whom he, like Wesley later, had grown up, the Marquis de Renty, Gregory Lopez, Mme Guyon, not to mention the New Testament record of Christ himself. At the same time he sought to consolidate the base of his work and to extend its circumference. In 1727 he set up his *Pilgerhütte*. This was a house built in the country by a Duisburg smith called Otterbeck; he shared it with his sister, both being unmarried. The house was now conveyed to a relative who was also a friend of Tersteegen, and adapted for the use of a brotherhood of kindred spirits who should leave the world and develop the life hid with Christ in God. Denial of world and self was to be the essence of the community. Tersteegen created no monastic rule, for he thought this a legalism ruinous to the monastic life and to interior Christianity. It caused surprise in the Reformed world, though such things had been tried or talked of among the quietists. And, in any case, Tersteegen was before long involved in his life's work, the *Select Lives of Holy Souls* (1733–53), all of them Catholic, and most of them hermits and members of religious orders of Counter-Reformation provenance, a testimony to his veneration of spiritual gifts, and a constant means of keeping him informed about the regular life.

In Tersteegen this withdrawal into community life was balanced by increasing itinerancy. He was constantly on the move around Berg, is said to have ventured into Denmark and Sweden, and in 1732 was invited to Amsterdam by a connexion of Wilhelm Hoffmann, Jonkheer Adriaan Pauw. From then until 1756 he visited Holland almost every year. Everywhere he went there were circles of friends kept together by spiritual correspondence with him and with each other; indeed at Krefeld, the refuge town of the North, and at half a dozen places in the Ruhr area, communities formed in which the spiritual life could be lived in common. At a distance Tersteegen maintained contacts by correspondence much like those of the radicals in the Wetterau (contacts which indeed included Dr Carl at Berleburg) – minor aristocracy, urban separatists, wealthy merchants in the big South German towns, emigrants from Krefeld to America. The variegated pattern of Dutch life opened his way into new circles, especially those convinced that the Dutch establishment and the Dutch way of life did not permit intimate fellowship with the like-minded, sanctification or serene withdrawal from the world. Tersteegen inherited not only the literary remains of mystic Pierre Poiret, but his band of followers. Coenraad Bosman was a Labadist, Jan Beets was a Mennonite pastor who later turned against Tersteegen and became a revival preacher of a more familiar style. Apart from Pauw, among the wealthy there were Catharina van Vollenhoven, a wealthy woman of Rotterdam, and Maria d'Orville, a member of an eminent patrician family; others flocked in from all round the country whenever Tersteegen came to Amsterdam. But Tersteegen did not aim at a fashionable congregation; his connexions included a few clergy, and his hearers many of the poor of the sort to whom he ministered in Berg. All found nourishment in his writings, and the club spirit thrived on mutual greeting with a verse from his *Blumengärtlein*. Tersteegen never aimed to create a new sect, but fellowship was one of the demands of his movement, and he was prepared to use the word 'membership'. His milieu in the Netherlands overlapped with that to which Zinzendorf appealed and into which Wesley was received in 1738. Some of his friends had been friendly with the Moravians before they met him, and he suffered some of the polemic directed against the Herrnhuters. His influence in Holland was strengthened by his excellent written and spoken Dutch, by the circulation of his writings – many of which appeared in Dutch without his knowledge – and not least by a firm structure of interlinked class-meetings which preserved his movement there when, in 1756, he announced that he no longer had the physical strength for journeys into the Netherlands.[56]

With the exception of two entirely different characters, Jonathan Edwards and Charles Wesley, Tersteegen was the only one of the revivalists whose literary memorial was more important than his pastoral and evangelistic work. This impression has been reinforced by the recent publication of Tersteegen's sermons. They create a

---

[56] van Andel, *Tersteegen* 197–201, 75–100.

vivid impression of his personal tranquillity and of a skill in the imaginative exposition of scripture in a class-meeting context which has probably never been equalled. Moreover he had a message of hope for Rhineland congregations which had lost political control of their future. Were they a heap of dry bones unmoved by their own need and danger, the wrath of God, fear of death or the Last Judgment? The love of Christ constrained even them. Would the faithful be judged according to strict justice on the Last Day? They would, yet not according to their own righteousness, but according to the righteousness they have put on through union with Jesus. The Christian is indeed (in the Reformed manner) a pilgrim on the way to eternity, but what 'glorious and comforting society' he enjoys on his journey; the continuous presence of Jesus in the cloud or the pillar of fire.[57] His hymns were soon taken up by the German Lutheran churches with which he never had any connexion, with such enthusiasm as to make him the fifth most numerously represented hymn-writer in the German Evangelical hymn-books. (Two were put into good English by John Wesley.) In Switzerland too the influence of Tersteegen was early and enduring, notwithstanding the hostility of Swiss Orthodoxy to the mystical approach. The passivity of the mystics was not without points of contact with what all the Swiss Reformed learned in their catechism and sang in their Whitsuntide hymns; in French-speaking Switzerland the ground was prepared by the French Catholic mystics and by Hector de Marsay; and Swiss Pietist refugees turned up constantly not only in the Wetterau, but also in Mülheim. The result was that Tersteegen was already appearing in Swiss hymn-collections in the thirties, exercised a constant literary influence throughout the century, had his Swiss disciples, and was used to produce revival in the Zurich Oberland in 1757.[58]

Tersteegen's literary output not only illustrates his peculiar attractiveness and helped to sustain his appeal, it is the tangible remnant of a steady work of religious consolidation in which the ground was prepared for a major revival when, very late, the impulse was provided by the Netherlands. The Dutch origins of the great revival movements of 1750 will concern us shortly. They evoked a response in many places in the Rhine valley, including Mülheim and its neighbourhood. The moment was seized by a Dutch theological

[57] G. Tersteegen, *Werke* I: *Geistliche Reden* ed. A. Löshhorn & W. Zeller (Göttingen, 1979) 270.
[58] P. Wernle, *Der schweizerische Protestantismus im 18. Jahrhundert* (3 vols. Tübingen, 1923–5) I:102, 141, 226, 249, 253, 317, 453–5, 458, 618; III:53, 57, 146, 170.

student, Jacob Chevalier, who came from a respectable Amsterdam merchant family, and was now studying at Duisburg. There were the usual revival phenomena of tears and mass conversions, and Tersteegen was drawn in. Much of the labour of dealing with those affected by Chevalier's message fell on him, and he found himself engaged in counselling from morn till night. Nor was this all. The counselling and the opposition which Chevalier received – his own professor described Tersteegen as 'the most dangerous heretic of our time' – convinced the mystic that Chevalier had the root of the matter in him, and that he too must join in the work. The house-meetings were packed out, and the addresses form some of the most interesting in Tersteegen's collection. Their success was only too palpable, for authority in church and state intervened. The revival meetings came to an end; Chevalier went back to the Netherlands, at the end of his study received a parish, and died a zealous adherent of the Orthodoxy of the Synod of Dort. What did not come to an end was the revival in a deeper sense. House-meetings had been in trouble with authority for some time, but now Tersteegen could not escape them. People thronged his house all day, barely leaving time for meals. Even when he rose in the morning there would be a queue of ten before the door waiting a word from the master. By this time it was public property that at least some of what Tersteegen had to offer could not be had from the parish ministry at all.

## REVIVAL IN THE NETHERLANDS

An impulse from the Netherlands was needed to set revival going on any scale in East Friesland or the Rhineland; when it came, after long delays, it illustrated how severe were the institutional barriers to be overcome. As revival moved westwards it had sought to get round the old confessional divisions. The balance in the Netherlands was tipped not by the efforts of Labadists, Herrnhuters or friends of Tersteegen, but by the outbreak of revival in the Reformed churches of New England and Scotland. It was, in this sense, a reassertion of Reformed confessional identity against the trend.

The movement of sentiment which was compacted in the case of Frelinghuysen may be further illustrated by the case of two men who within a few years of each other were pastors of Midwolda, near the frontiers of the Netherlands and East Friesland. Wilhelmus Schortinghuis (1700–50), a Voetian,[59] educated at Groningen, received his

[59] J. van den Berg, 'Orthodoxy, Rationalism and the World', *SCH* 10 (1973) 177, 184.

first pastoral charge as second preacher at Weener in East Friesland (1723–34). This appointment proved a turning point in his life. The pastor of Weener, Johann Klugkist, as appears from his gravestone, belonged to that class of Frisian preachers who were moving into revivalism, and were described as a Boanerges in the pulpit and a Barnabas in pastoral care. As such, he did not please part of the congregation, and Schortinghuis was expected to provide a counter-balance to him. In the event Schortinghuis proved one of Klugkist's most durable converts, and indeed wrote hymns for Klugkist's short catechism. Talmudic scholar, powerful preacher, a prolific hymn-writer who addressed himself to every stage of life, regenerate or unregenerate, Schortinghuis quickly came to exercise an enormous influence in East Friesland and across the Netherlands frontier. In 1734 the opportunity came for him to return as pastor of Midwolda across the border. From this point everything began to go wrong. What Schortinghuis had always pleaded for was an inward Christi-anity; what he denounced was an outward conformity, a trust in institutional allegiance; indeed he called on the church to repent. All this he poured into a book, *Christianity Resting on Inward Experience*, published in 1740. This book made Schortinghuis the leader of a party, but landed him in great trouble with the authorities in church and state. However large the congregation at Midwolda, the Netherlands church was not going to repent.[60] How the mood was running locally even amongst the non-Reformed came out in 1743 when Dreas, the second Lutheran preacher at Groningen, was convicted of *Pietisterey* by his church authorities for holding that man could not be born again except through despair, that an unregenerate preacher could not preach with fruit, and that articles of faith and forms of prayer were of small account, since they were often the work of men not demonstrably regenerate. Here was a cry of despair against the institutional church not unlike that of Schortinghuis; and, as in the latter's case, the institutional church showed that it was not prepared to accept the invitation to repent.

A change, however, was at hand. Schortinghuis was defended in print by the Reformed pastors of Emden. To the charge that he had put forward doctrine which had never been heard in the church before, they answered that his teaching was to be found in scripture, and, with varying degrees of force, in the early fathers, in the

---

[60] Hollweg, *Älterer Pietismus* 137, 134, 156–7, 168–79; Heppe, *Pietismus und Mystik* 421–459; *AHE* 7:983–1017.

Reformers, and in the churches of England and Scotland as well as the Netherlands.[61] In short a wider world was to be brought in to redress the balance against the Netherlands church which Friesland could not redress on its own. And the fact that religious revival was promoted by many of the best ministers of the Reformed churches of New England, and that it was eminently represented by Whitefield among the few remaining Calvinist clergy of the Church of England, impressed opinion in the Dutch church. Revival, it was clear by the early forties, was not necessarily the foible of separatists or neo-Labadists. And in 1745 (another dangerous year for the world of internationally guaranteed Protestantism) Amsterdam was shaken by the preaching of a candidate for the ministry, Gerardus Kuypers. Cries of distress from anxious souls interrupted his preaching, and enormously multiplied his congregations as people came to see what was going on. When in 1749 he obtained a living at Nijkerk op de Veluwe near Amersfoort, and informed an admittedly dead congregation that it had succumbed to the unrestrained domination of Satan, when he beat the drum about sin and grace, conversion and the New Birth, there were extraordinary scenes. In addition to the cries and groans, many members of the congregation collapsed, and others became incapable of leaving their seats at the end of the service, and had to be carried out. In what had been a dead congregation, the kirk sessions proclaimed on 29 October 1750, that church services must not be interrupted, and that elders must instruct the people that physical excitements were not of the essence of conversion. The movement, which, as in New England, sharply divided sentiment for and against, spread rapidly into every province in the Netherlands, and produced particularly striking results in the summer of 1751 in Hoogeveen and Zwartsluis.[62] The movement also illustrated how far the old party lines in the Netherlands had been confused in the last half-century. For Kuypers was a pupil of the moderate Orthodox van den Honert, a powerful opponent of Schortinghuis. But then van den Honert's work had been entitled *The Church in the Netherlands Considered and Admonished to Conversion* (1746) and this was what, in their different ways, Schortinghuis and Kuypers were calling for. Once again church discipline was brought into play

---

[61] Hollweg, *Älterer Pietismus* 172–3.
[62] Kuypers's account was translated for British readers by John Gillies in *Historical Collections Relating to Remarkable Periods of the Success of the Gospel* (4 vols. Glasgow, 1754–86) II:455–61, App:18–26. Cf. *Ibid.* II:9–18.

to restrain the worst excesses of the outbreak, and by the beginning of 1752 all was apparently over. Kuypers in 1759 moved on to Schortinghuis's old parish at Midwolda, before, like so many Reformed revivalists, accepting a university appointment. Heinrich Heppe concluded that 'the fire which mysticism had begun was not the fire to kindle which the Lord of the church came into the world; hence it must disappear like a breath'.[63]

This judgment was harsh. The revivals in the Reformed churches of New England and Scotland had already come to an abrupt stop, even while (as Wesley noted) Methodism continued to make steady progress. Revival had begun among Protestants deprived of their church system, and was never promoted for long by church establishments. The profoundest impact of the work of Schortinghuis and Kuypers was thus felt in East Friesland. People came across to see what Kuypers was up to, and enthusiastic reports were published in Bremen. Revival had begun independently in Manslagt even before this time, and the news from Nijkerk led to an outbreak in Leer and Reiderland which went on for three years and spread into the Krummhorn. The prominent name in this case was that of Helmer Schröder (1710–67), the son of an Emden textile manufacturer, and at the time pastor of Rysum; the notable features of his revival were that it was contained within the church, and that, in spite of receding after a time, it permanently raised the level of church attendance. Schröder was another preacher who combined the Boanerges with the Barnabas, and, as a preacher, is said to have been like Ezekiel, who struck with his hand and stamped with his foot, and called down judgment upon all abominations.[64] He too contributed to the forces of revival which had been building up in the Lower Rhine area.

[63] On Kuypers: Heppe, *Pietismus und Mystik* 459–64; Ritschl, *Geschichte des Pietismus* I: 347–52.
[64] Wesley, *Journal* IV: 54, 122; Hollweg, *Älterer Pietismus* 158–67.

# CHAPTER 7

# Revival in the American colonies

Revival in the American colonies shared the characteristics of revival in Europe; friends and enemies alike treated it as a pan-Protestant phenomenon. Jonathan Edwards discerned a distinct stage in the cosmic history of redemption in the reforms of Peter the Great, here regarded as a surrogate Protestant, the success of missions among the Tartars, the American Indians and on the Malabar coast, and of revivals proper in New England and most especially 'in Germany, through the endeavours of an eminent divine there, August Herman Frank, professor of divinity at Halle in Saxony'.[1] Conservative opponents of the revival also secured a European resonance for their views,[2] and put the synoptic vision of the revivalists to their own use. They perceived 'a wonderful WANDERING SPIRIT' which

now haunt[s] Moravia, and many other places in the German Empire; has of late been very troublesome in England; and has been seen, felt and heard by thousands in America...honest folks in Scotland...get by its influences such a second-sight, as they can easily see their neighbours' hearts and intentions...Such as have read the records of Germany and England al[l]edge that it was the same [spirit] who guided the incomparable Jacob Behmen in writing his religious jargon and dark nonsense: that possess'd the enthusiasts of Munster.[3]

The immigrant Babel in the Middle Colonies, especially Pennsyl-

---

[1] *A History of the Work of Redemption* (1773) in Jonathan Edwards, *Works* ed. S. E. Dwight & E. Hickman (2 vols. London, 1834; repr. Edinburgh, 1974) II:600. This treatise first published after Edward's death consisted of sermons preached to his congregation at Northampton in 1739.

[2] [Charles Chauncy] *A Letter...to Mr. George Wishart...* (Edinburgh, 1742).

[3] *The Great Awakening* ed. A. Heimert & Perry Miller (5th edn Indianapolis, 1978) 147–51. Both Chauncy (*The Wonderful Narrative* (Boston, 1742)) and Alexander Garden, the bishop of London's commissary at Charleston (*Take Heed how ye Hear* (Charleston, S.C., 1741)) made great play with the idea that the same 'wandering spirit' inspired the French Prophets.

vania, was certainly immense; it was here that revivalism was first developed, and that there were the greatest concentrations of the Dutch, German and Swiss peoples whose history in Europe has concerned us. With them it is convenient to begin.

### THE DUTCH REFORMED IN AMERICA

Religious dissidence had been an important factor in the early migrations of the Germans and Swiss, but it had been speedily overwhelmed in importance by economic motives. The sects got much of what they wanted by emigration, though not all succeeded in propagating their styles of the Christian life; by contrast the birthright members of the great European religious establishments did not find the religious ethos which they had left behind. When religious revival set in, it almost predictably affected church people in the main, and largely passed the sects by. The special feature of the history of the Dutch Reformed was that historical accidents left them as a religious establishment in important corners of what became, under British rule, New York State, without sparing them the disagreements usual among church people in America; and these disagreements were compounded by the arrival of representatives of hostile religious parties founded for other purposes in Europe.

In the days when New York had been New Amsterdam there had been constant dissonance between the aims of the Dutch West India Company to make a profit, and those of the Amsterdam classis to plant a Christian commonwealth on the Reformed pattern. When New Amsterdam surrendered to a British army in 1664, Dutch immigration ended and half the minuscule number of Dutch ministers were withdrawn; the province was put under the government of the duke of York, the future James II, and the prospects of the Reformed interest could hardly have looked worse. Under the terms of surrender, however, the Dutch church was permitted to maintain its public worship and church discipline and to hold its property. The oath of allegiance required to the British crown was held to be no bar to their remaining in a full sense members of the church of Holland, subject to the authorities of Amsterdam. The antics of James II caused alarm,[4] but the triumph of William of Orange in England opened the way in 1696 for a charter to the Dutch

---

[4] *Ecclesiastical Records of the State of New York* ed. Hugh Hastings (7 vols. Albany, N.Y., 1901–16) II:1041. The Dutch church did, however, pray for James II. *Ibid.* II:950.

Reformed church in New York recognising their right to hold property, exempting them from the ecclesiastical patronage of the governor, and permitting their worship 'according to the constitutions and directions of the Reformed Church in Holland, approved and instituted by the National Synod of Dort'. This charter proved to be a model for many others for Dutch churches in other parts of New York State and New Jersey. The Dutch Reformed were now British subjects but not dissenters; they were friendly with the Church of England in New York even while they blocked its establishment in the state (they could not prevent it in four counties). Nor was their subjection to the Amsterdam classis tempered, as it had been in the days of the Dutch West India Company, by the influence of the merchant patriciate in the Dutch capital; and in the transatlantic correspondence clerical concern about the threat of Labadism and Koelmanism to Reformed Orthodoxy on both sides of the ocean figures large.[5] Given the assistance of the Amsterdam courts in recruiting clergy and in other respects, it is not surprising that in New York, right up to the time of American Independence, there was a clerical party pledged to a Reformed Orthodoxy which was indissolubly linked with the supremacy of Amsterdam and even with the Dutch language, and with attitudes more exclusive than those now prevalent in the Netherlands.

This caricature Orthodoxy had even less to be said for it in the New World than the old. Internal migration produced a Dutch diaspora in New Jersey and Carolina; assimilation led Huguenots and Palatines to throw in their lot with the Dutch. On both fronts new needs must be met, and met especially in the Raritan valley. In the third quarter of the seventeenth century settlements of Dutch and Huguenots began in this part of New Jersey and in 1699 a church at Raritan was formally organised by Guiliam Bartholf, the pastor of the North Jersey churches of Hackensack and Acquackanock (now Passaic). This and other churches founded in the valley were long

---

[5] *Ibid.* ii: 746–7, 823–4, 831, 839, 874–6, 1004–5, 1051. Jacobus Koelman (1632–95), the most influential Voetian of his generation, was dismissed from the parish of Sluis in 1675. He was a notable translator into Dutch of Puritan works (including two by the New England divine, Thomas Hooker) and believed that the church consisted of visible saints. He was thus attracted to the Labadists, but finally repudiated them in polemic of extravagant proportions. He broke with the establishment by opposing synodical appointment of holy days other than the Lord's Day, and arrangements for the administration of the sacraments; he demanded free prayer. Some of his Puritan translations circulated among the Dutch in America.

served by Bartholf by itinerant visits twice a year.[6] This time Koelmanism really made an appearance. Bartholf had been born and baptised in Sluis, and instructed by Koelman himself. Coming to America as a cooper, he also served in the Dutch Reformed manner as a lay-reader and sick-visitor.[7] These services so endeared him to the pastorless Dutch churches of North Jersey, that they sent him back to the Netherlands for ordination, not to Amsterdam but to Sluis and the Classis of Walcheren. This procedure infuriated the Orthodox of New York, who suspected that a back door had been permanently opened to the ordination of unsuitable candidates for the ministry. Bartholf exercised a more informal ministry than seemed good to the New Yorkers, as, for fifteen years after his ordination in 1694, he was the only Dutch Reformed minister in New Jersey. Itinerating continually, he was the real founder of his church there. And when after five years' petitioning the Raritan churches received a pastor, Bartholf proved to be his firm friend.[8]

### FRELINGHUYSEN, HIS FRIENDS AND ENEMIES

Theodorus Jacobus Frelinghuysen (1692–1747) has already appeared as exemplifying in compacted form the steady progress of the Reformed ministry in East Friesland and the Lower Rhine towards revival. The case for having in the Middle Colonies a German Reformed minister intimately familiar with Dutch ways was obvious; and he came, not merely approved, but actually reordained, by Amsterdam. But the Amsterdam party in New York knew from at least the moment of his arrival that he would give them trouble and alleged that 'while on the sea Rev. Frelinghuysen condemned most of the preachers in Holland as not regenerated men', and intended to build up a party in America.[9] The fact was that Frelinghuysen brought with him Lower Rhine traditions of 'discriminating preaching', that is, addressing different sections of the congregation according to their presumed spiritual state; that these traditions had been given systematic shape at Groningen by Johan Verschuir

[6] A. Messler, *The Reformed Dutch Church of Raritan...* (Somerville, N.J., 1834) 5–6; *Forty Years at Raritan* (New York, 1873) 163.

[7] The *zieketroster* or *krankenbezoeker* were lay church officials much employed in Amsterdam in hospitals. They came frequently on board ship and in the colonies to act as a sort of unqualified and sub-standard clergy.

[8] Hastings, *Ecclesiastical Records* II: 1051, 1072–3, 1105–7; III: 1649; C. F. De Jong, *The Dutch Reformed Church in the American Colonies* (Grand Rapids, Mich., 1978) 76, 172–3.

[9] Hastings, *Ecclesiastical Records* III: 2182–4.

(1680–1737), to whom he was devoted;[10] and that Verschuir was a latter-day Koelmanite. In this tradition Frelinghuysen yearned for a church of visible saints with tight communion discipline and preached his heart out to get it. On the one front, Frelinghuysen, in his different context, is reminiscent of the doctrinaire young Wesley in Georgia fifteen years later; on the other he rapidly developed into a revivalist who deeply influenced Gilbert Tennent (whose strained relations with Presbyterians of New England and Scottish origin exactly paralleled those of Frelinghuysen with the New York Dutch), and won the approval of Jonathan Edwards and Whitefield.[11]

Frelinghuysen's ideas on communion discipline did not appeal to the more substantial Dutch of the Raritan valley, and the New York pundits did not care for his preaching. Bartholf found his early sermons 'learned, well-digested and thrilling', but was later reported to Amsterdam as saying that 'Frelinghuysen ought to know that the Raritan church was very feeble in spiritual knowledge…and that there was a danger by his harsh treatment, of making them into Quakers, or atheists, or suicides, or Pharisees.' And if Frelinghuysen gave offence where his views were narrow, he contravened church discipline where they were broad. He itinerated constantly, evoking charges that he was intruding on the parishes of other men; an accusation hard to bear from a party which was certainly fomenting opposition to him. The revival which he got going spread to English-speaking Presbyterians who began to organise themselves in the valley. Abetted, it seems, by Frelinghuysen's enemies, they called as a minister the young Gilbert Tennent. After some hesitation, Frelinghuysen formed a close relationship with him, lent him barns and churches which he himself used, and occasionally shared services, even communion services, the one speaking English, the other Dutch; in return, Tennent adopted Frelinghuysen's rather abrasive style. It was made a charge against Frelinghuysen that he was employing an English dissenter (i.e. a Reformed minister in like standing with himself) and even the English language. He was said to be insane with lucid intervals, to go in for 'howling prayers' and to deserve exclusion from the ministry on health grounds. The Amsterdam classis behaved prudently, shielding Frelinghuysen from the worst attacks of his enemies, while counselling him to greater

---

[10] M. J. Coalter, 'The Life of Gilbert Tennent' (unpubl. Ph.D. thesis, Princeton University, 1982) 46–8.
[11] George Whitefield, *Journals* (London, 1960) 351–2; Edwards, *Works* 1:349.

gentleness, and making clear the limits to his authority which he must not exceed.[12]

Revivalism and new growth exposed the constitutional arrangements of the Dutch Reformed church to the same strains as those of the English-language Presbyterians. A move was set on foot by Frelinghuysen's friends as early as 1737 for the creation of an American coetus, or ministerial advisory body, still subordinate to Amsterdam, without powers to ordain; this was granted in 1747. After Frelinghuysen's death an agitation for authority to ordain in America followed, which continued, furiously contested by the New York shellbacks, down to the time of American Independence. But the future cast its shadows before, and those shadows had been curiously anticipated by Frelinghuysen. In 1764 even New York had to resort to a minister who preached exclusively in English, and he was a minister of the Church of Scotland; and, as the condition precedent of Dutch recognition of American ordinations was improved theological eduction, a chair was created at Princeton for the purpose, the first incumbent of which was Robert Livingston, namesake and descendant of the hero of that distant Scots revival at Kirk o' Shotts. Moreover, among Frelinghuysen's offences had been to extend a hand to the likeminded among the German Reformed, and to union between the Dutch and German Reformed in America, to which the Amsterdam authorities proved more sympathetic than their protégés in New York.[13] To the fate of the Germans, the majority of whom originated in the West of the Empire, and were Reformed by tradition, we must now turn.

### GERMAN-LANGUAGE SETTLERS

In Europe the Mennonites had been the first target for Quaker evangelists; in Pennsylvania as in Germany the boundaries between the Mennonite and Quaker communities could be quite fluid, and the spiritual history of the Pennsylvania Mennonites mirrored that of the Society of Friends. Within forty years 'many of 'em were wealthy, having got the best land in the province',[14] and (Swiss though many of them were) they enjoyed the liberal support of the Dutch Mennonites in hard times. In America as in Europe the community

---

[12] Hastings, *Ecclesiastical Records* III:2179, 2319, 2466: IV:2566–7, 2466, 2566–70, 2640, 2351–6, 2363, 2381–8, 2413–24, 2459–68; De Jong, *Dutch Reformed Church* 175.

[13] F. Klees, *The Pennsylvania Dutch* (New York, 1952) 78; Hastings, *Ecclesiastical Records* IV:2987–8.      [14] S. Hazard, *Register of Pennsylvania* 15 (1835) 201.

gradually divided among those who sought survival for their fellowship in strictness of dress, conduct and separation from the world, those tempted by progressive intellect and those seeking a new inner impulse from Pietism or revival. In the Netherlands men of this latter mind provided Zinzendorf with major financial support; in Pennsylvania they did not make their mark for another decade, when a renewal movement began which was to take the local Quakers out of politics and into a more strenuous affirmation of the Peace Testimony and opposition to slavery.[15] Then under the impact of the revival in Virginia the Mennonites produced their own revivalist in Martin Boehm (1725–1812), who, with others, threw in his lot with an undenominational revival pioneered by the Reformed evangelist Philip William Otterbein. This movement issued eventually in the Church of the United Brethren in Christ. The outcome, which falls beyond the period of the present study, showed that the hopes which the revivalists of Switzerland and the Netherlands had conceived of the Mennonites were not misplaced; but that like other old denominations they were not able to contain revival ferment. The paradox was that the great old German denominations in Pennsylvania, the Reformed and the Lutherans, were able to do so not only better than the churches of their European heartlands, but better than their English-language counterparts in America, the Presbyterians and Anglicans. To stimulate revival among them, however, more activity on the part of new sects was required.

The great German influx of the eighteenth century raised what was called the 'German' proportion of the population of Pennsylvania to almost half by the time of the War of Independence, overwhelming the sects by newcomers of Lutheran and Reformed origin. Most of the reports, other than those spread by the recruiting agents, 'the Dutch traders in human beings and their man-stealing emissaries', were gloomy about their spiritual condition. Some were the work of men like Gottfried Mittelberger, the organ-builder, laudably anxious to warn his fellow-countrymen that America did not offer instant bliss, but totally unable to adjust to a society where *Obrigkeit* put its weight behind no particular form of Protestant religious observance, and German congregations hired preachers 'for the year like cowherds in Germany'; it followed, in his famous aphorism, that Pennsylvania 'was heaven for farmers, paradise for

---

[15] H. Wellenreuther, *Glaube und Politik in Pennsylvania* (Cologne, 1972) 323, 335.

artisans, and hell for officials and preachers'.[16] Other dark tidings
were designed to strengthen the hands of the European fund-raisers
or to get men to volunteer for the ministry in America by tales of
religious destitution. No one admitted that the early settlers had
consistently brought in books,[17] or damped the zeal of Dutch or
German patrons by confessing Whitefield's enthusiastic discovery
that 'some of the Germans in America are holy souls... They keep up
a close walk with God, and are remarkable for their sweetness and
simplicity of behaviour.'[18]

Even to the optimist, however, not all was well with the German
church people in America. Both the grind of getting started and the
temptations of success in what became the most prosperous of all the
colonies could be ruinous to the spiritual life. One anti-Moravian
tract put it very fairly:[19]

Many [Germans] were awakened before they came, others were awakened
and attracted through the instruction and advice of good souls, others by
God without human intervention through his living voice and word. But the
land is very productive and to those who seek a great deal of property
beyond their needs, it is a very busy country, and there is much heavy
physical labour. Many of the awakened of every nationality are subject to an
oppressive and spiritually weakening covetousness, desire for land... Notwithstanding this an often secret yearning after a new earnestness is
frequently aroused.

There were special difficulties for the German church people.
German was (so to speak) *lingua franca* only to those possessed of High
German, and this was quickly supplemented by a sort of German
franglais. Mühlenberg complained of one family in which 'I did not
know what language to speak to the young people whose parents
were German, for they could not speak proper English, German or

16 Gottlieb Mittelberger, *Journey to Pennsylvania* ed. O. Handlin & John Clive (Cambridge,
  Mass., 1960) 47–8.
17 S. G. Wolf found that one of her poorest Germantown testators, with no real property, left
  twenty books which constituted 5 per cent of his total worth. She also found, however, that
  as the century proceeded (and the immigrants came increasingly from established churches)
  books declined both in value and as status symbols. *Urban Village. Germantown...* (Princeton,
  N.J., 1976) 50.
18 G. Whitefield, *Works* (6 vols. London, 1771–2) 1:164–5. Writing on his return from
  Charleston, Whitefield may have had the Salzburgers in mind. Cf. G. F. Jones, 'Two
  "Salzburger" Letters from George Whitefield and Theobald Kiefer II', *GHQ* 62 (1978)
  51–2. Their admirable conduct was believed by Steinmetz to have contributed to
  awakenings not only among their brethren in the Baltic, but also in England.
19 J. P. Fresenius, *Bewährte Nachrichten von Herrnhutischen Sachen* (4 vols. Frankfurt, 1746–51)
  III:108.

Dutch, but mixed words of all three languages in such a way that I could not understand them nor they me', but he got into the same habits and periodically baffled his directors at Halle how to turn his reports into something they understood as German.[20] Even in Germantown, though both the major churches kept their registers and minutes in German, the rest of their administrative records were in English, wills were signed in English script, and the school was conducted in English from the very beginning. From this point of view, though neither Mühlenberg nor Halle would have admitted it, the Pennsylvania Germans were like the old Protestant Poles of Teschen. Those who supposed 'that German was probably the language which Adam and Eve spoke in Paradise, all contrary opinions of the *critici* notwithstanding'[21] were inconveniently few.

### THE LOWERING OF DENOMINATIONAL BARRIERS

Divided by Low German dialects, the Germans were further fragmented by religion, and this not just in the sense that the Lutherans must expect to encounter Swedish, Finnish and Dutch co-religionists, the Reformed their Swiss, French and Dutch brethren. The immigrants came from innumerable churches, Lutheran and Reformed, with a great variety of traditions, practices and ethos; it was fortunate that the bulk of them had come from the West of the Empire where Lutheran and Reformed often lived cheek by jowl, sharing many features of church life which distinguished them from the Saxon Orthodox. Partial assimilation in America only made things worse. Both Lutheran and Reformed feared losses to the Church of England, which, fortunately for them, was not much in evidence in Pennsylvania. But at the accession of George I a group of Lutheran and Anglican divines agreed that little divided their two churches other than episcopacy; the liturgy which Mühlenberg prepared for the German Lutheran church was based on that in use at the German chapel in the Savoy in London, which was a German version of the liturgy of the Church of England; even the Reformed church in Philadelphia proposed to adopt this in 1764. Some Lutheran ordinands accepted English orders while remaining Lutheran, among them Mühlenberg's son, Peter, who could see no

[20] *Journals of H. M. Muhlenberg* tr. T. G. Tappert & J. W. Doberstein (3 vols. Philadelphia, 1942–58) I:xiii–xiv, 287.

[21] C. H. Glatfelter, *Pastors and People: ... the Pennsylvania Field, 1717–1793* (2 vols. Breinigsville, Pa., 1980–81) II:261.

other way of legally preaching to Lutherans settled within the prickly English establishment of Virginia. The establishmentarian traditions of both the Lutheran and Reformed churches in Europe might therefore intensify the solvents applied by assimilation in America to their distinctive heritage; traditions which were particularly bizarre in a population which voted solidly for a Quaker government until the Quakers sought to replace the proprietary government of the province with direct royal rule.

Clearly in Pennsylvania the old denominational barriers were much reduced, as well as relativised by the extraordinary profusion of sects. Intermarriage between Lutheran and Reformed was frequent (even clergy taking marriage partners from the other camp), and clergy must frequently minister indifferently to each. When church-building began apace in the forties one fifth of the congregations provided themselves with union churches; by 1776 the proportion had risen to about 45 per cent. Many of these arrangements lasted into the twentieth century, and one early one, at Goshenhoppen, is reported still to survive.[22] Here economic convenience added greatly to the attractiveness of a polity with which few of the immigrants were familiar before they left Europe. The sense of denominational distinctiveness rapidly collapsed, showing incidentally how far the Orthodox platforms of Europe were simply clerical ideologies. From an Old World viewpoint, this looked like galloping religious decline; and much of it undoubtedly was. Unlike the sects, the church people had been for generations officially discouraged from self-help; and the learned parish ministry on which the Lutherans, especially, had staked everything was no longer to be had. The benign toleration of Pennsylvania seemed a better recipe for confessional liquidation than the bitter persecution of Silesia or Hungary.

There were just two positive features. There were evidences of religious hunger. Travellers told tales of being dunned for sermons in the backwoods; and German communities in both Pennsylvania and Virginia became adept at the higgling of the religious market. Schoolmasters were regularly employed to preach, and often to administer both sacraments; a whole army of characters assumed ministerial functions 'partly in compliance with the earnest solicitations of the people … and partly on account of having been destitute of any other means of support';[23] and a modest corps of European

[22] Wolf, *Urban Village* 129; Glatfelter, *Pastors and People* II: 162–3.
[23] T. F. Chambers, *The Early Germans of New Jersey* (Dover, N.J., 1895) 100.

clergy, regularly ordained but sometimes very irregularly behaved, came out to America and negotiated terms with a congregation without a call in due form. Hard liquor was often their undoing. Of the 167 German Lutheran and Reformed pastors who served in the Pennsylvania field over the whole period to 1776 no less than 56 began and continued their ministry without formal licence or ordination, while 25 were ordained men who came without a call. The second positive feature was implied in confessional decline; while there was no question of early eighteenth-century German-Americans, like their successors a century and a half later, developing a nationalism they had not had before they arrived, they were looked on by their neighbours and came to look on themselves not as Palatines, Württembergers or Wetteravians, but as a single cultural entity. Whoever tapped that market as a whole would reap a rich reward.

### SECTARIANS AND ESTABLISHMENT-MEN

So much of the doctrine of the sects in Germany had consisted of separation, indeed isolation, that they were not well equipped for this purpose. The Society of the Woman in the Wilderness, led by Johann Kelpius (1673–1708), a Transylvanian, took Cabbalistic and Rosicrucian traditions out of the circle of Spener himself in time for the millennium appointed for 1694. By the time Mühlenberg arrived in the forties, he could write as if the settlement on the Wissahickon creek was merely a memory. It nevertheless released two brothers, Daniel (1666–c. 1741) and Justus Falckner (1672–1723), of whom one (having received Swedish ordination locally) organised the first German Lutheran congregation in Pennsylvania, and the other ministered to German Lutheran congregations in the New York region.

There was, however, a small group variously known as German Baptists, New Baptists and Brethren, which had been deeply influenced in the Wetterau by the revivalist Hochmann von Hochenau; the organ of that milieu, the *Geistliche Fama*, distinguished them from the Mennonites by precisely this peculiarity. The Old Baptists withdrew from the world, the New evangelised within it.[24] The founder of the movement, Alexander Mack, was one of the

---

[24] M. G. Brumbaugh, *The German Baptist Brethren in Europe and America* (Elgin, Ill., 1899) 16; J. S. Carl, *Geistliche Fama* (n.pl, 1733–43) 1:86–9.

disillusioned Reformed of the Palatinate, who had withdrawn to Schwarzenau, and in 1708 covenanted with seven others to form the new church. Numbers multiplied and in 1719 many of the faithful came to Pennsylvania, at once encountering that fate that was to dog their sect and other small fellowships. Having scattered to settle they found their spiritual temperature declining; the evangelism required to keep in touch let alone make other converts was not easily combined with getting established. One who went out at the same time, Mathias Bauman, who had been commissioned in a fourteen-day series of trances to preach a simple gospel of repentance, became a vigorous, if unorthodox, evangelist, and annoyed the Quakers by doing what they would once have done, proclaiming judgment to the masses from the steps of the Philadelphia court-house. He died about 1727, and most of his followers were absorbed into the German Brethren or Moravians. Meanwhile the former had been organised by Peter Becker. In the autumn of 1724 Becker sent out a missionary party of fourteen, the entire male membership of Germantown, 'to undertake a general visitation of the hinterland'. This produced extraordinary evidences of religious revival, and was the forerunner of two other revivals at Germantown at decennial intervals.[25] Alexander Mack came out in 1729, and within a few years the fellowship in Pennsylvania was reinforced by virtually the entire strength of the original European movement.

The Brethren were now to exemplify both their native propensity to the solitary life, and a capacity for union created by revival and required by the decline of parochialism in the German community. Johann Conrad Beissel (1690–1768) had associated with the Inspired and the New Baptists in the Wetterau and Wittgenstein, and came to Pennsylvania in 1720 in the hope of joining Kelpius's community of the Woman in the Wilderness. By the time he arrived the community had been dispersed and he became an apprentice to the weaver Becker. Beissel, too conscious of his own spiritual gifts and too keen to strip Christianity of human accretions to remain subordinate for long, adopted the seventh-day principle and abandoned the scripture principle. Retreating into the wilderness, he gathered a group of men and women who formed what became the Ephrata community, an

---

[25] J. F. Sachse, *The German Sectarians of Pennsylvania* (2 vols. Philadelphia, 1899–1900) 1:73–5, 97–101, 273; F. E. Stoeffler, *Continental Pietism and Early American Christianity* (Grand Rapids, Mich., 1976) 234; F. Nieper, *Die ersten deutschen Auswanderer von Krefeld...* (Neukirchen, 1940), 197.

extraordinary centre of music and cultural achievement,[26] of spiritual sweetness and practical help to neighbours, of spiritual impulses which issued in revival, of theosophy, alchemy and magic. Alexander Mack's funeral in 1735 brought together not only the seventh-day and Sunday Baptists, but sects of all kinds. The fellowship was maintained by love-feasts, by common breaking of bread, by an itinerant ministry maintained by Mack's son, Alexander, junior. The Ephrata chronicle noted that between 1740 and 1750 'the fire burned in the Philadelphian church'. Of Reformed extraction, the Ephrata movement had a particularly powerful impact upon the German Reformed; and in mid-century Mittelberger still found 'many totally unlearned men preaching in the open fields. For the sectaries say and believe that today's scholars are no longer apostles, and have turned their living into a trade.' What undermined the fair prospects of the Brethren movement was a conflict with another revival fellowship dedicated to realising the unity of the Pennsylvania Germans, that of the Moravians, and the jolt which that gave to the confessional strategists in Europe. If any further impulse was needed, it was given by George Whitefield. In the glow of his first triumphal progress the legends multiplied as to his extraordinary influence over Germans who understood not a word of what he said; and, never backward, he too was prepared to offer himself as the uniting force of German America:

Nov. 27, [1739]. I preached at German Town...to above six thousand people. God strengthened me to speak nearly two hours, with such a demonstration of the Spirit, that great numbers continued weeping for a considerable time...After I had done, people came to shake me by the hand, and invited me to their houses...I had sweet converse, and felt a blessed union and communion with many souls, though of different nations and professions...Our hearts were knit together, and the God of love was with us of a truth. The Germans, I find, are about to translate my *Journals* into High Dutch.[27]

Halle was prepared to grant Whitefield the primacy in the Methodist movement, but not the assimilation of the Pennsylvania Germans. Again, long before Zinzendorf arrived in America, war had been declared on the Moravians by the Synod of South Holland, and in Germany by both the Orthodox and the Hallesian parties. None were prepared to allow him an uncontested advantage in America.

---

[26] In Thomas Mann's *Doktor Faustus* Adrian Leverkühn was introduced by his teacher to Beissel's theory of music.   [27] Whitefield, *Journals* 357–8.

To make the matter worse, it looked in 1740 as though Whitefield and the Moravians were hand in glove. Whitefield bought 5,000 acres in the Forks of the Delaware for an orphanage and school for blacks, not far from where the Moravians were to pitch their settlement at Bethlehem; he set them to build and before long sold them the whole estate. In fact in the middle of the transaction the two parties became estranged; but for a moment it seemed that two great rivals to the European establishments were making common cause.

Zinzendorf's attempts to unite the Pennsylvania Germans in a 'Congregation of God in the Spirit', and their fate, have already been described. Here it need only be said that the Moravian presence in Pennsylvania had begun in 1734 when Zinzendorf had sent in a group of immigrants with the missionary George Böhnisch. This body was reinforced two years later by Spangenberg and most of the Moravian settlers in Georgia and then by Peter Böhler, who had nursed John Wesley into his conversion experience. They went first to pastorless Lutheran and Reformed congregations, and further depleted the stock of clergy by taking into their service men like the Swedish Lutheran Laurentius Nyberg, or the Swiss Reformed Jacob Lischy.[28] Even more valuable was the prosperous layman Henry Antes, of Rhineland Reformed origin, who was brought by Spangenberg into the Associated Brethren of Skippack (who sought strenuously to raise the religious level of the Pennsylvania Germans on an undenominational platform) and was one of the staunchest supporters of Zinzendorf's Congregation of God in the Spirit.[29] But the Moravians annoyed the sects at the outset by claiming that 'they could make a Christian in three days' and clear up the Babel in Pennsylvania in not much longer; the sects came to the count's early conferences, but were the first to drop out, and the Ephrata community, encouraged by the appearance of the Great Comet of 1743–4, poured out propaganda against him. But until 1748 the Moravians made a noble revivalistic effort of their own. Failure to assimilate the German sects released a new energy of missions to the Indians, and a contingent of itinerant preachers was created to take the gospel to German and non-German alike, and to

---

[28] For biographies: Glatfelter, *Pastors and People* 1: 100–1, 83–4.

[29] E. McMinn, *A German Hero of Colonial Times...* (Moorestown, N.J., 1886). When Zinzendorf returned to Europe in 1743, he took with him Antes's second daughter, Margaret, to complete her education at the Moravian school in London; she later married Benjamin La Trobe, a leading Moravian minister in England. Her son, Benjamin Henry Latrobe, water engineer and architect, was commissioned by Jefferson to salvage the building of the Capitol in Washington.

assist especially Lutheran congregations; not surprisingly these itinerants were called 'fishers' in the diary of the Bethlehem community. But their *Singstunden*, love-feasts, preaching and teaching left their mark, and as the German and Swiss Moravian preachers were reinforced by Swedes and English, they influenced an ever broader area. In 1748, however, Mühlenberg noted in his Journal that Moravian activity was quietening, and very quickly they became just one more Pennsylvania sect, with a political importance confined to Northampton County.[30] This retreat was due partly to increasing popular suspicions of 'crafty Herrnhuters', and partly to three fresh European inputs into the situation: there was a new threat of war in Pennsylvania; in Europe the Moravians became consumed with that wave of enthusiastic self-absorption known as the 'time of sifting' which was the immediate prelude to financial collapse; and the European supporters of the Reformed and Lutheran churches in America had finally got their act together and were able to rival the Moravians at their own game. To this subject we must now turn.

## THE PENNSYLVANIA GERMANS AND THEIR EUROPEAN PATRONS

In the twenties and thirties the Reformed and Lutheran congregations of Pennsylvania and the other Middle Colonies were in a curious limbo; with no past and apparently no future, they found the New World a cold climate in which to organise themselves ecclesiastically. Their present largely pastorless existence in barns and farmhouses was nibbled away by a handful of active sects. They needed a revival in the Silesian style, but their situation differed in three respects from that of the Silesian Protestants. The Pennsylvania Germans lacked the goad applied to the Silesians by the loss of a great past; corporately speaking they had no past to salvage and no political patrons to encourage them. On the other hand, in Pennsylvania, at least, they were subject to no political oppression, and it was not treasonable to seek outside assistance. And, thirdly, while emigration provided one answer to the problems of the Silesian Protestants, the Pennsylvania Germans were constantly being reinforced by the mass immigration of church people, at least some of whom wanted to recover a religious ethos they had left behind. Thus

---

[30] Dietmar Rothermund, *Layman's Progress* (Philadelphia, 1961) 31, 117; Glatfelter, *Pastors and People* II:81–2; Mühlenberg, *Journals* I:211.

if Zinzendorf and Whitefield were trying to solve the problems of the Pennsylvania Germans in one way, the rise of the German churches in the middle of the eighteenth century offered a different solution, paralleling the long-delayed rise of the Church of England in America. But whereas a minority Anglicanism sought (like the New York Dutch) to find a role as a barrier against disorder and revival, the German churches, having no status in America as metropolitan institutions, sought to sweeten the attractions of order with some spiritual counter-attractions to sects and anglophone Presbyterians.

Moreover, the accident that a Dutch king, a Danish royal consort, and a whole German dynasty succeeded each other in England made it in some respects easier for the Reformed and Lutherans than for the Anglicans to raise help there; and, given the camaraderie which existed early in the eighteenth century among the progressive forces in church life, it was not thought bizarre for official organs of the church, like the SPG, to work together with the court chaplain, A. W. Böhme, a Lutheran Pietist, and the charitable institutions at Halle, to assist the German Reformed in America. Thus, for example, they provided pastoral assistance for the Palatines, rescued from the clutches of Louis XIV by the navy, and transported to New York State to support the development of a naval stores programme which was subsequently abandoned. In the long run, however, the chief advantage of the London network accrued to the Lutherans.

If Böhme became a public figure in England, his perdurable successor as court chaplain 1722–76, Friedrich Michael Ziegenhagen, was still more prominent. A loyal son of Halle, he actively assisted the settlement of the Salzburgers in Georgia, and cooperated with Samuel Urlsperger of Augsburg (himself a member of the SPCK) in securing them international news-coverage, charitable assistance and practical help of all kinds.[31] When Pennsylvania became the urgent problem, Ziegenhagen created another network, bringing Halle into play again, briefing pastors on their way out and teaching them English, writing a *Glaubenslied* or 'rhymes for the benefit of the youth in Pennsylvania... containing the most important contents of the order of salvation', which obtained such standing as to be

---

[31] J. G. Burckhardt, *Kirchengeschichte der deutschen Gemeinden in London* (Tübingen, 1798) 78ff. Correspondence of Ziegenhagen, Urlsperger, Whitefield and the Halle fathers about these matters is to be found in AFSt A171 nos. 157–8, 161; A177 no. 100; A174; C532 nos. 1–7; K20 nos. 30, 82, 101 (also K2, 7, 19, 25 26 *passim*); SPK Francke Nachlasse 21 (27); 32; 33. Cf. Samuel Urlsperger, *Detailed Reports on the Salzburger Emigrants who settled in America* ed G. F. Jones (6 vols. Athens, Ga., 1968–) II: 189; III: 46, 162, 184; IV: 104; VI: 126.

appended to Christoph Saur's American edition of Luther's Shorter Catechism. Ziegenhagen involved the other German pastors in London in the work, and a generation after Pennsylvania headed the agenda, one of them, Dr J. C. Velthusen, returning to Germany as a professor and superintendent at Helmstedt, did for the Lutherans of North Carolina what Ziegenhagen himself had done for those of Pennsylvania.[32] In minute ways deeds of kindness offered through these channels echoed down the years. Böhme, 'at the time of good Queen Anne', shipped out literature for the Palatines, including the *Postille* or lectionary sermons of August Hermann Francke; one copy led to the conversion of Conrad Weiser (1696–1760), who negotiated the Iroquois alliances for the Penns; he 'could never find a congregation and constitution of the same kind', and was for a time a member of the Ephrata community, but in 1750 his daughter married Mühlenberg, whose mission was to create just such a church.[33] More publicly these networks decisively strengthened the hands of those who wished to create a German (as distinct from Swedish or Dutch) Lutheran church in America, and diverted the currents of European influence upon them from Hamburg, one of the last great fortresses of Lutheran Orthodoxy, to Halle, the stronghold of church Pietism.

If the churches were to be reconstituted they needed more clergy. Even in 1740 there were reckoned to be only three German Reformed pastors for twenty-six congregations in Pennsylvania, and only one to twenty-seven Lutheran congregations.[34] The difficulties in the way were illustrated by Johann Christian Schulz, an Ansbacher. He was ordained in 1732 at his native town of Schainbach apparently for missionary service in Pennsylvania, and later in the year, again apparently without a call, was elected pastor of the congregations at Philadelphia, New Hanover and Providence. Almost at once he ordained the two Johann Casper Stoevers, father and son[35] (who were relatives of Johann Philipp Fresenius, senior of Frankfurt and ferocious anti-Moravian polemicist). According to all the ordinary rules a single Lutheran minister had no authority to ordain; and the proceeding was in any case odd since the younger Stoever, who had

---

[32] Henry E. Jacobs, *Evangelical-Lutheran Church in the U.S.* (New York, 1893) 145.
[33] *Die Korrespondenz Heinrich Melchior Mühlenbergs* ed. Kurt Aland (2 vols. Berlin/New York, 1986–) 1:365.
[34] W. J. Hinke, *Life and Letters of J. P. Boehm* (Philadelphia, 1916) 83, 88–9; Jacobs, *Evangelical-Lutheran Church* 191.    [35] Glatfelter, *Pastors and People* 1:126, 138–43.

begun by performing pastoral functions without any authorisation, and had not succeeded in obtaining ordination from Swedish Lutherans, was now in Reformed orders. Schulz, however, seems almost at once to have left him in charge of his congregations while he returned to Europe with two laymen to appeal for money to build a church and school for each of the congregations, and for more ministerial assistance. They made, of course, for Ziegenhagen in London, and he obliged by giving them a moving recommendation to a preacher in Hanover, to Gotthilf August Francke, and to other German theologians. Daniel Weissiger, one of the two lay deputies, had this material published at Hildesheim in 1734. After a fair start everything went wrong. Weissiger fell out with Schulz, who wished 'to be released from the work of collecting... he even wishes he were dead; for he cannot succeed in his crooked purposes'. Schulz, indeed, was subject to criminal arrest, was deprived of his credentials and never returned to America. Francke took the view that ordained men could not be asked to go to America without cast-iron guarantees of a salary which infant congregations were in no position to give, and they in turn were chagrined to receive only a small sum of money and a few books for the bread they had cast upon the waters.

## HEINRICH MELCHIOR MÜHLENBERG

In the longer run, however, a dividend accrued. Steinmetz, the old apostle of Silesia, reprinted the documentary material in his *Sammlung auserlesener Materien zum Bau des Reiches Gottes*, and, at a later date, it appeared again in the Weimar Orthodox *Acta Historico-Ecclesiastica*.[36] And the cause was furthered by personal recommendation by Francke, Urlsperger and their friends in different parts of Germany.[37] Once Zinzendorf appeared in America with his usual promises of instant achievement and instant conversion, rapid action followed on behalf of the church. Francke dropped his financial conditions, assumed that the call made in 1734 was still valid in 1741, looked for two ministers, and found one, Heinrich Melchior Mühlenberg, pastor of Gross Hennersdorf, the parish of Zinzendorf's aunt, next to Herrnhut itself. Money suddenly became available. Mühlenberg accepted the call for a trial period of three years, with a guarantee of

---

[36] *SMBRG* 3 (1734) 973–92; *AHE* 9:891–915.
[37] J. L. Schulze, *Nachrichten von den vereinigten deutschen Evangelisch-Lutherischen Gemeinen in Nord-Amerika* ed. W. J. Mann *et al.* (Allentown, Pa., 1886) 9–70.

travelling expenses in both directions. His salary for the period, together with a small but adequate sum for travelling in Pennsylvania, would be found from collections in the hands of Ziegenhagen in London. The latter provided spiritual counsel, disclosing 'one depth after another in the Passion History of our Saviour', instruction in English, and the suggestion that Mühlenberg travel via Georgia to receive a first-hand briefing on American conditions from Boltzius, still shepherding the Salzburgers.[38]

Originally intended by Francke for the East Indies mission field, Mühlenberg proved a good choice for America. A Hanoverian by birth, and educated at Göttingen, he might be acceptable to the British court; but he was so hostile to the entrenched Orthodoxy of the Hanoverian church as to have no future in its service. Even on the way out he was in trouble with its consistory; the consistory was desperately opposed to conventicles, while Mühlenberg held advanced views on their international significance as a means of raising the devotional level. After leaving Göttingen, he had taught in the Orphan House at Halle, and had received his preferment at Gross Hennersdorf through Count Henry XXIV of Reuss; thus he carried the seal of approval of the Halle circle and its lay backers. No great theologian, he was at least tough; and he needed all his native muscle when he arrived to find (not in principle surprisingly) that his three congregations were not expecting him, and that they had engaged themselves three preachers. One was Johann Valentin Kraft, who was always a thorn in Mühlenberg's flesh, and began by announcing that he had invented a consistory which would put the new young man where it saw fit; the second was Zinzendorf himself. Mühlenberg's reply was to produce his credentials, put on a great display of establishmentarianism, talking about his European superiors, and calling in Swedish Lutheran pastors to assist him. It is a commentary on German Lutheran mentality even in America that these tactics worked, though it cost Mühlenberg a desperate struggle with Zinzendorf to get hold of the Philadelphia church record book and chalice.

Mühlenberg's work in creating an organised Lutheran church structure in Pennsylvania with a ministerium (1748) which he managed falls outside the scope of our present inquiry. It was not open to him to be a simple bruiser, dragooning Pennsylvania

---

[38] Muhlenberg, *Journals* I: 7, 19–23; *Korrespondenz* I: 21.

Lutherans into conformity. If he preached that 'God is a god of order, and in His congregations everything must be done orderly', he also preached that 'there is more to true Christianity than merely saying "Lord, Lord" and continuing in the old groove'. He was sensitive to two of the things much in the mind of the German population. The Spanish threat to Georgia drove some Germans north to Pennsylvania; still closer to home, the great outflows from the Palatinate and Württemberg to Pennsylvania had begun largely in reaction to the miseries of French invasion; the peace settlement of Utrecht wound up this menace in Europe for a period, but did nothing to reduce Anglo-French rivalry in the New World. In Pennsylvania this was a special anxiety, because of Quaker refusal to provide defence against French or Indian incursions. Moreover Mühlenberg knew that if the Salzburgers in Georgia were thrilled by news of the revival in New England, and New England's preservation from her enemies; if they were indebted for many kindnesses to Whitefield, and were generating the proper prelude to revival in the shape of children's revivals;[39] the Pennsylvania Germans could not be immune to the high-pressure revival going on around them among the Presbyterians.

Mühlenberg's prescription has been described as 'revivalism within the liturgical framework of a structured, institutional church'. When he arrived some were lapsing into heathendom, or acquiring a taste for 'Arnold's *Kirchen-und Ketzer-Historie*... the oracle of many of the half-baked';[40] he must therefore revive a faith which had been neglected or perverted, and did so with the usual accompaniments of heightened emotional tension and tears, in the sort of itinerancy obligatory for clergy of every variety outside New England. The cells of lay piety which he sometimes encountered were the seedbed of revival right across Europe. At Hackensack, where in 1751 the clergy did not come often,

one man said they met every Sunday, sung a hymn, and had a sermon read to them. I asked them what sort of a sermon book they had. The man replied that the book had been written by August Hermann Franck[e] and sent to this country by the late Court Preacher Böhm[e] in the times of Queen Anne. They were of the firm belief that there was no better book under the

[39] Muhlenberg, *Journals* ii:200; 1:369, 61; *Korrespondenz* 1:34; Samuel Urlsperger, *Die ausführlichen Nachrichten von der Salzburgischen Emigranten* (19 parts Halle, 1735–52) ii/i:469, 562, 675–6, 341, 565, 362–75, 602–3; ii/ix:1752–6, 2107–9. For an English translation of part of this work see chapter 1 n. 2.

[40] Mühlenberg, *Korrespondenz* 1:250.

sun, because it went straight to the heart and pleaded for repentance. I was delighted, and...admonished them to treasure the contents.[41]

And a total of 53 congregations created by 1748 (almost all in the forties) and 126 gathered by 1776 would not have disgraced a revivalist anywhere.

The American Germanists have lately remarked that the German denominations were not split by revival as were the Presbyterians. The reasons for this are not far to seek. The revival among the Presbyterians was one aspect of a feud amongst clerical parties. At the crucial time the German denominations had too few clergy for organised warfare, and Mühlenberg's constructive work, supported by the recruiting of a substantial squadron of Hallesian clergy, a succession which continued till 1789, ensured the creation of a monochrome church in Pennsylvania. In the long run, however, Lutheran Pietist homogeneity was to divide the German nation in America. When the nineteenth-century successors of the old Lutheran Orthodox wanted to preserve a 'pure' church against the ravages of Prussian liberalism, they made off well to the West, creating new bodies like the Missouri synod.

## JOHANN PHILIPP BOEHM

In this period the Reformed were usually in a small majority among Germans in Pennsylvania, but their history may be treated briefly because it parallels very closely that of the Lutherans. The heroic figure here was an unordained man, Johann Philipp Boehm (1683–1749), the son of a Reformed minister in Hesse-Kassel, and himself a schoolmaster by profession. In 1720, however, he emigrated to Pennsylvania as a farmer, and almost at once began to take services for his neighbours. In 1725 he began to administer the sacraments, doing so reluctantly, there seeming to be no other way of obtaining them. This was the real beginning of the German Reformed Church in Pennsylvania, but it was soon challenged on two fronts. In 1727 Georg Michael Weiss (1700–61), a tailor's son educated at Heidelberg, was ordained by the upper consistory of the Palatinate in hopes of acquiring an American congregation. On arrival he appealed to the Heidelberg consistory for help to build a church; and

---

[41] J. B. Frantz, 'Awakening of Religion among the German Settlers', *WMQ* 33 (1976) 284; Muhlenberg, *Journals* 1:297.

Heidelberg confessed to the financial facts of life in the Reformed world by passing the request on to the Synod of South Holland. He also, as an ordained man, challenged the ministry of Boehm. Boehm, who could not stand Frelinghuysen's self-confident communion discipline,[42] appealed to the New York Dutch, who referred the case to the Classis of Amsterdam. This double appeal to the Dutch authorities effectively subjected the Pennsylvania German Reformed to them until 1793. The Dutch commenced a canny administration by recommending the New York Dutch to recognise Boehm's work by ordaining him, and advised Boehm to seek a reconciliation with Weiss. This reconciliation proved no more than skin deep, and the Holland fathers (exactly as with the American Dutch Reformed) were now in permanent receipt of two conflicting sources of information about the German Reformed. Weiss went off to Europe in the years 1730–1, collecting on behalf of the Philadelphia and Skippack congregations, and one of the consequences of the harsh picture he painted of Boehm was that no more funds were forthcoming for sixteen years. On his return, however, Weiss accepted a call to New York, and was off Boehm's back, at any rate locally, till 1746.

He was, however, soon replaced by another gadfly, Peter Heinrich Dorsius (1710–c. 1757), a Lower Rhine Reformed with Dutch education and ordination.[43] Dorsius was probably theologically alien to Boehm for he was highly spoken of by Frelinghuysen and taught at least one of his sons; certainly his policy for the German reformed was different. Boehm was exclusive in his churchmanship, particularly in regard to the sects ('the most horrible heretics, Socinians, Pietists etc., among whom dreadful errors prevail'); and had a growing battle on his hands with the Moravian union schemes. Dorsius took the view that since the Reformed people had long been going for the ordinances to English-language Presbyterians, the best solution both for ordination and for organised church life would be a union among the Reformed churches in the field, British, German and Dutch. He advocated these views in Europe, 1743–4, and was commissioned in 1744 by a South Holland synod already convinced that the Reformed

---

[42] Hinke, *Boehm* 33, 156, 325.
[43] On Dorsius, see Glatfelter, *Pastors and People* 1:31. Dorsius came to an unknown, but rather bad, end. His wife left him in 1748 owing to 'his shortcomings, including drunkenness', and was supported by Dutch charity. His congregation dismissed him, and he returned to Europe. Nothing is known of his death, but the coetus minutes of 1757 referred to his estranged wife as 'the widow Dorsius'.

cause in Pennsylvania was neither financially nor spiritually viable to put a proposal of union to the (Old Side) Synod of Philadelphia. To the Old Side, suffering at that moment the risk of extinction from the ravages of the revivalists, these proposals offered unexpected new hope; Boehm, who had consistently taken the view that the Reformed cause was through the worst and was establishing itself, refused to budge from the 'Church Order established from the beginning in our churches'.[44] The Dutch were now in clear need of a Reformed Mühlenberg if anything was to be done in Pennsylvania, and they opportunely found one in Michael Schlatter (1716–90).

MICHAEL SCHLATTER

Schlatter might well have been of the same dubious material as several of the other early Reformed ministers in German Pennsylvania. A native of St Gallen in Switzerland, he matriculated at Leiden at the age of twenty, later returning home to complete his studies. Finding no employment he returned to Holland as a tutor; but he was back in two small Swiss parishes, 1744–6. Then, apparently without giving much notice to anyone, he made off to the Heidelberg consistory in hopes of preferment in America, and was by them referred to Holland. The Holland fathers very properly inquired why he had left Switzerland in the dead of winter to seek his way in Pennsylvania. His answer was that he was young, unmarried, disposed to serve abroad, and almost completely lacking in seniority among the pastors of St Gallen. At the end of the examination, the Holland fathers 'conceived that through him they could organise the scattered Pennsylvanians', and dispatched him on a detailed fact-finding mission, to discover what the resources of the American congregations were in cash, buildings and manpower, to organise them on a proper constitutional model, and to create an upper tier of presbyterian structure, a coetus, and preside over it. Encouraged by the fact that clergy and people alike seemed willing to accept his authority, Schlatter plunged into a period of immense activity, travelling, sorting out disputes, preaching and organising on an heroic scale. He related well with Mühlenberg, recognising that they

---

[44] Hastings, *Ecclesiastical Records* IV:2740; Hinke, *Boehm* 161, 391; Hazard, *Register of Pennsylvania* 15 (1835) 201; Glatfelter, *Pastors and People* II:112–13; G. S. Klett, (ed., *Minutes of the Presbyterian Church in America*, 1706–88 198–9; H. Harbaugh, *The Life of Michael Schlatter* (Philadelphia, 1857) 43 n. 2. In 1751 the Pennsylvania Germans were more amenable to proposals of union, but the Dutch went cold.

had much in common in their missions, and outstripped him in his progress. Carrying both Boehm and Weiss with him, Schlatter created the impression that at long last the German Reformed church was getting its act together, and this not only evoked the usual revival phenomenon of enthusiastic tears, but was the best possible blow against the Moravians. Jacob Lischy, a Reformed pastor who had gone over to them, was won back. He launched his coetus in 1747, just a fortnight behind the Dutch Reformed in New York, who had been aspiring in this direction for over a decade. All this enabled Schlatter to give an encouraging account to Holland, and to back his demands for more ministers, for support for schoolmasters (some of whom he wanted to get out of the ministry), for religious literature and a printing press. During the forties the rate at which Reformed congregations were created outstripped even the rapid growth of the Lutherans, and did not fall seriously behind during the whole period up to 1776.

Schlatter's way was strewn with thorns as well as roses. Part of his own congregation in Philadelphia wanted to be rid of him, and in this they were assisted by another newly arrived Swiss minister, Johann Conrad Steiner (1707–62), to such effect that for a time Schlatter and his party had to take refuge in the church built in Philadelphia by Whitefield, the pulpit of which was then occupied by Gilbert Tennent. This conflict hastened, if it did not bring about, Schlatter's visit to Europe in 1751, and breathed new life into the idea of a union among all the Reformed churches in America. The Dutch authorities again commissioned Schlatter to go ahead, but then, for reasons that are not clear, backed down. In other respects Schlatter's visit was very successful, and shows how ties between the New World and the Old were getting closer. The South Holland synod got him to write a full paper on the needs of the German Reformed churches in America, and recommended it to their own churches. An Amsterdam bookseller printed it at his own expense and put it in circulation. Fresenius in Frankfurt received him well, helped him with the translation of his appeal into German, published a version in his own *Pastoral-Sammlungen*, and assisted with an independent publication in Switzerland. David Thomson, the English Reformed minister in Amsterdam, put the case before the Reformed churches of England and Scotland, an appeal which led to the beginnings of the charity school movement in America, and one of the professors at Herborn recruited ministers from the Lower Rhine area. Schlatter returned to

America in triumph with money, Bibles, six ordained men and the knowledge that the Dutch authorities had resolved 'that Pennsylvania be placed upon the list of needy churches'. A door had been opened through which endless treasure would pour.[45]

The later stages of Schlatter's career, in which he left the service of the church, devoted himself full time to the scheme for charity schools, and became the target of vicious attacks for promoting English assimilation, fall outside the present study. His career shows how the most conservative of Protestant ecclesiastical authorities had to compromise with the forces and techniques of religious revival when they wished to achieve a result in American circumstances. There is something comic in the Holland fathers employing an agent who took temporary refuge under the wing of Gilbert Tennent. Of course his position remained unstable, and the Dutch withdraw from schemes of amalgamation which would have involved some recognition of unpalatable forces in the Reformed world which were beginning to affect the Netherlands themselves. Nevertheless the compromise was made and the result appeared to strengthen Europe's foothold in America. To what had been happening among the English-speaking Reformed in America we must now turn.

### MIXED TRADITIONS AMONG THE SCOTS-IRISH

While the Dutch and Germans were resorting to a mixture of revival, organisation and foreign help, a flood of English-speaking but non-English Protestant immigrants had been pouring into the country on a scale even greater than the Germans: the Scots-Irish. Making for unoccupied lands on the Pennsylvania frontier, they ran up against the Indians and the mountains and spread out along the frontier from New York to Georgia. Politically they were poles apart from the Germans, having no use for the pacifism of the Quaker regime; but they were like the Germans in depending at first for religious provision on generosity overseas. One of the paradoxes of which the colonial history of American Presbyterianism is full is that many of the early ministers sent out to serve the Scots-Irish were recruited by London dissenting ministers. And the oldest Presbyterian congregations in the Middle Colonies were of English derivation, with their

---

[45] Schlatter's propaganda is largely reprinted in Harbaugh, *Schlatter* 118–234. See also J. P. Fresenius, *Pastoral-Sammlungen* (2 vols. Frankfurt, 1748–60) XII: 181–360. Cf. P. Wernle, *Der schweizerische Protestantismus im 18 Jahrhundert* (3 vols. Tübingen, 1923–5) I: 26 n. 1, 41 n. 4.

own understanding of what Presbyterianism was.[46] Settlers in New Jersey and Long Island had come down from Connecticut and bore the marks of that colony's criticism of the Congregationalism of Massachusetts. They did not care for the Congregationalist view that the ministry was made by and in the congregation; but English Presbyterians, their associational life notwithstanding, never succeeded in establishing the hierarchy of courts which characterised the fully fledged Presbyterian systems of Ireland and Scotland, and for an unhappily brief period in the 1690s it had been possible to arrange a Happy Union between them and English Congregationalists. When the Presbytery of Philadelphia was created in 1706 it was, despite its title, very like an English association (or its contemporary counterparts in New England), proposing 'to consult the most proper measures, for advancing religion, and propagating Christianity, in our various stations', and to improve 'our ministeriall ability'. It got control of ordinations, attempted to raise a new supply of ministers from England and Scotland, but not to exercise discipline in the manner of Scottish or Irish presbyteries.[47] Even so, increase in numbers led the presbytery in 1716 to transform itself into the Synod of Philadelphia, with three subordinate presbyteries of Long Island, New Castle and Philadelphia; and for a number of years after the Irish flood began in the twenties, the mechanism sufficed.

The Irish brought with them different notions of Presbyterianism; several different notions in unstable combination. The Reformed faith had so often come under the hammer of hostile governments that it had on occasions issued in revival phenomena of the sort we have encountered in Silesia; and nowhere more so than in Ireland in the middle of the seventeenth century. The Six-Mile-Water Revival which began among the Scots colonists around Antrim in 1625 generated the familiar evidence of abnormal religious psychology:

I have seen them myself stricken, and swoon with the Word – yea, a dozen in one day carried out of doors as dead, so marvellous was the power of God smiting their hearts for sin, condemning and killing.

About the year 1628...[there] was a bright and hot sun-blink of the gospel, yea, [it] may with sobriety be said to be one of the largest

---

[46] On the following L. J. Trinterud, *The forming of an American Tradition* (Philadelphia [1949]) is still useful despite sharp challenges from Elizabeth I. Nybakken, 'New Light on the Old Side', *JAH* 68 (1982) 813–32, and M. J. Westerkamp, *Triumph of the Laity* (New York, 1988).

[47] Jon Butler, *Power, Authority and the Origins of American Denominational Order* in *Transactions of the American Philosophical Society* 68/ii (1978) 52–60.

manifestations of the Spirit, and one of the most solemn times of the down-pouring thereof, that almost since the days of the apostles hath been seen...surely this was the very power of God...and...a terror to their adversaries.[48]

In short the forward policies of the Stuarts provoked a religious revival which lasted some eight years (1625–33); out of it arose the Irish Presbyterian church.

This revival could not be isolated from events in Scotland; it took place among recent Scots colonists, and the church in Scotland confronted the same Stuart forward polices as the Irish. Indeed preachers from Ireland, including Robert Blair and John Livingston, had been in Scotland in 1630 helping to launch another famous revival at the Kirk o' Shotts. The Scottish bishops alerted the English authorities to the fact that 'we stirred up the people to ecstacies and enthusiasms', and the Irish bishops put restrictions on their movements and dispossessed them of their parishes.[49] In the seventeenth, as in the eighteenth centuries, there were at least prospective links between Scotland, Ulster and the American colonies. Excommunicated and ejected, Blair, Livingston and others set out for America in the *Eagle-Wing* in 1635, only to be beaten back by the weather, and to take refuge in Scotland just as the crisis which led to the signing of the National Covenant was coming to a head there. Blair accompanied the victorious Scots army into England in 1640, and was one of the commission appointed by the General Assembly of the Kirk in 1648 to try to establish uniformity of religion in England on a Presbyterian basis; Livingston came into England with the Scots army in 1650, and on the Restoration went into exile at Rotterdam rather than take what he regarded as an Erastian oath of allegiance.

Thus from the beginning two quite different things were inter-mingled in an Irish Presbyterianism which, unlike that of Scotland, remained a dissenting faith. There was the unmistakable evidence of revival which had reappeared in the West of Scotland as 'the Stewarton sickness' and at the Kirk o' Shotts, to which both the eighteenth-century promoters of revival and the nineteenth-century tracers of revival pedigrees, appealed. But there was also a tradition

[48] P. Adair, *True Narrative of the Presbyterian Church in Ireland* ed. W. D. Killan (Belfast, 1866) 317; R. Fleming, *The Fulfilling of the Scripture* (n.pl, 1679) 418.
[49] *Brief Historical Relation of the Life of John Livingston* ed. T. Houston (Edinburgh, 1848) 81–3.

which became Cameronianism, which hankered after a single community profession of religion on the basis of the Westminster standards. This decision was never within the grasp of the Irish Presbyterians, but they helped to keep the ideal alive in Scotland as well as in Ireland. Their aspiration ensured that, dissenters though they might be, the Irish never pined for a church of visible saints, and though prepared to maintain communion discipline, did not believe, as Frelinghuysen's enemies had accused him of believing, that there was a way of seeing into the hearts of men so as to separate the church from the world. Equally, whereas over most of Europe revival offered a way of escape from Orthodoxy, in the Irish (and much of the later Scots) tradition revival had issued so quickly into the Westminster Confession, that it was not easily separated in anyone's mind from that high and scholastic statement of the Reformed faith. This was a matter of peculiar importance in the early eighteenth century as Presbyterian ministers began to respond to the Age of Reason and find difficulty with the doctrine of the Trinity. Ulster ministers, especially those who had been over to Glasgow as pupils of Professor Simson, began to reject not the Westminster Confession as a whole, but the idea of subscription. The result was that by 1726 a schismatic, non-subscribing, Antrim presbytery had formed. The Ulster synod was now more heavily committed to the Westminster Confession than ever; the Antrim presbytery and the friends it retained in the South of the country had taken up a position long since reached by the majority of the English Presbyterians from dislike of the Anglican formularies (to which selective subscription was still required under the Toleration Act of 1689). This cacophony of Presbyterian attitudes, Irish, Scottish and English, towards establishment, doctrine and subscription, was to reappear in Pennsylvania, yet further confused by the resurgence of revival.

No presbytery in America seems to have demanded subscription before the New Castle presbytery in the 1720s, but as the issue came to a head in Scotland and Ireland, that presbytery pressed the case in Pennsylvania. They were opposed by Jonathan Dickinson (1688–1747), the most impressive of the New Jersey ministers, and later the first president of Princeton. In his view church union was sufficiently guarded by accepting the scriptures as the standard of faith and practice; he confessed that he could not understand everything in the Westminster Confession, and was sure that new ordinands could not. What was needed was a strict examination not only of the candidate's faith but of his experience; here Dickinson might be justified not merely by the scandals in the German Reformed ministry in Pennsylvania, but by those developments in the Reformed churches of the Lower Rhine which lay in the immediate background to Frelinghuysen. He also put his finger on the fact that the Reformed world as a whole had become so clergy-ridden that everywhere the initiative was in the hands of the ministry; even Irish revivalism was interwoven with a tradition of communion seasons. Moreover the enthusiasm of American religious groups to subject themselves to European authority in return for practical assistance created a new urgency: some outside body, like the Ulster synod, might enforce subscription. At any rate the Adopting Act of 1729 was a compromise. It renounced a legislative power in the church, claiming only an administrative power; it recommended but did not adopt the Westminster Directory; and even within those standards, it distinguished essential from non-essential articles. Presbyteries must find their way within these guidelines. The New Castle and Donegal presbyteries continued to take an extreme subscriptionist line. These categories were to be quickly confused by the emergence of revival. In the English-language Reformed world in the Middle Colonies revival was, at least in part, the by-product of a clerical feud led on one side by the Tennent family, but it thrived on a native demand for revival amongst the Irish and upon the disagreements in the ministry.

### THE TENNENT FAMILY

The story of William Tennent (1673–1746), his gifted sons and his Log College, has been told so frequently that it may be briefly dispatched. William Tennent was an Irishman who had been in episcopal orders before he emigrated and had to give an elaborate account of his reasons for dissenting from the Irish church before the Philadelphia synod accepted him in 1718. Always of an evangelistic turn, Tennent served on both sides of the frontier between New York State and Pennsylvania, before settling at Neshaminy in the latter in 1726. Like leading ministers in New England and dissenting ministers in old England, Tennent was already privately educating candidates for the ministry, and at Neshaminy he built the famous Log College to develop the work. Tennent's most distinguished pupils were his three sons William, John and Gilbert, and Samuel Blair; but the college trained a whole school of practical evangelists and created a new party within the Presbyterianism of the Middle Colonies. What could be offered by a college staffed by one man whose own education had been completed a generation before must have been limited and there was not much in the way of mathematics or modern literature; but the curriculum was broad, and in a recognisable Presbyterian tradition. Though the alumni might lack the university cachet, they were not ignoramuses. Whitefield's assessment hit exactly the right note:

> it seemed to resemble the school of the old prophets...we are told that at the feast of the sons of the prophets one of them put on the pot, whilst the others went to fetch some herbs out of the field...Carnal ministers oppose them strongly; and, because people, when awakened by Mr. Tennent...see through them, and therefore leave their ministry.[50]

As the alumni of the Log College secured their converts, the college itself spawned academies in its own image, at Fagg's Manor, Nottingham and Pequea, all in Pennsylvania, at Hanover and Louisa counties, both in Virginia. The Log College helps to explain how the Tennent party altogether outstripped their opponents in ministerial recruiting.

The most important member of the party was Tennent's eldest son, Gilbert (1703–64), himself an Ulsterman. After suffering severely, Voetian style, from 'law work', he underwent a conversion experience, resolved to enter the ministry, obtained the M.A. degree from Yale, and was licensed by the Philadelphia presbytery in 1725. William Tennent broadened the party by getting Whitefield down to Neshaminy within about a fortnight of his arrival in Pennsylvania. Gilbert cast the net in another direction with results that were to leave a mark on Whitefield himself.[51] His first appointment was in Delaware, in an area well populated with English, Dutch and Scots-Irish settlers, to a congregation which disliked the nearest Presbyterian minister at Freehold. Tennent was at first less than happy with what he achieved; but another neighbour, T. J. Frelinghuysen, was doing well. This observation underlay an association and then an intimacy which changed Gilbert Tennent's ministry. What Frelinghuysen had that the young man lacked was that spiritual and

---

[50] Whitefield, *Journals* 354–5. Whitefield omits to say that a good portion of the Neshaminy congregation of William Tennent senior thought they had seen through him and were always trying to get rid of him. G. H. Ingram, 'Biographies of the Alumni of the Log College, 11. William Tennent snr', *JPHS* 14 (1930) 13–16.

[51] Gilbert Tennent is best studied by Coalter, 'Life of Gilbert Tennent'.

psychological analysis which underlay the 'discriminating' preaching of the Lower Rhine Reformed, addressing different sections of the congregation according to their spiritual state; and especially his method of dealing with those who were both ignorant and unconverted, preaching terror, holding up the mirror to the human soul, what he called 'the searching method'. There is no doubt that Tennent's father had opened Gilbert's mind to this approach, but he emerged from Frelinghuysen's tutelage a much more singleminded preacher of conversion than his father, a determined upholder of communion discipline, and a ferocious scourge of unconverted ministers. If he himself, after a conversion experience, had not understood the principles which distinguished the sheep from the goats, what could unconverted clergy do but imperil the salvation of their flock? On this method Gilbert Tennent became an effective evangelist, and left Frelinghuysen's precise mark on Whitefield himself. Tennent was appealing to the older strand in the Ulster tradition.

The recent trend in Ulster was to ward off the threat of Arianism by renewed emphasis upon subscription to the Westminster Confession; and in the thirties many of the Philadelphia synod saw in this a way to keep the revivalists in check, and the New Castle and Donegal presbyteries began to demand unqualified subscription. The liberal menace appeared in Pennsylvania in the person of Samuel Hemphill, whose trial was doubly embarrassing since he had subscribed the Westminster Confession both in Ireland and in Philadelphia, and was befriended by that successful printer and publicist, Benjamin Franklin. But the force which broke the Philadelphia synod was that of Tennent-style revivalism. Gilbert Tennent could not permit the creation of a Presbyterian hierarchy on the Scottish or Irish pattern to block his evangelism, any more than his father could afford continual appeals of the discontented faction in the Neshaminy congregation to presbytery and synod. Moreover Gilbert Tennent's programme, while not silent as to doctrine, put all the weight upon the practical discipline in the church. The young should be nurtured by catechetical training and family education; adults should be visited for close examination of their behaviour and during pre-communion seasons tested in their experimental knowledge of grace; ministerial candidates should be experimentally acquainted with the normal movements of the Holy Spirit in the sinful soul; ordained clergy should be subject to mutual self-examination, and their preaching should include essential doctrines. Tennent got this programme accepted by the Synod,[52] but the preference of all parties for uneasy unity collapsed in the face of Whitefield and the great revival of 1739–40.

Tennent himself delivered a ferocious attack on his opponents in the ministry.[53] Ulsterman as he was, Tennent here summoned to his aid authorities from other Reformed traditions in Baxter and Voetius, ascribed the 'great cause of the general spread of Armininianism, Socinianism and Deism' to 'the carnality of the ministry', and called on the congregation of the 'carnal' ministers to leave them; this, in the heat of the moment, many had already done. In 1741 the Synod of Philadelphia broke up, the New Side forming the New York synod of their own. The revival enjoyed what to the American English mind was the decisive evidence of divine favour, some success among the Indians; David Brainerd, the famous missionary to the Indians, was converted in one of the revivals conducted by Tennent at Yale, and championed by the New Side in his troubles with the Yale authorities. Besides leading to immense numbers of new conversions, the creation of new congregations, and the reshuffling of old, the revival broke the old Presbyterian party structure in the Middle Colonies. All the old cultural groups divided almost evenly between the two sides, the Ulstermen with a small majority to the Old Side. Only the New Englanders remained reasonably unanimous. Their dislike of subscription and Presbyterian hierarchy brought them down heavily on the New Side; and so things remained until, the New Side having drained all the life out of the Old, a reunion was arranged in 1758. The only difference at the later date was that the New Side having been the aggressive agency, they ensured that they were numerously reinforced by the local products of the Log Colleges and that all the ministers they imported from Scotland in the interim were of their own evangelical kidney. Tennent had provided a patchwork army of Irish, English, Scots, and native Pennsylvanians with a rhetoric and programme derived largely from Dutch and Lower Rhine sources.

Tennent had, however, salvaged one strand of the Ulster tradition and in so doing acquired a reputation second only to that of Whitefield himself; fittingly enough, in due course, he presided over the church built for Whitefield in Philadelphia. He had not, however, emerged unscathed. Even as the Philadelphia synod was collapsing

[52] Klett, ed., *Minutes of the Presbyterian Church* 122–3.
[53] G. Tennent, *The Danger of an Unconverted Ministry* (Philadelphia, 1740) 12–13, 19–21.

Zinzendorf arrived in that now unharmonious town apparently urging, in the interests of the Congregation of God in the Spirit, that congregations should leave their stated pastors, and join an amalgam in which with whatever circumlocution, he would be in effect bishop. This experience brought out the old Presbyterian rock in Tennent, and his blast against the Moravians took a stand on pure doctrine, 'truth, precious truth', which would not have disgraced the hardest of Ulster shellbacks.[54] An unconverted ministry might clearly take more forms than one; perhaps safety consisted in reknitting the severed wings of the Ulster tradition. At any rate in 1748 Tennent broached the possibility of Presbyterian reunion, and the following year put out an *Irenicum Ecclesiasticum*. Neither the Old Side ministry, nor the New Side adherents, thought much of this; but the Old Side had been so badly hollowed out that union had to come before long, and in 1758 communion was restored between the Synods of New York and Philadelphia in a church dominated by the New Side. It was now a question which element would predominate in another area where there was a strong new Ulster presence, Virginia.

## PROBLEMS OF THE NEW ENGLAND ESTABLISHMENTS. THE MATHER FAMILY

The revival in New England, which stands in the literature as the Great Awakening *par excellence*, is difficult to keep in proportion, for it has attracted far more scholarly attention than all the rest of the Protestant awakenings put together. Though it lasted only three or four years it has been given credit for the most far-reaching changes in American life from the American Revolution onwards, and has been subject to explanations (not excluding an outbreak of 'throat distemper') based on the sociology of the town or parish which start from the assumption that it was a local phenomenon. Yet it is quite clear that (as in every other Reformed country) a leading role in it was played by a ministry which shared fully in an intellectual and emotional heritage common to the Reformed ministry in the whole of Western Europe, and refused to accept the stigma of provincial status. Cotton Mather, the self-appointed spokesman for New England, devoted the two gigantic volumes of the *Magnalia Christi Americana* (1702) to rebutting the Orthodox libel that America was the outer darkness to which unprofitable servants were condemned,

---

[54] G. Tennent, *The Necessity of Holding Fast the Truth* (Boston, 1743).

and that his forebears were a 'company of asses' for entering it. He reported that, when passing Land's End in 1629, Francis Higginson had called his family and passengers

to take their last sight of England, [saying] 'We will not say, as the separatists were wont to say at their leaving of England, "Farewel Babylon!" "farewel, Rome!" but we will say, "farewel, dear England! farewel, the Church of God in England, and all the Christian friends there!" We do not go to New-England as separatists from the Church of England.'

Indeed, in Mather's view, New Englanders still 'humbly petition[ed] to be a *part* of it'.[55]

More generally, Mather made the secular history of New England impossible to expound on Puritan principles by the argument that the hand of God in the creation of New England had been specially manifest in the simultaneity of the discovery of America, the Reformation and 'the resurrection of literature', or Renaissance. Printing had denied the devil any possibility of excluding the new settlers from 'the two benefits, *Literature* and *Religion*'. If 'Mather obsessively wanted to put America on the cultural map' this was the price he must pay; and he must get a foothold in the most energetic spiritual movement of his middle years, that of Halle Pietism. He took up with Arndt, corresponded energetically with 'the incomparable Dr Franckius', became a propagandist for his institutions, and asked A. W. Böhme, the Pietist chaplain to Queen Anne's consort, Prince George of Denmark, to get a copy of the *Magnalia* to 'our [Hallesian] friends in the Lower Saxony', for it would 'be a little serviceable to their glorious intentions', 'the American Puritanism [being] ... much of a piece with the Frederician Pietism'.[56] Mather's self-conscious Europeanism is hardly surprising; his father, Increase, who did as much as anyone to shape the legend of New England as Immanuel's land, spent his life trying to get back to old England;[57] his uncle Nathaniel and his brother Samuel actually got back; while his son Samuel not only continued the correspondence with Francke's son, but published a life of the great August Hermann, *theologus incomparabilis*,[58] including material by the pro-rector of Halle, and an

---

[55] C. Mather, *Magnalia Christi Americana* (2 vols. 3rd edn Hartford, Conn., 1852; repr. Edinburgh, 1979) 1:27, 414, 362, 26. The same claim was made in 1743 in the 'Advertisement' to Thomas Prince's *Christian History* (2 vols. Boston 1743-5).

[56] *Selected Letters of Cotton Mather* ed. K. Silverman (Baton Rouge, La., 1971) xvi, 89, 215.

[57] M. G. Hall, *The Last American Puritan* (Middletown, Conn., 1988) 61-2, 65, 76, 269, 272-3, 280-82.

[58] S. Mather, *Vita B. Augusti Hermanni Franckii* (Boston, Mass., [1733]) 1.

account of religious events in the Lutheran world down to the revival in Livonia – all addressed to the college at Harvard. Even if the will to establish a European position had burned low, it would have been fanned into activity by the need to get a better charter for Massachusetts after the ravages of the Catholic James II and his agent Andros, and by the constant external pressure from France. 'Whether New-England may live any where else or no, it must live in our History' pronounced Mather desperately; and Edwards's enthusiasm for the War of the Austrian Succession shows how a revivalist millennialism might evolve into a civil millennialism with French and Catholic conspiracy playing a constant role throughout.

## JONATHAN EDWARDS

Edwards was of a later generation and a different character from Mather, but he (rightly) understood that the context of his ministry was no narrower than the whole Protestant world. In his *History of the Work of Redemption* (preached in 1739 and published only posthumously) Edwards perforce began with the fall, but had to strike a balance in the post-Reformation period. On the debit side 'the protestant church is much diminished', perhaps by half, especially in Germany, Bohemia, Hungary and France. It had often succumbed to heretical opinions and lost the power of godliness. Against all this were to be set the advances of the kingdom of God in America, the advances of Moscow against the Tartars, the successful Danish missions to the Malabar coast, and the remarkable movement set on foot by Francke.[59] It was but just that Edward's standing should be recognised at the other end of Europe; Fresenius published a translation of the *Life of David Brainerd* (1749) in his *Pastoral-Sammlungen*, Steinmetz, in the mass of his American reporting, published another, as well as a German version of the *Faithful Narrative*. The relevance of Edwards's kingdom of God was more sharply perceived in Eastern Europe than in his own congregation.

## THE ADVANCE OF THE CHURCH OF ENGLAND

Of course, in New England as everywhere else, the revival was shaped by local circumstances as well as general ideas. Cotton Mather might repeat the old Puritan claim not to have abandoned the Church of

[59] Edwards, *Works* 1:600–1.

England, but to have been abandoned by it. But, in a much more direct sense than the Kirk, the Standing Order in New England constantly feared assimilation or overthrow by the English establishment. Some of their complaints were exaggerated (as when the rector and tutor of Yale and a handful of other ministers seceded to the Church of England in 1722) or perhaps even calculated (as when, in the years immediately preceding the War of Independence, the Standing Order sought to divert the attacks of Baptists from themselves to the Church of England). But it was true that the bishops of London, through their commissaries or the SPG, made endless difficulties for colonial government; successive schemes for establishing a bishop in America looked like a stalking-horse for greater imperial control; in Boston as in every colonial capital (Edinburgh rather than Glasgow, Dublin rather than Belfast) there were those for whom an Anglican profession was the badge of a public yearning for a wider world,[60] and there were some everywhere who scented liberation in Anglican modernism. There were always those who could see no cure for the endemic disorder of colonial life except in adopting the whole range of metropolitan institutions, church included. When that disorder was aggravated by the disagreements engendered by the revival the number of Anglicans in public office increased, and, in many areas, those infuriated by the 'insufferable enthusiastick whims and extemporaneous jargon' of Whitefield and his imitators formed a new Anglican church.[61] Above all the English church reaped the benefit of a steady English immigration; on the eve of an American Revolution which decimated its Loyalist constituency and handed the Methodists the priceless advantage of offering a way to be English without being Anglican, the Church of England in America was stronger in numbers and organisation than ever before.

[60] J. W. Raimo, 'Spiritual Harvest: the Anglo-American Revival in Boston, Mass., and Bristol, England' (unpubl. Ph.D. thesis, University of Wisconsin, 1974) 46–7. In New England (as in nineteenth-century Belfast) Anglicanism also attracted much less genteel adherents who did not care for a Presbyterian or Congregational establishment. B. E. Steiner, 'New England Anglicanism: a Genteel Faith?' *WMQ* 27 (1970) 122–35.

[61] B. E. Steiner, 'Anglican Office-Holding in Pre-Revolutionary Connecticut', *WMQ* 31 (1974) esp. 381–2; Heimert & Miller, eds., *Great Awakening* xlvii, 397; R. Sklar, 'The Great Awakening and Colonial Politics', *CHSB* 28 (1963) 90–3.

## PROBLEMS OF SOCIAL ORGANISATION AND FAMILY CONTROL

Immigration pressed harder on the New England churches than establishments elsewhere, for the New England parish was more than a device for paying a minister; it was a social ideal. In the Connecticut valley, for example, an abundance of land made it relatively simple to keep the peace in seventeenth-century towns. There was no equality, but everyone had some land, including some of the better land. The object was to settle everyone in and about the town, and to enlarge their holdings by strips radiating outwards like the spokes of a cartwheel. This system of regulation fell foul both of the desire of sons to start economically where their fathers had left off, and of a dramatic increase in population. From 1670 to 1700 the population of Connecticut increased by 58 per cent and between 1700 and 1730 by 280 per cent. The result was that old parishes filled up with 'outlivers' who always bore a whiff of dissent and had less interest than the old settlers in paying for the central institutions of the town, including the church. But the regulation of economic appetites continued in the formation of new parishes until the Narragansett War in the mid-seventies. Then a huge area of Indian land east of the Connecticut River came into the hands of a few colonial leaders who were permitted by the Assembly to dispose of it as they wished without requirement of residence or price regulation. Speculation in property to which Indian titles were not good was an even surer recipe for conflict than the disruption of old settlement patterns, and clashes between factions in the town and between the town and the church became the order of the day. The ministry moved steadily away from Congregationalism towards a semi-Presbyterian church system in the hope of salvaging an authority which could no longer rest on consensus. Their worry was that a church polity originally designed to exclude all but the saints now served the idleness of the general public; church membership fell to very low levels. But, apart from the miseries inseparable from the creation of a new society, the people had reason for unease. Speculation, inflation and conflict underscored the failure of an ideal, a failure daily manifest in the shape of the parish.[62]

New Englanders were well aware of the prominent role of children

[62] On the above see R. L. Bushman, *From Puritan to Yankee* (2nd edn Cambridge, Mass., 1969); P. R. Lucas, *Valley of Discord* (Hanover, N.H., 1976); H. S. Stout, *The New England Soul* (New York, 1986) 175–6.

and young people in the story so far and had their own problems with them. There is no need to rehearse the Puritan obsession with 'breaking the will', nor even to debate whether the ministerial conviction that enthusiasm for catechising declined in the seventeenth century was well-founded or not. Certainly American children were targets for the English literature produced for children (like Janeway), and at the Peace of Utrecht the Connecticut clergy reported to the General Assembly in terms which might have been true of any generation: 'there was a great neglect of attending on public worship on the Sabbath and at other seasons. That catechising was much neglected in several places. That there was a great deficiency in family government'.[63] Judges and JPs, constables and grand jurors, were required to enforce the laws governing the education of children, the keeping of the Lord's Day and moral behaviour. Any Protestant prince aspiring to be the father of his people might have required as much. But that there was something adrift with the children and young people (this being a large age band going up to the time of marriage and church membership at about twenty-seven) was shown by the stir they made in the revival; and their restlessness sprang directly from the unsettled state of property relations.

The Connecticut concern for young people reappears prominently in Jonathan Edwards; his classic account of the revival in Northampton links failures of family management with the wider spirit of contention in the town. The galling part of it was that the 'frolics' commonly began after service or the midweek lecture, which provided one of the few natural occasions for the young people of both sexes to meet, and that the adults in the town were so divided over their own affairs that they would not unite to put a stop to the nonsense. The modern form of the adolescent problem was already encountered in Northampton; young people's resistance to parental control was reinforced by sufficient purchasing power to pay for some independent pleasure, and by the necessity to seek financial independence elsewhere when there was not enough land to go round.

By targeting this group Edwards brought about a revival in which the young people were prominent; meetings at his home replaced the tavern-haunting, and his personal authority sufficed, not indeed to replace lost communal control, but to rally a pressure-group of his

---

[63] B. Trumbull, *A Complete History of Connecticut* (2 vols. 1797; new edn New London, 1898) II:4–5.

own among the young. This is the meaning of a rather pompous description of the achievement of the evangelical clergy: 'the precariously seated clergy made an ally out of youth by evoking, interpreting, and legitimating its inner guilt, its public shame, and its ardent hopes for historical meaning and direction.' This caricature was itself caricatured by one of Edward's favourite converts, the four-year-old Phebe Bartlet. She endeavoured to pressure her sisters and adult neighbours into conversion by crying 'because she was afraid they would go to hell'. (Her mother, naturally enough, 'knew not what to make of it'.) After the revival Edwards had to leave his parish for a time to convalesce from illness; but on his return, Phebe 'told the children of it, with an elevated voice, as the most joyful tidings; repeating it over and over, Mr. Edwards is come home! Mr Edwards is come home!'[64] Pleasing to relate, Phebe Bartlet stayed the course and was reported sixty-five years later still to maintain 'the character of a true convert'; but youthful adulation did not secure Edwards's authority in the parish. He had provided an opportunity for the young to ventilate their generational grievances against their elders from within the religious tradition rather than from outside it, a process which became familiar within the evangelical world. But the peer group could be turned against him as well as the parents. In 1744 he took strict measures against a group of young men in their mid-twenties who had been annoying the girls of the parish with sexual information derived from a handbook of midwifery. It was now his turn to be told that they did not 'care a turd' or 'care a fart' for the committee of inquiry. The sad thing was that all but three of the accused were church members admitted after conversion in the revivals of 1735 and 1742. Worse was to come; in 1750 Edwards was dismissed from his parish, and the large number of young people he had admitted to membership in the revivals proved a broken reed in his own personal crisis.[65]

## BOSTON AND THE HALF-WAY COVENANT

This, however, is to anticipate a long story. New England was like other parts of a Reformed world which was rather short of royal courts, in granting a disproportionate importance to the metropolitan clergy, in this case the clergy of Boston. Boston was the Zion

---

[64] Cushing Strout, *New Heavens and New Earth* (New York, 1974) 44; Edwards, *Works* 1:361–3.
[65] P. J. Tracy, *Jonathan Edwards, Pastor* (New York, 1980) 4–5, 88–9, 106–8, 113, 160–5.

of New England Puritanism, the place where, in a dream, Samuel
Sewall beheld 'that our Saviour in the dayes of his Flesh when upon
Earth, came...and abode here some time...[and] admired the
goodness and wisdom of Christ in coming hither'.[66] To this Zion one
clerical dynasty was central as no other, the Mather family; and the
Mathers were not short of policy for the New England predicament.

In the last thirty years of the seventeenth century New England
ministers gave heed to the fate of the church, but also to the fate of
New England itself; had they not wished to do so, the pressure of
international politics would have compelled them. It was not always
clear how the idea that New England was in covenant with God
could be reconciled with the idea that the pure church was in
covenant with God, and attempts to harmonise them had unavoid-
ably to be made. Increase Mather (1639–1723), the second of the
great Mather dynasty, was a master of the jeremiad in its great days,
interpreting the troubles of New England as God's judgments upon
its sins, and prescribing accordingly. The civil authorities should do
what they could by enforcing wholesome laws for moral behaviour
and church attendance. The churches should play their part in all
this by getting the people publicly to renew each church's own
covenant with God. And the ministry should put the screw upon the
people by seeking to restore regeneration as the test for church
membership.

Under the first heading Increase was prepared to stimulate public
effort by private enterprise in the modish English manner; he had a
copy of the first edition of Josiah Woodward's *Account of the Rise and
Progress of the Religious Societies in the City of London* (1699) and both he
and his son Cotton encouraged the spread of societies of all kinds;
societies for the reformation of manners by enforcing the law, societies
for prayer and spiritual exercise. The second and third prescriptions
were to be controversial, and as the former of them, 'owning the
covenant', is unfamiliar to English readers it needs to be described.

The first Puritan settlers brought with them the federal or covenant
theology then current in the Reformed churches, and quickly grafted
on to it the requirement that to qualify for church membership
candidates must give an acceptable testimony to a work of grace
within. This immediately put a barrier to church membership to the
children of regenerate communicants who arrived already baptised,
and inhibited the administration of baptism to the children of non-

---

[66] *Diary of Samuel Sewall* (2 vols. New York, 1973) 1:91.

communicant adherents. Thus the small pool of church members in New England had to be reinforced from a very small pool of candidates baptised in infancy. When in 1662 a Massachusetts synod insisted that church membership was restricted to 'confederate visible believers...and their infant seed', they at the same time created a class of half-way members, subject to church discipline, and capable of transmitting baptism, but excluded from the Lord's Supper and from voting in church affairs. No testimony of regeneration was required from half-way members, simply the act of renewing or 'owning' the baptismal covenant made for them by their parents. By this device the churches enlarged their formal constituency, and the half-way members could secure baptism for their children.

The Half-Way Covenant focussed a long-running argument in New England between those, especially of Presbyterian tendencies, who wished to put the stress in the process of regeneration upon Christian nurture, and those who looked to conversion. It caught on in parishes piecemeal and in a remarkable variety of forms, some securing the promise of good behaviour and abstention from tippling, others the acceptance of an elaborate doctrinal statement. There was also a great variation in the ways the covenant was administered. At Hartford, Conn., the two ministers

with their deacons, went round among the young people and warned them, once every year, to come and publicly subscribe, or own the covenant. When such persons as had owned or subscribed it came into family state, they presented their children to baptism, though they made no other profession of religion...In other churches the covenant was owned by persons, sometimes before marriage, but more generally not until they became parents, and wished to have baptism administered to their children.[67]

At Taunton, Mass., in 1705, Samuel Danforth skilfully combined administering a covenant he had obtained from Boston, with religious societies and prayer meetings, to obtain a community response worthy of a revival.

[The Covenant] was read to the brethren & sisters in the forenoon, they standing up as an outward sign of their inward consent to the rest of the inhabitants...We give liberty to all men & women kind, from sixteen years old & upwards to act with us: & had three hundred names given to list under Christ against the sins of the times. The whole acted with such gravity

[67] Trumbull, *Connecticut* 1:400–1.

& tears of good affection, as would affect an heart of stone…Its almost incredible how many visit me with discoveries of the extreme distress of mind they are in about their spiritual condition. And the young men instead of their merry meetings are now forming themselves into regular meetings for prayer [and] repetition of sermons.[68]

Samuel Willard (1640–1707), the great systematician of New England, also came out strongly in favour of this system; the idea that baptism sealed the candidate into the covenant gave the ministry, at the very lowest, a homiletic lever to use at a later date. At all events the war years of the seventies saw a flurry of covenant renewals, and in 1677 Increase Mather began a campaign to persuade all the churches in Massachusetts to renew their covenants. This exercise of piety would save them from dying on their feet in the day of papal aggression and would renew the spiritual timbre of the founding fathers.[69]

Increase Mather, who at bottom did not care much for the spiritual realities of New England, outlived any conviction that New England would be saved or even improved by his policies; and his son Cotton also thought that the religious societies had done their work before the end of the War of the Spanish Succession. Even the pure church, it seemed, would not save New England. More and more it appeared to Cotton Mather that the pure church would not usher in the millennium; the millennium would have to usher in the pure church. Halle with its plans of universal regeneration, its efforts to convert the Jews, and the mission on the Tranquebar coast was less significant as empirical evidence of the way gospel work might be done, than as a sign of the end-time. In the years after the Peace of Utrecht when in England Archbishop Wake was seeking to dam the international tide of popery by negotiating Protestant Union, Mather in New England was pursuing Christian union on the basis of three simple 'MAXIMS OF PIETY' [always in upper case] as a certain sign that the millennium was near. This development in Mather was accompanied by a steady heightening of emotional temper, which was also to be observed in a section of English dissent in the same years. For all his hereditary championing of a pure and narrow church, and of owning the covenant, it is not surprising that the *Oxford English*

---

[68] J. M. Bunsted, *The Great Awakening and the Beginnings of Evangelical Pietism* (Waltham, Miss., 1970) 24–7. Cf. Prince, *Christian History* 108–12.
[69] E. B. Lowrie, *The Shape of the Puritan Mind* (New Haven, Conn., 1974) 146, 176; Hall, *Last American Puritan* 148, 153; C. F. Hambrick-Stowe, *The Practice of Piety* (Chapel Hill, N.C., 1982) 131–2, 248–52; D. D. Hall, *The Faithful Shepherd* (Chapel Hill, N.C., 1972) 244.

*Dictionary* attributes to him the first use of the word 'revival' in the technical religious sense. Mather, however, did not live to see the outbreak of revival on any great scale, and those who practised it on a small scale were his critics. To them we must now turn.

## SOLOMON STODDARD

The chief of these was Solomon Stoddard (1643–1729), minister of Northampton, Mass., from 1669, a man built on the large scale, physically, politically, ecclesiastically. Succeeding the first minister of the town, he married his predecessor's widow, added twelve children to her three, and reinforced his spiritual influence by a great network of family connections in the Connecticut valley. He got the town meeting to build a good road to Boston, and came down it annually until he was eighty to preach at the Harvard commencement when most of the ministers in the province were present; and when war broke out in 1675, he, almost single-handedly, forced the magistrates to drop their intention of abandoning the defence of Northampton. He thus acquired a singular resonance both southwards down the Connecticut valley, and eastwards towards Boston, the citadel of the Mathers. Stoddard was an innovator from the beginning. He began using the Half-Way Covenant when it was still a relative novelty. The church required its children, when they came of age, to present themselves to the elders, and, if found acceptable, 'publickly own the covenant'. A standard statement was prepared for this purpose in which the individual acknowledged the teaching and government of the church in return for its instruction, discipline and privileges. In three months 105 people owned the covenant, virtually all the eligible children of the parish. But over the next five years Stoddard admitted only 19 new communicants. As a 'state of education in Christ's house' half-way membership had failed, and Stoddard admitted as much in 1677 when he discarded it and the whole notion of church covenants as well.[70]

This was not all that Stoddard jettisoned. He was not interested in the millennial question; in this he was not singular in the Reformed tradition, but distinguished from many of his fellows in New England, especially the Mathers, and, in due course, from his celebrated grandson, Jonathan Edwards. And he put the doctrine of 'prep-

---

[70] J. W. Jones, *The Shattered Synthesis* (New Haven, Conn., 1973) 106; R. G. Pope, *The Half-Way Covenant* (Princeton, N.J., 1969) 251–3.

aration' to new use. The doctrine of the sovereignty of God as taught in New England, and not least by the Mathers had two pitfalls. The final consummation of this evil age, it was understood, was entirely in the hands of God; but Mather and others had been fertile in suggestions to induce God to bring it about more quickly; Stoddard provided relief by turning aside to the practical question of how to undo the ruinous effects of what amounted to a Protestant Jansenism, which narrowed the basis of the church at the very moment when it was on public trial. It was also understood that conversion was God's work alone; but the New England fathers like the Reformers before them had their proposals for preparing the heart to be effectually grasped by grace, as indeed had the scripture testimony. The Law was a schoolmaster to bring men to Christ, but how effectively did it do so? How long and imperceptible was the progress from conviction under the law to the assurance of saving grace? And there was the religious counterpart to the question discussed by the moral philosophers whether ethical issues concerned primarily the understanding or the will: how far did regeneration involve the affective side of human nature?[71] Puritan thinkers had worked out an elaborate series of stages on a man's journey from sin through preparation to assurance of salvation which, at least hopefully, would correspond to the three stages of God's relation with man, viz. vocation, justification and sanctification. Stoddard could not have repudiated this frame of mind and got a hearing; when he came out in favour of permitting all but the scandalous to partake of the sacraments, Stoddard was in effect pushing sacramental observance forward from the period of assurance into the period of preparation.

In seeking to have and to eat as many buns as possible, Stoddard did not mince words. Proclaiming that 'all men of competent knowledge' may come to the Lord's supper, 'though they know themselves to be in a natural condition', he held that 'this ordinance has a proper tendency of its own nature to convert men'. Preparation was indispensable and might take a long time, but conversion (and here Stoddard almost anticipated the objections which the Moravians would make to the whole Puritan scheme) was wrought in the twinkling of an eye. For this reason, if for no other, to subject candidates for church membership to an inquisition about the work of grace within, could not yield a useful result. If all this gave spiritual

---

[71] N. Pettit, *The Heart Prepared* (New Haven, Conn., 1966) 45–47; W. Walker, *History of Congregational Churches in the U.S.* (New York, 1894) 252–3.

relief, Stoddard could reintroduce a burden by sleight of hand: 'the use of this discourse [he concluded a vast sermon on the *Nature of Saving Conversion* (1719)] is of EXHORTATION to labor to be converted'. Nor was this all. If salvation was prepared by the ordinances of the church, and it was important to get as many people prepared as possible, the rational ideal was that of a national church and not the gathered community of visible saints. The 'light of nature' suggested to Stoddard that the ideal polity was that of the Church of Scotland. All this might be poison to the Mathers, and one of the objects of writing the *Magnalia Christi Americana* was to show that Congregationalism was the true New England tradition; but it became an orthodoxy in the Connecticut valley, and, as Jonathan Edwards related in a famous passage in 1736, by beating the drum of the Law, Voetian style, Stoddard produced results:[72]

he had five harvests, as he called them. The first was about 57 years ago; the second about 53; the third about 40; the fourth about 24; the fifth and last about 18 years ago... Those about 53, and 40, and 24 years ago, were much greater than either the first or the last: but in each of them, I have heard my grandfather say, the greater part of the young people in the town, seemed to be mainly concerned for their eternal salvation

Moreover, championing, as he grew older, a charismatic, spirit-filled ministry of a style becoming fashionable in the Church of Scotland, even more than he championed the sacraments, he almost brought the Mathers to terms. When he produced his *Guide to Christ* (1714), Cotton Mather wrote a preface asserting that the two were in complete agreement except on the matter of the use of communion. In 1716 Mather even urged revivals right across the province on a European pattern designed to secure the triumph of Protestantism over its Roman Catholic enemies. And as preaching began to compress the familiar progress from sin to assurance into the crucial phase of the New Birth, the revivals began, most notably at Windham, Conn., in 1721.[73]

The most famous of Stoddard's harvests, because it was described in the most famous tract of the whole revival, *A Faithful Narrative of the Surprising work of God...in Northampton* by his grandson and successor in the parish Jonathan Edwards (1737), occurred after his death. This tract gave a classic account of the diffusion of revival by

---

[72] Edwards, *Works* 1:346.
[73] C. Mather, *Menachem* (1716) 39–42; W. F. Willingham, 'Religious conversion in... Windham, Conn., 1723–4', *Societas* 6 (1976) 109–19; Prince, *Christian History* 129–34.

contagion, and has often been regarded as the beginning of the Great Awakening. This it clearly was not. Stoddard had been no more able than the Mathers to generate a great awakening as distinct from quite local revivals, and the outcome of Edwards's preaching in 'Northampton and the neighbouring towns and villages' differed only marginally in scale from that of his grandfather. Moreover the tract was the first published in England with a commendation by the eminent Congregationalists Isaac Watts and John Guyse; this showed, as Steinmetz's German edition showed still more clearly, that the significance of the pamphlet lay less in the importance of what it reported, than in the way it corresponded to hopes and fears much more widely held. Neither the impact on America of the constant reporting of developments in European Protestantanism, nor the direct transfer there of the activity of men like Frelinghuysen had been sufficient to generate a really great awakening. The heavy hand of the reformed ministry needed to be loosened before a dramatic result could be achieved. This happened with two surprise arrivals from the Middle Colonies, George Whitefield and Gilbert Tennent.

### GEORGE WHITEFIELD

In the strict sense Whitefield's arrival was not a surprise at all, for he had already acquired many of the arts of self-advertisement and campaign-financing which characterise the entrepreneurial evangelists of the present day. He had succeeded the Wesleys in Georgia, distinguishing himself honourably from them by his superior grasp of the means to survival in the wilderness. Intending to establish an Orphan House there, he had come back to England to beg for it, and inveigled Wesley unwillingly into field-preaching to look after groups who had responded to his preaching, while he extended his begging missions. The best and worst of Whitefield were already apparent: the power of work, the remarkable eloquence, the generosity of spirit, along with the readiness to trust his immediate religious impressions, and his exalted self-estimate. 'I have great assurances given me [he wrote to Charles Wesley of his Orphan House] that it will be a Pietas Georgiensis, equally remarkable with the Pietas Hallensis...I have written to the Bishop of Gloucester, and have delivered my soul, by meekly telling him of his faults.'[74] Before returning to America in

---

[74] Whitefield, *Works* 1:504.

August 1739 he had achieved prodigious success as an open-air preacher in London and elsewhere, triumphs liberally reported in the American papers. Once in America again he secured enormous press coverage and his itineraries through the Middle Colonies into the South were published in advance in the press[75] and filled out locally by personal invitation. The most famous and frequently reprinted example of this, Nathan Cole's vivid account of how thousands descended like 'cloud or fogg rising' on Middletown, Conn., to hear Whitefield in 1740, illustrates also something a good deal harder to understand, the extraordinary degree of religious longing to which Whitefield's presence gave vent.

When I saw Mr Whit[e]field come upon the scaffold, he looked almost angelical; a young, slim slender youth before some thousands of people with a bold undaunted countenance, and my hearing how God was with him everywhere as he came along it solemnized my mind; and put me into a trembling fear before he began to preach: for he looked as if he was cloathed with authority from the Great God.[76]

This from a man plunged by Whitefield's sermon into terror of damnation and two years of spiritual torment. Clearly the old New England religion had not been meeting the need. Professional critics were equally taken by surprise and delight. The Rev Samuel Smith had scruples about Whitefield, but found on inspection that:

He is of a cheerful, sprightly temper; and moves with great agility & life. The endowments of his mind are very uncommon; his wit is quick and piercing, his imagination lively and florid; and both, so far as I can discern, under the direction of an exact and solid judgment. He has a most ready memory, and, I think, speaks entirely without notes. He has a clear and musical voice, and a wonderful command of it. He uses much gesture, but with propriety. Every accent of his voice, every motion of his body, speaks; and both are natural and unaffected. If his delivery is product of art, it is certainly the perfection of it; for it is entirely concealed. He has a great mastery of words, but studies much plainness of speech... Mr Whitefield spoke as one having authority. All he said was demonstration, life and power. The people's eyes and ears hung on his lips... I came home astonished. I never saw nor heard the like.[77]

Franklin was more sceptical, and claimed, from frequent hearing, to be able to distinguish Whitefield's more polished stand-bys from his

---

[75] *American Weekly Mercury* 24 April–1 May 1740 p. 3; 1–8 May 1740 p. 3; 22 9 May 1740 p. 2.
[76] L. W. Labaree, 'George Whitefield comes to Middletown', *WMQ* Series 7 (1950) 588–91.
[77] Trumbull, *Connecticut* ii: 115–16.

occasional compositions, but his testimony to the former was like Smith's:

His delivery... was so improved by frequent repetition, that every accent, every emphasis, every modulation of the voice, was so perfectly well turned and well placed, that, without being interested in the subject, one could not help being well pleased with the discourse, a pleasure of much the same kind with that received from an excellent piece of musick.[78]

Whitefield's triumph in his second visit to America, 1739 to 1741, was to succeed in two quite different markets. Notwithstanding his constant and unqualified attacks upon unconverted clergy, he must succeed with the ministry. They knew that a variety of plausible policies had been tried in New England with only modest success. But if Whitefield could succeed with his conversions there would be no problem in satisfying the demands of the covenant in Matherian parishes and the objects of the preaching in Stoddardean ones would also be achieved. So far as the latter were concerned Whitefield was invited to Northampton by Jonathan Edwards and let loose a revival which lasted a couple of years; Edwards recalled that 'almost the whole assembly [were] in tears for a great part of sermon time', and, if Whitefield may be believed, 'good Mr. Edwards wept during the whole time of exercise'. Where the former were concerned, the outcome in Boston was singular. Whitefield was invited to the town by Benjamin Colman, minister of the Brattle Street church, who had encouraged Jonathan Edwards to write his account of the revival at Northampton. His was the most anti-Matherian church in Boston, founded by a group of merchants at the turn of the century on 'broad and catholick' lines. Communicant status was granted to all who made a profession of Christian belief; all who helped to support the minister were to have a voice in his call; the Lord's Prayer was to be used in worship; and the minister, Benjamin Colman, was a Harvard graduate with English presbyterian ordination. While in England he had mixed in latitudinarian circles and preached the excellencies of creation in fashionable Bath. Nevertheless, in keeping with his interest in Edwards, he now opened the door, and did the preliminary propaganda work to such effect that, when Whitefield arrived, the ministers were on his side by a majority of three to one, and, of those against, only Chauncy took up the cudgels in public. Whitefield brought with him not only a legendary reputation from Moorfields

---

[78] Benjamin Franklin, *Autobiography* ed. L. W. Labaree *et al.* (New Haven, Conn., 1964) 180.

and the Middle Colonies, but a claim like that which Cotton Mather had tried to sustain for the New England Way, a claim to represent the true Church of England against its modern self. Conveniently for Whitefield, the doors of the Anglican churches in America were closed against him from the beginning, and his clash with the Commissary Garden at Charleston which led to the summoning of what is said to be the first ecclesiastical court in the British colonies, did him even more good than being later denounced by Harvard College.[79] To cap all, shabby behaviour by John Wesley, whom he had left in charge of his work in Bristol, left him no choice but to write in favour of predestination and the doctrines of grace. To the New England Reformed Whitefield was a gift like that of the converted brewer to nineteenth-century temperance platforms. He did best where relations between the Reformed churches and the Church of England were worst, and worst where those relations were harmonious.

Whitefield, however, could hardly serve the ministry did he not possess an unsurpassed gift of addressing the people. Like Solomon Stoddard before him, he relieved them of religious burdens. In particular he turned the jeremiad upside down; the trouble with New England, he seemed to say, was not an unregenerate people but an unconverted ministry. Whitefield also developed a rhetoric for coping successfully with the new conditions of his mission. The 'distinguishing' preaching which Frelinghuysen brought with him from the Lower Rhine presupposed a pastor's intimate knowledge of his flock (indeed it presupposed a knowledge which Stoddard insisted it was impossible for anyone to have). Whitefield must succeed with a temporarily assembled multitude whom he did not know personally at all. He did so by dramatising his message, and doing so not in the analytical language of Puritan theology or homiletics but in a mixture of the familiar languages of the Bible, the market-place and human emotion (a mixture eroded by Whitefield's latter-day

[79] A. Dallimore, *George Whitefield* (2 vols. Edinburgh, 1970–80) 1:511–21; L. Tyerman, *Life of George Whitefield* (2nd edn 2 vols. London, 1890) 1:357–64, 396–401; W. H. Kennedy III, 'Alexander Garden and George Whitefield', *South Carolina Historical Magazine* 71 (1970) 1–16. Garden found Whitefield 'the most virulent, flaming, foul-mouthed persecutor of the Church of God that ever appeared in any age or country' (G. J. Goodwin, 'The Anglican Middle way in early eighteenth-century America' (unpubl. Ph.D. thesis, University of Wisconsin 1965) 275). For American episcopalian efforts to get the bishop of London to act, W. S. Perry, *Historical Collections Relating to the American Colonial Church* (5 vols. Hartford, Conn., 1870–8) 1:364; 11:203–9; 111:423–5; *The Testimony of Harvard College against G. Whitefield* (Boston, 1744) repr. in Heimert & Miller, eds., *Great Awakening* 341–3.

successors to that of the market-place alone). Whitefield's message of the New Birth was common to the Pietist and revival movements everywhere and had the advantage of being familiar to his hearers. But it was now shorn of the laborious Puritan morphology of conversion; it was a great self-validating event in which the Holy Spirit implanted itself in the soul. A new creation was unmistakable when it happened. Jonathan Edwards expounded this situation in terms comprehensible to both old-fashioned rationalists and new-style Lockeians by arguing that the Holy Spirit created a new faculty of spiritual discernment; Whitefield again took a more direct route, and paid the price. In his preaching, the Holy Spirit united itself with man at the moment of conversion and did its sanctifying work through the natural capacities of sense and intellect.[80] Thus by the logic of the New Birth all kinds of abnormal psychological phenomena which had been marginalised as enthusiasm in the old Puritan morphology of conversion became direct evidence of spirit-possession. There was so long a history of this in the Protestant underworld that Whitefield must have reopened many old doors in the minds of his hearers; but given the allies without whom his mission could not be accomplished he was laying up very speedy trouble for himself.[81]

### JAMES DAVENPORT

Whitefield was in a measure unfortunate in his collaborators. In England Wesley had undertaken to keep quiet on predestination and the decrees in Bristol, but had not done so. In America Gilbert Tennent was a tough well equipped 'to blow up the divine fire lately kindled' in a Boston suffering a long post-war recession, and to give it an edge of class-consciousness by snarling against the rich.[82] But abrasiveness made enemies as well as friends at the very moment when the mere fact of widespread itinerancy was giving an unpleasant jolt to the clergy and everyone in authority. For a short time it looked as if the regular ordinances were to be supplanted by a mass of itinerant preachers, clerical and lay, exhorting the flock to adhere to those of their taste. The result was an enormous outburst of clerical

---

[80] See the 'Indwelling of the Spirit' in J. Gillies, *Memoirs of the Late Rev. George Whitefield* ed. J. Jones (London, 1811) 423–33.

[81] For Whitefield's homiletic strategy: Stephen A. Marini, *Radical Sects of Revolutionary New England* (Cambridge, Mass., 1982) 11–17; Stout, *New England Soul* 194.

[82] Cf. *The Unsearchable Riches of Christ* (Boston, 1739) partly repr. in Heimert & Miller, eds., *Great Awakening* 19.

opposition to the notion 'that no other call is necessary to a person's undertaking to preach the gospel but his being a true Christian and having an inward motion of the spirit'.[83] This reaction was the easier to fan when the new preaching issued in the 'grosser' forms of enthusiasm. Here James Davenport (1716–57) formed a convenient focus for the conservative reaction, the more convenient because of the extravagant testimonials he received from the revivalists.

Mr. Whitefield declared in conversation, that he never knew one keep so close a walk with God as Mr. Davenport. Mr Tennent...affirmed Mr. Davenport to be one of the most heavenly men he ever was acquainted with. Mr. Pomroy... thinks he doth not come one whit behind Mr. Whitefield, but rather goes beyond him, for heavenly communion and fellowship with the Father and with the Son Jesus Christ... Mr. Owen... of Groton, said that the idea he had of the apostles themselves scarcely exceeded what he saw in Mr. Davenport.[84]

After such praise Davenport could hardly be disowned, and the conservatives aimed to get him to disown himself. Davenport undoubtedly came close to claiming direct inspiration; and he exhausted himself and his hearers in rambling discourses which might last twelve hours or more, and ended in a demand for conversion. He encouraged the faithful to come out from ungodly ecclesiastical fellowship, and he compounded the offence by helping to provide, in the Shepherd's Tent, alternative ministerial training which should concentrate on the development of spiritual gifts rather than carnal knowledge.[85] Still worse, in a piece of theatre of his own, on the authority of Acts 19: 19, he held a great bonfire of books including the works of past and present pillars of the New England Way. Davenport undoubtedly acted as a model for other exponents of what was later called 'wildfire', and supplied much of the febrile energy which transformed Whitefield's revival into a great revolt against the New England establishments.

### THE DECLINE OF THE REVIVAL IN NEW ENGLAND

The reaction of authority in Connecticut was short and sharp. While the Connecticut Association denounced 'the depending upon & following impulses & expressions made on the mind as tho' they were

[83] *Letter from the Associated Ministers of Windham* (Boston, 1745); *Records of the General Association of...Connecticut* ed. L. Perrin (Hartford, Conn., 1888) 14.
[84] J. Tracy, *The Great Awakening* (repr. Edinburgh, 1976) 230–1.
[85] R. Warch, 'The Shepherd's Tent', *American Quarterly* 30 (1978) 177–98.

immediate revelations of some truth or duty that is not reveal[e]d in the Word of God,'[86] and deplored ecclesiastical disorder, the government acted quickly to put down itinerant preaching and the Shepherd's Tent, and revoked the Toleration Act adopted in 1708. Davenport was twice judicially found insane, brought to recant his errors and transported back home to Long Island. By 1744 the Great Awakening in New England was virtually over, and both Tennent and Whitefield were apologising for breaches of charity. A movement professing allegiance to genuine evangelical union had so split the massive support it had received in the established churches as to be stopped in its tracks (at any rate in New England) until the time when the French Revolution made it possible for revival to take place on a conservative basis. The sight of Jonathan Edwards turning against the whining tone affected by the Davenport school as a badge of preaching in the Spirit, his desperate attempts to rebuff allegations by opponents of revival that the devil had been mimicking the work of God[87] and to distinguish between true religious affections (which issued in holy tempers) and the false, his writing the *Life of David Brainerd* (1749) to show that when Reformed doctrines were properly applied to the heart a man ran off neither into the moralism that Edwards called Arminianism, nor into experimental religion of either the excited or complacent variety, his insistence that, though the Puritan morphology of conversion was not normative, conversion was a lifelong affair, are very revealing. Most revealing of all was the plain experience in Edward's own parish (of what the conservatives claimed for New England as a whole) that in the heat of the revival too many members had been added to the church. Edwards concluded that he must scrap Stoddardeanism and require of postulants a strict testimony to the work of grace; this cost him his parish and exile to the remote Indian mission at Stockbridge.

### A BALANCE-SHEET OF THE REVIVAL

The result of the Great Awakening in New England was more of a drawn battle than appeared in 1743 when Edwards was encouraging Thomas Prince to get something going by collecting the eyewitness accounts of the progress of religion which he published as the *Christian*

---

[86]  *Records of Connecticut General Association* 12.
[87]  *Philosophy of Jonathan Edwards* ed. H. G. Townsend (Eugene, Or., 1955) 235; G. Gillespie, *Remarks upon Mr. G. Whitefield Proving Him a Man under Delusion* (Philadelphia, 1744) 22.

*History*. The qualified victory of the standing churches was won by a costly exhibition of Erastianism. The Protestant Dissenting Deputies in England sympathised with the churches' discomforts with Davenport, but did not mince the meat of the matter: any appearance of persecution would redound in England to the dissenters' disadvantage.[88] Nor, in such a case, would they 'vindicate such proceedings'. Isolated from their principal spokesman abroad, the New England churches found that the reaction of reasonable men at home to ecclesiastical disorder and to the methods used to remedy it was to go over to the Church of England by the score, and to the new Separate churches by the drove. Between 125 and 225 of the latter (according to the definition employed) came into existence, mostly in eastern Connecticut and south-eastern Massachusetts.[89] The Separates could not create a permanent alternative to the Standing Order. Ground between the upper millstone of unyielding public authority and church establishments which often tightened up the requirements for membership, and the lower millstone of the Baptists who offered a more consistent linkage of admission to the sacraments with profession of faith, and now became a major denomination for the first time, the Separates lasted barely a generation. But from the standpoint of the Standing Order, the Baptists were far more formidable enemies, while those Separates who pushed off in misery to the backwoods of Maine, New Hampshire and Vermont took with them habits of mind which enabled their successors in the latter part of the century to break with Calvinism altogether.

More generally, the revival had done best in those areas and social groups which had most severely perplexed the clergy in the previous generation. It was strong on the frontier, in second-generation towns settled between 1691 and 1715, and in urban areas where diversity, mobility and instability were greatest. The oldest towns and villages settled between 1630 and 1690 seem to have been the most immune to the upsurge in church admissions; there the existence of older forms of cohesion made the Matherian policy of reinforcing cohesion by 'owning the covenant' effective. In general the revival seems to have brought into the churches many of the young, especially young men, some of whom would normally have joined at a later date. In other unexpected ways too old and new continued to coexist. Much

---

[88] C. Bridenbaugh, *Mitre and Sceptre* (Oxford, 1962) 52.
[89] W. G. McLoughlin, *New England Dissent, 1630–1833* (2 vols. Cambridge, Mass., 1971) 1:346–7.

dramatic ink has been spilt on the theme of the 'shattered synthesis', the destruction of the creative tension in which faith and reason had been held in the old Puritan synthesis, and it is true that there could be little common ground between the polemics of Edwards on behalf of the one and Chauncy of the other. But what had kept the synthesis afloat was not so much logic as a ministerial consensus which had been adaptable to circumstances. The number of ministers ejected from their parishes during the struggles of the revival notably increased, but was not large; all ministers hoped to see a raising of the religious tempo in the churches, the bulk were prepared to make compromises to suit their parishioners and had never belonged to the extremer parties. The strength of their position was that the New England establishments had been more efficient than most, and that the evidence throughout the Reformed world was (to put it harshly) that the people were so priest-ridden that they knew not how to take a radically new line. The result was that after the revival neither the synthesis nor the ministerial consensus which made it plausible shattered, and Ezra Stiles in a famous *Discourse on the Christian Union* (1761) was able to restate the New England Way in the light of the balance of powers.

> Providence has planted the British America with a variety of sects which will unavoidably become a mutual balance upon one another. Their temporary collisions, like the action of acids and alcalies after short ebullition, will subside in harmony and union, not by the destruction of either, but in the friendly cohabitation of all... The notion of erecting the polity of either sect into universal dominion to the destruction of the rest is but an airy vision.[90]

Even when faith and reason parted company much more drastically in the nineteenth century Stiles's balance accommodated numerous effervescent newcomers – Baptists, Methodists, even Roman Catholics – though the victor was not, as he expected, 'resplendent and all-prevailing TRUTH', but a common civic religion.

If the revival was thus partly contained and partly assimilated in the churches of the Standing Order, there were other churches and other colonies on which it made no impact at all. The high and latitudinarian wings of the Church of England in the American colonies shut their doors against it more firmly than the English establishment could contemplate; while the Quakers were too near their own charismatic past to be affected by the latest spirit-filled

[90] Heimert & Miller, eds., *Great Awakening* 604; D. Harlan, *The Clergy and the Great Awakening* (Ann Arbor, Mich., 1980).

protests against unconverted ministers. The effect of the revival in New York and Delaware was patchy and in Maryland and Georgia almost nil. Nevertheless it taught important lessons about the way to appeal to a population increasing rapidly and constantly threatening to escape the influence of religious institutions. And in Virginia successive waves of evangelisation by Presbyterians, Baptists and Methodists made it possible to pull down an Anglican establishment. We have observed the impact of the American revival on the Netherlands and central Europe; it was also influential in every part of the United Kingdom.

# CHAPTER 8

# Revival in the United Kingdom

## CONTINENTAL INFLUENCES: (I) IMMIGRATION

Despite the enormous dominance of England in the cultural exchanges between Britain and the continent in the early eighteenth century, the British churches as a whole were subject to important continental influences, influences which helped prepare British opinion for the startling news, sedulously disseminated, of religious upheaval in the American colonies. Just as the revival in the Rhineland and the international activities of the Moravians had helped to bridge the chasm between the Lutheran and Reformed worlds, so too did the British churches. A central position in the propaganda for the revival came to be taken by a group of ministers of the Church of Scotland, John Gillies producing an updated version of the Acts of the Apostles in his *Historical Collections of Accounts of Revival*;[1] and the British Reformed churches fully and self-consciously shared in those changes of thought and sentiment in the Reformed world which had paved the way for revival in the Lower Rhine, Netherlands and New England. If August Hermann Francke, himself an apostle of reform and renewal rather than revival, had under-pinned the revival movements of the first generation, and the world-wide conflict between his son and Zinzendorf had given shape to the revival movements of the second generation, it was the eccentric English clergyman George Whitefield who established himself as the universal gospel salesman of the next generation, helping to unify both the friends and enemies of revival by focussing the division of spirits upon himself.

Britain had of course suffered many similar ideological alarms to her continental neighbours. The contest over what was called atheism had been as fiercely fought here as on the continent, and had

[1] 4 vols. Glasgow, 1754–86.

bequeathed both an abiding fear that mechanical philosophies would squeeze God out of the universe, and a radical determination to breach the institutional defences of orthodoxy more broadly than the Toleration Act had ever done.[2] In Quakerism England had produced the archetypal Philadelphian answer to the confessional conflicts of the seventeenth century. The older 'alternative' religion and science deriving from Jakob Böhme had its English following, and Wesley was not alone in being fascinated, like continental pietists, by those French and Spanish mystics who had fallen foul of the Roman Catholic Church. In a modest way Britain also felt the impact of European emigrations occasioned by religious persecution. The French Prophets had raised all the questions relating to spirit possession which were to be posed again by the revival, had reinvigorated the anti-enthusiasm lobby, and drove the point home by disturbing the early outdoor meetings of the Wesleys. Continental religious exclusiveness was in the immediate background to a number of the leaders of the revival in England. Philip Doddridge's maternal grandfather, John Bauman, had been one of the Protestant refugees from Bohemia, as Doddridge himself recorded in Bauman's Luther Bible. But then Doddridge had learnt his ethics from Grotius and Pufendorf, been raised on German polemical theology, recommended Pufendorf and Lampe's *Ecclesiastical History* to Wesley's Christian Library, and not only regarded support for the Silesian Protestants as a touchstone of the churches' mission,[3] but was approached for news of the revival in New England and Scotland by Abbot Steinmetz himself.[4] Steinmetz, of course, who had nine of Doddridge's books, had his *Family Expositor* translated into German as an antidote to Moravianism, and introduced it himself, pacifying Lutheran alarm by also translating Doddridge's 'sermons on the nature and efficacy of grace'.[5]

Then there were the descendents of the Huguenots, who seemed to cluster mainly round Wesley, occasionally with disastrous effect; the widow Mrs Vazeille whom he married (unhappily) in 1751, like her first husband, was of this extraction. Wesley had made his first personal contacts with Huguenots in Georgia, that refuge for

[2] M. C. Jacob, *The Newtonians and the English Revolution, 1689–1720* (Hassocks, 1976).

[3] *Correspondence and Diary of Philip Doddridge* ed. J. D. Humphreys (5 vols. London, 1829–31) 1:42–3; II:465, 471; IV:485; V:177, 179; *Calender of the Correspondence of Philip Doddridge D. D. (1702–1751)* ed. G. F. Nuttall (London, 1979) no. 1674.

[4] *Calendar of Doddridge Correspondence* nos. 1382, 1478, 1532, 1546, 1572; *Doddridge Correspondence* V:489.　　　　[5] *Doddridge Correspondence* V:145.

persecuted Protestants; his first hymn-book was produced by a Huguenot printer in Charleston, Lewis Timothy (Louis Timotheé). In England the names of those who assisted him at various stages tell the same tale, Walter Sellon, James Rouquet, the Delamottes, Mary Bosanquet, William Lunell in Dublin. The Perronets and John William Fletcher (de la Fléchère) were casualties of the high Swiss Reformed Orthodoxy of the Formula Consensus. Huguenot emigration had been sealed off by the government of Louis XIV, and the religious consequences of their slow assimilation were among the interesting conundrums of the second quarter of the eighteenth century. Some clung to the Book of Common Prayer in French (one group in the crypt of Canterbury Cathedral); some maintained Reformed worship and built chapels of their own; some threw in their lot with the French Prophets; many flooded into the religious societies; some took up with the mysticism of which their countryman, Pierre Poiret, had become a general mediator, and others with Moravianism. When Wesley encountered the Huguenot congregation at Portarlington in Ireland in 1750, revivalism seems to have been the order of the day.[6] The London Huguenots were very heavily concentrated in the west in the Savoy and Soho, and in the east in Spitalfields, Whitechapel and Wapping. During the period immediately after his conversion when Wesley's work was very closely based on the religious societies great numbers of Huguenot names appear in his diary, a sizeable minority of the early membership at his society at the Foundery (conveniently located for Spitalfields) were Huguenots, and when he began to administer communion to society members in premises not episcopally consecrated, he accepted the offer of Dr Deleznot, the pastor of a Huguenot congregation in Wapping, to his chapel. And in the mid-forties he put the London work on a firm base by acquiring the Huguenot chapels at West Street, Seven Dials, in the west, and, in the east, at Grey Eagle Street, Spitalfields, using them, amongst other purposes, gradually to educate dissenting Huguenots in the ways of Anglican liturgical worship. It was the same story in Bristol; and even in the fifties Wesley was grateful for the services of Fletcher and the Perronets in preaching to congregations in French.[7] The willingness of the

---

[6] Wesley, *Works* xx: *Journals* iii: 346.

[7] G. E. Milburn, 'English Methodism and the Huguenots', *PWHS* 45 (1985) 69–79; P. P. Streiff, *Jean Guillaume de la Fléchère. Ein Beitrag zur Geschichte des Methodismus* (Frankfurt, 1984); A. B. Sackett, *James Rouquet* (Chester, 1972). Even in 1765 Wesley preached a charity sermon for the Spitalfields weavers (*Lives of the Early Methodist Preachers* ed. T.

Huguenots to respond to a live religious appeal, however alien to their theological heritage, foreshadowed Wesley's later and much greater success among another unassimilated minority, the Palatines who had been planted upon estates in the South of Ireland early in the eighteenth century. Here was an almost Silesian situation of a German-language population deprived of their church but clinging to their Luther Bible. They detected echoes of Reformation preaching in Wesley, responded vividly, and made their own contribution to the history of religious revival, by taking Methodism to America. The two pioneers were Philip Embury and Barbara Heck. A half-length American portrait of the latter shows her piously clasping her Bible, the *Luther* Bible. To such a distance might the sorrows of Protestant Europe carry the cause of vital religion. And those sorrows seemed never to go away. As late as 1742, the Moravian James Hutton encountered a group of Salzburgers in the streets of London; they were immediately from the settlement in Zealand, and complained of being without pastoral oversight there. Hutton arranged for one of the Brethren in the Netherlands to take them on.[8]

CONTINENTAL INFLUENCES: (2) THE COURT

The major burdens of assimilation undertaken by the British state and churches in the eighteenth century were in Scotland, Wales and Ireland, and these will concern us later. Popular concern with confessional issues abroad was kept up, as we have seen, by the press, and kept up to such effect that when, during the Seven Years War, George Whitefield prayed publicly in Dublin 'for success to the Prussian arms' he was severely rabbled 'and almost killed' by a Catholic mob; each side understood quite clearly what was at stake, and Whitefield left well satisfied that 'thousands and thousands are now praying daily for success to the Prussian and Hanoverian arms'.[9] This result, however, was by no means what might have been expected at the beginning from the Methodist circle; their evolution in this respect is a striking illustration of the slow but relentless pressure on the elite of one of the institutions binding England to the continent which they liked least, the court.

Jackson (6 vols. London, 1872) VI:33. Another prominent evangelical of Huguenot descent was William Romaine.

[8] D. Benham, *Memoirs of James Hutton* (London, 1856) 81.

[9] G. Whitefield, *Works* (6 vols. London, 1771–2) III:207, 230.

Wesley's parents, ex-dissenters both, were equally high Tories and almost equally high royalists. Samuel, however, accepted William III as king; Susanna did not. The difference of opinion had a practical bearing upon the obligation to pray for the king, and, as is now well known, led to a breach of conjugal relations which was not healed by the death of William III. The fruit of the ultimate reconciliation was the birth of John Wesley himself, and, as if to make good any defect in his Toryism, old Samuel, if his son may be believed, helped write the defence speech in the trial of Sacheverell in 1710.[10] Wesley, in short, was born of the Jacobite issue, and born into a rabidly Tory circle which damned foreigners, foreign religions and foreign entanglements, kept up Jacobite sentiment far down the eighteenth century, united it with country-party principles to form a wide-ranging critique of British society and government, and persuaded themselves that the Restoration had led not merely to the reconstruction of the Church of England, but to a revival of morality, had been indeed a cosmic event modelled on the resurrection.

If morality had been in short supply in the public life of Queen Anne, it was still shorter under the Hanoverians. Wesley's family prejudices were confirmed by his Oxford education, and preserved into later life. Two contrasting quotations about Walpole, one from Wesley and one from Doddridge, illustrate how far they each had to move before they could be congenial companions in the work of revival. In 1776 Wesley wrote:[11]

At the accession of George II the nation had great reason to wish for an alteration of measures...The interior government of Great Britain was chiefly managed by Sir Robert Walpole, a man of extraordinary talents, who from low beginnings raised himself to the head of the Treasury. He was endowed with a species of eloquence, which though neither nervous nor elegant...was so plausible on all subjects, that even when he misrepresented the truth, whether from ignorance or design, he seldom failed to persuade that part of his audience for whose hearing his harangue was chiefly intended. He was well acquainted with the nature of the public funds, and understood the whole mystery of stockjobbing. This knowledge produced a connexion between him and the money corporations, which served to enhance his importance...He perceived the bulk of mankind were actuated by a sordid thirst of lucre; he had the sagacity enough to convert the degeneracy of times to his own advantage; and on this alone, he founded the

[10] H. D. Rack, *Reasonable Enthusiast: John Wesley and the Rise of Methodism* (London, 1989) 48–9, 46.

[11] J. Wesley, *Concise History of England* (4 vols. London, 1776) IV:160, 162–4.

whole superstructure of his subsequent administration...He knew the maxims he had adopted would subject him to the hatred, the ridicule and reproach of some individuals, who had not yet resigned all sentiments of patriotism...Nevertheless it required all his artifice to elude, all his patience and natural phlegm to bear the powerful arguments that were urged and the keen satire that was exercised against his measures and management [by Wyndham, Shippen, Pulteney and others].

This country-party pastiche of a septuagenarian is a fair representation of his views as a thirty-two-year-old seeking in 1735 the succession to Epworth Rectory through the interest of Lord Bolingbroke, or indeed those of his associate Whitefield, who was patronised by William Pulteney, earl of Bath.[12] Compare with this Doddridge in 1733, the year of the excise crisis:[13]

> You need not make any apology...for recommending us, at the approaching election, to evince the firmest and warmest attachment to a government, with whose security I think our own to be inseparably connected. I have the satisfaction to inform you that, in the present circumstances, it is as much our inclination and pleasure, as it is our duty and interest, to do our utmost for its service. Our good people here are most of them far from being polite; nor do they pretend to be acquainted with the depths of politics; but they have the common sense to see that it were madness to throw ourselves into the hands of the tories, and to seek our further establishment from those who are united in thirsting for our ruin. I suppose there is not one dissenter in a hundred who reads the Craftsman, or any of his associates; and those who do, read them only to despise their artifices, and wonder at their assurance.

Here Doddridge writes with the complacency of a man comfortably protected by the second-class establishment created by the Toleration Act, Wesley with the radicalism of a party defeated in the struggle for the control of the first-class establishment. It is Wesley, not Doddridge, who, like Jonathan Edwards in New England, has come to a view of the Walpole system not unlike that taken by those in Eastern Europe who were resisting assimilation by their 'well-organised police states'. It was, however, Doddridge, not Wesley who inherited with his politics an international perspective on the Protestant cause. Wesley had come out of the narrowest of Little England stables. Yet when Wesley returned from Georgia in February 1738 with his tail between his legs, he had attained an

---

[12] L. Tyerman, *Life and Times of John Wesley* (3 vols. 6th edn London, 1890) I: 102–3; *Life of George Whitefield* (2nd edn 2 vols. London, 1890) II: 193, 211, 318. Colonel Gumley, who was converted in the circle of the countess of Huntingdon, was the father of the countess of Bath.

[13] *Doddridge Correspondence* III: 125.

international perspective not characteristic of the party from which he had sprung.

> Hereby God has given me to know many of his servants; particularly those of the church of Herrnhut. Hereby my passage is opened to the writings of holy men in the German, Spanish and Italian tongues... All in Georgia have heard the word of God... A few steps have been taken towards publishing the glad tidings both to the African and American heathens. Many children have learned 'how they ought to serve God'.[14]

Here the Wesley who had confined his Oxford reading to English, French and the biblical and classical languages had broadened his vision; he had acquired the new Lutheran Orthodox appreciation of the New World, and the Lutheran Pietist appreciation of heathen and children's missions; one might guess that if he was to be converted it would in Moravian company and 'where one was reading Luther's Preface to the Epistle to the Romans', as was now very nearly obligatory in the Pietist world.[15] That such a development had been possible owed much to the hated foreign courts of the past generation.

## CONTINENTAL INFLUENCES: (3) THE SPCK

The reconstruction of English church life which had begun after the Restoration had perforce to be continued after the Revolution under different conditions. The statutory toleration of dissent set practical bounds to the church courts and the canon law, and a proliferation of society action bore witness not only to the gradual supersession of corporative society by informal fellowships, but to the application of the modish principle of contract to the work of the kingdom of God. Charitable societies, religious societies, reformation societies, and, at the top, the SPCK and SPG, bore witness to new necessities and a new frame of mind. The SPCK was originally intended by Thomas Bray to put down Quakerism at home and dissent generally in America. It was at first largely lay-dominated and gave its mind to the assimilation of Welsh Wales and the promotion of the church cause in England by largely educational means. From the beginning, however, the Society recognised that there were others in Europe with similar objectives. Francke was promptly elected the first of the Society's European corresponding members. The Society was also in

---

[14] Wesley, *Works* xviii *Journals* 1:222.
[15] M. Schmidt, *Wiedergeburt und neuer Mensch* (Witten, 1969) 299–330.

active touch with the rational orthodox in Switzerland, who, notwithstanding the criticism the Society incurred in high-church circles 'as a reviving of Presbyterian classes, encouraging fanaticism', thought its general respectability gave it a quasi-official standing which they could well use in their struggle with their own high Orthodox party.[16]

Both in public and in private, however, Halle was the great foreign fascination of the SPCK. The private pull may by gauged by a paragraph which Henry Newman, the New England-born secretary of the Society, penned to Francke in 1719 (though he finally did not send):[17]

While I write this, casting my eye on a mapp of the world, I could not help observing that Germany is near the centre of the extreams of the known habitable parts of our globe, and consequently by her situation the fittest country to invigorate the most distant nations with the most important truths. And as Hall is near the centre of Germany her situation with the vast accession of learning and other emoluments which Providence has graciously vouchsafed does not less adapt her to be the primum mobile of all intelligence for the improvement of mankind.

This somewhat extravagant endorsement of Francke's schemes for universal regeneration was hardly more extravagant than the public endorsement the SPCK gave Francke's chief programmatic and fund-raising tract, *Pietas Hallensis*, in a preface written by Josiah Woodward, the great spokesman for the religious societies, in 1706. 'If... anyone finds his trust in God beginning to waver in any pressing trial, and ready to stagger by reason of unbelief', wrote Woodward,[18] Francke's own 'mighty faith, constant zeal, unwearied diligence, entire self-renunciation, enlarged charity, and ...deep humility' would revive him.

The key to the intensity and duration of the SPCK's devotion to

---

[16] E. Duffy, '"Correspondence Fraternelle"' in *Reform and Reformation : England and the Continent* ed. D. Baker (Oxford, 1979) 251–80.

[17] W. K. Lowther Clarke, *Eighteenth Century Piety* (London, 1944) 49. Newman clearly did not think this paragraph too fulsome, for he had begun by comparing Francke favourably with Caesar and Alexander (and had been even more flattering in a letter of 14 July 1713. AFSt DIII pt. 1). Wake was still corresponding with Francke on matters of scholarship and missions in 1722 (SPK Nachlasse A. H. Francke K30 fascicle. II fos. 65–6, 835–40). For Francke's correspondence with John Chamberlayne, the first secretary of the SPCK and secretary of the SPG, *Ibid.* fos. 841–56.

[18] A. H. Francke, *Pietas Hallensis* (2nd edn London, 1707) iv–v. Woodward was a very active member of the SPCK, as were White Kennett and others who commended the book. Francke in turn made use of Woodward's puff in his *Grosser Aufsatz* ed. O. Podczeck ([East] Berlin, 1962).

Francke was revealed in the *Pietas Hallensis*; it was the translator of that tract and the author of another that was bound up with it, Anton Wilhelm Böhme. Böhme's misfortunes in Waldeck have been encountered in chapter 6. His contemporary biographer, Rambach, admits he obtained too close an insight into the destruction of modern Christianity, and 'with the unwisdom of youth [he] denounced it too freely'. Francke nevertheless now wanted him in England, and here he came in 1701. He had first to learn the language and in this he was assisted by members of the religious societies. He ran a school for the children of German families, but this was never enough to support him, and he was much dependent on charitable assistance dredged up from various quarters (including the court of Waldeck) by an extraordinary character he had met in Rotterdam on the way to England, Heinrich Wilhelm Ludolf. A professional traveller and orientalist, Ludolf had grasped the geopolitical connexion between Russia, the Balkans and the Near East, and the diplomatic, religious and economic importance of securing influence in the Orthodox churches. While one of the two contemporaries of universal vision, Leibniz, looked to China as the goal of his cultural mission, Ludolf persuaded the other, August Hermann Francke, to concentrate upon Russia, and those territories in the Balkans and Near East which bore on the Russia question. This was the origin of the Seminarium Orientale at Halle. England was also contesting the growth of French and Catholic influence at the Porte, and through this connexion Ludolf was taken into English service, became secretary to Prince George of Denmark, the consort of the future Queen Anne, published a Russian grammar at Oxford, and early joined the SPCK. Two of these connexions were crucial to Böhme. In 1705, through Ludolf's interest, he was appointed court chaplain to Prince George of Denmark, and in 1709 became a member of the SPCK, establishing himself (as the secretary of the SPCK accurately related) as 'the life and soul of our correspondence in religious affairs with Germany and Denmark'. Böhme was crucial in persuading the SPCK to adopt the Tranquebar mission, and give financial backing to a number of Francke's projects, including translations of the Bible into Arabic and Estonian, and the relief of persecuted Protestants.

Thus at the very moment when the party of confessional isolation into which Wesley was born was running amok in the interests of Dr Sacheverell, a powerful influence of a quite different kind was admitted by the back door of the SPCK. What could not have been foreseen was that the Böhme who had so quickly come to grief in Waldeck would, by great personal qualities and incessant literary activity, become important in English religious life. He kept the English editions of the *Pietas Hallensis* and the reports of the Tranquebar mission up to date; he made available in English texts of his own religious tradition, especially of Arndt and Francke, not to mention news of the children's revival in Silesia; he also acted constantly as a middleman in the opposite direction in works which interpreted the position of the Church of England to German readers, and left a history of that church which was published posthumously. (Of course he preached Ludolf's funeral sermon and published his remains.[19]) In the gigantic purge which befell the English court at the accession of George I he must have been the only survivor (continuing as court chaplain till his death in 1722); equally unforeseeably Wesley prescribed the reading of his sermons to his preachers at the Conference of 1746 and commenced his Christian Library with a two-volume abridgement of his translation from Arndt. Highly prized by Isaac Watts, his translations from Francke were formative reading of all the leading early evangelicals.[20]

Böhme doubtless owed some measure of his acceptability to Anglicans to his coming in at one remove, so to speak, under the aegis of good Queen Anne. The court of George I was a different matter. This court contrived the proscription of the Tory party, turning many of them into Jacobite mutterers and some into Jacobite conspirators. The Hanoverians brought with them continental entanglements in the Great Northern War which helped to split the Whig party and seemed outrageous to Tories. The abuse encountered by the king's two German mistresses, advanced as the duchess of Kendal and the countess of Darlington, was a measure of the revulsion of the political nation not for concubinage but for the loss of patronage to foreigners. They acted with some desperate politicians who seemed bent on remodelling church and state in the worst Stuart manner, and did no better than other governments in either preventing, or remaining unspotted by, the great speculative bubbles which followed the War of the Spanish Succession. To many, especially of Tory inclinations, who took it for granted that parties in

---

[19] *The Faithful Steward* (London, 1712); *Reliquiae Ludolfianae* (London, 1912).
[20] Wesley, *Works* IX:272, 335 n. 4; G. F. Nuttall, 'Continental Pietism and the Evangelical Movement in Britain; in *Pietismus und Reveil* ed. J. van den Berg & J. P. van Dooren (Leiden, 1978) 207–36.

church and state would interact, the spectacle of parties in the state interacting with parties in the City seemed proof positive of national decline, and the damage suffered in the South Sea Bubble did in fact lead to efficacious good resolutions not to visit the wilder shores of speculation again. And when political stability was re-established under the Walpole system, apparently by a mixture of shuffling and the manipulation of patronage, the cure seemed as bad as the disease. The only remedy seemed to be to tip the balance of the constitution against the court in parliament and in the country. Should anyone worry about the religion of the Hanoverian church, he would discover that there England's new Defender of the Faith presided over a system as drab as it was exclusive, as hostile to the ways of others as the narrowest of English high-churchmen.

Paradoxically the main hope for the English on the religious side lay in George I's streak of Machiavellianism. In England he did not need to make the concessions to Lutheran Orthodoxy he made in the electorate, and, if he was to realise his hopes of contesting the leadership of the Protestant interest in the Empire with Prussia, knew he must try another tack. Francke, not a man to miss a trick, put himself in touch at the outset with Bothmer, a central figure in the government of the electorate and in the London court.[21] Of the leading court figures on the distaff side the duchess of Kendal was a Pietist confidentially reported to be devoted to Spener's penitential sermons, who insisted on seeing off the Tranquebar missionaries herself,[22] while the countess of Schaumburg-Lippe, the consort of the ruler of a small North German Pietist principality, was another devotee of the Tranquebar missionaries, one of the Zinzendorf's first contacts in England, and had actually given employment to Böhme in his youth.[23] Böhme, of course, was retained, his correspondence to Halle multiplying the whole time, and ensuring that the interest of the SPCK in Francke's causes did not decay like its relations with the Swiss rational orthodox. Still more remarkably, when Böhme died, George I replaced him by a chaplain from the same Hallesian stable who became a still more firmly established figure in all the English

---

[21] AFSt A168 no. 49. Cf. A177 no. 100. Zinzendorf attempted to ingratiate himself in the same quarter a decade later. Herrnhut MSS R20 c4 no. 1.

[22] SPK Nachlasse A. H. Francke K30 St. 9, 23.

[23] *Ibid.* St. 22; Benham, *Hutton* 17; G. A. Wauer, *Die Anfänge der Brüderkirche in England* (Leipzig, 1900) 75–7; A. Sames, *Anton Wilhelm Böhme* (Göttingen, 1990) 67. On Schaumburg-Lippe, O. Bernstorff, 'Eberhard David Hauber (1695–1765)', *JGNSKg* 63 (1965) 169–93.

religious scene, Friedrich Michael Ziegenhagen, who held office 1722–76.

FRIEDRICH MICHAEL ZIEGENHAGEN

A Hanoverian by origin, Ziegenhagen won a complete spiritual ascendancy over the countess of Schaumburg-Lippe, continuing to minister to her after she had returned to Bückeburg, and attracting numbers of the awakened when he preached in Hanover.[24] But the great significance of Ziegenhagen even to the Hanoverian court in England was that he took Böhme's place in the SPCK and used it to act as an organising middleman between London and the Franckes, father and son, with their plans both to meet the Protestant crisis in Central Europe, and to provide for the needs of the rocketing German population in America. From the point of view of the Franckes, Ziegenhagen was indispensable at the precise point where their aspirations diverged most widely from the calculated ambitions of the Prussian monarchy. To George I and George II he gave some substance to transitory ambitions to head the Protestant interest in the Empire, and he was invaluable in the long haul of recruiting the population on which the future of the American colonies depended. And in due course he helped to change the outlook of a disaffected section of the church.

For some years before his appointment in England Ziegenhagen had been in touch with Francke by letter every few weeks and after his appointment the close contact continued.[25] Its principal substance in the twenties was formed by matters educational, and by keeping the principal lay member of the SPCK, the Welsh baronet Sir John Philipps of Picton Castle, Pembrokeshire, in touch with the Halle leaders. The latter was elected a member of the SPCK a month after it was founded, and he took the lead in it up till his death in 1737. He made Pembrokeshire and Carmarthenshire the chief centres of the Society's work in Wales, himself founding twenty-two schools in the former county, besides several more in the latter; and he did much to

---

[24] *Ibid.* 188; G. Meyer, 'Pietismus und Herrnhutertum in Niedersachsen', *Niedersächsisches Jahrbuch* 9 (1952) 108. Coaching in Ziegenhagen's house indelibly impressed the later distinguished theologian J. D. Michaelis. '*And Other Pastors of Thy Flock*' ed. F. Hildebrandt (Cambridge, 1942) 113.

[25] SPK Nachlasse A. H. Francke K30; AFSt A177 no. 100.

assist the educational work of his brother-in-law Griffith Jones of Llandowror. In due course he opened his own lines of communication with Gotthilf August Francke, to elicit practical information on the cost per head of maintaining orphans at Halle.[26] Philipps was also in correspondence with the Swiss rational orthodox, and must be numbered among the *fromme Adel* who in various parts of Europe were looking for new methods of enabling the Protestant establishments to work more effectively.

The great moment for both Ziegenhagen and the SPCK came with the Protestant crisis in Salzburg over the winter of 1731–2. In conjunction with another member of the Society, now senior of Augsburg, Samuel Urlsperger, they raised funds, created the organisation which shipped the British party of the Salzburgers out to Georgia, and found themselves committed in the long run to paying their pastors, reporting their progress, and through Ziegenhagen personally, rendering spiritual and administrative assistance to every individual and party that went out to them. The Society was now thoroughly indoctrinated by its German allies with the Pietist view of events in central Europe. The revolutionary Liberda was 'a very good man', 'a man full of faith and the Holy Ghost'; the Society was plied with information about Protestant sufferings in Slovakia, in Hungary, in Carinthia, in Bohemia; its response could hardly have been bettered: 'Happy Sufferers, Glorious Resolution! the genuine fruit of a true saving faith, wrought in their souls by the influence of the Holy Spirit'.[27]

In England the Salzburg crisis had a double significance. It compelled the SPCK to involve many more people in the rescue operation. They had to work hand in glove with the Georgia Trustees who were to settle the 'English' Salzburgers; here fortunately there was an overlap of managing personnel. They sent down a copy of an appeal on behalf of the Salzburgers to every Oxford college and canvassed for support on the Hebdomadal Board. The Salzburg affair was now a matter of common college gossip in circles close to Wesley; Thomas Wilson, son of the venerable bishop of Sodor and Man of the same name (himself a subscriber to the Salzburg cause),

---

[26] *Ibid.* A180 no. 31; c450 no. 1. Cf. c346 nos. 2–5; SPK Nachlasse A. H. Francke κ2 nos. 24–38. See also T. Shankland, 'Sir John Philipps, the S.P.C.K. and the Charity School movement', *THSC* 13 (1904–5) 74–216; M. Clement, *The S.P.C.K. and Wales* (London, 1954).

[27] *Henry Newman's Salzburger Letterbooks* ed. G. F. Jones (Athens, Ga., 1966) 256–7, 279, 232, 252–3, 282–3, 506–9, 511–13, 22.

'vindicated the Saltzburghers upon the footing of Riot and Resistance' to that partisan Whig, John Conybeare, about to succeed as dean of Christ Church, a very significant reversal of the usual roles. The net began to close round John Wesley himself. Oglethorpe, the governor of Georgia, wrote to old Samuel Wesley at Epworth that 'we should have been very happy had a man of your spirit health enough to have gone thro' the labours of a missionary'; Samuel offered his curate, John Whitelamb, a pupil of his son John.[28] Within three months Samuel Wesley was dead, and within seven John Wesley, who had saddened his father's last days by pleading the superior merits of Oxford as a theatre for sanctification, had been approached to go to Georgia and had declared his willingness to consider an offer. The extraordinary feature of all this activity, this justification of Salzburger resistance on Protestant grounds, was that it was the work of men who were supposed to be Jacobites. Oglethorpe had been christened James Edward for the Old Pretender, and his sisters devoted themselves to Jacobite conspiracy; Philipps, though the son of a Puritan and Whig MP and the cousin of Walpole himself, had gravitated in Oxford into very high Tory circles and had been immersed in the charity school movement, the political loyalty of which was very suspect; and Wesley was the son of non-juring parents, and a younger brother of a protégé of Bishop Atterbury.[29] Those who, during the 'Forty-Five, persistently accused Methodists of Jacobitism understood quite accurately the hole of the pit out of which they were digged.

[28] *Ibid.* 99, 104–5, 254–5, 514–18; *Diaries of Thomas Wilson* ed. C. L. S. Linnell (London, 1964) 63, 94, 95, 107, 85 (on the politics of Conybeare, W. R. Ward, *Georgian Oxford* (Oxford, 1958) 137–8); Adam Clarke, *Memoirs of the Wesley Family* (2 vols. 4th edn London, 1860) 1:337–9. For Wesley's increasing involvement with Philipps and the Salzburgers; R. P. Heitzenrater, 'John Wesley and the Oxford Methodists', (unpubl. Ph.D. thesis, Duke University, N. C., 1972), 172, 178, 281, 282. Fifty years later in his abridgment of Mosheim, Wesley emphasised the increase in Lutheran numbers and reputation effected by the Salzburgers. *Concise Ecclesiastical History* (4 vols. London, 1781) IV:164.

[29] Wesley, *Works* XXV: *Letters* 1:432 & n.; R. Wright, *Memoir of James Oglethorpe* (London, 1867) 187–8; L. Tyerman, *Life and Times of Samuel Wesley* (London, 1867) 425–8; Paul Kléber Monod, *Jacobitism and the English people* 1688–1781 (Cambridge, 1989) 272, 278; P. K. Hill, *The Oglethorpe Ladies and the Jacobite Conspiracies* (Atlanta, Ga., 1977); L. Colley, *In Defiance of Oligarchy* (Cambridge, 1982) 86, 113.

WESLEY AND THE PIETY OF CENTRAL EUROPE

The earliest activities of the Oxford Methodists had been reported privately to Francke apparently by Ziegenhagen.[30] Now Wesley took part of the company with him to Georgia, Whitefield following as he returned in 1738. The experience was in different ways to tie each of them more closely to the movements in Central Europe whose service was among the motives for their venture to the western frontier of the Protestant world. Wesley suffered the worse, and not just because in his bookish and rather pharisaical way he lacked Whitefield's practical understanding of how to survive. 'The genuine fruit of a true and saving faith, wrought in their souls by the influence of the Holy Spirit' which 'the gentlemen of the Society for Promoting Christian Knowledge' had perceived in the Salzburgers, he recognised on the outward voyage in the Moravians; and Spangenberg's inquiry on his arrival whether he had a personal knowledge of the saving power of Christ could hardly have cut more painfully. What aggravated the difficulty was Wesley's lesson at the hands of the Salzburgers (noted above in chapter 1) that there was now war to the knife between Halle and Herrnhut, incompatibility between 'true and saving faith' as he was now tempted to see it, and as his Franckephile patrons in the SPCK were tempted to see it. On the way to Georgia and after his arrival, Wesley learned German by the eccentric but only available method of studying German hymns, first in the Herrnhut hymn-book of 1735 and then in the Hallesian Freylinghausen hymn-book. This intense immersion in the modern spiritual verse of Lutheran and related German Protestant traditions was reinforced by reading in prose spirituality, Tauler, Jakob Böhme, Arndt, Meister Eckhardt, and the Luther Bible. In a measure he sought to work out his personal problem in terms of the thirty-three German hymns he translated while he was in Georgia. The spread is interesting. There are no Reformation hymns (he was not yet ready for Luther's Preface to Romans) and none from the Reformed tradition in the denominational sense. Confessional Lutheranism was there in its most devotional shape with Paul Gerhardt; Silesian mysticism with Johann Scheffler; Halle Pietism with Joachim Lange, Freylinghausen, Rothe and Winckler; Moravianism with Zinzendorf, Spangenberg, Anna Dober and Maria Böhmer (together contributing one third of the total); radical spiritualism with

---

[30] SPK Nachlasse A. H. Francke к30 fos. 539–49.

Gottfried Arnold; and contemporary mysticism of Reformed origin in Tersteegen.[31] Wesley, in short, initiated himself into the practical theology of virtually every school encountered in the present study, and made no choice among them. In so far as the balance was tilted, it was tilted by the fact that both he and his brother ran away from their Georgia mission, as the pastors of the Salzburgers, those Hallesian cynosures of the SPCK, Boltzius and Gronau, most notably did not. If Wesley was to be converted, and the impact of a devotional literature which as a whole had a much heavier soteriological concentration than the Anglicanism in which he had been raised, was that he must be, it was likely that this would happen under Moravian auspices.

The balance was also tilted by the fact that Wesley's personal misery on his return seemed to mirror that of the Church establishment at large. The Church of England was less short of policy in the early eighteenth century than it has commonly been since that time. There had been those at the beginning of the century who had sought to fertilise their world by the pure streams of modern knowledge, and appeal to reason as now understood; they had finally tied themselves in knots over the doctrine of the Trinity, and had let loose radicalisms in church and state which no one cared for. Wake had sought the way of Protestant union. This offered a means not only to shore up a Protestant succession, but to strengthen a church which had failed to secure comprehension. Moreover it embodied a latitudinarian principle and an escape from controversy which on religious grounds it would be foolish to do without. But Protestant union required action from princes, and they quickly spotted that the great Catholic forward move which had brought the Empire to the brink of confessional war in 1719 was over; and when, at the time of the Salzburg crisis, the Emperor Charles VI was bidding for Protestant support for the Pragmatic Sanction, Wake's policies had lost their political relevance. Wake was superseded as Church policy-maker in chief by Edmund Gibson, bishop of London. Gibson perceived that the Church had no option but to act with the Whig party as the only committed defenders of the Protestant succession, and did not shrink from using patronage to create them a following in the Church. The Church could be made more effective by improved organisation, an attack on non-residence, stricter discipline, canon law revision. These policies required parliamentary

[31] J. Nuelsen, *John Wesley and the German Hymn* (Eng. tr. Calverley, 1972) 17, 43.

assistance from the government, and, in 1736, while Wesley was in Georgia, Gibson bitterly concluded that Walpole had reneged on his share of the implied contract, broke with him, and in the following year was passed over for the succession to Wake at Canterbury. Of all the policy failures of the early eighteenth century Gibson's was the most public, and it came at a time when there was a deep and genuine revulsion against what Walpole had done with English politics.[32] If on the political side there was now no alternative to merging Tory and country traditions in a policy of reform and circumscription of the powers of the state, on the side of the Church the state was a broken reed; if the Church was to be saved, there was no alternative to private enterprise. This self-evident truth, unmistakable since the foundering of the confessional state at the end of the seventeenth century, was so unpalatable that the bulk of the clergy still held out against it, but Tory laymen, especially those used to society action in the SPCK, were coming round to this view. This is the explanation of the success of the Moravians in obtaining special privileges by legislation as late as 1749.[33] The average Tory squire was doubtless ill-primed with Zinzendorf's core claim to have discovered a more rapid method of conversion than the Halle Pietists, but he was well aware of the count's ability to get things done quickly in a more general sense, his combination of vision and the ability to borrow cheaply on the Dutch money market.

At any rate Wesley escaped (if only gradually) from personal fractiousness and the hopeless accumulation of religious claims he had taken on board[34] by the only possible way, by the way of conversion, in his case under Moravian auspices, on 24 May, 1738. This was speedily followed by a deeply impressive visit to Herrnhut which looked as though it might (as with many others) be the preface to seeking entry to the Unity of the Brethren. The journey to Herrnhut showed, however, that conversion had not yet brought Wesley to make his final choices. He visited Halle and recalled 'that August Hermann Francke whose name is indeed as precious ointment. O may I follow him, as he did Christ!' And he was denied communion by the Moravians as a *homo perturbatus*.[35] Moreover what Wesley discovered at Herrnhut and in his conflicts with Philipp Heinrich Molther on his return, was that 'Moravianism' was still as

[32] I. Kramnick, *Bolingbroke and his Circle* (Cambridge, Mass., 1968) 201–60.
[33] David Nitschmann's file of papers on this triumph is in Herrnhut MSS R13 A24.
[34] 'My weak mind could not bear to be thus sawn asunder.' Wesley, *Works* xviii *Journals* 1:254.
[35] *Ibid.*,1:263–4; ii:6; Benham, *Hutton* 40; *PWHS* 15 (1926) 209.

much an unresolved congeries of spiritual claims and counter-claims as was 'Methodism'. It was inevitable that he should get involved in polemics with them about degrees of faith when he found the original Moravian refugees claiming to renew the Church of the Brethren, while Zinzendorf was claiming that they were an interconfessional religious society.[36] As inevitable, indeed, that like other men of independent mind, he would not endure Zinzendorf for long. How the process looked from the side of the Moravians was vividly reported to Zinzendorf by James Hutton:[37]

*J. Wesley* being resolved to *do* all things himself & having told many souls that they were justified who have since discovered themselves to be otherwise & mixing the works of the Law with the Gospel as *means of grace* is at enmity against the *Brethren*. Envy is not extinct in him. His heroes falling every day almost into poor sinners frighten him; but at London the spirit of the Brethren prevails against him... I desired him simply to keep to his office in the Body of Christ i.e. namely to awaken souls in preaching, but not to pretend to *lead* them to Christ. But he will have the glory of doing all things... *J. W.* & *C. Wesley* both of them are dangerous snares to many young women, several are in love with them. I wish they were married to some good sister, but I would not give them one of my sisters, if I had many.

When the Fetter Lane Society divided, Wesley indeed took most of the women, leaving the count most of the men. So sharp was the severance that he also repudiated Luther's commentary on Galatians, with which Moravians had nursed his brother through conversion. The paradox was that the process which had begun with a Moravian conversion ended not only with Wesley's coming down on the other side of the Central European conflict (at the very moment the SPCK were cooling) but in his imagining that Halle had been engaged in the kind of revivalism which was now his life's work.[38] Most of the important British (as distinct from German) Moravian leaders in the British Isles were ex-Methodists, but when the Moravians fell into a financial crisis in the mid-fifties, the competition between the two bodies which had led to whole Methodist societies going over to the Moravians[39] came to an end; and if Wesley did not renew his proposals of union with the Brethren of 1745, he became in later life

---

[36] On these differences of view, W. R. Ward, 'The Renewed Unity of the Brethren' *BJRL* 70 (1988) 77–92. [37] Herrnhut MSS R13 A7. Briefe von englischen Brüdern no. 25.
[38] Wesley, *Works* xx: *Journals* III: 219–20. Halle was kept in touch with Wesley's doings by the German pastors in London. SPK Nachlasse A. H. Francke K31.1 fos. 164–6, 244.
[39] E. A. Rose, 'Methodism in Cheshire', *TLCAS* 78 (1975) 23. For more friendly intercourse including the Brecknock Gwynnes, one of whom was Mrs Charles Wesley, JRL English MSS 1065 fo. 20.

more kindly disposed to them, and in 1783 even paid a (slightly tetchy) visit to his old Georgia acquaintance Anton Seifert, at the Moravian settlement at Zeist in the Netherlands.[40]

## WHITEFIELD AND HALLE

The case of Whitefield, who came out of the same stable, was different yet reached much the same conclusion. Whitefield was less bookish than Wesley, and having been rescued in 1735 from complete emaciation and exhaustion by a joyful conversion experience which was a New Birth in an almost physical sense, was less open to the reconsiderations and the immersion in German Protestantism which Wesley had to undergo. Tyerman, who clearly found it hard to believe that any friend of the excellent Wesley could be a Calvinist, thought that Whitefield became a Calvinist in America; and some of Whitefield's own language when trying to make Wesley feel bad about breaching his promise to keep clear of the Calvinist question while deputising for Whitefield at Bristol lends colour to his view. The truth seems, however, to be that before he went to America for the second time Whitefield had acquired a working knowledge of modern systematic Calvinism from his reading, and from correspondence with the Erskine brothers, the would-be reformers of Scottish Presbyterianism. Ralph Erskine's last letter to him was virtually a theological treatise in itself, elaborately expounding the Calvinist position. The chief change was that Whitefield modified his preaching manner by contact with Gilbert Tennent, though he was not tempted to follow him in making physical emaciation not the preface to, but the fruit of, conversion.[41]

All the more remarkable therefore that the practical concerns of the Orphan House which Whitefield resolved on his first visit to Georgia in 1738–9 to create on the Franckean pattern kept him in much closer personal touch with the Halle interest on a number of issues than Wesley ever was. He corresponded with the younger Francke, usually directly, but sometimes through Ziegenhagen, sometimes in English but more often in Latin, frequently down to

---

[40] Wesley, *Works* XXVI: *Letters* II:172. Wesley complained that at Zeist he was not even offered a cup of tea (*Journal* VI:428, VII:89); Seifert's journal makes it clear that the visit was celebrated by the children with special music.

[41] A. Dallimore, *George Whitefield* (2 vols. Edinburgh 1970–80) I:405; M. J. Coalter, 'The Life of Gilbert Tennent' unpublished Ph.D. thesis, Princeton University 1982, 163; Tyerman, *Whitefield* I:335.

1750 and occasionally to 1760.[42] Would this curious combination between the self-appointed guardians of Lutheran Pietism and the divinely appointed spokesman for English-language Calvinism serve in the great battle with Zinzendorf?

Whitefield was noted for a virulent anti-modernism and, when acting with Gilbert Tennent on his second American visit, found it profitable to scourge unconverted ministers, and to create the impression that they were particularly thick on the ground in the Church of England. These phobias (both of which he later rued) apart, he was on the whole a less prickly man than Wesley, had the advantage of being much nearer the theological mainstream of the English-speaking revival on both sides of the Atlantic, and was generous in recognising the fruits of the Holy Spirit where he encountered them, not least among Moravians. During his time in England in 1739 between his first and second American journeys, he found no difficulty in acting with a now substantially Moravianised Fetter Lane Society, and 'could not avoid admiring their great simplicity, and deep experience in the inward life'. He was in touch with them when he was out preaching with Methodists, corresponded with Zinzendorf after his return to America, and wrote over fifty letters to James Hutton, the pillar of the London Moravians.[43] In America he did much service to the Brethren, providing financial assistance to enable Peter Böhler and his company in 1740 to escape from Georgia and military service against the Spaniards to Pennsylvania. In the North he provided employment and a temporary home for them at Nazareth, the abortive and ambitious settlement he planned in the 5,000 acres he bought at the Forks of the Delaware; and when the cost of the project got beyond his means he sold them the property to add to their adjacent estate at Bethlehem. For all this he had to put up with rumours that he had become a Moravian, and with Zinzendorf's claim, during his ill-fated effort to capture German America for his movement, that Whitefield was his spiritual son.[44] But he became increasingly disconcerted at Moravian doctrine and practice, especially during the time of sifting, and rightly suspicious

---

[42] Whitefield, *Works* (6 vols. London, 1771–2) 1:469–70 (the original of this letter survives as AFSt c532 no. 2 where it is dated 23 November 1742. The editorial gloss that 'Mr W—' in the printed version is 'Mr. Wesley' is not borne out by the MS); Whitefield, *Works* II:83, 279, 480; III:260; AFSt c532 nos. 1–7.

[43] George Whitefield, *Journals* (London, 1966) 266; MCH MSS AB 101 Packet 4, 12 February 1738/9; Packet 14; Herrnhut MSS R13 A17b Briefwechsel zwischen G. Whitefield und Zinzendorf, 1739–53.  [44] Dallimore, *Whitefield* II:214.

of their finances. Finally in 1753, when Zinzendorf was violently attacked by Henry Rimius, a former aulic councillor to the king of Prussia, Whitefield, who by now had suffered substantial losses from his London Tabernacle to his old colleague Cennick and the Moravians, weighed in with a sharp *Expostulatory Letter* which achieved the instant accolade of translation into German (of course at Halle). The Moravians' financial collapse seemed on a par with their spiritual extravagance. As Whitefield put it in a letter to the countess of Huntingdon which could be read literally or meta-phorically: 'The Moravians' outward scheme, I am apt to believe will soon be disconcerted. Strange! Why will God's children build Babels? Why will they flatter themselves, that God owns and approves of them, because he suffers them to build high? In mercy to them, such buildings, of whatever kind, must come down'.[45] Halle had again held its unlikely English allies, but the Methodist movement was now itself falling apart. To the means by which it had created a device to save the church from itself comparable with that of the Tory–country reform platform to save the state from itself we must now turn.

### THE SPCK IN WALES

Welsh Wales was spared the fate both of the Protestant Poles in Silesia, subject to both German and Catholic oppression, and of the Wends and Sorbs of Upper Lusatia, whose Pietist German masters were determined to put them to rights on the basis of literature in their own vernacular; but, like both, it felt the impact of the Halle propaganda. In many respects the efforts of the English state and church were like those of the Swedes south of the Baltic, and met much the same fate; but the English were less enterprising than the Swedes in exploiting the possibilities of a peasant vernacular. There were two great paradoxes in Wales. A sustained campaign to assimilate Wales to the English language, culture and religious establishment generated by way of reaction a religious revival which ended by being Welsh, evangelical and dissenting; though the elite which launched the revival was almost as anglicising as the official

---

[45] G. Whitefield, *Ein Bestrafungsschreiben an hrn ... Grafen von Zinzendorf* (Halle, 1753); Whitefield, *Works* III:5. Zinzendorf made only a feeble reply (MCH MSS Folder 9, Zinzendorf to Whitefield, 8 May 1753). The suggestions of Tyerman and Dallimore that the heroic efforts of the Brethren over the next fifty years to pay off Zinzendorf's debts owed something to expostulations from Whitefield are implausible.

policy it sought to supplement. And it was characteristic that the successes of a movement which, in the period of this study, was led by men with powerful English ties and a strong international awareness of what was happening in the Protestant world as a whole, were deeply marked by the highly decentralised, indeed tribal, structure of Welsh society. This was to be the special Welsh contribution to the almost universal history of revival as resistance to assimilation.

The ambivalence of the early revival in Wales is forcibly illustrated in the way Griffith Jones (1683–1761) launched the general propaganda for his 'circulating schools' in a publication justly bearing the Hallesian title of *Welch Piety*, for, like Spener, Jones was led into innovation by harrowing experiences in catechising people before sacrament Sundays. Instruction in Welsh, he argued, put a necessary brake on labour migration into England, and,

> with respect to a more important concern, our spiritual and highest interest of all, there are some advantages peculiar to the Welsh tongue, as being perhaps the chastest in all Europe. Its books and writings are free from the infection and deadly venom of atheism, deism, arianism, popery, lewd plays, immodest romances, and low intrigues [like too many books in English. Not only is it impracticable to teach all the people to speak English, but preaching to Welsh congregations in English] has in too many places, reduced the country to heathenish darkness and irreligion (and, what some are apt to declaim against as more damnable) into different communities and separations from the Established Church.[46]

There were reasons why a man who clearly recognised the folly of requiring the monoglot Welsh to drag through devotional and educational exercises by rote in English, had to argue that the change would be convenient for the Anglo-Welsh gentry and to support the *argumentum ad hominem* with the unlikely plea that the real language of Canaan was Welsh. By origin a Carmarthenshire shepherd, Griffith Jones had with difficulty obtained ordination and then modest preferment in the Church. In 1709 this preferment was reinforced by the mastership of a school founded by that cynosure of the gentry, Sir John Philipps. Predictably Jones became in 1713 a corresponding member of the SPCK, and revealed his knowledge of what was happening in the world by applying to join the Tranquebar mission. By now Jones was often in trouble with church authority for itinerant preaching, but in 1716 his patron, Sir John Philipps, presented him to the living of Llandowror, Carms. SPCK duties took up much of his

---

[46] W. M. Williams, *Selections from the Welch Piety* (Cardiff, 1938) 42–5.

time; he was amongst those who pressed for a new edition of the Welsh Bible. In 1718 he went on a seven-week preaching tour with Philipps in Wales, England and Scotland, and eighteen months later married Philipps's sister. In all manner of ways Jones was a herald of the Welsh revival. He was a thunderous preacher in the Voetian manner, but in the Pietist style he preached the indispensability of the New Birth; if he had converted no one else he would have left a mark on the revival by converting Daniel Rowland, esteemed by the enthusiast Howel Harris as 'in his pulpit... a second Paul'.[47] Then secondly, he had been active in the charity school movement backed by the SPCK since its palmy days. No one knew better that it had been flagging in impetus from the time of the Hanoverian succession and had run into the sands by 1730, and that it had deserved to do so because in South Wales the dominant language of instruction was English. This notwithstanding that (as he believed) even in the English counties of Monmouth, Hereford and Shropshire 'most of the inferior people speak Welsh'. In 1731 he sought SPCK backing for a 'Welch School' at Llandowror, and over the next six years created thirty-seven circulating schools, through which in that period 2,400 scholars passed, the masters being trained by him at Llandowror. Like the great communion seasons in Scotland, these schools were adapted to rural underemployment. They met for three months at a time, generally in winter, with evening classes for those at work in the day. Pupils were taught to read the Welsh Bible and to learn the Church catechism. The significance of this was that Sir John Philipps had found (as in their own way Lutheran pastors in the Lower Saxon areas which had gone over to High German had found) that in the SPCK English-language schools, pupils might recite the catechism impeccably but were 'literally ignorant of the meaning of the words, resurrection, saint, grace &c.'[48] The reason why Jones produced the first number of *Welch Piety* in 1738 with its curiously lame English apologetic for instruction in Welsh, was that in the previous year his patron Philipps had died, and that all Wales could produce to replace him was Madam Bevan of Laugharne (1698–1779), whose father had managed the SPCK schools in Carmarthenshire when he was working for them, and whose uncle had married Arabella Philipps, sister to Mrs Griffith Jones. He was going to be dependent upon English subventions, and appealed with such success

---

[47] *Selected Trevecca Letters* ed. G. M. Roberts (Caernarvon, 1956) 164.
[48] G. H. Jenkins, *Literature, Religion and Society in Wales* (Cardiff, 1978) 80.

to doctors, bankers, baronets and divines who were sympathetic to the movement of reform which was becoming the movement of Methodism and revival that by the year of his death, 1761, 3,495 of his schools had been set up and over 158,000 scholars had passed through them.

The SPCK campaign to civilise, christianise and assimilate Wales also incorporated an important holding operation. There was a great crescendo of Welsh-language publishing to save the souls of the monoglot Welsh until such time as the schools raised up a generation whose heavenly pilgrimage should follow the broader and safer paths of English civilisation. From 1546 to 1660 about 108 separate Welsh books had been printed; from 1660 to 1730 the minimum reckoning is 545, no less than three quarters of which were published after 1700, the output of the SPCK and presses at Shrewsbury (from 1696), Trefedhyn (from 1718) and Carmarthen (from 1721).[49] Almost half were books translated from the English. The bulk of the output was devotional prose or verse, justifying Griffith Jones's assertion of the superior chastity of Welsh literature, and the bulk of both the religious and secular works (including the inevitable almanacs) was directed towards the family, and especially the head of the family. Thus what was on a small scale a Halle-style drive to provide literature for a neglected ethnic group was directed to a market in some ways resembling that of the churchless Protestants of the Habsburg lands. The Welsh *paterfamilias* was not churchless, though the Welsh church was both impoverished and ill-organised, but, as the head of a natural community 44 per cent of whose members were supposed in 1695 to be under sixteen, had a prospectively priestly position of great significance. In 1809 Jabez Bunting received a letter from the Durham coalfield describing how the Methodist revival there was bringing in new members '*per stirpes* and not merely *per capita*', and it was the special character of the Welsh revival to do this on a large scale. The revival began by strengthening the centrifugal forces in Welsh life by adding public worship to the functions of the farm kitchen, and later contributed to the curious distribution of Welsh rural chapels. What appears gaunt isolation was often the intersection of routes linking the farms and avoiding the nuclear village with its church at the parish centre.[50]

---

[49] *Ibid.* 35.
[50] MCA MS John Ward to Jabez Bunting, 27 March 1809; A. D. Rees, *Life in a Welsh Countryside* (Cardiff, 1968) 102–6.

This barrage of propaganda, loyally supported by the London Welsh, the main beneficiaries of the union with England, included plenty of anti-Catholic polemic, but was directed mainly against the magic, astrology and witchcraft which constituted much of the popular *mores*. There was little to choose here between the establishment and the later evangelical dissent; each wished to blot out this side of Welsh life. The Welsh spirit, however, like that of Gaelic Scotland, which was much worse catered for, was sympathetic to the great quantity of religious verse which was poured into the country, to the not unmixed approval of the evangelicals. The Methodist Robert Jones of Rhoslan complained that in pre-revival Wales a religious verse or carol was reckoned to be the equal of a sermon; but verse was much used by the Carmarthenshire revivalists in particular, and in the work of William Williams of Pantycelyn contributed substantially to the fund of Welsh culture.[51]

### DANIEL ROWLAND AND HOWEL HARRIS

The limitations to what the old dissent could contribute to the origins of revival are instructive. Proportionally to the population as a whole, the Welsh dissenters were not much weaker than the English; but in absolute numbers they were very thin on the ground, and were hardly represented at all in North-East Wales. Their progress depended chiefly on gentleman-preachers with private resources, and was made principally on the fringes of the country, and in the main areas of dissenting strength in South and South-West Wales. It was achieved by itinerant preaching, by the gathering of new churches on a sort of circuit system, and, like the New Divinity parishes in later New England, by the training of a succession of capable preachers. Thus Stephen Hughes, the 'apostle of Carmarthenshire' (1622–88), kept eight Independent churches under his own charge, encouraged his followers to stick to the Welsh language, and trained half a dozen or more preachers. Henry Maurice, an Independent who worked into Brecknock from the borders, showed how the Puritan heritage was being adapted to the religious affections, revealing 'a wonderful skill in unravelling the very thoughts and inward workings of men's hearts, and was very particular and convincing as well as affectionate in his applications to

[51] On this: D. Ll. Morgan, *The Great Awakening in Wales* (London, 1988; original Welsh edn Llandyssul, 1981).

the consciences of his hearers'. Philip Pugh (1679–1760), an Independent of Cilgwyn, gathered five churches in the region of the upper Aeron and Teifi, and by 1715 was reckoned to have 1,000 hearers. But Pugh attained a much greater impact indirectly, by persuading Daniel Rowland, curate of Llangeitho in the established church, to change his style of preaching. Rowland (1713–90) had been converted under Griffith Jones in 1735, and powerfully mastered his mentor's denunciatory method. Pugh's counsel was:[52]

Preach the gospel to the people, dear Sir, and apply the Balm of Gilead, the blood of Christ, to their spiritual wounds ... If you go on preaching the law in this manner, you will kill half the people in the country, for you thunder out the curses of the law, and preach in such a terrific manner, that no one can stand before you.

This advice, well taken, marked one beginning, perhaps the beginning of the Welsh revival, though Howel Harris was loath to admit it.

Harris was a strange character who repeatedly wanted ordination and was refused it, and yet refused openings for ordination when they came his way. The issue was not fundamentally that the bishops were on the watch for devices which would stop the itinerant preaching he had begun after his conversion in 1735, for he was equally antipathetic to the discipline of Wesley's itinerancy. 'I said it could not be, my work was not theirs, and I could not slavishly be in subjection to men'; 'I could never call myself a preacher, but an exhorter, my gifts being so.' Again it was not that as a Calvinist he disliked Wesley: 'I saw him an honest spirit attacking the unbelief, pride, and sleep of the nation; and I loved him in that light though I differed in some things.' Nor was it that as a Welshman Harris disliked English interloping, still less that any propensity to dissent turned him against any renewal of the effort of the establishment in Wales. For whereas Rowland was only one stage removed from the monoglot Welsh, Harris wrote voluminously almost exclusively in English; he was everlastingly on visits to London, taking part in the religious societies and preaching, and not only bringing into Wales the whole English evangelical circus as it took shape, but helping to make Whitefield the leader of Welsh Methodism. Again no man strove harder than Harris to keep the Welsh Methodist movement within the pale of the establishment. Harris was indeed an enthusiast,

[52] E. Evans, *Daniel Rowland and the Great Evangelical Awakening in Wales* (Edinburgh, 1985) 43.

convinced of his calling to the New Testament office of exhorter, enjoying nothing better than the 'power' of exhortation which was the evidence of Spirit-possession.[53]

Like Rowland, Harris had to change, and did so under the combined effect of personal contacts, practical experience and reading. At first he had the simple exhorter's object ' to rouse all to fly from the wrath' of God; by 1744 his 'message [was] chiefly to preach Christ's Kingly Office, and deliverance to the captives and weak'. 'See I have had every truth gradually [he wrote in 1761]... first the thundering, then the spirituality of the Law... then of Christ doctrinally... then inviting to Christ... forgiveness of sins and assurance... a year after, holiness and pressing to perfection.' Enlargement of spirit was the offspring of breadth of vision. Harris knew what was happening in Central Europe. His settlement at Trevecca derived from Halle, his knowledge of the place coming not only from Griffith Jones, but from Anton Wilhelm Böhme, and Böhme's biographer, Jacobi. He was in touch with Zinzendorf by letter in 1738, and met him on his first visit to London the following year.[54] He thought well of the Moravians, and his biography was written by the Moravian LaTrobe. He read Jonathan Edward's *Surprising Work of God* at a very early stage, and perceived its relevance to Wales: 'Sure the time here now is like New England'; and weighed up Whitefield's fantasy that Cotton Mather had prophesied his birth, 'that in 1714 [Whitefield's year of birth] one should be born that should go like a seraph to set New England in a flame'. Certainly as one who had to deputise for Whitefield in London while he was in America, Harris could not fail to be apprised of the revival in New England. Whitefield put Harris in touch with the Scottish revival circle, with McCulloch of Cambuslang, and most importantly James Erskine, Lord Grange, secretary to the prince of Wales, who seemed to be on intimate terms with everyone (except, as we shall see, his own wife). Harris was one of the channels through which the Welsh Methodists resolved to produce Welsh translations of the works of the Erskine brothers, Scottish reformers and distant cousins of James.[55] And Harris had the same strong country view of English politics in

[53] G. F. Nuttall, *Howel Harris. The Last Enthusiast* (Cardiff, 1965) 13; T. J. Beynon, *Howell Harris, Reformer and Soldier (1714–1773)* (Caernarvon, 1958) 184; T. Beynon, *Howell Harris's Visits to London* (Aberystwyth, 1960).

[54] Nuttall, *Howel Harris* 14, 23–27; Herrnhut MSS R13 A 4 11b.

[55] Evans, *Rowland* 69 (cf. *Selected Trevecca Letters* 104), 247–54; Beynon, *Harris's Visits to London* 48.

the mid-forties as the other evangelicals. He was indeed on the way to joining that 'Grand Table' of opposition politicians which in the later forties gathered round Lady Huntingdon and the outskirts of Leicester House, and entertained pipe-dreams of having Whitefield made a bishop.[56]

Like some other men of irenical views, Harris could be an irascible curmudgeon, and the fuse to his powder was unnecessarily shortened by a lack of worldly wisdom and by a failure to pace himself as effectively as did Wesley. Nevertheless his breadth and generosity of vision were never in question, and down in Wales he formed an effective combination with Rowland, whom he met only a couple of years after they had both been converted. Whitefield helped to supply organisation in the Calvinistic Methodist Association, and, when he was present, a leadership they could both accept. They quickly secured the conversion of other lads like themselves, Howel Davies, Williams Pantycelyn, John Thomas and others, and obtained a notable response. They had their full share of the problems which beset the Methodist movement as a whole. Before long the Welsh Calvinistic Methodists cut their ties with their English brethren and went their own way. The protest against assimilation was not to be denied. Moreover the doctrinal differences between Calvinist and Arminian divided the religious societies even more sharply than the leadership; so Wesley, who was prepared to preach and travel in Wales, but not to organise societies against those who invited him, was left with a tiny handful of exclusively English-speaking and anti-Calvinist societies. The friends of Harris and Rowland also secured a larger response than they could organise even by liberally using exhorters, and many converts drifted off to the dissenters because, notwithstanding the assurances of the leadership, they could not find an evangelical message in the Church. But by the time that Rowland and his friends parted company from Harris on doctrinal and personal issues in 1750 there were 433 religious societies in Wales and the borders. Daniel Rowland must now hold this flock together until a fresh tide of revival set in with the war crisis in 1762, and Harris could be brought back into the work.

Even in 1750 many of the features of Welsh religious life as it emerged in the early nineteenth century were apparent. The

---

[56] G. F. Nuttall, 'Howel Harris and "The Grand Table"', *JEH* 39 (1988) 531–44; H. D. Rack, 'Religious Societies and the Origins of Methodism', *JEH* 38 (1987) 591–2. Harris had hopes of the prince of Wales even in 1742. Beynon, *Harris, Reformer & Soldier* 11.

Calvinistic Methodist movement was much the largest of the religious movements of principality. The Welsh sees could no more absorb this movement than the English sees could absorb any variety of English Methodism. The Calvinistic Methodists continued, however, to bear clear signs of their origins in the establishment: an allegiance to the Thirty-Nine Articles, men in holy orders at the helm, the enduring contempt of the more fastidious dissenters for their 'eagerness of zeal, devoid of the light of knowledge...which gained them...the reputation of wonderful men'. And these gifts, or failings, were being exported by their exhorters deep into England.[57]

The movement bore the clear marks of the tribal structure of Welsh society. Pembrokeshire was the stamping-ground of Howel Davies, an unbeneficed clergyman, but, with its substantial English population, it also attracted Wesley, Whitefield and the Moravians. Cardiganshire and Carmarthenshire were pre-eminently the territories of Daniel Rowland and William Williams of Pantycelyn. Radnorshire, Montgomeryshire and Brecknock were the original mission fields of Howel Harris, the work in the last proving more permanent than the others because the Welsh language was more deeply rooted there. Glamorgan and Monmouth were the most densely populated, and felt the power of the revival more deeply than anywhere except Carmarthenshire. This was partly because English penetration encouraged the attention of Wesley and Whitefield, and partly because the relatively numerous dissenters of that area were unusually receptive to the Methodist appeal. Thus accommodation was as much as feature of the revival as transformation.

## PROBLEMS OF RELIGIOUS ESTABLISHMENT IN SCOTLAND

The history of the Church of Scotland and those related to it by way of opposition and secession has rarely been more ambiguous than in the first half of the eighteenth century. Both Kirk and seceders retained a proud sense of belonging to an international fellowship extending from Lithuania to New England,[58] in which, in a practical sense, all were members one of another. As recently as the Restoration Scots Presbyterian ministers had come under the hammer and had

[57] D. Bogue and J. Bennett, *History of the Dissenters* (2 vols. 2nd edn London, 1833) II:46; MCH Box A3 Parcel Y. Extracts from John Cennick's diary, 1742.
[58] Wodrow, *Analecta or Materials for a History of Remarkable Providences* (4 vols. Edinburgh, 1842–3) III:327–8; H. Davidson, *Letters to Christian Friends* (Edinburgh, 1811) 119–20. Cf. 126–8.

themselves been indebted to the fellowship; driven from what was to become the key revival parish of Cambuslang, Robert Fleming (for example) became a 'shining light' at Rotterdam, the ministers and elders of the Scottish church there being prominent among the subscribers to his apocalyptic speculations. Scotland had its high Orthodoxy in the Westminster Confession; but the Scots Orthodox were less parochial, in both senses of the word, than Orthodox parties elsewhere. For although the Kirk was among the vested interests on which the sun shone at the Revolution, and although it received every conceivable guarantee in the Union of 1707, it still had a tremendous struggle to add substance to its constitutional privilege. There were episcopal ministers to get out of parishes, the power of the chiefs of Catholic clans, and the chivalry and Gaelic culture which propped them up, to break, the patronage question to sort out. A variety of policies were available here, all of which must take into account the restlessness of armed Jacobitism in the Highlands, and, after the Union, the long arm of the London government. Amongst these policies was one, discounted in other European Orthodox establishments, afforded by the vivid and living memory of mass revival in the seventeenth century in Ulster and in parishes in the West of Scotland, some of them deeply affected by Irish exiles. It was universal for Orthodox establishment men in the early eighteenth century to bewail the degeneracy of the times; it was, I think, unique for Scots Orthodox like Wodrow to measure the decline by the falling off of communion conversions and the disappearance of the extraordinary scenes which gave rise to them.[59]

If ministers did not secure the desired result it might be because they were becoming addicted to the early Enlightenment (which could be assumed to be an English fashion) or that they were the wrong kind of ministers, appointed under the Patronage Act of 1712, an act passed by a Tory government in England in defiance of the promises of ecclesiastical autonomy made at the Union, and of every shade of anti-patronage opinion in Scotland.[60] There was not much democracy about the two viewpoints from which patronage was most strenuously contested in the first half of the eighteenth century. One view was that the minister should be selected by male heads of

---

[59] *Correspondence of the Rev. Robert Wodrow* ed. Thomas McCrie (3 vols. Edinburgh, 1842–3) 1:55–8.
[60] R. Sher & A. Murdoch, 'Patronage and Party in the Church of Scotland', in *Church, Politics and Society:Scotland, 1408–1929* ed. N. Macdougall (Edinburgh, 1983) 197–220.

households in the congregation, that 'selection was a function of election'. This view could find support in John Knox, was upheld by Ebenezer Erskine and the first seceders of the thirties, and cherished by innumerable devout Presbyterians; it was never operated in the church and went back to Covenanting congregations meeting outside the church. It found favour with the supporters of the 'Praying Societies' which bridged the gap between the Covenanters and the eighteenth century, and to Scots who viewed the decline of the Kirk as a function of English assimilation the Covenanting connexion enhanced the attractiveness of this protest against patronage. Hence when revival began, much heartache was created by the fact that the Erskine brothers went further than anyone in seeking to mobilise English support for their cause. There was a second type of opposition to patronage based on the view that ministers should be selected by the presbytery and kirk session, with heads of households restricted to a qualified veto. This view went back to Melville, but it was Orthodox in the sense that it embodied the exalted clericalism of the Westminster Confession and associated documents. It was particularly important after the middle of the eighteenth century, and afforded an outlet for the kind of high-church sentiment rampant in the Lower House of the Convocation of the Church of England while that unruly body was permitted to do business. Meanwhile patronage was overwhelmingly exercised by the crown, nobility, and baronets and gentlemen, each presenting to almost one third of the livings; it was perfectly plain both that crown and aristocratic patronage were among the resources exploited by Walpole to create a following for English political purposes, and that the defenders of the system were most aggressive when they thought they had the sympathy of the English government. Mercifully for the Kirk the threefold agony of determining how to improve, how to be Scots, and how to be Presbyterian, which led to the growth of Presbyterian dissent on a substantial scale, was altogether absent in the Highlands, where the Kirk itself was an agent of assimilation in the interests of Lowland religion and the English Bible.

### REVIVAL IN (I) THE HIGHLANDS

The problem tackled by the Kirk in the Highlands was more acute than that which confronted the SPCK in Wales. The separateness of a primitive society was guarded by a language with little prose literature. Many parishes were at first in the hands of episcopalians, and the allegiance of the upper classes was episcopalian where it was not Roman Catholic. These confessional differences were an element in persistent Jacobite rebellion which threatened not only the Kirk but the international confessional balance. The work of the Kirk was independent of the economic changes which were transforming Highland life; but to the average Highlander both looked like Whig contrivances, and newly arrived Presbyterian ministers were often rabbled like the later Methodists south of the border. It took till 1730 before they could gain access to the lands lately dominated by the Seaforth family. In the Highlands, however, there was no doubt as to the identity of the enemy, and the Kirk sharpened his definition. By establishing Sabbath discipline it created a public benchmark distinguishing the loyal from the disloyal, and by using the preaching, in the North German Reformed manner, to address the regenerate and the unregenerate separately, it created another of potentially great importance. The General Assembly treated the area north of the Tay as a mission area, and reinforced the efforts of ministers, on the one side by catechists, and, on the other, by schools which, though bad, were good enough to produce children who could give current translation from the English Bible into spoken Gaelic. In an age when ministers were often not literate in Gaelic, this artificial exercise was indispensable to Highland worship; but it drove home the need for a more effective penetration of Highland society.

The means for doing this were developed in part of the Highland with special assets and special problems. Sutherland and Easter Ross preserved memories of the Covenanting tradition and of recruiting for the Protestant crusades of Gustavus Adolphus. In the former, the head of the clan MacKay, General Hugh MacKay, embodied a piety of the Dutch evangelical type. Ross was the scene of the bitterest post-Revolution struggles between episcopacy and Presbyterianism. In 1724 the Presbytery of Tain appointed meetings for prayer and fasting in three of their parishes, and, at the same time, the people of Nigg, led by the 'elders and serious people', did the same. The Nigg meetings grew more numerous and more intense over the next fifteen years. Then, in 1730, John Balfour became minister of the parish and began systematically to develop the eldership. He formed a fellowship meeting of his elders and a few others which gave an impulse to the other meetings, enabled the elders, 'the Men', to acquire a real expertise in prayer, exposition of the scriptures and experimental religion. Moreover, 'the Men' came to apply the public benchmarks by which Highland society was distinguished. On the Fridays of communion seasons, when people flocked in from all parts, fellowship meetings were held in which 'the Men' resolved cases of conscience and determined who might communicate and who might not. This situation was clearly open to abuse, and in 1737 the Synod of Caithness and Sutherland attempted to suppress it, only to be required by the General Assembly, after a twenty-one-year conflict, to give way. 'The Men' had won a resounding victory over the clergy. More importantly they had discovered how to plant Presbyterianism within the Gaelic community, and to sustain its distinguishing features, the Sabbath, family worship and the rest.

Having developed his own version of Spener's prescription for checking Lutheran decline, Balfour found that it issued in deep and genuine revival. This had the usual contagious effect and from 1739 onwards influenced a series of neighbouring parishes. Moreover the revival among the Ross-shire 'Fathers' provided the power and set the standard for the evangelical conquest of the Highlands as nothing else could have done. The Highlands of Scotland were won for the Kirk as the highlands of Wales were lost to the Church. And the pioneers understood themselves as part of an international revival fellowship, what Balfour called 'the Communion of Saints upon Earth'. They took in the international journalism of the Awakening, sent out David Brainerd as missionary to the Red Indians, and had an impact on the revival in the Netherlands. The revival in the Highlands differed in two important respects from that in New England. It was free from the psychological abnormalities which accompanied that outbreak; and it was not a convulsive and short-lived affair. Like the English revival it lasted well into the next century, and indeed responded to English influences. It had also the usual Reformed characteristic of being in general managed by the ministry, though 'the Men' had given early warning of how truculent they were to become in the nineteenth century. But the ministry formed the piety of 'the Men', and through them, of the flock. The best of them had New Testament Greek and a substantial body of Reformed divinity at their elbow from Switzerland, the Netherlands and Puritan England; in 1729 the Presbytery of Gairloch resolved to discuss the main heads of doctrine in Latin. In most parts of the Protestant world revival offered some release from the niceties of confessional Orthodoxy, but in the Highlands it helped to root them in a popular milieu. In 1717 the Presbytery of Tain initiated proceedings against the modernising Professor Simson of Glasgow, and in due course 'the Men' kept their scruples alive in the flock long after the ministry had moved on to something else.[61]

### REVIVAL IN (2) THE LOWLANDS. WAS THE ASSOCIATE PRESBYTERY A FAILED REVIVAL?

Though the Highlands comprised one third of the population of the Scotland of that day, the dramatic events there could not decide the destinies of church and nation. In the strategically decisive Lowlands revival took another, less elemental shape, and almost took more than one shape. Here the patronage question was more important, and it became entangled with changing currents of thought and feeling. Early in the eighteenth century a group of ministers became attracted by an old book, Edward Fisher's *Marrow of Modern Divinity* (London, 1646), which was republished with a preface by James Hog of Carnock in 1718. The *Marrow* (in which Luther was cited twice as often as Calvin) found room for a tenderer piety than was then usual in Scotland and took seriously the missionary vocation of the church. But Hog and three of his colleagues were examined by a commission of the General Assembly, and in 1720 the book was savagely condemned by the Assembly itself. The contrast between the lax treatment of the rationalising Simson and the heresy hunt mounted against the *Marrow* men was very striking; it brought them Cameronian support, and turned the man who led the defence of the *Marrow*, Ebenezer Erskine, irreconcilably against the Assembly on a relatively moderate patronage question in 1732. He, his brother Ralph, and Thomas Mair seceded in 1733, and were everywhere welcomed by the Praying Societies. A new denomination was rapidly created, fifteen congregations in 1737, thirty-six in 1740, forty-five in 1746, ninety-nine in 1766, and more in Ireland and England.

Was this revival or was it not? Gilbert Tennent and the Philadelphia synod thought it at least worthy of 'their hearty approbation' and wrote to say so. John Muirhead, another revivalist in America, went further: 'Go on, blessed champions in the cause of God. Your trials are not greater than those of Zinzendorf, White-fiel[d], Tennant [sic], and the poor unworthy instrument that is now writing to you... sing for joy... to the blessed Lamb of God, who

---

[61] A. Stewart, *A late revival of Religion in... the Highlands...* (Edinburgh, 1800) 11, 14, 16. The Highland revival is memorably treated in J. MacInnes, *The Evangelical Movement in the Highlands of Scotland* (Aberdeen, 1951).

seems to have begun his millennium at this time in America.' From the beginning of the Welsh revival the works of Ralph and Ebenezer Erskine were translated into Welsh by Williams Pantycelyn and others, their definition of faith as 'an act of the heart or mind, whereby the soul under the influence of the Spirit, sweetly and irresistibly returns to God in Christ as its only centre of rest' being irresistible to the enthusiastic Welsh.[62] Wesley also wrote in 1739 to Ralph Erskine for advice on the strange psychic phenomena which accompanied his preaching in Bristol, clearly supposing him to be expert in revival matters; in return Erskine convinced Wesley that congregations had the right to choose their own ministers, and the two seemed on the way to establishing a useful occasional correspondence when the link was broken by the controversy surrounding George Whitefield.[63] This put not only personal relations but the Erskines' self-understanding to the touch.

Whitefield had begun correspondence with Ralph Erskine in March 1739, and had included his business manager William Seward in it. He seems to have approved the Erskines as field-preachers and as zealous men under the ban of a case-hardened church government like the Tennents in America and the Methodists at home. And he was exposed to a degree of flattery.

As... the Messrs. Erskines gave me the first invitation to Scotland, and hath been praying for me in the most public, explicit, I could almost say extravagant manner, for near two years last past, I was determined to give them the first offer of my poor ministrations.

However, both flatterer and flattered had reservations. Ralph Erskine's invitation was warm but ambivalent:

Come, if possible, dear Whitefield, come. There is no face on earth I would desire more earnestly to see. Yet, I would desire it *only* in a way that, I think, would tend most to the advancing of our Lord's kingdom, and the reformation work, among *our* hands. Such is the situation of affairs among us, that, unless you come with a design to meet and abide with us of 'The Associate Presbytery'... I would *dread* the consequence of your coming, lest it should seem equally to countenance our persecutors.

Whitefield replied to Ebenezer with complete candour:

---

[62] D. Fraser, *Life of Ralph Erskine* (Edinburgh, 1834) 281–3; Morgan, *Great Awakening in Wales* 158; Evans, *Rowland* 247–53.

[63] Wesley, *Works* xxv–xxvi *Letters* 1:680; ii: 16–17, 48, 92. John Cennick had no doubt that Erskine encouraged Wesley in his bad habit of reducing people to fits by thundering the law. *PWHS* 6(1908) 108.

This morning I received a kind letter from your brother Ralph, who thinks it best for me wholly to join the associate presbytery, if it should please God to send me into Scotland. This I cannot altogether come into. I come only as an occasional preacher, to preach the simple gospel to all that are willing to hear me, of whatever denomination.

To this Ebenezer replied with the most liberal interpretation his brother's letter would bear.[64] Whitefield, after triumphant progress in America, was naturally reluctant to forgo an opening in Scotland and admit that his view of the Erskines was mistaken; they wanted his assistance and persuaded themselves that his original taint of English birth might be purged by a gentle education in the delights of the Solemn League and Covenant. This was an unreasonable expectation of a man who was in Anglican orders, had pleaded against separation from the establishment at home, confessed lucidly to a vocation as a universal evangelist, and, though English, had the wit to understand that the system of religious compulsion embodied in the Covenant was unlikely to benefit a small body of dissenters. Moreover, Whitefield's public doctrine that 'nothing has render'd the Cross of Christ of less effect...than a supposition now current among us that most of what is contain'd in the gospel of Jesus Christ was design'd only for our Lord's first and immediate followers' was particularly unpalatable to men whose view of the Pastoral Office was based on the *Form of Church Government* (1645).

The result was almost instant disaster. Whitefield found himself before a meeting apparently bent on exercising Presbyterian discipline, control of which was lost by the Erskines to Cameronian hotheads to whom 'every pin of the tabernacle was precious'.[65] Whitefield went his way to great triumph under the aegis of the establishment, his passage eased by a torrent of abuse from the Associate Presbytery. An olive branch generously extended by the Englishman in 1742 was met by a fast in repentance for the revival at Cambuslang and 'the fond reception given to Mr George Whitefield'.

Whitefield was in a measure unfortunate in the moment of his arrival. Ralph Erskine had felt most like a revivalist when he had preached the Covenant, but he had not found a way of combining the constituency in the Kirk which sympathised with much that he said

---

[64] Fraser, *Ralph Erskine* 287; Whitefield, *Journals* 275, 244; Whitefield, *Letters* 1:304, 262, 268; Tyerman, *Whitefield* 1: 504–5; D. Fraser, *Life of Ebenezer Erskine* (Edinburgh, 1831) 425–6.
[65] Whitefield, *Works* 1:307–9; Fraser, *Ralph Erskine* 330–44.

with the quick way of beating up a party by rallying Cameronian irreconcilables out of their parishes. Originally the Erskines[66]

declared that they did not secede from the sound part [of the Kirk] which concurr'd not with, but opposed the defections complained of, but only separated from those as went along with these abuses. They were favoured by many of the serious people...Flushed with this success they separated more and invented more causes for it, and to find them searched back for near a century, and revived disputes long forgot and out of head; and, notwithstanding their solemn and public declaration that they did not seceed [*sic*] from the sound part of their Brn. still remaining in the communion of the church, they now openly separated from everyone who did not with them leave the church.

Whitefield arrived just as this point had been reached, to find, of course, that there was even less room for him than for non — separating ministers. There would in any case have been discomfort, since what he preached was a 'simple gospel', what in the early twentieth century would have been called 'the essence of Christianity', built, in his case, round the core of the New Birth, while the spirits now dominant in the Associate Presbytery took their stand on systematic scholastic Calvinism and a doctrine of the relations of church and state that went with it and was entirely incompatible with the Union of 1707. Ebenezer Erskine is said to have regretted 'the eagerness with which [the Covenant] was inculcated on the members of the Secession Church'.[67] Well he might, for in 1745 when the whole Protestant cause in Scotland was in jeopardy, and Ebenezer himself had raised a corps of 600 volunteers to face the foe, his followers began to debate the burgess oath which required an acknowledgement of 'the true religion professed within this realm', and in 1747 the Antiburghers brought the Burgher leaders to the bar of their synod and, when they failed to appear, deposed and excommunicated them, not excepting the Erskine brothers, the fathers of the secession.

## JACOBITISM AND THE REVIVAL IN SCOTLAND

In the end a movement which was almost a revival and might have been a revival contributed to revival in Scotland in three ways. The fact of secession increased the anxieties in the establishment; by turning in upon itself, the secession encouraged the search for a

[66] Herrnhut MSS R13 C4 fos. 13–14.        [67] Fraser, *Ebenezer Erskine* 436.

different way to combine for forces to which it appealed–a way actually discovered at Cambuslang; and there were fresh appeals to bring outside forces to bear in the shape not only of Whitefield and the Leicester House circle of alternative religion, but even of the Moravians. The key figure here was a distant cousin of the seceding Erskines, James Erskine, Lord Grange (1969–1754).[68] Even in that age no man was more equivocal than he. The younger brother of the earl of Mar, he was rapidly advanced under Queen Anne to lord justice clerk with a Scottish title on the strength, it was said, of his brother's vote for Sacheverell, but lost the office in the Hanoverian purge of 1714. A strict Presbyterian who in 1736 vehemently opposed the repeal of the statutes against witchcraft, he professed equally strict loyalty to the Hanoverian line. His elder brother, however, having failed to make his way with the court of George I, became the leading organizer and general of the Pretender in the rebellion of 1715, and then his secretary of state abroad, organising non-legitimist Jacobite propaganda in England. Grange stood aside from this adventure, but his relations to it remained a matter of conjecture.[69] The wives of both brothers were difficult. Mar's wife suffered occasional insanity, and Grange was thwarted in an attempt to carry her off to Scotland in 1731 by her sister, Lady Mary Wortley Montagu, armed with a warrant from the King's Bench. At the same time Grange's relations with his own wife reached a stormy climax. Violent, drunken and an occasional imbecile, she is said to have accused him of treason and stolen letters to prove it. At any rate in 1732, Grange celebrated her death, having in fact had her abducted by men in Lovat (Jacobite) tartan to confinement for many years in St Kilda, and later in Assynt and Skye where she truly died in 1745. The simplest explanation of these adventures is that both wives had access to secrets ruinous to the Erskine family.

Erskine certainly had public grievances against the order in the British state and Scottish church. He was one of those who contested the patronage question in the interest of the utmost liberty for ministers and presbyteries, and was so strongly against the patronage

---

[68] Grange's mother, the countess of Mar, was godmother to Ebenezer Erskine, while he himself was groomsman to Ralph. A. R. MacEwen, *The Erskines* (Edinburgh, 1900) 19.

[69] Recent scholars have no doubt about Erskine's 'sinister' manoeuvres to save the Jacobites from the full penalty of their failures (Bruce Lenman in *Britain in the Age of Walpole* ed. J. Black (London, 1984) 88). In 1745 Grange encouraged the Pretender's adventure, but condemned his arrival without an army. *The History of Parliament. The House of Commons 1715–54* ed. R. Sedgwick (3 vols. London, 1970) II: 14–17.

measure of 1731 which brought the Erskine brothers to secession as himself to be accused of causing schism in the church. When Walpole, whom he described as 'an insolent and rapacious minister',[70] passed a measure excluding Scottish judges from the Commons, Erskine resigned his judgeship, secured election for Stirlingshire, and became one of the principal advisers to the opposition peers. Appointment as secretary to the prince of Wales meant that Erskine had successfully made the transition to legitimate opposition, and he helped to whip in the Scottish members for the final defeat of Walpole. By the early forties he was engaged in this capacity building up the broad-bottomed Methodist coalition around the countess of Huntingdon, bringing in Howel Harris and the Wesleys[71] on a Catholic-Christianity and anti-bigotry platform. He was invited to Wesley's Bristol Conference in 1745, and actually attended the London Conference in 1748. He and Charles Wesley seemed able to reduce each other to happy tears at will; he helped to get John Nelson out of pressed service in the army by providing a substitute; Charles Wesley redeemed a lost daughter of his from deism and reconciled her with her father.[72] Once again Jacobitism was coming to the aid of revival.

But before any of these connexions had formed Erskine was in touch with the Moravians, first with their London pillar, James Hutton (in 1741), then with Spangenberg and Isaac Lelong, the Amsterdam Moravian whom Wesley visited on his way to Herrnhut, and in 1743 with Zinzendorf himself. A correspondence which began with offers of assistance to Moravian exhorters taken up by the press-gang turned speedily to an attempt to use the Moravians to capitalise the new situation in Scotland; in particular Erskine presented Zinzendorf with a huge analysis of the religious situation there which has lain unused at Herrnhut since Spangenberg saw it when writing his *Life* of the count.[73]This report is the best exposition of the outlook of a man who professed to have 'amused [himself] long with a variety of studies and projects' but now desired 'to be wholly taken up with the gospel and...the advancement of it'. The tragedy of Scotland, but not Scotland alone, was the 'bad and mischevious way that those who profess Christ have almost in all ages and places treated one

[70] 'Letters of Lord Grange' in *Miscellany of the Spalding Club* II (Aberdeen, 1846) 56.
[71] Wesley, *Works* XXVI *Letters* II:124, 128–36. In 1745 Erskine made it possible for Wesley to answer the *Craftsman*'s sceptical attacks on Methodism. *Ibid.* 146–7.
[72] C. Wesley, *Journal* (2 vols, London, 1849) I:364, 367, 389, 393, 451; II:73–4.
[73] *ZW* Series 2 V:1479–80; MCH Packet I Folder 7 (Letters of James Erskine); Herrnhut MSS R13 C 4 Corr. des ehemaligen Sekretairs des Pr. v. Wales. The report is in no. 6.

another...so flagrantly opposite to our blessed Lord's precept'. But even among the Scots, 'blessed be God, this bigotry is much abated, since Mr Whit[e]field's labours were so signally blessed among them, whereby they found to their sweet experience how eminently the Lord might be taken with an episcopalian of the Church of England'. By the same token the Scots might now waive their objections to Moravian bishops, while Moravian inter-confessionalism was just what the situation called for, and their stress upon receiving Christ into the heart by faith would endear them to those orthodox Presbyterians uncorrupted by the rationalising influence of government. Whitefield had brought the long dry time in Scottish religion to an end; now was the moment to strike. None of this resembles the strict Orthodoxy with which Erskine has usually been credited, but it made good sense as an attempt to shift the balance in the Scots church ahead of the shift in government to be expected when the accession of the prince brought the reversionary interest to power. This invitation tempted Zinzendorf to send an agent, but his preoccupations first with the American Germans, and then with the legal standing of his own flock diverted him from seizing the iron while it was hot. What achievement of Whitefield was it that thus brought Scotland into the strategy of Leicester House?

### CAMBUSLANG AND KILSYTH

In the short run the opponents of rationalising ways had the laugh upon their opponents. David Hume had no sooner pronounced that enthusiasm, Cameronianism, had gone soft and genteel than revival broke out powerfully, and was carefully weighed and measured by those who took part in it. 'To what purpose [crowed Alexander Webster] are we entertained with trembling Quakers, deluded Camizars, prophesying enthusiasts, fainting hypocrites, and short-lived convictions', when those now being converted were carefully recorded as not 'under the power of Satan and the dominion of their lust'.[74] Kirk o'Shotts was reproduced at Cambuslang, a parish which encapsulated the problems of the Scots establishment at large.

After the Toleration Act, the minister of the parish, Archibald Hamilton, refused to take the oaths, and the Perthshire catechist Addison itinerated through it, rousing the restless Covenanting

---

[74] *Hume on Religion* ed. R. Wollheim (London, 1949); A. Webster, *Divine Influence the True Spring of the Extraordinary Work at Cambuslang...* (Edinburgh, 1742) 33.

element with sermons on the blind man who came to Christ and cast away his garments. He 'began with the garment of the Union, that of toleration, that of the Oath of Abjuration'. This evoked a 'Protest and Testimony' to the kirk session from Hugh Cumin, inveighing against 'all defections contrary to the Word of God and our Covenant engagements'. Addison eventually turned Independent, but as late as 1739 Cumin was a trouble-making elder in the parish. When Hamilton died in 1723, it took the patron, the duke of Hamilton, a long time to replace him; by the time his nominee Thomas Findlater arrived, the Praying Societies had had ample time to stir up opposition, and troops had to be called in to keep the peace. In 1731 Findlater left for another parish pursued by unproven charges of misconduct. The duke now presented the kind of minister the parishioners wanted, William McCulloch, receiving his first parish at the age of forty. McCulloch was of strong Covenanting Galloway stock, the tradition which now presented him with his worst problems. In 1739 Cumin got up a faction in the kirk session against an apparently blameless elder, made it impossible for him to exercise his communion functions and took another stand on the Covenant. At this point the Seceders of the Associate Presbytery were condemned by the General Assembly, and joined by the firebrands of Cambuslang. Most of the kirk session were suspended.

If ever a parish needed the New Birth it was Cambuslang, and, much moved by the news of the revival in New England, McCulloch made regeneration his theme. McCulloch was more than a retailer of New England gossip; he was the editor of a Whitefieldite newspaper, reporting revival on the Atlantic rim, begun in Glasgow in December 1741, *The Weekly History*. This journal was a forerunner of James Robe's *Christian Monthly History* (1743) and Gillies's *Historical Collections*, which attempted to give a synoptic, even cosmic, view of the revival as a whole. This propaganda had a speedy response in Cambuslang. Ninety heads of families asked McCulloch to hold a weekly weeknight lecture. At the third meeting there were strange spiritual signs, and fifty people came for counsel. McCulloch began to preach daily, the crowds flocked in, the more remarkably in that he had 'but a weak voice, no violent action, and [was] far from endeavouring to stir up unreasonable passions'. High-pressure revival began in mid-February 1742 and it was not till mid-July that Whitefield, the greatest awakener of them all, now anathema to the seceders, arrived to try his hand. Whitefield's influence, however, had preceded him. When McCulloch began to record the results of the work, he found that many had heard Whitefield in Glasgow on his previous visit and had been impressed by his preaching of the New Birth. But the scenes after his arrival had no parallel in Scottish history. He began by preaching to 20,000 the day before communion. The sacrament was perforce celebrated in the fields, evoking nostalgic memories of the days of persecution. 'People [he noted] sat unwearied till two in the morning to hear sermons... [and in witting emulation of the Saviour in Luke 12:1] you could scarce walk a yard but you must tread upon some.' This sensation occasioned another; the kirk session decided to hold another communion the following month, and this time 30,000 people appeared. Whitefield and other evangelical ministers preached in turn; 3,000 received communion in tents. John Erskine, later the famous minister of the Old Greyfriars Church, Edinburgh, thought that events in New England and Scotland together were a prelude to the end-time, and could find no evidence for the Lockeian objection to the revival that [75] 'the faith of the new converts is not founded on the Word, but visible representations or imaginary ideas of an amiable object which the Devil suggests to them is Christ'. Whitefield took good care to report the news to America, and the newspapers run by his sympathisers were of course full of it. Events in Cambuslang had the usual contagious effect upon all the parishes within a dozen miles, and by means scarcely indirect on parishes at a distance, most notably James Robe's parish at Kilsyth.[76] Kilsyth, by contrast, was a parish in fair shape, where Robe had organised a generation before an elaborate system of Praying Societies. It was Robe's impression that the heart had been taken out of the enterprise by a fever epidemic at the turn of the years 1731–2 which carried off many of his best leaders. But at the crucial moment the question whether the parish should hold a second communion, Cambuslang style, was referred to the Praying Societies; the evangelical clergy gathered to assist and the floodgates opened.

Kilsyth in its turn influenced other local parishes, and also Muthill in southern Perthshire, where the trouble had been not Cameronianism but violent episcopalianism. Contact was made with the North-East. John Sutherland, minister of Golspie, visited Cambuslang,

---

[75] *Ibid.* 15; J. Erskine, *The Signs of the Times Considered* (Edinburgh, 1742) iii.
[76] On Cambuslang: A. Fawcett, *The Cambuslang Revival* (London, 1971). James Robe's account of Kilsyth was recently republished as *When the Wind Blows* (Glasgow, 1985).

Kilsyth and Muthill in 1743, and the news he brought back
stimulated revival in his own parish. John Willison, the respected
minister of Dundee, who had long suspected that 'Satan [was]
carrying on a deep and subtile plot for shaking our covenanted
Reformation', saw in the revival the Christian balm of Gilead,. the
Old Testament type of the blood of Christ shed for the healing of
diseased souls, in gospel seasons for which the harvest was the type.
When in 1742 this blessing was confirmed by a favourable turn in
politics he broke into memorably wretched verse:[77]

> In mercy, God preserves our crown,
>    In the reformed line,
> French schemes and projects he breaks down
>    When hell and Rome combine.
>    Hallelujah, Hallelujah,
>    Hallelujah, Amen.

We have seen that American conservatives were not backward in
putting the case against revival, their own or anyone else's, and in
bombarding the Reformed churches of Scotland and the Netherlands
with it. This proceeding was counterproductive, for Robe was
spurred to produce as circumstantial a report on the revival as
possible by proto-evangelicals in Holland anxious for ammunition to
use in return. Even England felt the tremor. The eccentric William
Darney, supposed to have been converted at Kilsyth, played a
notable roving part in the Lancashire–Yorkshire border country, was
instrumental in the conversion of Grimshaw of Haworth, dithered
between Methodism and Moravianism, and had his societies finally
taken over by the Wesleys. He was also distinguished by perhaps the
worst religious verse ever produced. The work of the Praying Societies
was transformed by agreements between Jonathan Edwards and the
Scots evangelicals into the Concert of Prayer for the revival of
religion and the extension of God's kingdom upon earth. In the long
run this system caught on in England, especially in the South
Midland country of evangelical dissent, and was developed into
regular prayer for overseas missions. In the changed circumstances of
forty years later, this gave rise to the Baptist Missionary Society and
a reverse impulse into Scotland in the cause of foreign missions.

Yet in Scotland the convulsive excitements of the summer of 1742
did not herald the glories of the last days. The evangelical party

[77] J. Willison, *Whole Works* (Aberdeen, 1769) iii (cf preface dated 1727), 'Hymns of The Love
and Sufferings of Christ' no. 89; J. Willison, *The Balm of Gilead* (Glasgow, 1765) 4–5.

remained a minority in the Kirk, and could neither prevent a steady increase in secessions nor dim the lustre of the Scottish Enlightenment. The patronage question remained painfully divisive, and the next vacancies in the parishes of Cambuslang, Kilsyth and Nigg alike were the signal for dreadful conflicts. Without the elemental simplicities of the struggle in the Highlands, the Lowland church could neither sublimate its policy disagreements in revival, nor sustain revival itself. A valuable check to secession, the revival movement forfeited the freedom of enterprise which secession might have given. Like the revival in New England to which it was so closely linked, the revival in the Lowlands bloomed but for a day. And in so far as the Lowland revival succeeded in a milieu distracted by fear of assimilation, it assimilated its adherents into a broad fellowship not of confessional solidarity, but of unconfessional and international revival. Ralph and James Erskine had both cast a fly over Wesley, so too did James Robe.[78] His arrival in 1751 brought with it not only red-blooded Arminianism, but a movement which had no obvious place in the Scots establishment or the world of indigenous religious societies; it could hardly develop except into a form of non-Presbyterian dissent. On this point the Associate Presbytery spoke more truly than they knew.

THE METHODIST MOVEMENT AND THE RELIGIOUS SOCIETIES

One of Howel Harris's older biographers justly remarks that 'despite their doctrinal differences Harris kept in touch with the two Wesleys, and he attended many of their Conferences; he always endeavoured to heal the breach between them and Whitefield. Harris's role was that of a peacemaker... This, perhaps, was his greatest contribution to British Methodism. '[79] Once it is recognised that there was a 'British Methodism' which was a movement, not a denomination, and which never became a denomination, the contribution of the others towards keeping their sometimes sharp differences within bounds is easier to perceive. To say that the pioneering elites of establishment men in England, Wales and Scotland constituted interlocking directorates would be to affirm greater unity than there was; but the roles played in succession by Sir John Philipps, Harris, Whitefield and the Scots evangelicals, with their networks extending from Eastern Europe to

[78] J. Whitehead, *Life of John Wesley* (2 vols. London, 1793–6) II:195.
[79] R. Bennett, *The Early Life of Howell Harris* tr. G. M. Roberts (London, 1962) 178.

America and their common 'myth' about the regenerating work of Halle, have something of this character about them. Wesley, the most difficult of them, did not push competitively in Wales; and the fund of charity uniting him with Whitefield was never quite exhausted. Since all were establishment men there was no question of their organising a denomination; in Scotland they were episcopalian dissenters, but Whitefield perforce acted within the Scots establishment, and Wesley tried to do so, even seeking (it seems) some kind of recognition from the General Assembly.[80] Exactly as the revivalists in Germany and Switzerland tended to make for known cells of religious virtuosi, they began work mostly on the basis of the religious societies, especially in places like London, Bristol and Newcastle where anti-court sentiments were strong, and the clergy enjoyed nothing like the hold on opinion enjoyed by the ministers of, for example, Boston, Mass.

How, especially in London, the religious societies created a constituency ripe for the revivalists is made clear by William Holland in a MS 'Short Account of some few matters relating to the work of the Lord in England' (1745)[81] which is modelled on his own Anglican progress through them into Moravianism (which he left in 1747). Having long felt a lack of religious fellowship he was delighted in 1732 to be invited to join a London religious society.

There were thirty or forty of these societies in the City and suburbs of London, the members were all of the episcopal church... At the expense of these societies the sacrament was administered every Sunday morning at 6 o'clock in one or two churches where many members of the Society used to receive it... [in the mid-thirties they heard of the Oxford Methodists, and as they looked out for 'religiously disposed' persons to invite to their society, they invited the Rev. Mr Broughton of that company] Although most of the members of the Societies used to go to their own parish church in the morning on Sundays, yet in the afternoon they went to hear such ministers whom they thought preached most spiritual & lived also according to their doctrine. As many had gone to hear Dr. Gascoith [John Gaskarth M.A., vicar of All Hallows, Barking 1686–1732] who believed a millenium, so after his decease several used to go to hear Dr. Heylin & others, and hereby members of the different societys became more intimately acquainted with each other. It was by... going to hear Dr Heylin that I was lent to read Mr. Law's *Serious Call to a Devout and Holy Life*... it had a very great effect on me. [He spoke of it in his society, always carried a copy in his pocket, and it was

---

[80] It could hardly have been accidental that Wesley was in Edinburgh at the time of the General Assembly in four successive years, 1763–6, though he does not reveal what his hopes were.          [81] MCH MS Fetter Lane Diary 1.

in buying another volume of Law that he became acquainted with James Hutton, bookseller, later the leader of the Moravians.]

Mr Broughton … got Mr. Whitefield (who just before had been ordained a deacon) to come to London to officiate for him in those churches where he preached &c. Some of the societys soon became intimately acquainted with him and he came to our meetings & expounded the Scripture in a sweet manner and we could plainly see that the Lord had bestowed grace and gifts upon him, and we got him leave to preach in many of our parish churches … [Howel Harris occasioned a great stirring in Wales, and when Whitefield returned to London in 1737 he had spectacular success.] He had leave to preach two quarterly sermons before all the religious societys in and about London … This was a very blessed period for the Holy Ghost worked powerfully on many hearts and a great stirring and awakening appeared. This year Mr. Ingham preached in Yorkshire and a great stirring and awakening appeared there also. [In 1738 the Wesley brothers returned from Georgia and preached much in Law's style in the societies.] Some few members of the society who were particularly intimat[e] together used to meet at Br. Hutton's of a evening where Esq$^r$ Thorold would some times expound & pray for Mr. Whitefield, Ingham &c. and for the work of the Lord in different places … [In this group he first heard of the Moravians and loved them on account of their persecutions. When Böhler and Neisser arrived Wesley met them providentially and brought the former to the group which met at Hutton's.] Then and at other times Br. Boehler spoke as well as he could in English, but explained himself when particularly asked about any matter in Latin … Many found there was a short way to salvation … [Böhler continued to work with Wesley, and took Holland through the eighth chapter of Romans, which made him very uneasy.] In my search I providentially found Martin Luther's comment on the Epistle to the Galatians. I conveyed it immediately to Mr. C. Wesley who was then sick at Mr. Bray's [house] as a very precious treasure that I had found & we three sat down together & Mr. Westly began reading Luther's preface to his Comment and at the reading of these words, 'What have we then nothing to do? No, nothing, but only to accept of him who is made unto us of God Wisdom, righteousness, holiness & redemption.' There came such a power over me that I cannot well describe. My great burden fell off in an instant, my heart was so filled with peace & love that I burst into tears & I thought I saw our Saviour at some distance. Mr. Westly & Bray perceiving me so affected fell on their knees and prayed. When I went afterwards into the street I scarce could feel the ground I trod upon … Mr Charles Westly afterwards read Luther's Comment with blessings to several persons …

Both Mr Westlys preached up faith &c. as also did B$^r$ Oxlee. The Religious Societys were divided in their opinions. Some with Mr. Broughton asserted that forgiveness of sins and being born again was in Baptism and that if souls who had been baptised fell into sin afterwards that they were to be renewed again by repentance. [Various parties, including John Wesley, set out for Herrnhut, but Holland's business did not permit him to go. When Whitefield returned from America they explained Böhler's doctrine to him.] He was very cheerful & loving & ... began soon to preach again in the churches & his doctrine was now something more evangelical. The latter end of this year [1738] or the beginning of the next the Fetter Lane Society having a Watchnight (Mʳ Whitefield, Westly, Ingham & I think Hall being present) a sudden effusion of the Holy Spirit was said to be experienced by many. [Preaching now began on a much bigger scale in the country, and the Wesleys and Whitefield created many societies elsewhere.] This summer [1739] some of the Fetter Lane Society thinking they had a call from the Lord went to Moorfields to preach, it being holiday time ... when all the ridiculous sports and pastimes were exhibiting, but the mob gathered about them & soon put them to silence ... [After Wesley's separation the Fetter Lane Society became a Moravian congregation and down to 1745 almost all the members were members of the Church of England and about half had been members of religious societies.]

Here vividly depicted in one man's experience was a religious pilgrimage diverted from the Church of England (temporarily) into Moravianism by a liberating conversion experience without any sense of institutional discontinuity; the way the religious societies were becoming a consolidated market even before Whitefield speeded the process up; the way they provided a springboard for revival and a model for religious organisation elsewhere; and a forcible indication of the fact that in London there was no possibility that religious societies would generate a revival on the community basis after which the New England fathers hankered. Finally Holland's narrative shows how the defence of the Protestant cause enabled other things to slip into a movement chiefly led and manned by disaffected Anglicans. A little must be said about the place of the Moravians and dissenters in the early Methodist movement.

### MORAVIAN DIPLOMACY

The Moravian presence in England originally owed everything to the diplomatic necessities and ambitions of Zinzendorf himself.[82] The count's first concern was to establish a foothold at court and here he followed the route taken by the Halle party, corresponding with the countess of Schaumburg-Lippe. In 1728 he sent a party of three with the Philadelphian object of seeking out the children of God and informing them of the movement of the spirit in Herrnhut. This time

---

[82]  For the following: Wauer, *Die Anfänge der Brüderkirche in England*: C. J. Podmore, 'The Fetter Lane Society, 1738', *PWHS* 46 (1988) 125–53.

the hope was to make a beginning with the University of Oxford like that which had been successfully made in Jena; indeed the party came armed with a recommendation from Buddeus to Ziegenhagen and with Latin translations of their other testimonials made by his students. But they were also to visit the SPCK, and the countess of Schaumburg-Lippe was requested to present them to the queen. When Spangenberg came in 1734–5 and when Zinzendorf came in person in 1737 the chief business was to negotiate with the Georgia Trustees about the settlements in America, and when in the same year the count assisted Ochsen (or Oxe), an impoverished Swedish baron brought up in Silesia, to recoup his fortunes here, the list of contacts he gave him reflected his own negotiations. They fell into four main groups: the court (the prince of Wales, the duchess of Kendal, Ziegenhagen); the SPCK–Georgia Trustees connexion (SPCK, Oglethorpe, Vernon, Newman, Albemarle, governor of Virginia); useful businessmen (John Furly, banker and Francis Weinantz, the naturalised Danzig merchant at whose home Wesley met the Moravian deputation of 1738); and long shots like Isaac Watts, the dissenter, whom he had consulted on the existence of the church of Christ in England before the Reformation, and Sir Robert Walpole. But the count also came to negotiate with the primate, Potter, about Moravian orders and his own intention to enter the episcopacy. This ended successfully with Potter's acknowledging the validity of the Moravian line and the soundness of their doctrine, and raising no objection to Moravian clergy officiating in the colonies. Henceforth Zinzendorf was in frequent touch with English bishops (especially Thomas Wilson of Sodor and Man, who eventually accepted the presidency of an English Tropus), with important clergy in the country like the Oxford circle, Dr Legh of Halifax, and a few dissenters like Watts and Doddridge.[83]

The mission of Böhler, Schulius, Neisser and Richter, who arrived in February 1738, was of a similar diplomatic kind. The Georgia Trustees and Dr Bray's Associates had invited Zinzendorf to supply two catechists to instruct the negroes of Purysburg in Christianity; to this Böhler and Schulius were appointed, with Neisser to accompany them to visit the Moravians in Georgia. Richter was to visit a minuscule German society founded in London. Meanwhile Böhler was to resume the unfinished work of 1728 and make contact with

[83] Herrnhut MSS R13 A 18 no. 14; R20 C 4 no. 62; R13 A 11 no. 1; R13 A 14 (55 items).

Oxford, the link man to be John Wesley. That the Fetter Lane Society would be formed as a virtual Moravian society from the beginning, and that through it the Moravians would be drawn into the world of English revival was entirely unexpected; but, at least in retrospect, it may be regarded as always a possibility. For the Moravians were where they were in England because of the assistance of the political milieu out of which that revival had sprung. The life of faith and the quick method of conversion as Moravians understood them met English needs, but were made more readily acceptable by the quarter from which they came.

And thus things continued for more than a decade. Zinzendorf pursued largely diplomatic interests. In 1747 the Moravians in America were exempted by parliament from the oath of allegiance on conscientious grounds; in 1749 they received legislative recognition as an ancient Protestant episcopal church,[84] and Zinzendorf seemed to have made the same profitable bargain with the British as with the Saxon and Prussian governments. The moving spirits were again Oglethorpe and the familiar Tory and Leicester House connexions with which Zinzendorf maintained his correspondence, even while speciously promising the Primate to stop Moravian poaching from the Church of England.[85] On the ground interchangeability continued to be the name of the game. Benjamin Ingham, the loyal Oxford Methodist (who married the sister-in-law of the countess of Huntingdon), handed over his societies in Yorkshire and Lancashire to the Moravians, and established them at Fulneck. No one became more incensed with the Moravians and with Zinzendorf personally[86] than Wesley, but he said he wished for union with them in 1744-5. Like all the rest of this old Jacobite network, the Moravians found good Protestant reasons for taking a public stand against the Pretender. Despite all the rubs Moravianism was sufficiently part of the Methodist movement for its headquarters to be appropriately housed in England from 1749 to 1755.[87]

---

[84] The papers of this negotiation are filed in Herrnhut MSS R13 A 24. See also Cossart's reports in R13 A20.

[85] Herrnhut MSS R13 A 15; R13 A 11 no. 10. The prince of Wales secured the support of the duke of Argyll and other Scots peers. Benham, *Hutton*, 215.

[86] With good reason, for Zinzendorf would advertise himself to the bishops as anti-Methodist (i.e. anti-Wesley) when he thought it would pay (Herrnhut MSS R13 A 12 no. 5) and astutely used the term 'Methodism' in Moravian synods as an opprobrious designation of a new legalism which embraced both Halle and Wesley. Benham, *Hutton* 112-13; Wesley, *Works* XXVI: *Letters* II: 172.

[87] Herrnhut MSS R13 A 10 no. 3: MS Neue Brüdergeschichte von J. Plitt v fos. 5, 57.

## THE ORIGINS OF EVANGELICAL DISSENT

Might dissenters also become Methodists? Apart from any other considerations, dissenting hostility to the political context of early Methodism made it quite certain that many would not; others would be deterred by the positions they had taken up in the course of that process of rebalancing the claims of orthodoxy, reason and life in which the whole Reformed world, English dissent included, had been engaged for a couple of generations. Even Isaac Watts could regard revival when it came as an Anglican gimmick, pray for it as though it had not come, and make mincemeat of Whitefield behind his back to Bishop Gibson. 'He has acknowledged to me in conversation, that it is such an impression upon his own mind that he knows it to be divine, though he cannot give me any convincing proof of it. I said many things to warn him of the danger of delusion...and told him plainly...I was not convinced of any extraordinary call he had to some parts of his conduct.'[88] Watts himself stood in the tradition lamented by the High Reformed Robert Wodrow as 'the Baxterian looseness', while Zinzendorf, having received various favours from Watts, dismissed him in a letter to Steinmetz as 'a Christian and a good man [who] lives in cosy comfort in the world', and 'a presbyterian, erroneous in doctrine, and English as well'. Watts had, indeed, produced *An Humble Attempt towards the Revival of Practical Religion among Christians* in 1731. His use of the word 'revival' here had much in common with the Hallesian sense of renewal and improvement, and opened the way to revival of the Whitefieldite stamp only through the usual interest of English moral philosophers in the passions, those God-given powers 'to excite the will to superior vigour and activity to avoid the evil and pursue the good. Upon this account the preacher must learn to address the passions in a proper manner.'[89]

Two different things had been happening among the dissenters. In the latter part of the seventeenth century notions of faith had changed in response to general changes in the intellectual atmosphere and styles of preaching had incorporated some of those changes in the worship of the Lower Rhine churches which Frelinghuysen had

---

[88] I. Watts, *Works* ed. G. Burder (6 vols. London, 1810–11) I:lxviii–lxix.
[89] Wodrow, *Correspondence* I:493; Herrnhut MSS R20 C 30a no. 23 (17 April 1746); Watts, *Works* III:25.

taken to New Jersey.[90] A comparison of Philip Henry (1631–96), one of the ejected ministers of 1662 with his more famous son, Matthew, will illustrate the point. Philip's view of faith was that of 'assent to what is spoken, as true, either from the evidence of the thing itself, or upon the account of the veracity of him that speaketh it'. This acceptance of propositions in effect on the authority of those who made them was a different thing from the personal trust implied in the New Birth. His son Matthew Henry depended heavily on Baxter, and his own Bible commentary was for generations valued by those who came to regard themselves as evangelicals, i.e. as continuing the middle way which Baxter had proposed between Arminianism and Calvinism. Baxter's middle way and his efforts in the cause of church union also compelled him to think what the essentials of Christianity were, and this pursuit of essence might also develop to two ways. It might be regarded rationally as Christianity with disputed doctrines omitted, and lead in the eighteenth century to demands for more generous subscriptions under the Toleration Act. Or it might be treated existentially as the evangelicals treated it when they saw the ground of Christian unity, the essence of Christianity, in the New Birth. Even in Matthew Henry the claims of reason were beginning to divert the Baxterian middle way, and a new concept of faith was becoming harder to hold in tandem with it. He found the heathenism of the villages round Chester at the end of the seventeenth century so oppressive that he established an itinerant ministry there. 'The vehemency of his affections both in prayer and preaching was such as, occasionally at least, to transport not himself only, but his auditory, to tears', and he was warned to go steady with small beer and sack when 'warmed with preaching'. He repudiated his father's deference to public authority: 'he would call no man *master*... He regarded implicit obedience to human dictates... as in direct hostility to the claims both of reason and revelation.' The pressure of progressive reason in Matthew Henry was evident less in the substance of his doctrine than in his style, which partook 'largely of the improvement of the times', and 'triumphed over the forced conceits and deformities' of his predecessors. Yet he exploited the techniques of his Lower Rhine predecessors in preaching that was 'pointed, discriminating and applicatory', i.e. addressed with the

[90] Doddridge's tutor was an advocate of the 'distinguishing and applicatory' style of preaching. A Boston edition of his sermon bound it up with Francke's *Letter to a Friend Concerning the Most Useful Way of Preaching*. J. Jennings, *Two Discourses* (Boston, 1740) 43.

maximum personal directness to different sections of his congregation.[91]

The middle or synthetic way became harder to hold as time proceeded. The hyper-Calvinists clung to sovereign grace with increased ferocity, and republished the works of Tobias Crisp. The men of reason found difficulties with the doctrine of the Trinity and could be passed off on both sides of the Atlantic as Arminians. The demands of 'life', for which Baxter had lavishly catered with practical theology, seemed to Watts to have led Richard Davis the High Calvinist evangelist of Northamptonshire of the 1690s[92] to breach of union and order, and Whitefield to stark fideism. The issue of principle in each case was made harder to solve by the constitutional status which the dissenters had securely achieved by the reign of George I. It was much easier to settle on the lees than to raise issues which might reopen the question of subscriptions under the Toleration Act. The effect of doing so was that the dissenting interest declined, and its ministers absconded to the greener pastures of the Church by the dozen. What changed Watts's view was the outbreak of revival in New England approved by many of his oldest friends and contacts there. It was he who got Jonathan Edwards's *Faithful Narrative* first published in London, and in his commendatory preface he maintained that Edwards's preaching embodied 'the common plain protestant doctrine of the Reformation, without stretching towards the antinomians on the one side, or the Arminians on the other', i.e. that Edwardsian revival actually was the Baxterian middle way.

Doddridge, the next in this succession, a universal man in terms of literary influence in the revival, held together a stronger impulse to Enlightenment and a more pronounced inclination to affective religion than Watts, at the expense of being himself regarded as disorderly, though both he and Watts had their doubts about the Wesleys.[93] But a man who in 1730 had reached the position that no one would do for dissenters but 'an evangelical, an experimental, a plain and an affectionate preacher', who became more evangelical

---

[91] M. Henry, *Life of Philip Henry* (London, 1698) 175; G. F. Nuttall, *Richard Baxter and Philip Doddridge* (London, 1952) 3; J. B. Williams, *Memoirs of... Matthew Henry* (London, 1828) 137–40, 114, 118, 181, 249, 125.

[92] For him: R. Tudor Jones, *Congregationalism in England* (London, 1962) 114–17; G. F. Nuttall, 'Northamptonshire and *The Modern Question*', *JTS* ns 16 (1965) 101–23.

[93] *Doddridge Correspondence* IV: 274, 277, 288, 290, 294–6; G. F. Nuttall, 'Methodism and the older Dissent', *URCHJ* 2 (1981) 272.

and Calvinist in the thirties and forties, had no difficulty in 1741 in holding 'a kind of council [of dissenting ministers]... concerning the methods to be taken for the revival of religion'. By this time he itinerated regularly around Northampton, and had long been on kindly terms with all the revivalists including Zinzendorf and Hutton.[94] Still more important, he seems to have deserted Walpole before the end, and to have pinned his faith to Frederick, Prince of Wales.[95] Doddridge, moreover, was intimately drawn into the web of the countess of Huntingdon. Impossible as it had seemed in the early thirties, Doddridge in the forties was a Methodist in the sense of an adherent of the movement of revival and reform.[96] And in this, though not typical of dissent as a whole, he stood for a growing number of others like the Gloucestershire minister Thomas Cole, who aided the young Whitefield and his converts, or Joseph Williams, the Kidderminster merchant who maintained a lively interior life, and stole off to commune with Charles Wesley. He found he 'could not fall in with their way of singing in the field, for they sung German tunes, keeping very quick time', but was greatly elevated by 'such evident marks of a lively fervent devotion [as] I was never witness to before'.[97]

## THE DECLINE OF THE METHODIST MOVEMENT

By 1750 the first great awakening in America was over, indeed, on a strict interpretation had been over for some years. By the same date the British Methodist coalition was in being, had overcome its worst hazards from mob violence, and had laid the foundations of some very durable constitutional mechanisms. Yet as a 'country' reform movement, somewhat in the Württemberger style, its course was almost run, undone by a combination of death, disaster and opposition. Doddridge died in 1751; much more importantly, so did Frederick, Prince of Wales, whose untimely end broke the normal cycle of British politics, and ensured that the revival movements would never be more than movements in the country. Had Wesley died in 1753 when he was seriously ill and wrote his own epitaph, most of the evangelical legends about the revival would never have

[94] *Doddridge Correspondence* IV: 38; *Calendar of Doddridge Corr.* no. 711; Herrnhut MSS R13 A 18 nos. 19–26.
[95] *Calendar of Doddridge Corr.* nos. 482, 492, 522, 1028, 1035, 1375, 1720.
[96] *Ibid.* nos. 953, 968, 1164, 1222, 1228, 1257, 1369, 1373, 1375–7, 1392; A. C. Clifford, 'Philip Doddridge and the Oxford Methodists', *PWHS* 42 (1979) 75–80.
[97] G. F. Nuttall, 'Charles Wesley in 1739', *PWHS* 42 (1980) 181–5.

been written. Nor were the chances of mortality the only problems of leadership which the Methodist movement encountered. Most public was the open breach between Howel Harris and Daniel Rowland; to some extent the breach simply re-emphasised the tribal nature of the Welsh revival, but for a dozen years it removed Harris from the fray, and with him the most powerful force keeping the revival within the pale of the establishment. Most disastrous was the financial crisis precipitated in the Moravian movement by the collapse of their Jewish financial correspondent in 1753, but prepared by years of borrowing too heavily on the Dutch market. The days of heroic enterprise and joyous abandon in the Moravian movement were over. Spangenberg wrested survival from the disaster, but did so by a strict system of intellectual and financial control which transformed the Brethren into *die Stille im Lande* and kept them for half a century at the grindstone of paying off Zinzendorf's debts.

Wesley too had made mistakes which came home to roost. Whatever their origin all the evangelical leaders had made anti-Jacobite demonstrations at the time of the 'Forty-Five, demonstrations which illustrate the fundamental inability of the Stuarts to cope with the Protestant convictions even of sympathisers. In this Wesley, whose personal safety and the freedom of whose preachers from the press-gangs were at stake, did no more than might be expected. But in 1747 in *A Word to a Freeholder* he urged his followers to prove their loyalty by voting for government candidates. This was more than the country party would stomach, and the peculiarly sour tone of the references to the Moravians in Wesley's Journal over the next three years in part reflects his chagrin at the fact that the Moravians were now much more able than he to secure favours from his old political friends. It was of course also true that the English of independent mind (like others) were coming to the end of their patience with Zinzendorf. Doddridge, pained by the loss of a pupil and part of a congregation and mortified at the extravagances of the 'time of sifting', denounced him from the pulpit, and as part of his personal balance sheet for 1749 'prepared...a Letter to Count Zinzendorf, *whose enormous errors and enthusiasm have filled the whole Protestant world with wonder and with horror*'. Whitefield had also had enough of Moravian sheep-stealing[98] even before he kicked them when they were down for financial impropriety in 1753.

The serious aspect of Wesley's rebuff to old friends was that, after

---

[98] *Calendar of Doddridge Correspondence* nos. 1163, 1239, 1612; *Doddridge Correspondence* v:488; Whitefield, *Works* II:214.

a reasonably friendly beginning, the bishops and other forces in possession in the Church were increasingly turning against the Methodist movement on much the same grounds as the Methodists were turning against the Moravians. Even in 1747 Zinzendorf had concluded. that 'we gain certainly' more 'when they [the bishops] attack' by resisting than by submitting. Bishop Gibson was being particularly stiff: 'I thought all churches had a right to make rules of discipline & administration for themselves; but that it was not fair to endeavour to introduce them into other churches, as we found Moravians doing.'[99] Wesley too was in the toils and was undergoing a change of view of episcopacy itself. The main fact was that with the defeat of the 'Forty-five and the collapse of the reversionary interest, authority in church and state had nothing to fear. The forces in possession in the Church did not have the sharp doctrinal profile of the Lutheran Orthodox, but in a characteristically Anglican *sotto voce* style they behaved in much the same way, pushing disagreements towards the schism they purported to deplore. Here Wesley had put himself in a cleft stick. He had created a non-denominational religious society, under a personal Anglican management by himself, so authoritarian that it could not possibly double as a church constitution. His preachers could see the writing on the wall, and many thought (not unnaturally) that if life in the Church was not to be available to them, life outside on the model of the dissenting ministry offered advantages which their present status did not. Charles Wesley made it all worse by organising vociferously on behalf of the Church, while insisting to his brother that the embarrassment was all of his making. 'I am told from Bristol, "You rule the preachers with a rod of iron: they complain of it all over England, etc., etc."'[100] By 1755 the game seemed to Wesley himself to be almost up: 'My conclusion (which I cannot give up) that it is lawful to continue in the Church stands, I know not how, almost without any premises that are able to bear its weight.'[101]

Unforeseeable circumstances came to his rescue. The Seven Years War broke out in 1756, the initial line-up of the powers creating the impression that the long-delayed day of reckoning between Catholic and Protestant had at last arrived, and evoking new revivals in both England and Wales. As early as 1758 he noted that 'controversy is

[99] MCH MS Gemeinhaus Diary 19 May 1747; Herrnhut MSS R13 A 12 no. 2. Cf. N. Sykes, *From Sheldon to Secker* (Cambridge, 1959) 139.
[100] F. Baker, *John Wesley and the Church of England* (London, 1970) 58–73, 146 ff. 160.
[101] Wesley, *Works* XXVI: Letters II:594.

now asleep, and we in a great measure live peaceably with all men, so that we are strangely at leisure to spend our whole time enforcing plain, practical, vital religion'.[102] The national rally induced by the war was crowned by a splendid series of victories engineered by Pitt. This began the process by which old irreconcilables came back to court, more came with the accession of George III, and still more (including Wesley himself) came back with the outbreak of colonial revolt in America and associated troubles in Ireland. In no part of Europe did politics look the same after the Seven Years War; and relations between Wesley's followers and Church authority remained easier, until the time, after his death, and in the shadow of bitter differences about the French revolution, they mostly decided to separate. And then the problems of authority which Wesley had kept at bay, instantly surfaced and divided the flock for almost a century.

Wesley was too convinced that nothing was properly done unless he did it himself to be a successful administrator; but, while also lacking Whitefield's gifts as a preacher, he did what he did with an intensity and regularity which was something new in the public life of the eighteenth century. And one thing at which he excelled was taking over and managing the work initiated by others. The small connexions created in the Midlands and North by John Bennet, David Taylor, William Darney and Benjamin Ingham were at various dates absorbed into his machine. Along with the work the Wesleys themselves opened in the Newcastle region, they got the Wesleys off the unadventurous London–Bristol axis, and, like the coalescence of the London religious societies at the very beginning, provided the impetus for expansion into every part of the Union. The outcome of the expansion, however, was not the original Methodist hope of reform of church and nation but a new kind of nonconformity, and one which ran the constant risk of becoming a holiness sect. The brilliant success of Methodism in America after the Revolution which derived from the opportunity it afforded the English to affirm their ethnic origin on an anti-Anglican basis was almost the inverse of the original intention. Whitefield's achievement was not the rope of sand imagined by later Wesleyan propagandists, though it did not include a bishopric for himself. Apart from playing an important role in short-lived revivals in America and Scotland, he brought about the conversion of many in England who subsequently appeared as Independent ministers, helping to transform the size, ethos and

---

[102] Wesley, *Works* (14 vols. London, 1872; repr. Grand Rapids, 1958) VIII: 225–6.

administrative assumptions of the community to which they gravitated. Lady Huntingdon's Connexion had to seek dissenting status in
order to secure the protection of the Toleration Act for its buildings,
but was rapidly surpassed in the nineteenth century by denominations of very humble social origin. In many respects the original
meaning of the word 'Methodist' was most accurately preserved in
Wales, where the Calvinistic Methodist Association also came much
nearer producing a national revival than any of their English
counterparts. But in the end this triumph of 'colonial' resistance
could be achieved only on an anti-Church basis, and even the
honourable name of CMA was ultimately dropped in favour of the
misleading designation of 'Presbyterian'. The historical propaganda
which dissolved the Methodist revival into the founding myths of a
number of accidentally created denominations has been unable to
preserve even the names, let alone the substance, of the original
movement.

# Conclusion

To assess the effects of the Great Awakening would require a further and much longer volume than the present attempt to explain its origins. Almost everywhere the revival began in resistance to a real or perceived threat of assimilation by the state in its modern shape, and the timetable of the revival, even in the West, was set by the timetable of the Protestant crisis in Eastern and Central Europe where that threat was most raw and crude. 'Awakened' religion had little direct success against the New Leviathan, but Joseph II's Toleration Patent (1781) was a monument to the lesson learned by the Leviathan to proceed, not generously, but more slowly and gently. Equally the religious agents of Habsburg policy had little success in recatholicising areas where Protestantism was forcibly broken; it took another and much later live religion, that of socialism, to succeed here.

As revival moved westwards its nature gradually changed. What had begun as an effort to revive the smouldering embers of religious faith in the absence of the ordinary ecclesiastical mechanisms, and had impressively demonstrated the real force of that Cinderella of Protestant doctrines, the priesthood of all believers, was increasingly taken over by the clergy as a device for solving intractable pastoral problems. Their enterprise was warranted by the evident power of revival in breaking the old paganism of the Baltic lands and the antique mixtures of old forms of Christianity with popular paganisms in the highlands of Wales, Scotland and Bern. America offered the general priesthood an apparently perfect second chance: widely scattered Protestant communities with thinly spread church organisations, little in the way of real persecution, and the one deeply rooted church establishment in New England burning its fingers early. The result was indeed that the characteristic American Protestant denominations became not Presbyterian or episcopal but Methodist and Baptist; for they were the most pragmatic in their approach and the most ready to employ lay agencies. But when, in the middle of the nineteenth century, the success of these methods enabled them to finance a professional ministry on a big scale, they altogether exceeded the bounds accepted by their spiritual forebears in Old England, became highly bureaucratic machines, and domesticated revival to an ecclesiastical routine. The bulk of the German immigrants in America were not there to escape priestly authority, and indeed sought to restore it as a proper constituent of their rebuilt corporate life abroad; the pastors they recruited, however, 'were increasingly drawn from Pietists who stood close to the world of revival, and drew on it to fan the dormant embers of old faith and practice.

In England the movement for reform of church and nation was so total a failure as to be entirely forgotten, and dissolved historiographically into the founding legends of new or reconstituted denominations. Those denominations never became characteristically English as they became characteristically American (or Welsh); but the Religious Census of 1851 found that while 520 of every thousand church attenders were Anglican (an unknown number with roots in the revival), 109 were Congregationalists, 81 Baptists, and 215 Methodists of one kind or another, a fair reward for the labour of taking religion to the people. This labour certainly postponed the day when church attendance in industrial England would sink to levels notorious in industrial Saxony, and bore fruit in a major missionary effort overseas.

The drawn battle, here reflected in institutional terms, was repeated at an intellectual level. Revival reinforced the Pietist struggle for survival against the onslaughts of the Orthodox parties, and ensured that theological pluralism would in future be the public condition of the Protestant churches. In the East, however, public authority was in general too strong to permit the rout of Orthodoxy, and at the end of the eighteenth century the xenophobia which was a usual ingredient of the new religious movements predisposed them against modernisms under the patronage of the French Revolution which were even more unpalatable than Orthodoxy. The paradox was that the massive blows dealt by the Revolution at institutional stability gave evangelical religion the best opportunity it ever received, and opened the way to another *Erweckungsbewegung* even on the continent of Europe.

The revival and Pietist movements also did much to redress the one-sided emphasis of the Orthodox upon pure doctrine, but did not resolve the conundrum they had set themselves about the relation between conversion and the pursuit of spiritual gifts. Whether either tradition can excogitate an effective approach to populations with no smouldering embers of faith to revive is doubtful; what both traditions show very clearly is the chameleon-like capacity of religious belief and practice to acquire new social roles. Their history since the Enlightenment has not been a simple story of secularisation, though secularisation there has been; the Great Awakening with its combination of theological conservatism and practical innovation was a fitting preface to the history of a very tangled web indeed. However ruthlessly cut down to size, the Great Awakening is not to be dismissed by critics as 'invention' or 'interpretative fiction'.

# Index